1996

Readers, Teachers, Learners

Expanding Literacy in Secondary Schools

Second Edition

William G. Brozo
Texas A&M University—Corpus Christi

Michele L. Simpson
University of Georgia

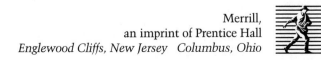

Merrill,
an imprint of Prentice Hall
Englewood Cliffs, New Jersey   Columbus, Ohio

Library of Congress Cataloging-in-Publication Data
Brozo, William G.
    Readers, teachers, learners : expanding literacy in the secondary
schools / William G. Brozo, Michele L. Simpson.—2nd ed.
        p.   cm.
    Includes bibliographical references and index.
    ISBN 0-02-315661-9
    1. Reading (Secondary)—United States. 2. Language arts (Sec-
ondary)—United States. I. Simpson, Michele L. II. Title.
    LB1632.B7   1995
    428.4'071'273—dc20
                                                                94-16927
                                                                CIP

Editor: Linda James Scharp
Production Editors: Jonathan Lawrence and Louise N. Sette
Text Designer: STELLARViSIONS
Cover Designer: Brian Deep
Production Buyer: Deidra M. Schwartz
Electronic Text Management: Marilyn Wilson Phelps, Matthew Williams, Jane Lopez,
    Karen L. Bretz

This book was set in Kuenstler 480, Avant Garde, and Swiss 721 by Prentice Hall and was
printed and bound by Book Press, Inc., a Quebecor America Book Group Company. The
cover was printed by Phoenix Color Corp.

 © 1995 by Prentice-Hall, Inc.
A Simon & Schuster Company
Englewood Cliffs, New Jersey 07632

Earlier edition © 1991 by Macmillan Publishing Company.

Printed in the United States of America

10 9 8 7 6 5 4 3 2

ISBN: 0-02-315661-9

Prentice-Hall International (UK) Limited, *London*
Prentice-Hall of Australia Pty. Limited, *Sydney*
Prentice-Hall of Canada, Inc., *Toronto*
Prentice-Hall Hispanoamericana, S. A., *Mexico*
Prentice-Hall of India Private Limited, *New Delhi*
Prentice-Hall of Japan, Inc., *Tokyo*
Simon & Schuster Asia Pte. Ltd., *Singapore*
Editora Prentice-Hall do Brasil, Ltda., *Rio de Janeiro*

Preface

As we put the finishing touches on this second edition, we once again realized how much more we could have said; how many more scenes of quality teaching and learning we could have shared; how many more literacy innovations we could have described. Four years have done little to alter our view that to publish is less an end point in the writing process than a place for rethinking, redefining, and planning for an even better text the next time.

As authors of this text, we remain readers, teachers, and learners who have learned from each other, from users of the first edition, and most of all, from our students. Our hope continues that the readers, teachers, and learners of this text will remain open to the mind-expanding possibilities and personal pleasures of change.

Although change and transition are obvious themes in this second edition, the overarching goal—to communicate to teachers *through* teachers—has been reinforced. With fresh and exciting reading, writing, and literacy research as a backdrop, we have tried in a collaborative spirit to empower teachers with the confidence to make their own best decisions about the learning that goes on in their classrooms. As in our first attempt, we have made a serious effort to avoid prescribing, offering "canned" answers, or demanding certain behaviors from teachers that ignore the realities of the everyday world of secondary schools, whose major goal is to teach content-area concepts.

We hope another clear message of the book is that teachers inform *us* as much as we inform *them*. In a very real sense, the growth and improvement of students' language processes in secondary schools will depend on the strength of the transaction between teachers in higher education and teachers in public schools.

This edition includes even more actual teaching scenarios and examples than the first. We demonstrate the valuable lessons to be learned from those content-area teachers struggling and triumphing as they implement stimulating reading, writing, and learning strategies. Theory and research are embodied in these scenarios and examples, which provide glimpses of teachers making literacy learning and content acquisition work.

Assumptions Underlying the Reading and Writing Strategies in this New Edition

A major theme of this book is that teachers who employ language-based strategies are more likely to build active learners and expand literacy in secondary schools. Throughout the book we describe strategies that exploit students' beliefs and backgrounds and provide students with new, imaginative experiences that will help them find reasons to learn. The strategies we discuss demonstrate how teachers can move students to become active learners by building independence. Above all, the strategies in this book strive to make learning fun and accessible for all.

We believe students develop misconceptions about literacy and learning as a result of their experiences in school. The strategies and ideas in this second edition stem from the belief that students can become interested and enthusiastic users of literacy to expand their sense of reality and their sense of themselves. Students are touched and moved by learning when teachers bring together teaching and learning experiences in positive and authentic ways, when learning is meaning centered, when teachers and students work together to shape the learning environment, and when students are given real-world reasons to learn.

Several assumptions, therefore, underpin the strategies in this book. These assumptions form the theoretical foundation on which our ideas for teaching and learning rest.

1. Teaching is more than dispensing information, because learning is more than receiving and remembering information.

    Learning is the construction of meaning, an active process on the part of the learner. Teaching is creating classroom contexts that support the acquisition of new knowledge through literacy.

2. A major goal of education should be the development of critical thinkers and active, independent learners.

    Students should be provided opportunities to play active roles in the meaning-making process. Students should be engaged in learning experiences that help them critically evaluate their worlds and participate in active problem solving of real-world concerns.

3. To be literate is to use literacy as a tool for learning.

    In supportive learning environments, students can learn to use literacy as a vehicle for meaningful and functional learning.

4. Content and process can be taught simultaneously.

   Students should be led to see that *what* is learned is inextricably tied to *how* one learns.

Organization and Special Features of the Book

This text is designed to help you to teach your content more effectively and to help you develop independent learners who can think about your content in creative and critical ways. This text is also designed to help you envision the possibilities for exciting teaching and learning in your classroom. To this end, we have filled the book with actual, practical examples, teaching scenarios, and classroom dialogues. Using an informal tone, we share our own teaching experiences as well as those of many secondary classroom teachers like yourself. We provide many alternatives, not with the intent that you should adopt every one, but with the expectation that you will select the strategies that best suit your subject area, your students, and your teaching style.

New to this edition, Chapter 1 provides a thorough description of major trends in literacy, themes in this book, and principles of language-based teaching and learning, as well as a much expanded explanation of cooperative learning. Chapters 2 and 3 are critical in that they explain the processes involved in developing active learners. We recommend that you read these first three chapters before reading the others, because the remaining chapters build on this foundation.

Regardless of the content that you teach or plan to teach, each chapter can provide you with insights into effective classroom interactions and practical examples of teaching strategies. Even when these examples of strategies and classroom applications do not come from your particular subject area, they can be invaluable as guides for helping you modify instructional practices within your own classroom context. Therefore, we recommend that you read each one, and as you do, rather than implementing the strategies exactly as explained and presented here, consider how the strategies can be adapted to your content, students, classroom, and teaching style.

Woven throughout the 11 chapters of this edition are many common threads. For instance, although we devote an entire chapter to writing in the secondary school (Chapter 7), writing strategies—in combination with other literacy processes as vehicles for learning in a variety of classroom contexts—are offered in nearly every chapter. The same holds true for using young adult literature and trade books to engender interest and spice up content learning (Chapter 8).

Readers of this second edition will be especially pleased with all of the updated references to professional literature. In addition, we have added a major section on authentic assessment, including portfolio assessment/teaching, in Chapter 4. New also to this edition are the case study sections in Chapters 3 through 10. The case study format asks you to consider a particular problem or issue from an actual teaching scenario related to the content of the chapter. At the conclusion of the chapter, the case study is revisited, and you are invited to offer teaching or problem-solving suggestions. This feature makes the second edition more interactive and hopefully a more useful text for secondary school teachers.

It is with great confidence that we stand behind the methods and strategies discussed within this book. In fact, many of the teaching scenarios and examples come from our own teaching and research experiences with middle school, junior high, and high school teachers and students. Other examples come from past students who have told us about or invited us to view their successful creation of literacy innovations or application of strategies.

We have taken great pains not to write another instructional recipe book that lists activities without connections to actual classroom environments, without a grounding in theory and research, without a focus on process. Dorothy Watson suggests that "instructional cookbooks carry teachers from one activity to the next, but do not empower them with knowledge that leads to flexibility in future decision making" (in Gilles et al., 1988). Instead, we have tried to provide the encouragement, strategies, and examples needed to help you transform your classroom world into a learning place where you and your students' mutual desire to learn will never disappear.

These opening remarks would be incomplete without a very special thanks to Jeff Johnston and Linda Scharp, our editors at Merrill. Without their unflagging confidence in us and their prescience in recognizing the need for secondary school teachers to become more knowledgeable of holistic literacy strategies, this second edition would never have become a reality. Thanks as well go out to our production coordinators, Jonathan Lawrence and Louise Sette, and to our copy editor, Luanne Dreyer Elliott. We are, of course, indebted to our diligent reviewers—Carolyn S. Andrews-Beck, Southern Illinois University at Edwardsville; Gerald Calais, McNeese State University; J. Richard Chambers, Boston University; Patricia N. Chrosniak, Western Illinois University; Dennis J. Kear, Wichita State University; Lorita G. Manning, Baylor University; and Judity B. Schaumberg, Carthage College—whose helpful insights made this second edition a better text. We thank all the students and teachers whose experiences inspired us and whose wisdom mentored us, especially, Dr. Keith Thomas, Dr. Ned Ratekin, and Hannah Katherine Brozo. Finally, we thank with all our hearts the two special teachers to whom we are married, Carol and Tom, for their love and support during the past 4 years of writing.

In physics they call it the "butterfly effect"—small influences creating dramatic effects—derived from the idea that the mere flap of an insect's wing in your backyard can cause a hurricane on the other side of the globe. This book is dedicated to small influences that can bring about big changes in the way students and teachers in secondary schools interact and the quality of student learning.

Reference

Gilles, C., Bixby, M., Crowley, P., Crenshaw, S., Henrich, M., Reynolds, R., & Pyle, D. (1988). *Whole language strategies for secondary students*. New York: Richard C. Owen.

Brief Contents

Contents

7   The Active Learner and Writing in the Secondary Classroom   201

8 Literature Across the Curriculum and Throughout Life 239

9 Strategic Learning Across the Content Areas 279

10 Expanding Literacy for Students With Special Needs   323

11   Becoming an Effective Literacy Professional   355

1

Readers, Teachers, Learners: An Introduction

A . . . plausible argument, substantiated over three hundred years of insight and research, is that knowing is an activity, not a condition or state, that knowledge implies the making of connections, not an inert body of information, that both teachers and students are learners, that discourse manifests and realizes the power to learn, and that teaching entails creating incentives and contexts for learning, not a reporting of data. Specifically, learning is the process of an individual's mind making meaning from the material of its experience.

—Knoblach & Brannon (1983)

This book is about readers, teachers, and learners in the secondary school; it is about contexts for learning; and it is about how students can be supported in their use of language processes for learning course content and expanding their sense of self.

Our purpose for this chapter is fourfold: (a) to share our philosophy of literacy; (b) to build a case for why literacy processes should be integral to secondary-content classroom instruction; (c) to describe what we believe to be important principles of language-based teaching; and (d) to lay down the assumptions about literacy and learning underpinning the strategies and ideas contained in this text.

What Is Literacy and Its Role in the Secondary School?

To be literate in the secondary school means many things. It means using literacy to bring pleasure and expand one's sense of self. It means using literacy to become a more fully realized and participatory citizen in a democratic society such as ours. And it also means being able to use reading, writing, speaking, and listening to acquire and apply knowledge in content-area classrooms.

With regard to using literacy for pleasure and personal growth, it seems to us that secondary school teachers must take as much care in reaching adolescents as they do in teaching them the curriculum. A big part of reaching students is to trust the voices of our students, to be learners ourselves, and to take risks. Charlie Reed (1988) says one of the best ways to reach young adults is through books. Sharing books that help students work through a personal or interpersonal crisis, that excite their imaginations, or support their own "need to know" communicates the clear message that you care about students and that you value reading and learning outside the strict and traditional boundaries of the school or class curriculum. To be a companion in literacy, however, requires that we ourselves read and know books. Linda Rief, a junior high school teacher, talks about how she rediscovered reading in a summer course, and how she was shocked into awareness of her own reading habits:

> She asked each of us to bring five favorite books we were currently reading, or had recently read, to the first class. I couldn't find five recently read books. I realized I wasn't reading. I thought I didn't have time. That scared me. Reading was part of my curriculum. How could I have neglected it so badly? (1992, p. 3)

Becoming knowledgeable about books, and regularly reading and writing ourselves, puts us in the perfect position to introduce young adults to the pleasures and functional uses of literacy.

Helping students become critical, participatory citizens may be one of the most important, yet neglected aspects of literacy teaching and learning in secondary schools (Willinsky, 1990). We believe our prescient forebears, such as Thomas Jefferson and Benjamin Franklin, foresaw the critical role schools could play in preparing students to be intelligent, functioning members in the democratic process. In fact, 200 years ago, they suggested that the biggest threat to national security was an uninformed populace. Literacy teaching and learning in junior and senior high schools could provide the necessary experiences for adolescents to take on the political, social, and economic challenges in the near and long term. Making literacy and learning meaningful on a sociopolitical level could help students look more critically at their own lives as well as the lives of their neighbors and society and imbue them with the courage to become involved in helping to improve our political, social, and economic condition (King & Brozo, 1992).

With regard to learning content material, unfortunately, students are rarely taught reading, writing, and reasoning processes that enable them to use these literacy skills as tools for learning in their daily schoolwork. A traditional perspective of reading development assumes that students become fluent readers by third or fourth grade, just about the time they begin encountering textbooks in science, social studies, health, and so on. But the processing demands of simple stories, which comprise nearly all of the material for reading instruction in the early grades, contrasts sharply with the processing demands of expository texts from which secondary students are expected to read and learn. Consequently, when students experience difficulty with expository reading in their content classes, it is often assumed that they have not learned to read properly, and they may be recycled through a program of basic reading skills. This practice leaves little hope of ever developing interested or sophisticated readers. When we consider the complexity of textbook reading, even greater time should be devoted to providing instruction in processing expository text at the secondary level than is provided for story reading at the elementary level.

Thus, reading is meaningful for older students when they can apply literacy processes for pleasure and personal growth, to better understand and influence their world, and to expand understanding of content textbooks and other school-related reading materials. The development of these critical reading, writing, and reasoning skills cannot be left to the reading teachers or English teachers alone. Teachers across all academic areas should be responsible for reinforcing literacy skills as they apply to the understanding of their particular content, as well as helping adolescents appreciate the personal pleasures of literacy. While we are certainly not the first to make these admonitions, the idea that all teachers should assume responsibility for supporting students' various needs to be literate is difficult for some to grasp. We ask you to accept the following premise as critical for secondary literacy learning: None of us—teachers and students alike—at any point in time have "arrived" as readers, writers, and thinkers. Instead, our literacy skills are in a continual process of growth and refinement.

Definition of Literacy: A Modest Proposal

Given the multifarious nature of literacy, perhaps it is futile to attempt to include all of its dimensions in a single, terse definition. We believe, therefore, that it is more helpful to define literacy by sharing scenes and instances of literacy teaching and learning. In other words, we try in this book to make the concept concrete by demonstrating how teachers and students in secondary schools continually stretch the boundaries of literacy possibilities. As you might infer, we believe there is no single best static definition of literacy. Nonetheless, we outline in general terms the variables inherent in literacy acts in schools. Following is our modest definition of literacy, which will form the basis for all of the discussion and methods in this book. This definition is a hybrid that combines current theory and research with our own and others' teaching experiences.

Literacy (including reading, writing, speaking, and listening) is a meaning-making and meaning-using process. Meaning is constructed through the interaction between the learner (in all of his complexities), the text (in all of its complexities), and instructional variables within the context of the learning situation. Meaning is used in direct relation to the level of interest in the learner and the level of functionality of the learning. The degree of interaction and use varies as a function of factors such as the learner's culture, prior knowledge, skills and strategies, motivation and interests, the type of text, the classroom environment, the instructional strategies, the meaningfulness of learning activities, and a host of other contextual factors.

Notice in this definition that our overall goal as learners is to make sense of our world through the use of literacy. Like all good thinkers, your ability to make meaningful interpretations of this book and use what you learn from it is directly related to (a) how much you already know about the topic of literacy (prior knowledge); (b) your experience with printed language (prior knowledge about the organization and structure of texts); (c) your interest in and motivation for reading this text; (d) your strategies for studying and retaining the ideas and information; (e) your purpose for reading it in the first place; (f) if you are reading it for a university course, how the instructor uses the book and the kinds of classroom experiences you are provided for learning the concepts and strategies in the book; and (g) how well we as authors have communicated to you as the reader. As classroom teachers, the more instruction we provide that braids literacy processes with the curriculum, that is connected to the interests and experiences of the learner, that allows for the exploration and generation of engaging texts, and that makes learning meaningful and functional, the more we improve how students make and use meaning (Calkins & Harwayne, 1991; Harste, 1989; Lipson & Wixson, 1991).

The remainder of this chapter is devoted to first describing some growing concerns about literacy trends and habits for American youth and adults to better understand why literacy in the secondary school is so important. We conclude the chapter by describing important principles of language-based teaching that underpin the scenes and strategies in this text.

The Literacy Landscape

Three ominous trends are growing on the American literacy landscape. First, national assessment data of reading and writing continue to point to the fact that many junior and senior high school students cannot read or write beyond basic levels of literacy. A second and insidious trend is that greater and greater numbers of able readers are choosing not to read. Finally, ample evidence supports the contention that students' levels of critical literacy are falling. Taken together, these trends pose many awesome challenges for secondary school educators concerned about the literacy growth of their students. Each is developed in more detail in the following discussion.

Low Levels of Literacy

The National Assessment of Educational Process (NAEP), a congressionally mandated project, has been conducting national surveys of the reading competency of 9-, 13-, and 17-year-olds since 1969 and of the writing competency for grades 4, 8, and 11 since 1984. In its most recent assessment for which analyzed data are available (*Trends in Academic Progress*, 1991), it was found that since 1971:

> virtually all students displayed rudimentary reading skills and strategies, characterized by the ability to perform relatively uncomplicated, discrete reading tasks successfully. [However], very few students in any assessment reached the highest levels of reading proficiency, reflecting their difficulty in comprehending passages that are more lengthy and complex or that deal with specialized subject matter. (pp. 122–123)

The report's authors make the following assertion about writing progress:

> The substantially larger percentages of students achieving the minimal, as compared to the adequate, level indicate that students had great difficulty communicating effectively in writing. (p. 7)

Together, these findings make clear that no real improvement has been made in overall reading proficiency for 9- and 13-year-olds between 1971 and 1990, and only slight improvement for 17-year-olds. Also, the few changes in writing proficiency since 1984 suggest that not enough attention to writing as a regular and important form of communicating and meaning making is being given in junior and senior high schools. Attention to fostering higher levels of literacy and problem-solving capabilities among young adults seems imperative, because our world is becoming increasingly complex and increasingly challenges the intellectual and creative energies of all our citizens.

Advanced literacy skills will not result simply from reading instruction provided in isolation from the reading, writing, and thinking requirements placed on secondary students in their daily schoolwork. Every teacher must place a special emphasis on helping students make thoughtful, critical elaborations of ideas and understandings that come from the materials they read and from their prior knowledge and experiences. To accomplish this, classroom teachers must shift away from learning that requires only simple memorization and superficial reading. Recently, the National Science Teachers Association met to respond to former President Bush's call for improving students' science and math skills. Their major recommendation centered on moving away from teaching science as a collection of minute facts and details, which students tend to memorize for quizzes and tests and then forget, toward improving the way students think and reason about science and making science learning more functional and meaningful. We strongly endorse this recommendation, because like these science educators, we believe that as students' thinking abilities improve, their interest and motivation to learn science will increase, and their ability to learn and retain important science facts will improve as well. Science educators are not alone in their pronouncements for transforming science learning from a rote exercise to a functional, problem-solving process; similar curricular recommendations have been made by national social studies organizations under the rubric of "globalism" and by mathematics organizations with math learning tied to the students' everyday experiences.

In all the subjects students study, countless opportunities exist for developing higher-level literacy skills. Experiences that allow them to tap their own prior knowledge, to connect their experiences with the topic, to develop their own interpretations of what they read, to question, rethink, self-assess, and elaborate on text information and ideas are what literacy instruction in the secondary school classroom is all about.

Aliteracy

Barbara Hoover (1989), a syndicated journalist, tells a seriocomedic story of falling in love with an attractive, fun, and affectionate guy. Not long into the relationship, however, she discovered that he owned just four books—a couple of business manuals, a dictionary, and a success guide. Her better judgment clouded temporarily by the newness of the romance, she minimized this observation, and started bringing her own books to read during idle moments in their time together. After a couple of difficult years, they finally broke up. It was then, she says, that she realized an important truth—"There are two kinds of people: those who read and those who don't. And sometimes they run out of things to say to each other" (p. 3B).

While more and more money is spent on remedial reading and learning disabilities programs in public schools and on adult functional reading programs, a growing number of people, like Hoover's ex-boyfriend, are in fact reading less, and in some cases, choosing not to read at all. This phenomenon of literate individuals who choose not to use their literacy has come to be known as **aliteracy**. Evidence for this growing phenomenon abounds.

Past presidents Ronald Reagan and George Bush might be characterized as aliterates. Of course they knew how to read, they simply chose not to. When interviewed at the end of his administration, Reagan was hard-pressed to remember the last time he'd read a book, let alone what it was. And Bush boasted that he read fishing magazines (even as his wife, Barbara, headed a national drive for literacy). We are not trying to single out these two presidents for criticism as much as we are trying to draw attention to how pervasive aliteracy has become in our country.

Statistics from the American Enterprise Institute (AEI), a Washington-based organization involved in extending public familiarity with contemporary issues, reports that by age 15, the average American child has spent more time in front of a television set than in the classroom or in doing homework (Thimmesch, 1985). Our current generation of youngsters also spends many additional hours playing games in video arcades or at home. Not only are children watching more and more TV, so are adults. Interior decorators and home builders in wealthy suburbs report that large homes are being built and remodeled without libraries, studies, or bookshelves. The owners simply aren't reading. Instead, these homes are being furnished with lavish entertainment centers (Hoover, 1989).

Television news programs claim as many viewers as this nation's approximately 1,700 newspapers have readers. Yet, while television news is expanding, newspaper circulation has been steadily declining. From 1970 to the present, the daily circulation of newspapers has dropped by nearly 1 million. Studies have shown heavy TV viewers to be more suspicious of people than those described as avid readers. People who rely exclusively on television to size up political candidates make far more subjective judgments than people who rely largely on written accounts about those candidates and the issues (Thimmesch, 1985).

AEI also reports on a recent study that found that the average college graduate had not read a book in 4 years after graduating. Another study found that less than a majority of Americans read books regularly, with less than 25% characterized as moderate-to-heavy readers (defined as 10 to 30 books or more per year) (Campbell, 1985).

Finally, Duffey (as reported by Campbell, 1985) conducted a study indicating that for the most part teachers do not read. It is difficult for adults, whether they are parents, teachers, successful business people, or politicians, to impart the love of reading or even a positive attitude toward reading to American youth unless they value literacy enough themselves to make it an integral part of their lives.

We argue that aliteracy is, in large part, the legacy of reading and writing instruction received earlier. Students develop concepts about literacy based on the way in which it is offered them. If reading and writing are taught without meaningful and functional applications in content-area learning, if emphasis is placed on memorization of endless facts, if the only materials students are exposed to are lifeless, abstract, and disconnected from their own experiences, then students may learn to "play the game," regurgitate information, but disdain reading and never find a reason to make reading an integral part of their lives.

No Place for Critical Literacy

Giroux (1987) talks about **critical literacy** as a process that "educates students to be critical citizens capable of exhibiting civic courage" (p. 181). In his view, as well as the views of Goodman (1992) and others (King & Brozo, 1992), school learning should provide the context for students to be critical and self-determined thinkers. Unfortunately, as increasing economic and political pressures dictate the teaching and learning possibilities for teachers and students, curriculum in many secondary schools has been reduced to a warehouse of knowledge merely to be passed on to waiting customers. Teachers often find themselves in the roles of information disseminators, forced to find ever more efficient means to "cover the material."

Symptomatic of a curriculum that has become devoid of a critical component is the preoccupation among adolescents with "getting a job" or "doing better than Japan." This single-minded thinking about the purpose of schooling reflects the prevailing condition of much of our secondary school curriculum. Secondary schools that make it a priority to educate students to make choices and think critically can help students develop the confidence and conviction that they can make a difference in the world. This sense of power can result from instruction concerned with making connections between and among teachers and students, within and among classrooms, and inside and outside of schools. Critical literacy fosters an understanding of the ways we are all interconnected and interdependent and teaches that in caring for others we are in fact caring for ourselves (Goodman, 1992).

When conceptualizing a curriculum of critical literacy that attends to the real-world needs, concerns, and aspirations of youth, we can't help but think of all of the monumental problems facing us as a nation and a people that beg for creative and humane solutions. Those same problems could be the focus of our curriculum in secondary schools: for example, conditions of urban and rural poverty, overpopulation and world hunger, environmental degradation, unresponsive government, and the energy crisis. We believe that schools can become sites for entertaining, working toward, and remedying social, political, economic, and environmental ills of our communities, nation, and world.

In the concluding section of this chapter, we outline essential principles of language-based teaching. Based on our experience as teachers and our knowledge of the research and applied literature in literacy, we believe that these principles hold the most promise for meeting the challenges posed by aliteracy, falling levels of literacy, and a lack of critical literacy.

Principles of Language-Based Teaching

Language-based teaching is much larger than the narrow notion of reading and writing techniques. It is a philosophy of teaching that sees the teacher's role as one of agitator, creator of conceptual conflicts, challenger of conventional wisdom, and above all, facilitator of students' own knowledge construction and use. Within language-based learning environments, students should be allowed to grow into critical-thinking members of society, while teachers engage in the process of reflecting, researching, and learning in order to become more effective teachers.

Following are the principles we consider essential for effective language-based teaching:

1. Language-based teachers understand that learning is a social process.
2. Language-based teachers know that the best learning occurs when it is whole, functional, and meaningful.
3. Language-based teachers know that students improve their reading and writing when given abundant opportunities to use reading and writing as vehicles for learning.
4. Language-based teachers are in a continual process of making transitions to better literacy and content teaching.

Principle 1: Language-Based Teachers Understand That Learning Is a Social Process

It has long been recognized that we only know what we know when we reflect our knowledge in others (Blumer, 1969). Harste (1988) offers these insights in the significance of the social nature of learning:

> I am convinced that we know nothing by ourselves. It is only in juxtaposition with others that we know, and know what we know differs from others' knowledge. (p. 13)

Literacy is a social process (Green, 1990; Myers, 1992). Even when you curl up with a book in the "private" act of reading, you are not alone—you are interacting with an author who holds other ideas, points of view, styles of expression. A useful construct here is **intertextuality**, or ways in which an individual's construction of meaning depends on other meanings (de Beaugrande & Dressler, 1981). Rowe (1987, 1989) has demonstrated that when teachers provide for intertextual tying between and among students in the social world of the classroom, greater language learning takes place. In her research, students made obvious connections between their written texts and those of classmates because they were provided opportunities to observe another author at work and to talk with that author to develop and expand on their own ideas. Similar discoveries of the power of cooperative meaning making have been made by Fine (1987, 1989).

The instructional implications of the social nature of learning are many and varied. On a general level, students can build shared meanings of literacy, language, and concepts when they are encouraged to make use of demonstrations provided by their peers and teachers and are given opportunities to interact informally with other authors and learners in the classroom community. On a practical level, the classroom itself should be arranged to encourage social interaction among student meaning makers. Instead of desks in rows where students are forced to talk to the back of others' heads and can make easy eye contact only with the teacher, we recommend a more flexible seating arrangement that encourages student–student dialoguing and problem solving. One such approach that has been found to improve not only the academic achievement of students but also their level of interpersonal attraction (Jules, 1990) is cooperative learning.

Cooperative Learning.   Johnson and Johnson (1989) describe three basic learning experiences that students are likely to have in schools: individualistic, competitive, and cooperative. Of the three, **cooperative learning** better facilitates a teacher's constructive use of student interaction and gives rise to an "increase in the pro-social orientation among students" (Kagan, 1990, p. 9).

Cooperative learning groups consist generally of three or more students grouped heterogeneously and linked by a common goal. The emphasis in the groups is both the completion of an academic assignment as well as the promotion of social skills. Cooperative learning has become immensely popular since the early 1980s because of its positive effect on achievement, self-esteem, interpersonal dynamics, and motivation. Figure 1–1 presents the essential elements for successful cooperative learning.

**Figure 1–1   Essential elements
of cooperative learning**

1. *Positive interdependence:* "We sink or swim together!"
   Methods to promote this attitude include

   • Mutual goal
   • Group accountability
   • Shared/limited materials
   • Group rewards
   • Complementary and interconnected roles
   • Division of labor

2. *Individual accountability:* "No hitchhiking!"
   Methods to promote this attitude include

   • Individual tests
   • Random selection of a group member
   • Random selection of one paper

3. Face-to-face interaction

   • Eye to eye, knee to knee
   • Oral exchange
   • Conducive physical arrangement

4. Appropriate use of collaborative skills

   • Skills should be taught
   • Skills should be practiced
   • Students should be motivated to use skills
   • Skills should be assessed by teacher or group members

The use of cooperative groups as a dynamic method for teaching content-area comprehension and learning has been consistently supported by a fairly long history of voluminous research (reviewed by Johnson & Johnson, 1987; Manning & Lucking, 1991). Cooperative learning enables students to assume responsibility for their learning and to develop confidence in their ability to learn. In heterogeneous classroom situations, where social interaction plays an important role in the facilitation of learning (Durojaiye, 1988), cooperative learning provides students who view themselves as unsuccessful learners—when grouped with others of low ability (Roller, 1989; Stanovich, 1990)—the opportunity to make significant contributions to group decisions. Further, cooperative learning gives students the opportunity to share what they have learned, to listen to the ideas and opinions of fellow students, to be taught by their peers, and to assume the role of teacher (Jules, 1990; Kagan, 1990; Sapon-Shevin & Schniedewind, 1990). As a result of cooperative learning, greater literacy and content learning have been observed in a variety of classroom contexts (Eeds & Wells, 1991; Jacobson, 1990; Slavin, 1987; Thistlewaite, 1990). Cooperative learning has also been shown to promote active comprehension and develop the language abilities in the content areas (Uttero, 1988; Wood, 1991). When teachers use cooperative learning, they communicate to students that their input is valued and that their contributions broaden the understanding of the topic for the community of learners in the classroom. We demonstrate applications of this powerful teaching and learning strategy throughout this book.

Principle 2: Language-Based Teachers Know That the Best Learning Occurs When It Is Whole, Functional, and Meaningful

The term *whole* in this principle has many different aspects. In one sense, it refers to complete and genuine text sources that students read and write. Commercially prepared learning materials, such as textbooks, are bound by countless restrictions that result inevitably in "pointlessly arid prose" (Tyson-Bernstein, 1988). Genuine text, on the other hand, is created by authors who simply have an urge to communicate their perspectives and information on a topic. Consider, for instance, the difference between the treatment of the topic of the Vietnam War in a 10th-grade history textbook as compared with Elizabeth Becker's (1992) *America's Vietnam War: A Narrative History*. The textbook, because of space limitations, offers only a few pages on the topic. The textbook publisher assures that issues about the war that might be considered too "controversial" are not included; concerns about "readability" force the authors of the textbook to exclude certain imaginative terms and phrases. By comparison, Becker's informational book provides an in-depth and critical view of the issues surrounding the Vietnam War from the history of American involvement to the fall of Saigon. Unbounded by publisher restrictions, such as those placed on textbook authors, Becker presents the topic in a lively and engaging way that is sure to draw adolescent readers into a more thoughtful study of Vietnam. So although textbooks often form the core of learning in most secondary classrooms, we suggest that textbooks alone aren't enough, because they fail the test of wholeness.

With respect to writing, we advocate that teachers allow students to compose complete texts through the writing process (discussed in detail in Chapter 7). Instead of being confined to certain topics and forms of writing, as often as possible, students should be free to select the discourse mode best suited to their needs of expression. For example, in writing about the Vietnam War, students required to write a two-page report on the battle of Dien Bien Phu or the Gulf of Tonkin incident would likely be less engaged and enthusiastic about learning than if they were asked to put themselves in the place of a participant in the war or a victim of war circumstances (e.g., Viet Cong villager, witness to the My Lai massacre, an American living in Canada to avoid the draft, parent of an MIA) and write, for instance, a letter, diary, or story. Better yet, students could be asked to respond in writing from a variety of discourse options that help them rework the content. When given options, students may choose to write poetry, song lyrics, or dialogue for drama to be enacted impromptu by a small group. In this way, students become much more invested in the learning process as they develop a sense of ownership of their ideas and their learning.

Another aspect of whole learning is the notion of integrated learning. Students should be involved in activities and projects that require integrating reading, writing, speaking, and listening. Writers workshops (see Chapter 7), for example, can be used as an outstanding way of bringing all the language systems to bear on the learning of content material. Integration also refers to tying together learning from many areas of the secondary school curriculum. This aspect of holistic teaching can be the most challenging for secondary teachers to pull off, largely because of the highly departmentalized nature of most junior and senior high schools. Consider this example of integration: Students learning about the Vietnam War could be learning about the U.S. government's evolving foreign policy as it relates to Southeast Asia in one classroom, the culture and customs of Southeast Asia in another, and the economic ramifications of the war in another. Students meanwhile could read works of fiction by Southeast Asian authors or about this region and its people. Making the curriculum whole allows students to see the interconnectedness of content to develop a broader understanding of topics. We present strategies for teachers working together to bring cohesion to the curriculum in Chapter 11.

Webster's defines *functional* as "connected with." We like this definition because it implies that when teachers make learning functional, students connect with it, they find linkages between classroom content on the one hand and needs and purposes in their personal lives on the other. We agree with Edelsky, Altwerger, and Flores (1991), who argue that "learners' purposes and intentions are what drives learning" (p. 25). If the sole purpose for learning is external to the learner (e.g., pleasing the teacher, getting a good grade, etc.), then it doesn't really matter what is learned. In secondary school classrooms where purposes for learning are always and unilaterally made by the teacher, we have seen a condition of "learned helplessness" (Diener & Dweck, 1978) set in. Students can become so conditioned to respond only to teachers' directives that they rarely if ever initiate learning, attack problems independently, or seek out information on their own. Students in classrooms that support their own explorations of functional learning can be characterized as engaged, enthusiastic, and independent.

An excellent example of functional learning comes from a senior high French class where the teacher provided the necessary support for students to explore their career options in a French language profession or aspects of French culture about which students desired more information. One student, Deanna, interviewed translators from international businesses (e.g., Michelin) and gained insights into the educational and experimental prerequisites for such a career. Terrell read about and spoke directly to French poets and writers whose topics dealt with race relations in France. Kimme's interest in becoming a buyer for a major department store led her to study the French fashion world. And Charles looked into French wines and cuisine with the intent of using this knowledge to conduct eating tours in France. These students kept a log of their information-gathering process, including following leads, phone conversations, and written correspondence, as well as personal reflections on their research. They also shared their findings with the class. Their demonstrations clearly reflected the power of making learning functional.

Meaningfulness simply refers to ways of making learning personally meaningful for the learner. If we assume that the only way to make students learn is to force them to learn, then we may be left with no choice but to use force every time we try to teach. Think about an alternative self-fulfilling prophecy. What if we demonstrated a trust in students' own natural curiosities, their own needs to know more, their abilities to make meaning? Imagine the transformation that might take place in classrooms where students are supported in their efforts to find meaningful connections to their own lives and their realities outside school with topics and content being considered in school? In working with Chicago youth, we discovered that students who were considered "problems" could become engaged in learning when they were sanctioned in their efforts to bring their real-world issues and concerns into the classroom. Using a reader-response writing strategy (described in detail in Chapter 7), students in an eighth-grade social studies class read magazine and newspaper articles about problems common to most inner-city communities and then wrote responses connecting their own experiences with those in the readings. Raymond, a former "graffiti artist," responded to an article in the *Chicago Tribune* about gangs and graffiti by relating it to his experiences. Raymond claimed that while most graffiti artists were not gang members, the mayor was linking all of them to gangs to mobilize more resources to eradicate graffiti. The teacher of this class found that by supporting her students' efforts to bring their lives into the content of their writing, students like Raymond became more engaged learners and more animated participants in class discussion.

Principle 3: Language-Based Teachers Know That Students Improve Their Reading and Writing When Given Abundant Opportunities to Use Reading and Writing as Vehicles for Learning

We described earlier the fallout of aliteracy: children and youth adopting the attitude that using literacy is not critical to function in the adult world. As one avoids literacy experiences more and more, one's skills of reading, writing, and critical thinking wither. Frank Smith's (1985) pithy axiom "We learn to read by reading" (p. 88) captures the essence of this principle. All of us must take responsibility for expanding literacy for our students. It is not the purview of any single teacher or of parents alone. And to do so, we must all be prepared to involve students in literacy experiences that contribute to their language development and their abilities to think more expansively about themselves and their worlds.

Secondary school learning environments that embody this principle of language-based teaching possess characteristics of immersion, demonstration, interaction, and transaction. **Immersion** refers to immersing students in environments that are language-rich with real-world artifacts of the adult literate community and filled with opportunities for critical analysis of school, text, and personal truths. **Demonstration** reminds us that teachers should know the literacy processes from the inside out to credibly model teaching as learning and teaching as inquiry. **Interaction** refers to opportunities given to students to learn from one another, value one another, and critique one another's truths. The teacher's truths should be subject to the same level of scrutiny as anyone else's. **Transaction** suggests that for students to learn principles of cooperation, participation, and critical citizenship, they should be directly involved in shaping the curriculum so that it is more aligned to their personal and career needs and goals.

In secondary classrooms, this principle translates into teachers creating supportive learning environments for students to use the language processes of reading, writing, speaking, and listening to better understand the curriculum. Such an environment would likely include process writing (see Chapter 7) wherein students can work together to write drafts, receive feedback, and rewrite until their work is ready to be graded and/or published. A secondary school teacher who encourages students' literacy growth while expanding their knowledge of content would also make available to students and make integral to the curriculum a variety of resources, such as trade and reference books, and as mentioned, a variety of literacy material from the adult world, in addition to the textbook. Not only can these alternative reading materials generate more enthusiasm for reading and learning, but they are also excellent resources for broadening students' understanding of topics as they read and consider the topics from various perspectives.

In secondary classrooms where this principle is practiced, teachers of all content provide sustained, uninterrupted periods for students and themselves to read and write. In this way, a literate culture is developed wherein teachers model healthy, adaptive literacy behavior while nurturing the literacy habits of their students.

Virtually every chapter of this book is devoted to offering ideas and strategies for getting students more actively and frequently involved in using the language systems as vehicles for learning and for personal growth and pleasure.

Principle 4: Language-Based Teachers Are in a Continual Process of Making Transitions to Better Literacy and Content Teaching

A theme running throughout this book is that language-based teaching is a process. This book is meant to encourage and support secondary school teachers as they move from teaching practices that focus exclusively on content to those intended to develop and apply students' language processes, and in this way, help students come to value literacy as an integral part of their lives. Advocates of a content/process model of secondary school teaching for improving students' abilities to learn content material, as well as for expanding students' sense of themselves as learners and critical, independent decision makers, have been around for some time (cf. Herber, 1978). Nonetheless, changes in the ways teachers teach junior and senior high students have been slow and painstaking. Administrators, professors, "experts," teachers, and students all share some of the responsibility for this uneven progress. O'Brien (1988) and others (Moje, Brozo, & Haas, in press) explain how the realities of secondary school teaching, including curricular demands and institutional and peer pressures, can seem to leave secondary teachers little choice but to employ efficient but unengaging and unauthentic instructional methods (e.g., lecturing, objective testing, etc.). We understand the realities of change and, therefore, emphasize the value of making transitions.

After working with a junior high teacher, Robin, for a year as she implemented cooperative learning for the first time after 12 years of teaching, we found that two overarching generalizations hold true with regard to making transitions in teaching: transitions take time, and they involve helping students make transitions.

Transitions Take Time.   Robin wanted to change but found that when her students didn't respond in ways she had expected, she became filled with self-doubt and wondered about returning to an information-dissemination model of teaching. It was only after 3 or 4 months of the school year, as her students began to take on their cooperative roles with enthusiasm and independence, that she saw the tangible benefits of this new approach to teaching and learning. Robin realized that through exploration, experimentation, and reflection she eventually appreciated the powerful transformation taking place in her classroom. So, by allowing time for change, students began to change; these positive changes in students then made it easier for Robin to accept and support further transitions toward more language-based, cooperative teaching.

Transitions Involve Helping Students Make Transitions as Well.   We often forget in our enthusiastic support of teacher change that as challenging as it may be for teachers themselves to make transitions toward new models of teaching, it may be even more challenging for students in a changing classroom environment. We discovered in Robin's classroom that students were not prepared initially for the demands of cooperative learning and, therefore, could not make an abrupt transition from their postures as receivers of information to active participants in shared learning. As discussed, the interrelationship between the students' reluctance to change and Robin's perseverance to work through change was critical. What helped was Robin's willingness to provide more modeling, more opportunities for students to take risks and experiment with their new roles. Perhaps most critical, however, was the self-assessment that was built into the process of cooperative learning. Through this process, students were able to take a new look at themselves as learners and turn to Robin for support. In this process, too, Robin watched herself change from "purveyor of truth" to someone who created the process and environment that allowed students to see each other as learning resources.

Summary

This opening chapter has set the stage for the ideas, examples, and strategies in this book. We have discussed the challenges all of us must face in attempting to encourage secondary students to become active, full participants in the learning process. Findings from national reports on literacy skills and habits of adolescents and adults paint a rather disturbing picture. Low levels of literacy are apparently becoming acceptable standards in our schools, and an attitude of indifference toward reading appears to be growing among adults, while our youth become increasingly passive learners. We have argued that low levels of literacy and aliteracy are largely due to the kinds of learning experiences students have in schools. At the same time, the potential power of literacy as a tool for social, political, and economic transformation is largely ignored in secondary schools. To reverse these trends, we suggest that teachers, with the help of their students, create learning environments in content classrooms where students use literacy to acquire new knowledge, to grow personally, to find pleasure, and to transform themselves and their world.

References

Beaugrande, R. de, & Dressler, W. (1981). *Introduction to text linguistics.* New York: Longman.

Becker, E. (1992). *America's Vietnam war: A narrative history.* New York: Clarion Books.

Blumer, H. (1969). *Symbolic interactionism: Perspectives and method.* Englewood Cliffs, NJ: Prentice-Hall.

Calkins, L., & Harwayne, S. (1991). *Living between the lines.* Portsmouth, NH: Heinemann.

Campbell, J. (1985). The "reading to learn" approach. In N. Thimmesch (Ed.), *Aliteracy.* Washington, DC: American Enterprise Institute.

Diener, C., & Dweck, C. (1978). An analysis of learned helplessness: Continuous changes in performance, strategy, and achievement cognitions following failure. *Journal of Personality and Social Psychology, 34,* 451–462.

Durojaiye, M. O. (1988). *A new introduction to educational psychology.* London: Evans Brothers.

Eeds, M., & Wells, D. (February 1991). Talking, thinking and cooperative learning: Lessons learned from listening to children talk about books. *Social Education, 55,* 134–137.

Edelsky, C., Altwerger, B., & Flores, B. (1991). *Whole language: What's the difference?* Portsmouth, NH: Heinemann.

Fine, E. (1987). Marbles lost, marbles found: Collaborative production of text. *Language Arts, 64,* 474–487.

Fine, E. (1989). Collaborative writing: Key to unlocking the silences of children. *Language Arts, 66,* 501–508.

Giroux, H. (1987). Critical literacy and student experience: Donald Graves' approach to literacy. *Language Arts, 64,* 175–181.

Goodman, J. (1992). Towards a discourse of imagery: Critical curriculum theorizing. *The Educational Forum, 56,* 269–289.

Green, J. (1990). Reading as a social process. In J. Howell, A. McNamara, & M. Clough (Eds.), *Social context of literacy.* Canberra, Australia: ACT Department of Education Canberra.

Harste, J. (1988). Tomorrow's readers today: Becoming a profession of collaborative learners. In J. Readence & R. S. Baldwin (Eds.), *Dialogues in literacy research.* Chicago, IL: National Reading Conference.

Harste, J. (1989). *New policy guidelines for reading: Connecting research and practice.* Urbana, IL: National Council of Teachers of English.

Herber, H. (1978) *Teaching reading in the content areas.* Englewood Cliffs, NJ: Prentice-Hall.

Hoover, B. (1989). Is anybody reading? *The Detroit News,* April 16.

Jacobson, J. (1990). Group vs. individual completion of a cloze passage. *Journal of Reading, 33,* 244–251.

Johnson, D., & Johnson, R. (1987). *Learning together and alone: Cooperative, competitive, and individualistic learning.* Englewood Cliffs, NJ: Prentice-Hall.

Johnson, D., & Johnson, R. (1989). *Cooperation and competition: Theory and research.* Edina, MN: Interaction Book Company.

Jules, V. (1990). Cooperative learning and work-mate preferences in classrooms in secondary schools. *Contemporary Education, 61,* 65–70.

Kagan, S. (1990). On cooperative learning: A conversation with Spencer Kagan. *Educational Leadership, 47,* 8–10.

King, J., & Brozo, W. G. (1992). Critical literacy and the pedagogies of empowerment. In A. Frager & J. Miller (Eds.), *Using inquiry in reading education.* Oxford, OH: College Reading Association.

Knoblach, C. H., & Brannon, L. (1983). Writing as learning through the curriculum. *College English, 45,* 465–474.

Lipson, M., & Wixson, K. (1991). *Assessment and instruction of reading disability: An interactive approach.* New York: Harper Collins.

Manning, M. L., & Lucking, R. (May/June 1991). The what, why, and how of cooperative learning. *The Social Studies,* 120–124.

Moje, E., Brozo, W. G., & Haas, J. (in press). Portfolios in high school classrooms: Recriminations and rewards. *Reading Research and Instruction.*

Myers, J. (1992). The social contexts of school and personal literacy. *Reading Research Quarterly, 27,* 297–333.

O'Brien, D. (1988). Secondary preservice teachers' resistance to content reading instruction: A proposal for a broader rationale. In J. Readence & R. S. Baldwin (Eds.), *Dialogues in literacy research.* Chicago: National Reading Conference.

Reed, A. (1988). *Comics to classics: A parent's guide to books for teens and preteens.* Newark, DE: International Reading Association.

Reed, C. (1988). *Comics to classics: A parents' guide to books for teens and preteens.* Newark, DE: International Reading Association.

Rief, L. (1992). *Seeking diversity: Language arts with adolescents.* Portsmouth, NH: Heinemann.

Roller, C. (1989). Classroom interaction patterns: Reflections of a stratified society. *Language Arts, 66,* 492–500.

Rowe, D. W. (1987). Literacy learning as an intertextual process. In J. Readence & R. S. Baldwin (Eds.), *Research in literacy: Merging perspectives.* Rochester, NY: National Reading Conference.

Rowe, D. W. (1989). Author/audience interaction in the preschool: The role of social interaction in literacy learning. *Journal of Reading Behavior, 21,* 311–349.

Sapon-Shevin, M., & Schniedewind, M. (1990). Selling cooperation without selling it short. *Educational Leadership, 47,* 63–65.

Slavin, R. (1987). *Cooperative learning.* Washington, DC: National Education Association.

Smith, F. (1985). *Reading without nonsense.* New York: Teachers College Press.

Stanovich, K. (1990). A call for an end to the paradigm wars in reading research. *Journal of Reading Behavior, 22,* 221–232.

Thimmesch, N. (1985). *Aliteracy.* Washington, DC: National Enterprise Institute.

Thistlewaite, L. (1990). Critical reading for at-risk students. *Journal of Reading, 33,* 586–593.

Trends in academic progress (1991). Educational Testing Service.

Tyson-Bernstein, H. (1988). *A conspiracy of good intentions.* Washington, DC: Council for Basic Education.

Uttero, D. A. (1988). Activating comprehension through cooperative learning. *The Reading Teacher, 41,* 390–395.

Willinsky, J. (1990). *The new literacy.* New York: Routledge.

Wood, K. (1991). Meeting the social needs of adolescents through collaborative learning experiences. In J. Irvin (Ed.), *Transforming middle level education.* New York: Allyn & Bacon.

2

Readers, Teachers, Learners: A Model of Active Learning

The direction is toward researching and understanding the cognitive and affective language processes of learners and teachers that mediate achievement in language learning and language teaching. The move is . . . to . . . how students and teachers think and feel, about how they use their background knowledge and strategies to generate or construct meaning and interpretations from literature and expository text.

—Wittrock, 1991

Recent national reports on literacy habits of schoolchildren and young adults point to the need for schools to do more to improve the development of higher-level reading and reasoning skills (cf. *Trends in Academic Progress*, 1991). Critics of reading taught in the middle and upper grades claim that too much emphasis is placed on the minutiae of reading, on skill building, and on factual recall of information, and that in the name of comprehension instruction, we do everything *but* teach comprehension (Dole, Duffy, Roehler, & Pearson, 1991). We contend that higher-level comprehension can be taught directly. This chapter explains a model of comprehension that can apply to all content-area classrooms where readers and teachers focus on learning. In Chapter 3 we demonstrate how this model and the guidelines for active learning that are associated with it can be used to develop effective comprehension and learning strategies.

19

Four Theoretical Principles That Promote Active Learning

Principle 1: Active Learners Use Schemata and Prior Knowledge in the Meaning-Making Process

Active learners know that reading is an interactive process, a coming together of the reader, the text, and the context of the learning situation. What they take from the page depends on how much they bring to the page. Hence, what readers already know and what they want to know will affect the ease or difficulty of their comprehension and subsequent learning. This premise is consistent with a **schema-theoretic** perspective of comprehension (McNamara, Miller, & Brandsford, 1991). **Schemata** (plural of schema) are abstract frameworks that organize knowledge in memory by putting information into the correct "slot," each slot containing related parts (Wilson & Anderson, 1986). For instance, your schema for going to an airport probably includes taxis, ticket counters, crowds, the smell of jet fuel, baggage claim, and so on. These clusters of related knowledge in memory—of experience, ideas, and feelings—guide our interpretations, inferences, expectations, and attention as passages are comprehended. It is theorized that readers comprehend a text when they bring to mind a schema that gives a good account of the objects and events described in the message. Schemata guide comprehension, and without them we could make little sense of text. Quite literally, without some kind of unifying idea to help tie together the information in a passage, without connections with the passage to our own prior knowledge and experience, without a foundational understanding of the concepts in the text, we might as well be looking at words in a foreign language.

To demonstrate the important role schemata play in text comprehension, read the following passage and see if you can activate an appropriate schema to help you understand it.

> The southpaw touched the rubber, kicked, and dealed. The big number 38 sent one up the chute. Smith raced from the hot corner and camped under it. He tripped, however, on the artificial turf, and it fell behind him and just in front of Murphy from left—38 had a two-bagger on a Texas leaguer. Cries of "kill the bum" echoed throughout the place as number 16 strode up. He was a sub for the dh and stood in brandishing a 40 ounce stick menacingly. He crushed one through the hole at short. Perez stabbed at it, but it rolled all the way to the warning track. 38 touched home, and it was over.

Did you understand this passage? What does it mean if you can't understand it? Chances are, you had no difficulty with decoding, so a good part of the difficulty you may have had making sense of this short passage can be attributable to an underdeveloped schema, a lack of knowledge about baseball, especially baseball terminology.

Prior knowledge may be one of the most potent variables in the overall comprehension process (McKeown, Beck, Sinatra, & Loxterman, 1992). As they read, active learners will consciously or unconsciously use their schema or prior knowledge in many ways. For example, a student with diabetes who has been assigned to read a chapter on the endocrine system would probably already possess a partially developed schema for this content. This schema would assist the student in assimilating any new information into what she already knows about the pancreas gland and the hormone it secretes, insulin. She would cautiously approach the reading task as one in which she knows some related information but needs to learn a great deal more. Perhaps the student might even take the time to preview (see Chapter 9) the chapter to determine what glands and hormones in the endocrine system the author deemed important and compare that information to what she already knows.

Active learners also use their schema to make inferences or to fill in gaps in text comprehension (Pressley, Johnson, Symons, McGoldrick, & Kurita, 1989). They know that textbooks are never completely explicit, and they will often have to read between the lines and piece ideas together to construct a full interpretation of the text. For example, if the political science chapter cursorily refers to the confidence levels of polls, such as the Gallup, but does not fully define confidence levels, active learners would use their prior knowledge to construct a definition. Active learners who had never heard of a confidence level in polling would seek alternative information sources such as the glossary, dictionary, index, or teacher to fill this gap in understanding.

Secondary students often experience difficulty comprehending technical content-area textbooks because of their limited prior knowledge for the topics. Conversely, students with extensive prior knowledge for a given topic will likely understand and learn from a textbook discussing an aspect of that topic. Of course, prior knowledge occurs in degrees and is not necessarily an all-or-none condition. In a fascinating study of prior knowledge, Brandsford and Johnson (1972) presented the following statement to students from differing sociocultural backgrounds:

> Jane decided not to wear her matching silver necklace, earrings, and belt because she was going to the airport. (p. 719)

Readers from backgrounds that had provided them many direct and related prior experiences with airports and jet travel had no problems explaining Jane's reasoning—the heavy jewelry could trigger the metal detector; therefore, she left it at home. Readers from backgrounds that precluded opportunities for visiting airports and flying, however, came up with explanations such as, "She was afraid of getting ripped off." The point of this research as well as other related studies is that the amount of information students possess on any topic may vary widely, leading to alternative interpretations. What is more, many students do not automatically draw on their prior experiences when reading in school settings; it must be cued (Pressley et al., 1990).

Although most researchers agree that prior knowledge for text topics facilitates comprehension, some researchers have shown that students may possess "incorrect" prior knowledge (Marshall, 1989) or "naive" conceptions (Alvermann & Hynd, 1987, 1989) that can interfere with learning important information. What is more, Hynd and Alvermann (1986) and Marshall (1987) found that many older readers were likely to hold on to their misconceptions even after reading well-written text that clearly refuted their misconceptions. These findings reinforce the critical importance of exploring students' prior knowledge for and conceptions of topics before reading. In this way, you can discover any misconceptions and create instructional conditions that enable students to reject their existing misconceptions (Alvermann & Hague, 1989; Hynd & Alvermann, 1989).

Finally, active learners use their schema or the textbook writer's schema in trying to summarize and recall important information. In this way, they can see the big picture instead of countless arrays of seemingly unrelated facts and details. If active learners know they have little or no information about a topic, then they will choose to use the author's schema by remembering the chapter's organizational structure. If, however, learners have considerable relevant prior knowledge and a clear purpose for reading, they will choose to organize recall around their own knowledge structures.

To summarize, active learners use their schema or prior knowledge flexibly to construct meaningful interpretations of texts.

The instructional implication of the importance of prior knowledge for secondary teachers can be simply put: Teachers must explicitly assist students in developing relevant prior knowledge for reading selections and in relating their own background information to their reading (Alexander & Kulikowich, 1991; Pritchard, 1990). In the next chapter we examine some teaching strategies for helping students activate and use relevant prior knowledge when interacting with text.

Principle 2: Active Learners Use Text Structure to Guide Their Meaning Making

Are you surprised that the reading materials that children in first grade are introduced to are stories? Can you imagine passing out science books to children and welcoming them to their first readers? We begin teaching children to read with stories because they are already very familiar with the structure of stories. Narrative, according to Sawyer (1987), is a fundamental mode of meaning making through language.

Interest in story reading rarely wanes throughout our lives; but do you relish the opportunity to crack open one of your textbooks before turning in? We have observed high school students plow through their assigned government and science reading, anxious to finish just so they can put the book down. Students in junior and senior high must learn to deal with the formal expository prose of textbooks if they are to be successful readers and learners.

Text structure refers to the discernible organizational patterns of narrative and expository texts. Within the past 10 years, researchers have been identifying the general structures of text and demonstrating the importance of using knowledge of these structures for effective comprehension (Armbruster, Anderson, & Ostertag, 1989; Graesser, Golding, & Long, 1991; Kieras, 1985; Mandel, Stein, & Trabasso, 1984; Meyer, 1985; Roller, 1990).

If a text is well organized, active learners will capitalize on those positive and facilitative features to improve their understanding (Armbruster, Anderson, & Meyer, 1991). If, however, the text is poorly organized or discusses complex and unfamiliar concepts, then active learners know it is appropriate to slow down, reflect, and use any necessary fix-up strategies to ensure adequate comprehension. For example, the active learner studying a biology chapter on glands and hormones for the first time might preview and then map the chapter to determine the author's overall organizational structure before proceeding to read. Active learners realize that texts are written by authors who have their own biases and schemata.

A useful frame of reference for characterizing the extent to which a text is organized is by describing its degree of **considerateness**. According to Anderson and Armbruster (1986), a considerate text is textually coherent, a characteristic of text they claim plays a prominent role in students' comprehension and learning. For a text to be coherent, it must cohere both globally and locally. When texts are **globally coherent,** the ideas are arranged logically in an easily identifiable organization. Research indicates that well-organized text is better understood and more easily recalled than poorly organized text (Sinatra, 1991). When the organization of prose is implicit, that is, less obvious, the text is more difficult to understand (Horowitz & Samuels, 1987).

Although several organizational relationships of expository text adhere globally (Weaver & Kintsch, 1991), Meyer's (1979) system, which examines five groups of logical relationships, is very representative:

- Antecedent/consequent or covariance showing a causal relationship between ideas
- Response relationship including problem–solution, question–answer, and remark–reply
- Comparison relationships dealing with likenesses and differences between ideas
- Collection relationship showing that ideas are related to each other by a common factor or factors
- Description relationship presenting attributes or explanations about a topic

When Bartlett (1978) trained ninth graders to identify and use these five organizational relationships, their comprehension and memory dramatically improved. Most secondary textbooks, however, are not as conveniently and clearly organized as the artificially constructed passages that researchers use in their studies (Armbruster, Anderson, & Ostertag, 1987). Chapters that appear in secondary textbooks rarely conform to one organizational pattern (Estes, 1982).

Stories or narrative text are also organized according to predictable patterns, called *story grammars* (Mandler, 1987). For instance, stories have settings; they have characters; the main character is usually en route to a goal; to reach his goal the main character must confront obstacles (essentially conflict); and conflict is resolved in some way. Apparently, as readers receive constant exposure to well-structured stories, they internalize these grammars in the form of story schema, which assists them in understanding and writing stories. Theoretical and instructional aspects of story schema are developed in Chapter 9.

Active learners are sensitive to a text's global organization through the use of signaling devices (W. Kintsch & Yarbrough, 1982; Meyer, 1979). Signals tell students something about a text's organization or emphasize certain ideas in the content. Types of signals include the following:

- Summary statements
- Previews or introductory statements
- Typographical clues such as underlining, italics, and boldfaced print (see Chapter 9)
- Pointer words and phrases, such as "the most important reason why . . ."

Local coherence, the other factor of textual coherence, is the linguistic mortar that connects ideas together in a text (Tierney & Mosenthal, 1982). A text will be locally coherent if the pronoun referents, substitutions, connectives, and conjunctions are explicitly stated and clear to the reader. When textbook writers fail to be locally cohesive, their texts are less structured, the ideas are not woven together, and there is no flow of meaning from one idea to the next. This kind of text places a particularly heavy burden on students, because it forces them to bridge many ideas inferentially that could have been tied together more explicitly by the author. The point here is that the more inferences the reader has to make, the greater the chance for the author's message to be misconstrued (Pearson & Camperell, 1985).

Fortunately, active learners can "realize" text structure in spite of its disconnectedness (Brozo, 1986; Brozo & Curtis, 1987). The two paragraphs that follow provide an example of a disconnected text and how active learners normally impose their own structure on the text to understand it.

Disconnected Text

In the evening, the light fades. Photosynthesis slows down. The amount of carbon dioxide in the air space builds up again. This buildup of carbon dioxide makes the guard cells relax. The openings are closed.

How the Good Reader Makes Connections

The fading light of evening causes photosynthesis to slow down. A plant's ability to "breathe" *however* [italics added here and following], does not depend on light and thus continues to produce *carbon dioxide*. The *carbon dioxide* in the air spaces builds up again, which makes the *guard cells relax*. The *relaxing of the guard cells* closes the *leaf openings. Consequently,* the *leaf openings* close in the evenings as photosynthesis slows down. (Anderson & Armbruster, 1984, p. 206)

In the first example, the author's use of short, simple sentences can often obscure the relationships among the ideas in the text. Notice also how the reader echoed words that ended the previous sentence by placing them at or near the beginning of the following sentence and inserted, inferentially, words that tied together the text and made the relationships more obvious (see italicized words).

When a textbook has global and local coherence, it becomes considerate and, thus, more readable for students. Unfortunately, many secondary-level textbooks have a high degree of inconsiderateness: They contain misleading titles and subtitles, lack explicit main ideas, omit crucial information, contain contradictory information, and are ambiguous (Anderson & Armbruster, 1984; Estes, 1982). Many textbook writers, editors, and publishers have attempted to deal with these inconsiderate and difficult texts by altering the surface-level features of sentences and word length, two indices typically used in readability formulas. Readability formulas such as Fry's (1968) and Gunning's (1952) use these easily quantifiable indices to yield either a grade level or a score on a scale roughly correlated with a grade level. Often textbooks are purposely rewritten or written with short, simple sentences and few multisyllable words to superficially simplify their difficulty level so a match can be made between students' supposed reading levels and a text's estimated readability. The rewritten text, while judged to be easier by a readability formula, often becomes more ambiguous and difficult for students (Davidson & Green, 1988). The first paragraph in the preceding example vividly illustrates this phenomenon. This paragraph has only four sentences, 35 words, and 52 syllables, yet remains inconsiderate and difficult to understand for its intended audience.

Thus, when selecting a textbook, teachers should focus on the features of global and local coherence and the students' prior knowledge rather than superficial features that may give the impression of considerateness but actually make the text less readable. Although no textbook is perfect, certainly some are more considerate, coherent, and have better learnability characteristics than others. Sometime in your teaching career, if you have not been asked already, you probably will be asked to be a member of a committee to select that "perfect" new textbook for your students. Do you know what you should look for beyond content that would promote learnability? Theresa, a health education teacher, was given the checklist in Figure 2–1 by her district-level curriculum coordinator. She found it extremely helpful in reviewing the many textbooks the publishers had sent her. With the checklist she had specific characteristics to evaluate that exceeded content and concepts in the field of health. You may wish to use this checklist to analyze the textbooks you are using, to review possible new adoptions, or even to critique this book.

In Chapter 3 we discuss some specific teaching strategies that can help your students overcome comprehension barriers of inconsiderate text by becoming more actively involved in the text-comprehension process.

Figure 2–1 Criteria for measuring a textbook's learnability

Directions: Check the column that best describes the textbook's use of these characteristics that promote active and successful learning.

	Excellent	Good	Poor
1. Difficult new vocabulary words are highlighted, italicized, underlined, or defined in the margins.	____	____	____
2. Concepts are presented clearly in relatively direct and understandable sentences.	____	____	____
3. The chapter's main idea(s) or purposes for reading are explicitly stated at the beginning.	____	____	____
4. The authors present a list of objectives, questions, or organizational structure to guide the students while reading/studying.	____	____	____
5. The authors use explicit and appropriate words to signal the text's structure and organization (e.g., *on the other hand*)	____	____	____
6. The authors use practical real-life situations, examples, or analogies that students can relate to and have an interest in.	____	____	____
7. The authors use boldface headings and subheadings that are logical to the concepts being discussed and useful to students with little or no prior knowledge.	____	____	____
8. The authors internally summarize key concepts and present useful summaries at the end of the chapter.	____	____	____
9. The authors help students use appropriate prior knowledge by reviewing or reminding readers of previously learned concepts (e.g., *in the last chapter we discussed . . .*)	____	____	____
10. The text includes quotations from primary sources and authorities to support and add interest.	____	____	____
11. When there are questions at the end of the chapter, different kinds (e.g., true–false) of questions are supplied that require higher levels of thinking (e.g., on my own) and responses using students' own words.	____	____	____
12. The table of contents shows a logical development of the subject matter.	____	____	____
13. Captions under graphs, tables, diagrams, and pictures are clearly written.	____	____	____
14. Math and science problem examples match the concepts and steps previously discussed.	____	____	____
15. The authors inform the students when information contained in graphs, tables, or diagrams is not also contained in the text.	____	____	____
16. When the text refers to a graph or table, that aid is on the same page as the textual reference.	____	____	____
17. The authors suggest other resources and activities for students motivated to explore the area or for students who have difficulties with specific objectives or specific tasks.	____	____	____

Principle 3: Active Learners Process Text in an Elaborative Fashion

Active learners who process text in an **elaborative** fashion focus on key ideas, construct internal connections among those ideas, and then integrate that information into their own schemata (E. Kintsch, 1990). As a consequence of these elaborations, they improve their comprehension as well as their interest and enjoyment in their reading (Garner, 1990; Garner, Alexander, Gillinham, Kulikowich, & Brown, 1991; Irwin & Baker, 1989; Wittrock, 1991). Learners who actively elaborate on text while they read are distinctive. Figure 2–2 illustrates this belief. In it are the summaries by two different students of a section in their science chapter dealing with water and land pollution. Can you pick out the active learner? What did that student do to make his or her comprehension more elaborative?

As you probably determined, Susan's summary reflects a much greater degree of elaboration than Derrick's for several reasons. What did you list as your reasons? If you listed any of the following, you identified some of Susan's most effective elaborative processes:

- Susan focused on the overall structure of the section—the four types of pollution and the solutions to water pollution. Derrick focused on details and facts with no sense of organization.

Figure 2–2   Susan's and Derrick's summaries on water pollution

Susan's Summary

According to this section of our textbook, there are four sources of water pollution: agriculture, industry, domestic, and other sources such as oil spills. Perhaps the most dangerous source of pollution comes from industry, though oil spills, such as the one in Alaska, have certainly had a large impact on our wildlife and on our economy. Pesticides, fertilizers, and animal waste, the three types of agricultural pollution, are usually not direct, but indirect. A notorious example of a pesticide is DDT. There are three kinds of industrial pollution; chemical, thermal, and radiation. The problems associated with radiation seem to be the most severe in that skin cancer and leukemia are possible results of exposure. Organic waste and detergent builders are the main sources of domestic pollution. Both seem to have an adverse effect on our lakes and rivers so that the balance of nature is upset. This section of the chapter ended by discussing some solutions to the problem of water pollution—all of which are costly but very important.

Derrick's Summary

This section of the chapter discussed different kinds of water pollution. Pesticides such as DDT are dangerous to use because they are not biodegradable. Some nitrates are toxic to animals and humans. Nitrates can be reduced to nitrites, which interfere with the transport of oxygen by hemoglobin in the blood. Mercury vapor is highly toxic and can be absorbed through the lungs. There are two types of radiation cell damage, direct and indirect. Detergents and organic wastes can also harm our water sources. Oil spills hurt our aquatic life.

- Susan used personal examples (e.g., the Alaskan oil spill and Alar) that were not included in the text. Derrick's summary used only textbook information, even though water pollution is a highly controversial and often-debated topic in the news today.

- Susan made some conclusions and inferences. For instance, she inferred that radiation is the most dangerous form of water pollution.

Wittrock (1990) has enumerated several learner-generated elaborations that include many of Susan's processes and many others that Susan did not use. Following is a modification of Wittrock's list.

Compose titles, headings, and subheadings when they are missing.

Underline, circle, or *check* words and sentences that are important or troublesome.

Develop questions.

Paraphrase key ideas in own words.

Relate text to personal experiences.

Seek interrelationships among ideas and across text.

Sense the overall structure of the text.

Create examples, analogies, or metaphors.

Make predictions, inferences, or conclusions.

Draw pictures, tables, or graphs for difficult operations.

Solve problems, create new problems.

Apply principles to new situations.

Not all learners need to elaborate in the same manner or in the same degree of intensity. Active learners know that their interest, prior knowledge, purposes, and the task will determine how much to elaborate. For example, a student who has avidly read fiction and nonfiction books on World War II will probably not need to do as much elaboration as the typical sophomore who knows only that Hitler was in some way involved in this conflict. The student with little or no background knowledge about World War II would probably have to do some extensive summarizing, outlining, or mapping to adequately prepare for an upcoming examination, while the well-versed student may only need to briefly review the key concepts and information.

Most secondary students do not have a repertoire of efficient, elaborative strategies. Several studies have demonstrated that secondary and postsecondary students frequently rely on lower levels of processing, such as rereading, to remember and understand the information (Garner, 1990; Nist & Simpson, 1988). Fortunately, teachers have a variety of strategies at their disposal (Alvermann & Swafford, 1989) with which they can help students move toward more elaborative processing by initially providing elaborations and then gradually phasing in student responsibility for their own elaborations through modeling and demonstrating. In Chapter 3 we discuss how classroom teachers can model and directly teach students to elaboratively think about content-area texts.

Principle 4: Active Learners Have Control and Knowledge of Appropriate Strategies

Thus far, we have discussed three characteristics of active learners. Briefly, the active learner is one who understands the interactive nature of the reading process, the unique characteristics of texts, and elaborative strategies for text comprehension. The fourth characteristic—**metacognitive awareness**—is the cognitive process that directs and orchestrates the other active learning processes.

Think about a typical reading experience—you're moving through a passage on automatic pilot, absorbing information and ideas, seemingly without effort. Suddenly, your eyes fix on the word *propinquity*. Within the span of a mere 2 or 3 seconds, you realize you don't know what the word means, quickly reread the sentence in which it was found, and decide that at least for the time being, its definition is not critical to your present level of comprehension. Back on automatic pilot, you realize after a couple of more paragraphs that the meaning of *propinquity* has taken on more significance. You return to the word, frame its meaning in context, guess, and finally consult a dictionary.

This scenario essentially describes the process of metacognition. According to Baker and Brown (1984), **metacognition** is the "knowledge and control we have over thinking and learning activities" (p. 2). Active learners who have knowledge of the reading process are acutely aware of their cognitive resources and know how to regulate those resources. They can detect errors or contradictions in a text, engage a repertoire of efficient text-processing and study strategies, and take advantage of their strengths while remaining sensitive to their weaknesses as learners. Metacognition involves planning strategies, allocating effort and resources, and evaluating the success of strategies in accordance with goals and assigned tasks (Garner, 1987).

Metacognitive awareness plays a vital role in whether or not students have successful reading experiences. In fact, research indicates major differences between the metacognitive abilities of novice and expert readers (Garner & Alexander, 1989; Schommer & Surber, 1986). There also appear to be developmental differences in metacognitive awareness. Researchers have found that older students seem to be better able to regulate and control their comprehension processes than younger students (Brown, Armbruster, & Baker, 1986; Pressley, Goodchild, Fleet, Zajchowski, & Evans, 1989). These findings do not mean, however, that you can expect your secondary students to possess sophisticated metacognitive strategies. On the contrary, research studies with entering college freshmen have found them to be very passive learners who lack awareness and control of their own learning strategies (Simpson, 1984; Weinstein & Rogers, 1984). Fortunately, secondary students can profit greatly from metacognitive strategy training (Brown & Day, 1983; Garner, 1990).

The extensive research on metacognition conducted since the late 1970s provides considerable insight into how active learners process text (Garner, 1987) and the instructional contexts that best support independent learning (Irwin & Baker, 1989; Perkins & Salomon, 1989). Active learners intuitively understand and coordinate the four variables that interact to promote learning. Each of these variables is considered next: the text, the task, strategies, and the learner.

The Text.   As discussed earlier, active learners are sensitive to the characteristics of text and use that knowledge as they plan their reading and learning. They analyze the vocabulary, clarity of presentation, and organizational structure of the texts they read. They assess their own interest in and prior knowledge of the topic. Finally, they ask themselves how each reading task differs. With this information, active learners set meaningful purposes for reading.

The Task.   Active learners realize that the primary purpose of reading is to construct meaning. They know that there are many different kinds of tasks that demand different levels of elaboration. One way readers determine the extent of their elaborations is by determining how the information from the reading will ultimately be used. Will there be a test? What kind of test? Will there be an assigned paper or project? A class discussion? A second way to characterize a task is to examine the levels of thinking it demands. Will a memory-level understanding be sufficient, or will the task also necessitate a synthesis of the key ideas and application of information to different situations? Active learners know that understanding directions to a physics laboratory experiment, for example, requires a different kind of reading than a poem, such as "Richard Cory," so that they can write a paper for their English teacher.

Strategies.   Weinstein and Mayer define a strategy as "cognitive behaviors that a learner engages in during learning that are intended to influence the encoding process so as to facilitate the acquisition, integration, and retrieval of new information" (1986, p. 1). Active learners have a repertoire of elaborative strategies and know when to select the most appropriate one(s) for the text and task.

To select the most appropriate strategy, active learners must have three different kinds of strategic knowledge (Paris, Wasik, & Turner, 1991). The first is **declarative** knowledge. For example, a student with declarative knowledge of previewing would know that previewing is done before you read and that it involves such steps as reading the introduction and summary. The second kind of strategic knowledge is **procedural**. Active learners with declarative and procedural knowledge of the preview strategy can preview and describe the idiosyncratic procedures for previewing in detail. In addition to these two types of strategic knowledge, students must also possess **conditional** knowledge, perhaps the most critical form of strategic knowledge (Paris, 1987). When active learners have conditional knowledge, they know when and why to use various strategies. Thus, with the previewing strategy, they know that it may be appropriate to preview only certain texts. Active learners know that the time involved in previewing a chapter before they read is time well spent, because they will be able to check the author's organization, establish what they might already know about the topic, set purposes for reading, and divide up the reading into meaningful chunks. Students must develop all three kinds of strategic knowledge if they are to control and transfer the strategies we teach them to their own reading and learning tasks.

The Learner.   The fourth variable is the learners' awareness of their own characteristics. These characteristics include prior knowledge, interest, motivation, attention span, learning style, and skill strengths and needs. Active learners use information about themselves and information about the text and task before selecting a plan of action or strategy to meet their purpose for reading. For example, active learners might choose to map a history chapter to prepare for an essay exam because they know that they need to see the "big picture." Such reasoning and strategy selection involve the task (the essay exam that focuses on general issues), the text (the history text is arranged in hierarchical fashion), and the learners' characteristics (they know they learn best when information is represented visually or diagrammatically).

The Influence of Context on Active Learning

In Chapter 1 we gave considerable attention to the idea that learning does not take place in a vacuum; rather, students become active learners within supportive learning environments that teachers create. It is important to keep in mind, therefore, that students will not come to possess all of the characteristics of active learners described previously unless teachers actively promote independent learning within a classroom context that is inviting, engaging, and nurturing of students' risk taking.

Most secondary students have, at best, only a partial understanding of the four interacting variables that impact successful independent learning. Even the brightest students probably earned their high grades through diligence and memorization, not through an analysis of the most appropriate strategies for the task and content area being studied. You can help students become more sensitive to these four variables in a variety of ways. Most importantly, you need to model or demonstrate the strategic behavior you want your students to emulate. For example, if there is a specific strategy you want them to use in solving math story problems, you must demonstrate and talk through that process so it becomes external and accessible. The mental steps you intuitively employ must in some way become visible to your students, or the chances of them understanding and applying your suggested strategy to their own story problems will be greatly reduced (Dole et al., 1991; Vygotsky, 1978). In the next chapter, we will share the teacher-directed strategy of reciprocal teaching as one way to encourage students to become more active learners who possess knowledge and control of text-comprehension strategies.

Summary

In this chapter we have proposed a holistic perspective of active learning. We have suggested that active learners are strategically involved in the reading process. More specifically, we outlined four important principles that characterize active learners. These four principles are not discrete and mutually exclusive, as in the skills model of reading comprehension, but rather are interactive and interdependent. The first principle concerns learners' use of prior knowledge to interact with text. The second principle focuses on active learners' use of text structure to guide their meaning construction. The third principle explains how active learners process text in an elaborative fashion to improve their understanding and recall. The fourth and final principle explains how active learners possess knowledge and control of appropriate strategies for independent learning.

In Chapter 3 we address these four principles within a methodological framework. We explain and demonstrate how you can use and devise many specific strategies for your classroom. Some of these strategies will be teacher directed and some will be student initiated. As you read the remaining chapters of this book, you will be frequently reminded of how a particular strategy is intended to force students out of familiar passive roles and impel them to become active participants in the learning process.

References

Alexander, P., & Kulikowich, J. (1991). Domain knowledge and analogic reasoning ability as predictors of expository text comprehension. *Journal of Reading Behavior, 23,* 165–190.

Alvermann, D., & Hague, S. (1989). Comprehension of counter-intuitive science text: Effects of prior knowledge and text structure. *Journal of Educational Research, 82,* 197–202.

Alvermann, D., & Hynd, C. (1987). *Overcoming misconceptions in science: An on-line study of prior knowledge activation.* Paper presented at the meeting of the National Reading Conference, St. Petersburg, FL.

Alvermann, D., & Hynd, C. (1989). Study strategies for correcting misconceptions in physics: An intervention. In S. McCormick & J. Zutell (Eds.), *Cognitive and social perspectives for literacy research and instruction.* Chicago, IL: National Reading Conference.

Alvermann, D., & Swafford, J. (1989). Do content area strategies have a research base? *Journal of Reading, 32,* 388–395.

Anderson, T. H., & Armbruster, B. B. (1984). Content area textbooks. In R. Anderson, J. Osborn,

& R. Tierney (Eds.), *Learning to read in American schools: Basal readers and content texts.* Hillsdale, NJ: Lawrence Erlbaum.

Anderson, T. H., & Armbruster, B. B. (1986). Readable textbooks, or, selecting a textbook is not like buying a pair of shoes. In J. Orasanu (Ed.), *Reading comprehension: From research to practice.* Hillsdale, NJ: Lawrence Erlbaum.

Armbruster, B., Anderson, T., & Meyer, J. (1991). Improving content-area reading using instructional graphics. *Reading Research Quarterly, 26,* 393–416.

Armbruster, B., Anderson, T., & Ostertag, J. (1987). Does text structure/summarization instruction facilitate learning from expository text? *Reading Research Quarterly, 22,* 331–346.

Armbruster, B., Anderson, T., & Ostertag, J. (1989). Teaching text structure to improve reading and writing. *The Reading Teacher, 43,* 130–137.

Baker, L., & Brown, A. (1984). Metacognitive skills and reading. In P. D. Pearson (Ed.), *Handbook of reading research.* New York: Longman.

Bartlett, B. J. (1978). *Top level structure as an organizational strategy for recall of classroom text.*

Unpublished doctoral dissertation, Arizona State University.

Brandsford, J., & Johnson, M. (1972). Contextual prerequisites for understanding: Some interesting investigations of comprehension and recall. *Journal of Verbal Learning and Verbal Behavior, 11*, 717–726.

Brown, A., Armbruster, B., & Baker, L. (1986). The role of metacognition in reading and studying. In J. Orasanu (Ed.), *Reading comprehension: From research to practice.* Hillsdale, NJ: Lawrence Erlbaum.

Brown, A., & Day, J. (1983). Macrorules for summarizing text: The development of expertise. *Journal of Verbal Learning and Verbal Behavior, 22*, 1–14.

Brozo, W. G. (1986). Recognizing and manipulating connectives: A reading/writing strategy for secondary students. *Reading Improvement, 23*, 7–11.

Brozo, W. G., & Curtis, C. L. (1987). College readers' comprehension of connected and disconnected text. *Research and Teaching in Developmental Education, 3*, 21–26.

Davidson, A., & Green, G. (1988). *Linguistic complexity and text comprehension: Readability issues reconsidered.* Hillsdale, NJ: Lawrence Erlbaum.

Dole, J., Duffy, G., Roehler, L., & Pearson, P. D. (1991). Moving from the old to the new: Research on reading comprehension instruction. *Review of Educational Research, 61*, 239–264.

Estes, T. H. (1982). The nature and structure of text. In A. Berger & H. A. Robinson (Eds.), *Secondary school reading.* Urbana, IL: ERIC Clearinghouse on Reading and Communication Skills.

Fry, E. B. (1968). A readability formula that saves time. *Journal of Reading, 11*, 513–516, 575–578.

Garner, R. (1987). *Metacognition and reading comprehension.* Norwood, NJ: Ablex.

Garner, R. (1990). When children and adults do not use learning strategies: Toward a theory of settings. *Review of Educational Research, 60*, 517–529.

Garner, R., & Alexander, P. (1989). Metacognition: Answered and unanswered questions. *Educational Psychologist, 24*, 143–158.

Garner, R., Alexander, P., Gillingham, M., Kulikowich, J., & Brown, R. (1991). Interest and learning from text. *American Educational Research Journal, 28*, 643–659.

Gunning, R. (1952). *The technique of clear writing.* New York: McGraw-Hill.

Graesser, A., Golding, J., & Long, D. (1991). Narrative representation and comprehension. In R. Barr, M. Kamil, P. Mosenthal, & P. D. Pearson (Eds.), *Handbook of reading research* (Vol. 2). New York: Longman.

Hynd, C., & Alvermann, D. (1986). The role of refutation text in overcoming difficulty with science concepts. *Journal of Reading, 29*, 440–446.

Hynd, C., & Alvermann, D. (1989). Overcoming misconceptions in science: An on-line study of prior knowledge activation. *Reading Research and Instruction, 28*, 12–26.

Horowitz, R., & Samuels, S. J. (1987). *Comprehending oral and written language.* San Diego, CA: Academic Press.

Irwin, J., & Baker, I. (1989). *Promoting active reading comprehension strategies.* Englewood Cliffs, NJ: Prentice-Hall.

Kieras, D. E. (1985). Good and bad structures in simple paragraphs: Effects on apparent theme, reading time, and recall. *Journal of Verbal Learning and Verbal Behavior, 17*, 13–28.

Kintsch, E. (1990). Macroprocesses and microprocesses in the development of summarization skill. *Cognition and Instruction, 7*, 161–195.

Kintsch, W., & Yarbrough, C. (1982). Role of rhetorical structure in text comprehension. *Journal of Educational Psychology, 74*, 828–834.

Mandel, H., Stein, N., & Trabasso, T. (1984). *Learning and comprehension of text.* Hillsdale, NJ: Lawrence Erlbaum.

Mandler, J. (1987). On the psychological reality of story structure. *Discourse Processes, 10*, 1–29.

Marshall, N. (1987). *When text fails to meet reader expectations.* Paper presented at the meeting of the National Reading Conference, St. Petersburg, FL.

Marshall, N. (1989). Overcoming problems with incorrect prior knowledge: An instructional study. In S. McCormick, & J. Zutell (Eds.), *Cognitive and social perspectives for literacy research and instruction.* Chicago: National Reading Conference.

McKeown, M., Beck, I., Sinatra, G., & Loxterman, J. (1992). The contribution of prior knowledge and coherent text to comprehension. *Reading Research Quarterly, 27*, 79–93.

McNamara, T., Miller, D., & Brandsford, J. (1991). Mental models and reading comprehension. In R. Barr, M. Kamil, P. Mosenthal, & P. D. Pearson (Eds.), *Handbook of Reading Research* (Vol. 2). New York: Longman.

Meyer, B. J. (1979). Organizational patterns in prose and their use in reading. In M. L. Kamil

& A. J. Moe (Eds.), *Reading research: Studies and applications.* 28th Yearbook of the National Reading Conference. Rochester, NY: National Reading Conference.

Meyer, B. J. (1985). Prose analysis: Purposes, procedures and problems. In B. K. Britton & J. B. Black (Eds.), *Understanding expository text: A theoretical and practical handbook for analyzing explanatory text.* Hillsdale, NJ: Lawrence Erlbaum.

Nist, S. L., & Simpson, M. L. (1988). The effectiveness and efficiency of training college students to annotate and underline text. In J. Readence & R. S. Baldwin (Eds.), *Dialogues in literacy research.* Chicago, IL: National Reading Conference.

Paris, S. (1987). *Does metacognition inhibit or facilitate reading comprehension?* Paper presented at the National Reading Conference Annual Meeting, St. Petersburg, FL.

Paris, S., Wasik, B., & Turner, J. (1991). The development of strategic readers. In R. Barr, M. Kamil, P. Mosenthal, & P. D. Pearson (Eds.), *Handbook of reading research* (Vol. 2). New York: Longman.

Pearson, P. D., & Camperell, K. B. (1985). Comprehension of text structures. In H. Singer & R. Ruddell (Eds.), *Theoretical models and processes of reading* (3rd ed.). Newark, DE: International Reading Association.

Perkins, D., & Salomon, G. (1989). Are cognitive skills context-bound? *Educational Researcher, 18,* 16–25.

Pressley, M., Goodchild, F., Fleet, J., Zajchowski, R., & Evans, E. (1989). The challenges of classroom strategy instruction. *Elementary School Journal, 89,* 301–342.

Pressley, M., Johnson, C., Symons, S., McGoldrick, J., & Kurita, J. (1989). Strategies that improve children's memory and comprehension of text. *The Elementary School Journal, 90,* 3–32.

Pressley, M., Woloshyn, V., Lysynchuk, L., Martin, V., Wood, E., & Willoughby, T. (1990). A primer of research on cognitive strategy instruction: The important issues and how to address them. *Educational Psychology Review, 2,* 1–58.

Pritchard, R. (1990). The effects of cultural schemata on reading processing strategies. *Reading Research Quarterly, 25,* 273–295.

Roller, K. (1990). The interaction of knowledge and structure variables in the processing of expository prose. *Reading Research Quarterly, 25,* 79–89.

Sawyer, W. (1987). Literature and literacy: A review of research. *Language Arts, 64,* 33–39.

Schommer, M., & Surber, J. R. (1986). Comprehension-monitoring failures in skilled adult readers. *Journal of Educational Psychology, 78,* 353–357.

Simpson, M. L. (1984). The status of study strategy instruction: Implications for classroom teachers. *Journal of Reading, 27,* 136–142.

Sinatra, R. (1991). Integrating whole language with the learning of text structure. *Journal of Reading, 34,* 424–433.

Tierney, R. J., & Mosenthal, P. J. (1982). Discourse comprehension and production: Analyzing text structure and cohesion. In J. H. Langer & M. T. Smith-Burke (Eds.), *Reader meets author/bridging the gap: A psycholinguistic and sociolinguistic perspective.* Newark: DE: International Reading Association.

Trends in academic progress (1991). Princeton, NJ: Educational Testing Service.

Vygotsky, L. S. (1978). *Mind in society: The development of higher psychological processes.* Cambridge, MA: Harvard University Press.

Weaver, C., & Kintsch, W. (1991). Expository text. In R. Barr, M. Kamil, P. Mosenthal, & P. D. Pearson (Eds.), *Handbook of reading research* (Vol. 2). New York: Longman.

Weinstein, C. E., & Mayer, R. E. (1986). The teaching of learning strategies. In M. C. Wittrock (Ed.), *Handbook of research on teaching.* New York: Macmillan.

Weinstein, C. E., & Rogers, B. T. (1984). *Comprehension-monitoring: The neglected learning strategy.* Paper presented at the American Educational Research Association, New Orleans, LA.

Wilson, P. T., & Anderson, R. C. (1986). What they don't know will hurt them: The role of prior knowledge in comprehension. In J. Orasanu (Ed.), *Reading comprehension: From research to practice.* Hillsdale, NJ: Erlbaum.

Wittrock, M. C. (1990). Generative processes of comprehension. *Educational Psychologist, 24,* 345–376.

Wittrock, M. C. (1991). Contemporary methodological issues and future directions in research on the teaching of English. In J. Flood, J. Jensen, D. Lapp, & J. Squire (Eds.), *Handbook of research on teaching the English language arts.* New York: Macmillan.

3

Comprehension Strategies: The Tools of Literacy

To fail to teach students strategies they do not use and from which they could benefit is to fail the students, to neglect to show them ways of reaching reading and studying in optimal ways. To teach crops and arithmetic facts and science principles and battles without teaching students how they can learn more about any of this or about other content is to risk that children will not become effective independent learners.

—Ruth Garner (1988)

As discussed in Chapter 1, we believe that the major goal of education should be the development of critical thinkers and independent learners so that students can use literacy to pursue knowledge on their own to the depth they desire. We also outlined our ideas about the importance of teachers' developing and expanding their own knowledge and abilities to facilitate students' independent learning and make transitions toward creating learning environments wherein student independence is enthusiastically supported. To become independent learners, students need strategies that actively involve them in the process of constructing meaning in reading and writing and using new understandings in a functional way. In this chapter we present teacher-directed and student-initiated comprehension strategies for facilitating the growth of independent learners. The four principles outlined in

Chapter 2 provide the organizing framework for our discussion. These principles, however, are not mutually exclusive. That is, a strategy discussed under the first principle—helping students use prior knowledge and schemata in the meaning-making process—could easily help your students with the second, third, and fourth principles describing active learning. In fact, each chapter in this book will in some way present another approach to helping your students become active readers and writers and, thus, effective independent learners.

Case Study

Charles teaches 10th-grade general biology in a large consolidated high school in the Midwest. After 3 years of teaching, he has noticed that many of his students (a) generally have a difficult time understanding the textbook, (b) do not complete homework reading assignments, and (c) seem to be trying to memorize information while failing to learn to observe and think about scientific phenomena. Charles is highly interested in discovering ways to help his students become more enthusiastic about science learning and better able to deal with and benefit from textbook reading.

Midway through the first semester of the new school year, Charles has begun a 2-week unit on genetics. Within the unit he wants to emphasize students' understanding of genetic engineering and the implications of this technology for their personal lives. In the preceding 2 months, his students studied the scientific method, the cell, and classification of living things, including the life cycle and basic requirements of life.

To the Reader: As you read and work through this chapter on comprehension strategies, think about and be prepared to generate some strategies that could help Charles accomplish his goals. Consider how the strategies described in this chapter and those from your own experience and imagination could be adapted to the teaching and learning of science material.

Active Learners Use Schemata and Prior Knowledge in the Meaning-Making Process

The principle that active learners use schemata and prior knowledge in the meaning-making process (as discussed in Chapter 2) is concerned with the extent to which readers *apply* appropriate schemata in meaning making. You can use many strategies to help students engage and use relevant prior knowledge as they read. In this section, we discuss three very effective ways of helping students access and use their relevant prior knowledge to comprehend and make meaning of the texts they read. We demonstrate how teachers implement these strategies in their high school classrooms to meet their students' needs. Teaching considerations related to prior knowledge are taken up in other chapters in this book as well (e.g., Chapters 4 and 5).

The Anticipation Guide

Using a series of statements, **anticipation guides** (Readence, Bean, & Baldwin, 1985) actively involve students by asking them to make predictions or take stands about ideas they eventually will be reading, listening to, or viewing. These guides not only are excellent stimuli for subsequent discussion and writing, but they also provide teachers with considerable diagnostic information. By examining answers to the statements in the anticipation guide, you can detect students' beliefs, the extent of their prior knowledge, and misconceptions about targeted concepts. As discussed in Chapter 2, this latter concern has been identified with problems in reading comprehension (Alvermann & Hague, 1989; Alvermann & Hynd, 1989; Hynd & Alvermann, 1989; Marshall, 1989). With this important diagnostic information, you can then make on-the-spot instructional adjustments in lesson and unit plans. An anticipation guide for the chapter you are now reading could look like the one in Figure 3–1.

Figure 3–1   Anticipation guide for Chapter 3

Directions: Before you read Chapter 3 any further, read each of the following statements and answer YES or NO in the space marked "Before Reading," depending on whether you agree with the statement or not. After you have finished Chapter 3, return to these five statements and in the space marked "After Reading," answer YES or NO. Now, compare your two responses. Did you change any of your responses? If so, why or why not?

	Before Reading	After Reading
1. Testing is the most efficient way to discover your students' misconceptions or lack of knowledge about a concept.	————	————
2. For students to use the structure of their textbooks to guide their meaning making, they should learn how to identify organizational patterns.	————	————
3. The best way to teach students how to monitor their learning is by assigning them to answer the questions/problems at the end of a chapter.	————	————
4. Most students believe that answers to teacher-posed questions will be found right in the text.	————	————
5. Almost all students can be taught to comprehend and think on higher or more elaborative levels.	————	————

How many statements in Figure 3–1 could you agree with? You probably guessed on a few and felt comfortable with the rest of the statements. Perhaps your careful reading of Chapter 2 or a recent related lecture/discussion helped you with this task. In other words, you were using your prior knowledge to take a stand on an issue. When you have finished this chapter, return to this anticipation guide to see if you have made any changes in your positions about how to develop active readers and learners.

Anticipation guides can appear in many different formats. The guide in Figure 3–2 was designed and used by Leslie, a business teacher, with her 12th-grade students during a unit entitled "Using Credit Wisely" in a consumer economics course. Leslie developed this guide as a result of discovering that many students have misconceptions about credit. The guide is helpful as a tool for students' self-assessment of their current knowledge and attitudes toward credit. Leslie has also

Figure 3–2   Anticipation guide for "How Do You Feel About Credit?": 12th-grade business

---

How Do You Feel About Credit?

Directions: Indicate your reaction to each of the following statements by stating whether you:

Always agree	Never agree
Usually agree	Are uncertain
Occasionally agree	

For each statement, write one of the words: *always*, *usually*, *occasionally*, *never*, or *uncertain* in the answer space provided.

(Note that *always* means that you agree wholeheartedly. *Usually* means you agree for the most part, with minor exceptions. *Occasionally* means that you agree under some conditions but not under others. *Never* means that you disagree entirely.)

1. Wise buyers do not use charge accounts. _____

2. Buying for cash is always the best policy. _____

3. People who use credit have a tendency to buy more than they really need. _____

4. Using credit encourages people to buy items on impulse. _____

5. Customers who buy on credit should be charged more than those who pay for cash. _____

6. People should not buy on credit because it discourages the practice of thrift. _____

7. Persons who buy on credit are less likely to search for the best buys. _____

8. Stores that offer credit are likely to charge more than those that sell only for cash. _____

---

found it helpful in activating students' prior knowledge and gaining their interest in the topics of the unit.

The guide in Figure 3–3 was constructed by Chris, an 11th-grade English teacher, for the poem "War Is Kind" by Stephen Crane. Chris used this poem and several short stories for his themed unit on war and conflict.

Chris and Leslie used the following procedures in constructing and using the anticipation guides with their students. We recommend that you follow a similar set of procedures in constructing and employing your own guides.

1. They identified the major concepts they wished to emphasize from the assigned text selection that related to the unit's theme.

2. They identified and described what they believed were their students' experiences, beliefs, and prior knowledge that would be challenged or supported by the assigned text.

3. They generated three to five statements that challenged and confirmed their students' present beliefs and wrote a brief set of directions to accompany those statements.

4. They prepared a handout and transparency for overhead projection with the statements and asked students to respond.

5. They polled the class on their responses and then engaged them in a prereading discussion, which clarified and highlighted how they felt.

6. They asked their students to read the assigned text.

Figure 3–3   Anticipation guide for "War Is Kind": 11th-grade English

---

War Is Kind

Directions before reading: Read each statement and answer YES or NO in the space provided, depending on whether you agree with the statement or not.

_____ 1. Wars destroy the unity of a nation.
_____ 2. Wars can be fought in a humane fashion.
_____ 3. The long-term advantages of war usually outweigh the short-term disadvantages.
_____ 4. A war like Vietnam is not justifiable in terms of money and the loss of manpower.

Directions after reading: React to the four statements from the perspective of the following individuals. Put YES if that person would agree and NO if that person would disagree. Be prepared for class discussion.

Statement 1	_____ You	_____ Stephen Crane	_____ Phil Ochs
Statement 2	_____ You	_____ Stephen Crane	_____ Phil Ochs
Statement 3	_____ You	_____ Stephen Crane	_____ Phil Ochs
Statement 4	_____ You	_____ Stephen Crane	_____ Phil Ochs

---

7. They assigned the students to return to the anticipation guide and respond again.

8. Students discussed the changes, if any, that occurred and explained and elaborated on the changes.

Both Chris and Leslie like the anticipation guide because their students become more actively involved in the lessons. The students like the guides because they can see that they are learning. They have learned that the anticipation guides work best when used with some units but not all. By not overusing the guides, Chris and Leslie have preserved their full impact as an active learning strategy. For variety, in other units, Chris and Leslie employ alternative, but equally effective, strategies that help students interact with text, such as the one discussed next.

The PReP Procedure

PReP, the Pre-Reading Plan (Langer, 1981), is an instructional procedure that can help you assess your students' text-related prior knowledge. In addition, through Prep you can determine how prior knowledge is organized and the quality and quantity of language that students use to express their knowledge about a particular topic. According to Langer, the PReP procedure has three phases: the initial association with the concept, reflections on the initial associations, and reformulation of knowledge.

Initial Association With the Concept.   Ask students for their **initial associations with a concept** or topic by saying "Tell me anything that comes to mind when. . . ." For example, you might ask students to say anything that comes to their minds when they hear the words "stock market." As students respond, you or another student record these comments on the board. During this phase, students have an opportunity to find associations between the topic about to be studied and their own prior knowledge for that topic, as well as the benefit of hearing their classmates' associations.

Reflections on Initial Associations.   Ask students for their reflections on those initial associations with a question such as "What made you think of . . . ?" This phase not only helps students develop an awareness of their network of associations but also provides opportunities for them to hear their classmates' explanations.

Reformulation of Knowledge.   In the third phase, reformulation of knowledge, you might ask "Based on our discussion and before we read the text, have you any new ideas about . . . ?" This question gives students the opportunity to verbalize associations that have been elaborated or changed through the discussion. By the close of this phase, students are usually making more refined statements about the concept to be studied.

Langer (1981) claims that students' responses to these questions can be classified into three distinguishable levels. The first level of response indicates that the students have "much prior knowledge" about the concept being discussed. Students with a great deal of prior knowledge will respond in the three phases of PReP with superordinate (main idea) concepts, definitions, analogies, or linkages of one concept to another. For example, for the concept of pollution, a student with considerable prior knowledge might respond as follows:

> There are three kinds of pollution—air, water, and land. All three deal with the process of harming our environment by making it unclean. Land and water pollution are closely related through the hydrologic cycle.

The second level of response, "some prior knowledge," indicates that students can discuss the concept in terms of examples, attributes, or characteristics. A student with some prior knowledge might state that pollution is bad because it ruins our air, land, and water with impurities. Students at both this level and the first level should be able to successfully comprehend the assigned text with some guidance by the teacher.

Students responding at the third level, "little prior knowledge," have underdeveloped schema for the topic to be studied. Their responses focus on low-level associations such as other words that sound like the targeted word, or unrelated firsthand experience. For example, a student operating at this level might say this about pollution:

> Pollution—yes, I have seen pollution at my grandmother's lake in southern Georgia. I used to fish there during the summer.

Students responding in this manner will likely need additional information to fill in gaps in their prior knowledge to ensure adequate understanding of the assigned text.

Interacting With Text Through Writing

Too many students have become passive learners and are likely to remain so if teachers assume the role of "filling heads" with knowledge. Meaningful learning grows out of experiences with the content that require active involvement and decision making. Writing forces participation and helps students increase their metacognitive awareness of what they know and their learning decisions through self-reflection, which is inherent in the writing process (Atwell, 1987; Calkins & Harwayne, 1991). Romano (1987) says "Using language makes us think, and writing makes us use language."

The Anticipation Guide, PReP, and Writing.   Both the anticipation guide and PReP strategies can be modified in many ways and used as stimuli for student writing.

The guided writing procedure (see Chapter 7) can be used as a natural extension of the reading and discussion stimulated by the anticipation guide. PReP can also be modified and used with student writing. Ann, a ninth-grade mathematics instructor, asks her students to make a journal entry for each unit of study. Her students respond to a variety of open-ended questions similar to those contained in PReP. For a unit on the real-number system, she asks her students to respond to the following questions before they begin to read:

> What do you think of when I say "whole numbers," "rational numbers," and "irrational numbers?"
>
> If you wrote anything to my first question, tell me, Where or what or who made you think of that response?

Ann believes that writing activities such as these help her plan her lessons because she learns so much about her students' prior knowledge or lack of knowledge. (Some of her other excellent ideas for the use of writing in the mathematics class can be found in Chapter 7.)

Learning Logs.   Toni introduces her 10th-grade biology students to learning logs (for further discussion and examples see Chapter 5) by sharing her own log. Her entries are based on scientific readings and laboratory and field experiences. **Learning logs** take the form of questions about terminology, reflections on experiments, musings on observations, and missives on new learning. Toni demonstrates how her rough and often messy entries provide a mirror for her thinking, which often leads to deeper understandings and more refined thinking. Toni then asks the class to examine the organization of the upcoming reading by looking at titles, headings, and subheadings, and chapter questions or objectives. Based on this preview, students brainstorm what they already know or think they know about the topic. These brainstormed ideas are recorded in students' logs. After reading the text chapter or a section of it, students are asked to write another entry focusing on what they learned and noting any misconceptions in their original entries (Santa & Havens, 1991).

The following example shows one student's entries before and after reading a chapter on the human brain.

Before-Reading Entry

In this chapter I'm going to learn about the human brain. I know the brain is split into a right and left half. I think the halves control different things, but I'm not sure what. I also know that when someone has a stroke, blood vessels break in the brain.

After-Reading Entry

I learned that the two halves of the brain are called the right and left cerebral hemispheres. But, really, there are four main parts of the brain: the medulla oblongata, which controls involuntary movements like breathing, the pons, which controls auditory and muscular coordination, the cerebellum, which controls fine motor movements, and the cerebrum, which is the largest part, made up of two hemispheres, and controls speech, intelligence and emotions. I also learned that a stroke is caused by a blockage in the arteries in the brain. This keeps the brain from getting enough oxygen, and it becomes damaged.

As these entries demonstrate, the student was able to use writing as an aid in the process of meaning making. The first entry served as a reflection of prior knowledge, whereas the second entry allowed the student to reconsider his initial understandings (e.g., about the nature of strokes) and derive new understandings based on text reading. Toni reinforces this reader–text interaction and metacognitive processing by asking students to include in their logs process comments that answer the broad question "How did writing about your ideas before and after reading affect your ability to learn the content?" Here is what the same student wrote in response:

Process Comments

I felt more interested in reading about the brain because I thought more about it before I read the chapter. I was surprised I knew even the little bit I did know about the brain before reading. Writing helped me think about what I already knew. It also made me more curious about what I was going to read because I wanted to find out if I was right. Knowing that I was going to have to write after reading made me read more carefully than I usually read stuff for school. I got more out of it. I wasn't real happy about doing it at first, but I think it helps.

Toni invites students to share their process comments with the whole class, which often sparks lively discussion about strategies for learning. Toni tries to focus class discussion on how writing helps connect prior knowledge to the ideas and information in the text, promotes active reading, and can lead to self-monitoring of learning.

The anticipation guide, PReP, and learning logs are strategies that can provide not only considerable diagnostic information about students and their prior knowledge but also, because they are excellent stimuli for student discussion and writing, can promote more elaborative levels of comprehension and thinking. In the next section, we discuss strategies that help students use the structure of content-area texts to improve their understanding and learning.

Active Learners Use Text Structure to Guide Their Meaning Making

Teachers who want their students to be more sensitive to the structure and characteristics of text have a wide range of strategies available. In this section, we first discuss two methods of teaching students how to capitalize on local coherence of text and three methods for teaching them about global coherence (see Chapter 2 for a discussion of local and global coherence). These strategies, as well as the related strategies of previewing and mapping (see Chapter 9), are intended to help students use a text's structure and organization to locate key ideas, understand relationships in the text, and store information in long-term memory for future recall. This section concludes with some suggestions for teachers who want to become more sensitive to the structures of their own textbooks.

Creating Local Coherence With Connectives

Rita teaches 9th- and 10th-grade history in a large suburban high school, where she has developed a method for helping her students use **connectives** in comprehending their history textbook. The following example describes her work in teaching connectives to students at the beginning of a unit over the American Civil War.

In groups of three to four, students were asked to generate a couple of statements about the Civil War that reflect what they already know about the topic. Afterward, the groups read their statements to the whole class. Rita copied the statements on the board. She studied the list for a moment, then placed stars next to six of the sentences:

> The Civil War was fought for many reasons.
> The major reason the Civil War was fought was to free slaves.
> The Civil War was not fought with a foreign country.
> American fought American in the Civil War.
> Abraham Lincoln was president during the Civil War.
> Many soldiers from both sides died in the Civil War.

Besides laying the foundation for manipulating connectives, Rita provided students with a stimulus for prior knowledge activation with this activity. Plenty of interesting discussion ensued as groups of students offered their statements. For instance, when the statement "The major reason the Civil War was fought was to free slaves," was read, another student quickly commented that she didn't think that was quite true, and a small debate commenced over that issue. The students finally agreed that the slave issue was one of the significant reasons for the war. During this period, Rita did not direct the discussion but facilitated it by prodding and asking open-ended questions.

Rita then passed out a list of connecting words (see Figure 3–4), provided information about the significance of the words, and modeled how she would use them in her speaking and writing. Then she wrote these two sentences on the board:

> The wine glass broke.
> Mary grabbed the broom.

Figure 3–4   Connectives used to join ideas

then	in the meantime	in order to	notwithstanding	so
moreover	however	so that	in comparison	how
also	although	thus	instead	until
likewise	on the other hand	as a result	finally	already
for this reason	in spite of	at last	next	but
because	by this time	subsequently	furthermore	otherwise
hence	another	meanwhile	and	nevertheless
accordingly	besides	even though	since	rather
soon	in addition	yet	therefore	that
at that time	as well as	on the contrary	consequently	even so
while				

Rita described how important it is to understand how sentences relate and mentioned that the ability to connect sentences with a word that accurately reflects the relationship between sentences is part of what good readers do. She asked for some possibilities from the students' list of connectives that would join the sentences. Some said *"so"* and *"therefore,"* which created one meaning, while other students offered *"as"* and *"when,"* which created another meaning. Rita capitalized on these responses by pointing out how important it is to have a connective to join these sentences to more closely match the author's intended meaning.

Next, Rita asked her students to open their history textbooks to the Civil War chapter and identify any connectives they could find on the first couple of pages. As connecting words were found, Rita and her students discussed the role each played in context by considering the meaning of adjoining ideas and their relationship as signaled by the connective.

At this point, Rita asked students to work in small groups and write a paragraph using connecting words to join together the statements the class generated about the Civil War. The groups then shared their paragraphs by reading them aloud. After each reading, Rita asked for reactions, especially comments about whether the connectives signaled the correct relationships among the sentences. Here is the way one group connected the statements:

> *Although* the Civil War was fought for many reasons, the major reason the Civil War was fought was to free slaves. The Civil War was not fought with a foreign country, *rather,* American fought American, *and* many soldiers from both sides died. *At that time,* Abraham Lincoln was president.

After reminding the students to keep a watchful eye out for structures provided by the author that help explain how ideas are related and that they would be working with connectives throughout the year, Rita proceeded with the unit. With only about 10 minutes left in the period, she began to read aloud from a book containing letters written by and to soldiers and officers during the Civil War. Not wishing to waste an opportunity to reinforce her recent instruction, she paused after reading a connective or some other structure of cohesion and, thinking aloud, modeled why she thought the author chose that structure.

Rita also takes some time within every unit to reinforce students' knowledge of how connectives operate in text. She gives students passages from their textbooks with the connectives removed. Students are expected to supply these missing links. Rita has found that by sensitizing her students to the role of connectives in text, students not only improve their comprehension by becoming better able to compensate for disconnected text, but they also compose more cohesive themes, essays, and stories.

Interlocking Guide

Another way to teach students to become more sensitive to connectives is through the use of an interlocking guide (Thomas, 1979). Thomas coined the term "**interlocking guide**" for a guide that brings together text information and the reader's text structure schema. The following example from a business textbook employs an advantage/disadvantage organizational pattern. The key connectives are in italics in the example but would be omitted from the students' copy.

> Every household has at one time or another received some type of advertising message sent directly to the home, such as a catalog, a circular, a letter, or a free sample. Direct-mail advertising is *advantageous* if an advertiser desires to get a wide coverage for products. The circulars announcing a grocer's specials for the week, the catalog announcing a summer or spring sale of merchandise, or a letter offering a special purchase are *examples* of direct-mail advertising. There are *two* major *advantages* of direct-mail advertising. *First,* the message can be directed to specific customers and thus it is selective; *second,* it can be spread over a wide territory. Both large national companies and small, local retails effectively use direct-mail advertising (Pickle & Abrahamson, 1980, p. 71).

As you can see from the example, the selections used for the modified cloze are brief and require students to replace the omitted word. The following steps the business teacher used in constructing this interlocking guide can be followed for developing your own guides:

1. He located a passage that represented a prevalent organizational pattern of the textbook and/or chapter.
2. He typed the passage on a separate sheet of paper, placing a blank of uniform size in place of the connectives. He then made handouts and a transparency for overhead projection.
3. Before students were assigned to read the chapter, he introduced the concept of connectives, similar to the way Rita did with her 9th and 10th graders. Then he asked his students to read the passage and alerted them to the fact that some of the words were purposely left out.

4. After the students read the excerpt, he asked them to reread and fill in the blanks with the appropriate words. He emphasized that the excerpt must make sense with their inserted connectives.

5. He read the excerpt aloud, pausing at each blank and asked students to insert their connective and provide a rationale.

6. He summarized the strategy and experience by reminding them of the usefulness of connectives—information can be more easily recalled when a structure is imposed on a text.

The business teacher provided an excellent follow-up to this activity by asking students short-answer questions about the excerpt that required them to integrate text structure knowledge with textual information. For example, one of the questions he asked was "What is one advantage and one disadvantage of direct-mail advertising?"

Creating Global Coherence With Charting

A critical aspect of instruction designed to promote active learning is for teachers to phase out of their instructional role and for students to phase in and take on more responsibility for their own learning. One strategy that supports this transfer is charting, which eventually can be used by students in their own learning once teachers have provided sufficient examples and guided practice.

Charting is a strategy that helps students summarize key ideas and visually sense the interrelationships between these ideas. The chart in Figure 3–5 is one that Tad, a biology teacher, used with his sophomores to help them understand the textbook's explanation of the pituitary gland. Tad first distributed the partially completed chart and described how the act of creating a chart can help improve understanding and recall. He then assigned his students to complete the chart after reading the assigned pages discussing the pituitary gland. The next day in class, he asked his students to work in small groups to check and discuss the information in their charts. After allowing students time in small groups, he brought the class together for a discussion of the function and location of the pituitary gland. During the rest of the unit entitled "Hormones, Nerves, and Muscles," he created a variety of charting formats for his students so they could see their versatility. Tad's long-term plan was to require his students to work in pairs to create their own charts for the next unit of study.

Tad relied on the textbook's structure to organize the charts for his units of study. Although this organizational structure suited his instructional objectives and his students, you may have to make some adjustments, depending on the extent to which the information in your textbook is explicitly organized. Charting then becomes one way of imposing order on information that may not be organized in a suitable way for your students.

Figure 3–5   Sample chart for biology chapter

The Pituitary Gland				
Hormone	**Function**	**Location**	**Scientific Name**	**Chemical Composition**
TSH	influences the thyroid by negative feedback	anterior lobe; 1 of 4 tropic hormones	thyrotropic	glycoprotein
FSH	stimulates ovarian follicle	anterior lobe; 1 of 4 tropic hormones	follicle stimulating	glycoprotein
ACTH				
LH				
Growth				

Ann, the math instructor referred to earlier, uses charting to improve her students' skills in solving word problems. The following motion problem is typical:

The speed of a stream is 4 miles per hour. A boat travels 6 miles per hour upstream in the same time it takes to travel 12 miles downstream. What is the speed of the boat in still water?

To help with the precision reading necessary for motion problems, Ann asks students to organize the data in a chart with the headings, *t*, *r*, and *d*, representing *time*, *rate*, and *distance*. She explains her lesson in this way:

My students already know that $R \times T = D$. I also have them represent rate downstream as $b + c$, where b is the rate of the boat, c is the rate of the current or stream, and $b - c$ is rate upstream. I point out how the boat and current work together downstream, hence $b + c$, and against each other, $b - c$, upstream. Therefore, before looking at the specifics of the problems, the student can make a chart as follows:

	t	r	d
upstream		$b - c$	
downstream		$b + c$	

My students then can read further and fill in the appropriate information so the chart looks like this:

	t	r	d
upstream	$\dfrac{6}{b-c}$, or $\dfrac{6}{b-4}$	$b - c$, or $b - 4$	6
downstream	$\dfrac{12}{b+c}$, or $\dfrac{12}{b+4}$	$b + c$, or $b + 4$	12

Here is the process they follow. Four is substituted for the stream speed. Six and 12 are substituted for distance up and downstream, and the time is represented as distance divided by rate. To set up an equation, students must look for a relationship, and hopefully they read "same time," so they set the representations for time equal to each other. In other words, the equation is:

$$\frac{6}{b-4} = \frac{12}{b+4}$$

My students seem to catch on to these motion problems much quicker with the charting idea.

Ann knows that she needs to maximize the interactions between her students and their math textbook by employing a variety of strategies. While some would suggest that good textbooks should take care of that interaction, we know that textbooks do not teach, teachers do.

Expository Passage Organizers

Another useful way to help students become more aware and take advantage of a text's global coherence is with **expository passage organizers (EPOs)**. EPOs were designed to help students see the structure of expository text and how the organization of ideas in text can affect comprehension (Miller & George, 1992). The proponents of EPOs have documented their utility for (a) focusing attention on critical components of expository text structure and (b) providing students models for organizing their ideas for writing exposition. Providing organizers for expository text reading and writing has been shown to improve students' comprehension and recall (Duffy, 1985; Slater, Graves, & Piche, 1985) as well as writing and attitudes toward writing (Miller, 1988).

Teachers from a variety of content classrooms can design EPOs that match their particular texts and lessons. For example, in the EPO in Figure 3–6, an eighth-grade health teacher provided his students an EPO for a problem–solution text on AIDS. Here is how the EPO was generated and how the teacher used it with his students:

First, he identified the various structural elements of the text, in this case, a chapter from an informational book entitled *AIDS: How It Works in the Body* (Greenberg, 1992) by: (a) listing the overall passage pattern (problem–solution); (b) labeling the critical components of the text structure (e.g., introduction, problem, body, etc.); and (c) providing partially completed main idea and detail statements within each of the critical components. As students work through the chapter, they fill in the remaining information on the EPO, such as additional details and/or main idea statements.

The teacher uses EPOs such as the one on AIDS not only to promote students' understanding and recall of text material but also to further develop students' expository writing skills. The organization of the EPO helps students conceptualize the overall structure of the author's ideas about AIDS from the specification of the problems to a discussion of particular solutions. The teacher extends the utility of EPOs by writing an essay himself using an expository text pattern consistent with the cause–effect patterns in the text, then fashioning an EPO for it. Both the essay and EPO are shared with students and critiqued. Using EPOs to interact with text on a global structural level helps students recognize that their expository writing should have an overall organizational pattern as well. In recognizing how authors produce well-written exposition, students learn to model their compositions after these excellent examples. For instance, in the problem–solution essay on AIDs, students see how the author's citing of the problem is a main idea and her elaborations on the problem are supporting details. They notice how

Figure 3–6   Expository passage organizer (EPO) for a problem–solution text

AIDS: How a Virus Becomes an Epidemic

Directions: Complete the following EPO by looking back at the passage.

Passage Pattern: Problem–Solution

Introduction—Problem—Paragraph 1

Detail: HIV can be passed to another in sexual intercourse if body
fluids are exchanged.
Detail: Blood-to-blood contact _____
Detail: Mothers with AIDS _____
Main Idea: HIV enters the body in only three main ways.

Body—Solution—Paragraph 2

Main Idea: _____
Detail: AZT has been shown to interfere with the production of HIV.
Detail: Natural immune substances _____

Body—Solution—Paragraph 3

Main Idea: Scientists continue to search for better ways to treat
the infections that attack people with AIDS.
Detail: Chemotherapy, radiation _____
Detail: Antibiotics _____
Detail: Early detection of HIV can improve chances for successful
treatment.

Conclusion—Result—Paragraph 4

Main Idea: With no scientific cure in sight, changing behavior in
the face of this growing danger may be the best
preventative tact.
Detail: _____

the author uses examples to support points and become better at providing appropriate supporting examples when composing their own expository texts (Miller & George, 1992).

Visualizing Text Organization

Another method for helping students better understand the organization of expository text is a holistic strategy that helps students visualize the abstract structures of exposition (McNeil, 1987; Sinatra, 1991).

One of the best ways we have seen to assist students in **visualizing text organization** is with pictures. You can use visuals to assist in the learning of text organization in a couple of ways. First, students can make their own visual essays with photographs, slides, or magazine or newspaper pictures and arrange them to form visual compositions. A visual display that is shared with the whole class can serve as a powerful organizer for students' oral presentations and written compositions. Second, you can help students prepare their visual essays and teach them to use frames and storyboards in representing text organization. The process of selecting pictures and arranging visuals that tell or imply how an expository text is organized reinforces for students a sense of global coherence, a sense of text structure (Sinatra, 1986).

We recommend you share with students a guide to structuring visual compositions for text organization such as the one in Figure 3–7. With this guide, students could be asked to work in small groups to prepare visual essays. On large charts, they can arrange and attach their pictures while planning their verbal accounts to accompany the visuals. Students can be shown how to draw lines to connect pictures and show relationships; in this way, they create a kind of visual

Figure 3–7   A guide to visual displays for expository text structure

Text Structure	Visual Display
Cause and Effect	Suggest with pictures of slides that an event took place as a result of a prior event. For example, a cause-and-effect relationship can be portrayed by showing melting snow and heavy rain and then the resulting damage from river flooding.
Enumeration	Arrange a display that shows a picture that represents a group or class surrounded by a variety of pictures that exemplify that class. For example, a picture of a weasel could be surrounded by other animals in the weasel family.
Description	Pictures should be organized so that each adds a bit more detail to the overall display. For example, in a horizontal plane, pictures showing the process of recycling aluminum or paper could be arranged.
Problem–Solution	Pictures of a problem situation or event should be followed by pictures showing how the problem was resolved. For example, photos depicting the size and complexity of early computers followed by today's PCs would demonstrate how computers have been made more accessible and "friendly" by their reduced size.
Comparison–Contrast	Pictures should be displayed that show likenesses and differences among events, people, and places. For example, British soldiers in battle formation and dress could be accompanied by the battle tactics and dress of the Colonial army.

schemata for particular discourse types. Before writing compositions that mirror the text structure inherent in the visual essay, students should be given opportunities to share their displays with the class. During the "talk-through" period, they can refine their thinking as a result of questions and feedback from their peers.

Assisting students in becoming more sensitive to the structure of text or imposing structure on a text that lacks considerateness (see Chapter 2) can lead them to active and meaningful learning.

Active Learners Process Text in an Elaborative Fashion

If asked, many teachers will tell you that the students who frustrate them the most are those passive students who rarely do the reading or assignments but listen well enough in class to "just get by." For these passive nonparticipants, learning is memorization of facts, and teachers are the dispensers of information. Teachers are always earnestly searching for solutions to problems associated with passive learners. Although there is no panacea to passivity, the strategies included in this next section invite students to be active participants in their own learning. We discuss teacher modeling, cooperative learning, question–answer relations, and study guides.

Teacher Demonstrating Active Reading Processes

To actively process main or key ideas is to get at the very heart of comprehension, because good readers think at the idea level. Recently, there has been a resurgence of research activity concerned with how readers construct main ideas for paragraphs and passages (Afflerbach, 1990; Hare, Rabinowitz, & Schieble, 1989). This interest in main idea comprehension is not surprising when we consider the following: (a) National reports on literacy habits conclude that students in the middle and upper grades cannot think inferentially about text (*Trends in Academic Progress*, 1991); (b) direct teaching of comprehension skills rarely takes place in reading and content classrooms (Dole, Duffy, Roehler, & Pearson, 1991); and (c) analyses of textbooks that students must read have shown that a minority contain topic sentences or explicit main idea statements (Baumann & Serra, 1984).

To find out how readers construct main ideas, researchers are investigating how a reader thinks while reading (Kintsch, 1990). Brown and Day (1983) and more recently Afflerbach (1987) asked a sample of mature, expert readers to verbalize aloud their thought processes while they read. This technique, known as "verbal reporting" or "think alouds," afforded the researchers the opportunity to eavesdrop on how good readers make sense of text. They discovered that good readers use certain rules in the construction of main ideas for paragraphs and passages, including:

- Deleting irrelevant or unimportant information
- Generalizing categories for lists of items or actions
- Selecting a main idea statement when the author provides one
- Constructing a main idea statement if none is provided

These research findings have profound instructional implications. For instance, Brown and Day (1983) found that when less able readers were trained to use the same procedures used by experts they made significant gains in their ability to summarize and comprehend expository text. Furthermore, these rules of main idea construction can be modeled by the teacher. Thus, thinking out loud becomes a means of reading comprehension instruction.

Sandy's seventh-grade social studies class was confronted by the following passage about the Bay of Pigs Invasion in their textbooks. Sandy's interaction with her class exemplifies the power and effectiveness of modeling and demonstrating comprehension processes for teaching students to focus on key ideas in text.

In 1959 a revolution, led by Fidel Castro, had taken place in Cuba. At first, the United States supported the revolution. But when Fidel Castro was shown to be a communist, the United States withdrew its support for him and starting planning ways to overthrow him.

Under President Eisenhower, plans were made to overthrow Castro by starting another revolution in Cuba. The U.S. gave arms, money, and training to a number of Cubans who had left their country and had come to the U.S. during the revolution because of their dislike for Castro and communism. After Eisenhower, John Kennedy was elected President. He continued to support the Cubans in the U.S. who were planning to overthrow Castro.

In April 1961, the Cubans with U.S. assistance landed at the Bay of Pigs in eastern Cuba. But because they were not well prepared, they were quickly defeated by Castro's soldiers. Shortly afterward, Kennedy went on television to accept the blame for the defeat of the Cubans at the Bay of Pigs (Graff, 1980).

Sandy:	Okay, let's see if we can make sense out of this passage. First of all, let's talk about some of the words in here and some of the words referred to.
Student 1:	I know what a "revolution" is. . . . It's when the people of a country go against their president.
Sandy:	Great, so how does that fit with the first sentence?
Student 1:	Well, there was a revolution in Cuba.
Sandy:	Okay, who is Fidel Castro?
Student 1:	He must be from Cuba if he led the revolution.
Sandy:	Did Castro revolt by himself? No, of course he didn't. Other Cubans helped him. How do we know this?
Student 2:	He "led" people.

Sandy:	Right. Does anyone know anything else about Castro?
Student 3:	Isn't he still the president of Cuba?
Sandy:	Yes he is, and he's considered a communist. Do you remember reading about communism a few weeks ago? What did you learn?
Student 3:	The Russians were communist.
Student 4:	It's when everyone works for the government.
Sandy:	Okay, I've heard two things about communism. How does communism compare with how we live in the U.S.?
Student 4:	People work for themselves here. . . . They can keep their own money.
Student 5:	In some communist countries there's no religion . . . nobody believes in God.
Sandy:	Okay, so that's another difference when compared with our system. . . . We have freedom of religion. Now, what do you think the topic of this passage is?
Student 3:	The Bay of Pigs.
Sandy:	Can anyone be more specific?
Student 4:	What happened before and after the Bay of Pigs?
Sandy:	Excellent, so the first paragraph is talking about what happened before. . . . Can someone give me the main idea for the first paragraph?
Student 6:	The U.S. supported Castro until they found out he was a communist. . . . Then they stopped.
Sandy:	How many agree with Todd's main idea? Excellent, Todd. Do you now see why we would reject Castro? What does the passage say that supports this main idea?
Student 6:	It says we didn't support him anymore when we found out he was a communist.
Sandy:	Great. Now, what can you tell me about Presidents Eisenhower and Kennedy?
Student 2:	I know, Kennedy was shot by Oswald.
Student 5:	Eisenhower was some kind of general or something . . . before he was president.
Sandy:	Okay, who can tell me what's going on in the next paragraph?
Student 5:	Well, it sounds like some Cubans who had left Castro didn't like him and wanted to go back to Cuba.
Sandy:	Right. Why do you think these Cubans who had left Cuba didn't like Castro?
Student 5:	Because they liked our government?
Sandy:	Very good answer. . . . So what can we say is the main idea for this paragraph?
Student 7:	Eisenhower helped Cubans overthrow Castro.

Sandy:	Okay, does anyone disagree with this?
Student 6:	And Kennedy helped too.
Sandy:	So give me a complete main idea.
Student 6:	Eisenhower and Kennedy helped Cubans overthrow Castro.
Sandy:	The overthrow didn't actually happen, did it?
Student 3:	No.
Sandy:	So what if we say Eisenhower and Kennedy helped Cubans who were living in the U.S. plan the overthrow of Castro.
Class:	That's good.
Sandy:	What support do we have for this main idea?
Student 1:	It says the U.S. gave arms and training.
Sandy:	It sure does. Excellent work, group!

It is important to notice that Sandy does not tell students the key ideas, nor does she simply hand out chapter questions. Instead, she teaches students how to develop key idea statements. Notice, too, how Sandy's interaction with her students stimulated their prior knowledge for the topic, regulated their attention to the important points and supporting information in the text, provided a model of her own thinking about main ideas, and reinforced students' main idea thinking. Sandy spends a few minutes during nearly every class discussion in a similar way, collaborating with students in the process of generating key ideas while assisting them in the overall task of making sense out of the entire text. She solidifies the importance of reading for key ideas with homework, papers, and tests that require students to demonstrate elaborate levels of comprehension.

We have seen that modeling and demonstrating comprehension processes are very effective strategies for Sandy. Her students are overtly aware that she is their partner in constructing meaningful interpretations of their class texts. These teaching strategies, however, have broad applications for helping improve students' thinking and learning. As you will see, examples of teacher modeling and demonstrating appear in nearly every chapter of this book with a wide variety of content and in a number of classroom settings.

Identifying Sources of Information in Question Answering

Another way you can encourage deep and meaningful processing of text is through a questioning strategy that sensitizes students to the interaction of the text with their prior knowledge during question answering. Using a questioning framework known as **question–answer relations (QAR)** (Raphael & Pearson, 1985), students can learn how to locate and use many **sources of information** when answering comprehension questions along the continuum of text processing:

- *Right There:* The answer can be found in the text. The question cues the reader by echoing words from the text. The information source is mostly text based.

- *Think and Search:* The answer is not directly stated but requires the reader to combine ideas in the text with prior knowledge to form inferences.

- *On My Own:* The source of information for answering this type of question is the reader's prior knowledge. Processing is nearly entirely reader based.

QAR refutes the common misconception held by students that the text tells all. Reliance on the text as the sole source of information limits students' interactions with text and consequently their depth of understanding. A study with college remedial readers (Brozo, Stahl, & Gordon, 1985) found that before training in QAR most students believed the answers to all reading comprehension test questions could be found directly stated in the passages. Their comprehension scores reflected this faulty line of reasoning—all had failed a state-mandated reading test for matriculation into college. However, after 4 weeks of developing their question-answering abilities based on QAR, significantly more of these students passed the reading test as compared with a control group. In a study by Wixson (1983), fifth graders were conditioned to answer questions about an informational passage on either the reader-based end of the continuum or the text-based end. Then after a week, the students were asked to recall the passage. Recalls were provided at a level of understanding consistent with the level of questions students had been trained to answer. In other words, students who had answered text-based questions gave superficial, detail-level recalls, while elaborate and meaningful recalls were provided by students who had answered questions that required more reader-based processing. This finding demonstrates the powerful learning potential of questioning. If students are asked questions at the think-and-search and on-my-own levels of processing, they will remember textual information and ideas at those levels; if they are asked questions at the right-there level, then they will likely remember only information at the verbatim-recall level.

To provide you firsthand experience with identifying sources of information for questions, following is a QAR activity for you to complete. The experience will give you a much better grasp of the processing requirements placed on students in a typical QAR exercise. Read the following passage; then group the questions and answers according to the source of information for answering them (right there, think and search, on my own).

The Story of Buck Billings

"Buck" Billings left Teddy's Rough Riders the very day peace was signed with the Spanish. There were wild stories about gold in the Klondike, and he couldn't wait to claim his stake. In the port of Havana he planned to pick up a boat to Tampa, then head north by train. After 3 days' trek through mosquito-infested swamps, he found that all the boats were packed with soldiers and civilians leaving for the states. He hopped aboard a ship bound for Venezuela. From there he found passage on a banana boat heading for South Carolina. The boat was turned back by a hurricane and forced to dock in Santiago Harbor. On a small sailing vessel he was finally able to reach the southern coast of Florida. He walked for 2 days to a train depot. After several weeks, he made it through the southern plains, and eventually arrived in Denver, the town of his birth. Since it was already November, he moved back into his Aunt Dolly's boarding house, where he planned to stay for the next 4 months. During that winter, however, his yellow fever returned, and he succumbed to it on the first of the new year.

1. Why was the boat forced to turn back? (Because of a hurricane.)
2. Where is Aunt Dolly's boarding house? (Denver.)
3. Where is the Klondike? (In Alaska.)
4. Where was Buck's ship forced to dock after the hurricane? (In Santiago Harbor.)
5. If Buck intended to head back to the states, why did he take a boat to Venezuela? (Because all the boats heading for the states were packed, and he thought he could get back to the states from Venezuela.)
6. Where did Buck get yellow fever? (Cuba.)
7. What was the boat carrying that was heading for South Carolina? (Bananas.)
8. Did Buck make it to the coast of South Carolina? (No, the boat was forced back by a storm.)
9. Where was Buck the day peace was signed with the Spanish? (Cuba.)
10. Who is Teddy? (Teddy Roosevelt.)

Think about how you categorized these questions and answers as you read our categorization and rationales. We placed questions 1 and 4 in the right-there category because the questions cue the reader to the answers with words taken directly from the relevant sentence in the text.

Questions 2, 5, 7, and 8 we identified as think-and-search questions. Question 2 requires the reader to combine ideas from two sentences—the one stating that Buck arrived in Denver, and the next one stating that Buck moved back with his aunt. The inference is that Buck is from Denver and has lived with his aunt before. To answer question 5 also requires some inferential reasoning. Buck was unable to go directly north to the states because all the ships were filled. By heading south first, he hoped to get there from Venezuela by avoiding Cuba altogether. Unfortunately, he found himself back in Cuba anyway. Question 7 asks the reader to make a low-level inference that connects the words in the question "What was the boat carrying?" to the sentence in the text that refers to the boat heading for South Carolina as a "banana boat." To answer question 8, the reader must combine information from two sentences—one stating that Buck was on a boat bound for South Carolina and the next one stating that the boat was forced to dock in Santiago Harbor. To answer "no" to this question requires more inferencing than may initially meet the eye. Notice that the reader must realize that Santiago Harbor is not in South Carolina, and because no other mention of South Carolina is made in the passage, it can be assumed that Buck never arrived there.

We grouped questions 3, 6, 9, and 10 in the on-my-own category. Certainly, to answer question 3, the reader must already know the geographical location of the Klondike. The text provides no clue. If the reader also realizes that peace with the Spanish over Cuba was signed around the turn of the century, then this knowledge could reinforce the time frame for the Alaskan gold rush. To know that Buck proba-bly contracted yellow fever in Cuba (question 6) means that the reader has prior knowledge for the fact that yellow fever is a tropical disease and that many soldiers suffered and died from it as a result of their experiences in the war with Spain over Cuba. To answer question 9, the reader must integrate several bits of textual infor-mation with a great deal of prior knowledge. The reader must possess knowledge about the "Rough Riders" and Teddy Roosevelt and that they fought the Spanish in Cuba. Question 10 requires related prior knowledge to question 9; certainly, the reader must know that it was Teddy Roosevelt who commanded the "Rough Riders."

Teaching Question–Answer Relations Using Cooperative Learning

The ultimate goal of QAR is not simply to train students to identify information sources for answering questions. Instead, QAR training should be seen as a method of sensitizing students to the idea that there are various ways of thinking about a text. Through QAR they can engage their existing knowledge to interact more deeply and meaningfully with the texts they read.

Following is a description of an actual eighth-grade science classroom in which students were involved in **cooperative learning** experiences for reinforcing their understanding of QAR. Beth, the teacher, exploits the powerful learning potential of cooperative groups throughout the school year with nearly every topic she and her students explore. Students in this class develop a deeper understanding of sci-ence content through interactions with their peers via speaking, listening, read-ing, and writing. All students are provided greater opportunities to articulate and reinterpret text concepts and vocabulary, raise questions, discuss answers, and become more active class members.

The topic the class was considering was "What Makes Ice Ages?" Beth first asked students to form into their **study reading groups**, three to a group. Her stu-dents were used to many different grouping arrangements that allow them to move in and out of groups, interacting with different students, depending on the purpose for the group. For instance, two other common grouping patterns in Beth's classroom were **interest groups** and **research groups**. Beth briefly rehearsed the "Rules for Group Membership," which students had in their notes and were also written in bold letters on the side wall bulletin board.

- Each member must be strongly committed to doing the work and carry-ing out his or her specific roles within the group.

- Each member should understand and follow the directions for completing assigned work.

- Each member should respect other members' input.

- A member who disagrees with another member should defend that point of view, giving specific reasons based on the text or on personal experience.

- No member should dominate or withdraw; every member should add something to the discussion.

- Each member should be positive and encouraging of other members.

Beth then introduced the idea of QAR using an overhead transparency to focus the discussion. She discussed with the students how becoming more sensitive to the sources of information for answering questions can improve their abilities to get more out of their textbook reading. She discussed each of the levels of QAR and provided a handout with the labels and explanations. Beth asked students to open their science textbooks to the beginning of the section on ice ages. She presented on overhead a series of questions accompanied by answers covering the first page of this section. In their groups, students discussed among themselves why a question belonged in a particular category. Afterward, students shared their responses and rationales with the whole class. Beth allowed students to debate their answers, providing support, feedback, and demonstrations of her own thinking in identifying information sources for the questions.

The next phase of QAR instruction involves assigning individual responsibilities for each of the three group members. Beth asked each student in the groups to generate questions with answers for one of the three levels of QAR. The questions were written over the next page of the text. The groups then went over their questions, helping each other focus on the appropriate question for the assigned level. Beth then asked groups to exchange questions, emphasizing that the questions not be labeled. The groups worked with their new questions, determining sources of information and rationales. During this time, Beth sat in on each group's discussion, answering questions, providing necessary input, and reinforcing group efforts. Questions were then given back to their owners with comments. Students then reworked their questions based on input from the other groups.

To get a better idea of the kinds of group discussions students had as they worked cooperatively on identifying QARs, refer to the following excerpt. This discussion took place between three students trying to determine whether a question required think-and-search or on-my-own processing.

Student 1:   The question is, "If the greenhouse effect is true, what kind of climate will Chicago have in 50 years?"

Student 2:   What's the answer?

Student 1:   It says "6 to 12 degrees warmer. Like Florida."

Student 3:   How are we suppose to know that?

Student 1:   We can figure it out. . . . We have to look in the book first to make sure it doesn't tell us about Chicago.

Student 3:   I don't remember anything about Chicago.

Student 2:   It doesn't, I'm looking right now. I can't find anything about it.

Student 1:   It does say that if carbon dioxide keeps getting worse the world temperature is going to go up. You see where I am, on page 128.

Student 3:   It's for sure not a right-there or in-the-book question.

Student 1:   Does it say by how many degrees. . . . I'm looking down here. Yeah, here it is, it says that "if carbon dioxide levels continue to increase at the present rate, in 40 to 50 years the greenhouse effect will cause temperatures worldwide to increase by about 6 to 12 degrees centigrade."

Student 2:   So big deal, that doesn't sound like very much. How could that make us as warm as Florida?

(Students attend to the text.)

Student 3:   Look, I found this part up here that says that a 100 million years ago the earth was a lot warmer even at the poles. So maybe if the poles were warm, we would be really warm too. What do you think?

Student 1:   I like it. . . . This is a hard one.

Student 2:   So we're saying it's what, an on-my-own type or a think-and-search?

(They ponder.)

Student 3:   I think it's sorta like both. You can find some of the information in the book, but you have to figure it out by yourself when it comes to the part about Chicago.

Student 1:   Don't we have to say one or the other?

Student 3:   I don't think so. . . . She said they could be one or the other or anywhere in between.

(Student 1, designated as the recorder, writes down the group's rationale. They move on to the next question.)

QAR training promotes sensitivity to various information sources for answering comprehension questions; thus, students learn to process text in a more elaborative fashion. To move them to greater independence in reading comprehension, students should be generating their own questions that reflect the important information and ideas in the text.

Using Study Guides

Another versatile tool designed to promote more student involvement in learning is the **study guide**—a teacher-directed activity that can encourage students to think at more elaborative levels.

To facilitate elaborative processing of text and to promote higher levels of thinking, teachers can provide students with study guides (Herber, 1978). Study guides are designed to stimulate students' levels of thinking during and after reading. Guides also help students focus attention on important information and ideas, making their reading more efficient and simplifying the difficult task of reading complex texts (Herber & Nelson-Herber, 1993).

If you are not familiar with study guides, we invite you to complete the sample in Figure 3–8. First, look at the guide and directions. Then read the passage that accompanies it. After reading, complete the guide.

Now that you have finished the guide, a few comments are in order. Did you notice that, like QAR questions, the statements seemed to require a greater degree of mental activity as you moved from level I to level III? The reason for this is that the statements were written to tap various levels of comprehension. The way we think about a text can be conceptualized as a sliding scale or continuum. On one end of the continuum is the kind of text processing that requires recall of directly stated material. We might call this **text-based processing** because the information is based almost entirely within the text. To respond to level I of the study guide, you employed mostly text-based processing, because the answers were basically right there. As we move along the continuum, processing becomes less and less text based and increasingly reader based. By **reader based**, we mean that comprehension requires readers to connect their prior knowledge about a topic with the textual information. Level II of the guide required you to combine your prior knowledge with textual information to form inferences. At level III, comprehension of these statements that seem to go far beyond the directly stated information in the text required you to rely heavily on prior knowledge and to process text in an elaborative fashion by applying and predicting. Thus, the goal of a study guide is to help learners assimilate information and ideas into their existing schemata to make learning more meaningful and useful.

Something else you may have noticed about your study guide experience is that the statements in the guide form an excellent basis for class discussion. In fact, we urge you to take advantage of the discussion-generation potential of study guides, otherwise students might eventually come to view them as just more busy work. The important advantage of study guides for teachers is that students must read the assigned textbook and think about the assignment rather than skim or scan the pages for answers to text-based questions. In short, students who are required to complete study guides cannot come to class unprepared; the guides force them to become active learners.

A few other important features of study guides are especially pertinent. To make guides more motivating and attractive to students and, consequently, increase the likelihood that they will complete them and use them, the response formats should require students to do very little writing other than a simple mark, check, or a few words. The idea is that guides should not resemble typical kinds of discussion questions students are used to seeing and are forced to respond to with extensive written answers. The extent of the response on the guides should not, however, be thought of as indicative of the extent of thinking demanded of students. A

Figure 3–8   Sample study guide activity

Directions: Read the following passage; then read the statements about it. In the space to the left of each statement, put an *A* if you agree with the statement and a *D* if you disagree. Base your decisions on the information and ideas in the passage as well as what you already know about the topic.

Jesse Jackson's Broadening Political Base

In 1984, during his first presidential campaign, Jesse Jackson identified a constituency of the American public he believed had been, up to that time, underrepresented. Minorities of all colors and ethnic backgrounds as well as women, the poor, and other groups rallied around Jackson and were to become his "rainbow coalition." Jackson claimed that politicians had forgotten about these groups of Americans. He charged that many were victims of poverty, homelessness, joblessness, poor working conditions, low salaries, sexual harassment, and subtle and overt racism. Many had chosen not to vote out of hopelessness. They looked at the slate of presidential candidates, claimed Jackson, and despaired, realizing that none had their concerns at heart.

In spite of grass roots support and impassioned oratory, Jackson lost his bid for the presidency in 1984. Many said the country was not ready for a black president. However, political analysts speculated that Jackson's lack of success was attributable more to his narrow appeal than to his color. Indeed, in the 1988 presidential election, Jackson broadened his political base of support and mounted a far more serious challenge for the Democratic nomination. While holding on to the "rainbow coalition," he reached out to farmers, factory workers, and the Democratic mainstream. He brought many delegates to the Democratic national Convention in Atlanta, where he brokered his political power and exerted leverage on Michael Dukakis to help shape the Democratic planks and platform.

Level I

_____   Jackson broadened his political base of support in 1984.
_____   Jackson first ran for president in 1984.
_____   The Democratic National Convention was held in Atlanta in 1982.
_____   The rainbow coalition was made up of the white middle class.

Level II

_____   Jackson might have been more successful in 1984, but the country was not ready for a black president.
_____   Jackson charged that the presidential candidates engaged in racism.
_____   Jackson supported equal pay for women.
_____   Affordable housing would not have been on Jackson's platform in 1984.

Level III

_____   Presidential candidates who appeal to farmers and factory workers are likely to be fairly successful.
_____   Jackson should continue to broaden his political base of support if he expects to be successful in 1996.
_____   The United States. will not vote in a black president in the foreseeable future.
_____   Jackson lost his bid for the presidency in 1988.

colleague puts it well, describing study guides as "Short on responding but long on thinking." As you undoubtedly noticed when working through the level-III statements of the Jesse Jackson study guide (see Figure 3–8), your single-letter or -word responses were made after considerable mental activity. In the directions to the guide, you are asked to be prepared to defend your responses with evidence from the text and your prior knowledge. Emphasis on this point will discourage students from responding arbitrarily, especially when they will be held accountable for their work in small-group or whole-class discussions.

Finally, as with most strategies, even the best can become drudgery if misused or overused. Be discretionary about when to employ study guides. Not every text lesson or topic will demand or lend itself to guides. A science teacher's point about study guides is instructive: "I use them with topics that typically give my students the most difficulty. They agree that it helps them organize the information and ideas and prepares them for my tests. But I don't use them all the time, because other approaches work really well too." Study guides are only one way to promote elaborate text processing.

Designing and Teaching With Guides.   There are no set procedures for creating study guides. Types of guides are as varied as the teachers who construct them. In this sections, we share a range of examples of teacher-constructed study guides from a variety of content areas. Although guides can take on a number of different forms, nevertheless, you must make some important and necessary decisions before designing them:

1.   Read the text material thoroughly and decide what information and concepts need to be emphasized. You will be reminded of this step at several points throughout this book because it is the same process you should go through when, for instance, deciding key vocabulary to teach, appropriate readiness activities, and relevant trade books to accompany the text.

2.   Determine how much assistance your students will need in order to process the information at a deep and meaningful level. If students already possess foundational understanding of the content, then your guides can focus on reader-based processing and higher levels of thinking. If, on the other hand, your students lack a basic understanding of the content, then guides should also be designed to facilitate text-based processing.

3.   Ask yourself, "What kind of format will stimulate my students to think about the content in an elaborate fashion as well as motivate and appeal to them?" In our experience, the more imaginative the guide, the greater the chance that students will be enthusiastic about the guide and use it appropriately.

It is critical to prepare students to use study guides. If you simply distribute guides and tell students to complete them, you are setting yourself up for disappointment. Students need grooming and coaching to take full advantage of study guides. We recommend that you begin by "walking through" one of the guides, explaining its features, intent, and benefits. Allow students to meet in small groups and complete the guide in class under your supervision and with your assistance. Engage the class in discussion based on their responses to the guide, and use this feedback for providing additional explanation and for making any necessary modifications to the guide. Above all, keep in mind your purpose for using study guides. They should not be used as tests, because promoting a right-or-wrong mentality among students undermines the intent—to encourage higher levels of thinking. It is important, however, that students be responsible for rationalizing and defending their responses to the guide. Make this an integral part of the study guide activity. Finally, at every opportunity, reinforce the connection between the mental activity required to complete the guides and your expectations of how and what students should be learning.

Examples of Guides From Various Content Areas.   Study guides have been used successfully by teachers and students in nearly every content area with a wide variety of topics. As you look over the following guides, reflect on how higher levels of thinking are engendered, and consider how you can adapt their formats to fit your content textbooks and other reading materials.

Literature.   The study guide in Figure 3–9 was developed by a teacher for her sophomores as they completed their analysis of characters in *To Kill a Mockingbird*.

Driver's Education.   For a unit in a driver's education class, students were provided the guide shown in Figure 3–10 to help them better compare and contrast the characteristics of motorcycles and automobiles. The information was presented in a film rather than a textbook. After the film, the students were asked to answer the questions that followed each section. These questions then served as a stimulus for classroom discussion.

Journalism.   A high school journalism teacher provided his students the study guide shown in Figure 3–11 to help them think deeper about the philosophies of various photojournalists so that they might begin to formulate their own ideas about photojournalism.

Social Studies.   The study guide in Figure 3–12 proved extremely useful for bringing the concepts of sectionalism and nationalism down to earth. The guide helped students realize how easy it can be to place individual interest over group interests. The discussion that evolved from using their guide contributed greatly to students' understanding of one of the major issues underlying hostilities between northern and southern states that led to the Civil War.

Science.   For a unit on archeology, students were provided the guide in Figure 3–13 to help them better understand the idea of stratification in archaeological digs. Rather than put the items in a simple time line, the students had to think in terms of strata, or layers, and write the names of the objects on the correct stratum of deposit site. The students' defenses of their decisions not only led to a better understanding of stratification but also stimulated a discussion of what tomorrow's archaeologists might learn from today's landfills.

Figure 3–9   **Study guide for literature: *To Kill a Mockingbird***

Directions: Below you will find a copy of today's want ads from the *Maycomb Daily Times,* a fictitious newspaper straight from the pages of *To Kill a Mockingbird.* Below each ad, write the name of the character from the novel that you feel would best fit the ad's description. All ads apply to at least one character, and some ads may have more than one responder. Be prepared to justify your answers.

Wanted: Individual who is interested in donating baked goods to be sold at the next PTA meeting to raise money for a school function.

_____

The Caucasians of America need information on the ghetto life of Negroes in contemporary America. Only those with personal experience need apply.

_____

Needed: Local newspaper is in need of an owner. Must have experience in printing, distribution, and sales.

_____

Gun Club looking for good shooter to give seminar.

_____

Help! The Kane County Rehabilitation Center is looking for a spokesperson for its drug unit.

_____

Child abuse is a crime. Report all cases to authorities.

_____

Wanted: A disciplinarian. A child who everyone considers a BRAT needs some old-fashioned disciplining.

_____

Teacher needed. Patience a plus but not necessary. Will train.

_____

The rape crisis hotline is a free public service for the community. If you know of anyone who needs our help, encourage them to call us.

_____

Penpals are wonderful. If you know of anyone who is interested in being a summer friend, a winter writer, send us his/her name.

_____

Seamstress Opening. Easy mending duties. Pick your own hours. Work at home if it's more convenient.

_____

Stop being a neighborhood gossip. Join Tale Enders today. Nobody likes to hear what everyone else has been up to.

_____

Figure 3–10   Study guide for automobile and motorcycle safety

Check which vehicle is affected most by the following adverse surface conditions.

	Automobile	Motorcycle
1. Loose gravel		
2. Gravel surface		
3. Sand on pavement		
4. Snow		
5. Mud		
6. Washboard		
7. Pot holes		
8. Wet pavement		

How can a motorcycle operator compensate for the shortcomings of the machine under adverse surface conditions?

Foreign Language.   In the final example of content-area study guides shown in Figure 3–14, you can see that guides can even be applied to foreign languages to promote deep and meaningful levels of learning. The Spanish teacher who constructed this guide found it to be a very useful strategy for helping her students expand their understanding of the central character. The guide is presented in English, but was, of course, given to her students in Spanish.

A Final Word About Study Guides.   As this section has demonstrated, study guides can be a very effective and versatile means of promoting higher-level reading and thinking about the concepts in your content area. In addition to their usefulness in learning from text, they can be used for lectures, films, and demonstrations. But they are just one means. And, as we have pointed out, they are teacher initiated. Here and in other sections of this book, we emphasize the importance of developing independent readers and learners. Therefore, we present a variety of strategies for teaching students how to generate their own guides and study aids such as maps, summaries, and other study products that reflect elaborative processing of text and promote long-term retention (see Chapter 9).

Figure 3–11   **Study guide for journalism: Photojournalism philosophies**

Directions: The following is a list of photojournalists whose work we have read about in "The Story of American Photography." Match their names to the philosophy you feel best represents their work and ideals based on the reading you have done. These philosophies are not "spelled out" in the reading but can be put together from their comments, actions, and photos. Be prepared to explain your answers in class discussion.

A. Margaret Bourke-White
B. Murray Becker
C. Weegee (Arthur H. Fellig)
D. Eddie Adams
E. Henry Luce
F. Alfred Eisenstaedt

_____   1. There are events that occur only once in a lifetime, and as news photographers we owe the public that documentation, regardless of the danger it may afford.

_____   2. The photograph is a dramatic essay, a study. It should possess a fine sense of composition and detail so as to make it truly memorable.

_____   3. Photography is a sort of candid eavesdropping. In some cases you feel you have stepped right into the lives of the people you are photographing.

_____   4. A photograph may be shocking, but if it causes viewers to pause and reflect on what they are seeing and the reasons for it, then it has served a vital purpose.

_____   5. To see life, to see the world, to eyewitness great events; to see things a thousand miles away, things hidden behind walls and within rooms, things dangerous to come to . . . to see and take pleasure in seeing; to see and be amazed; to see and be instructed.

_____   6. The news photograph should be a mirror of ourselves; our responses—our reactions and interactions. It should cause us to see our lives and our society as they truly are.

Figure 3–12   **Study guide for history: Sectionalism and nationalism**

Directions: In the mid-1800s, the United States became divided as a result of sectional interests taking precedence over national interests. This eventually caused the Civil War. The following activity is designed to help you get a better idea of sectionalism versus nationalism on a more personal basis.

For each of the following statements, you are to decide whether it will benefit an individual or society in general. Put *I = Individual, S = Society in general,* in front of each statement. Be prepared to explain your choices.

_____   1. Boy, does my grass look great. I found a new sprinkler with a mist so fine I can water every day and no one even knows.

_____   2. Hey, I know how to save some money. The four of us could carpool to school.

_____   3. I found a great way to get the library books out of the building without using my library card.

_____   4. I know how to get out of wearing our school uniforms next week. Let's have a "Change for Charity" week and buy some non-uniform days.

_____   5. It's going to cost 500 bucks to fix the antipollution device on my car, so I had the mechanic disconnect it!

_____   6. My dad found a great way to lower his taxes. He filled a few plastic bags with newspapers and donated them to the charity clothing drive. He still got an official receipt for estimating the value of the stuff, and he put down a lot more than 57¢

_____   7. My class went on a nature walk today and filled two litter bags at the park.

Directions: Stratify the following objects as they were probably found. Place them in correct order on the diagram. Caution! Check the "HELP" story first for clues. Be prepared to defend your stratification decisions.

OBJECTS

campaign button for F.D.R.
steering wheel with no horn
jelly shoe
White Sox pennant
wooden buckboard wheel
Cabbage Patch doll
crystal from a crystal set
bobby socks
autographed picture of Hank Aaron
Beatles' album
computer keyboard

"HELP"

I am an archeologist.
The year is 2010.
My team and I discovered a most unusual site.
For years, this particular group of humans had deposited objects at a central location.
My co-workers were not very conscientious. Instead of carefully mapping the area, they just started digging.
Could you help my scientific investigation?

Figure 3–13 **Study guide for science: Archeology**

Figure 3–14   Study guide for foreign language: Spanish article "Sor Juana Ines de la Cruz: Monja y Feminista"

Directions: In your reading about Sor Juana, you discovered that she could be considered one of the first advocates of the Feminist Movement. In addition, she was a very caring person, and her strong convictions often led her to step into situations on behalf of other people. *Evaluate* the following statements according to whether Sor Juana would agree or disagree with them. Just for fun, also consider your own reactions. Use the numbers 0–5 (5 = *total agreement;* 0 = *total disagreement*). You will be asked to justify your reactions in class discussion.

Sor Juana   Me

_____   _____   1. The greatest contribution of women to society is that of producing babies.

_____   _____   2. Although men and women are physically different, there is very little difference in their intellectual capacities.

_____   _____   3. If a job that a man holds is essentially the same as the job held by a woman employed by the same company, the man should receive a greater salary because he is most likely the main bread winner for his family.

_____   _____   4. There is no excuse for racial or religious discrimination. If you suspect that either of these situations is occurring in your community, you should talk to your neighbors about it.

_____   _____   5. If you are passing in front of a store and see a robbery taking place, you should discreetly enter the store, assess the situation, and if possible, somehow try to overcome the thief.

_____   _____   6. Because of past discrimination, society should now make certain allowances to women. For example, companies should be strongly urged to hire a female when given the choice between a male and a female of equal qualifications.

_____   _____   7. Although both men and women are eligible for the armed services, only men should be assigned combat roles.

_____   _____   8. If a company is marketing something that you believe may be harmful, you should discuss your feelings with the manager of a store that is selling the product. If he continues to sell the product, you should picket his store.

Active Learners Have Control and Knowledge of Appropriate Strategies

As discussed in Chapter 2, active learners are those who understand and coordinate the four variables that interact to promote successful, independent learning. Active learners are sensitive to the characteristics of the *text* from which they will be learning, whether written, oral, or visual. They capitalize on the considerateness of that text or, if necessary, impose their own structure in the meaning-making process. Active learners are aware that *tasks* vary across learning contexts and content areas, but the ultimate goal for all content is understanding and thinking on levels beyond memorization. Active learners can elaboratively think about concepts so they can develop questions, paraphrase, seek interrelationships, make predictions, and apply principles to new situations. Active learners understand themselves as *learners.* In Chapter 2 we described this learner characteristic as metacognition. To think metacognitively is to be aware of one's own strengths and needs in each content area and for each learning context. Active learners realize when their interest is minimal or when their prior knowledge is extensive and use that self-knowledge during reading, studying, and learning. Most importantly, active learners have a repertoire of strategies to use when reading and learning. They can select and employ strategies based on their own needs and the requirements and characteristics of the text and context.

In this chapter we have presented strategies to help students successfully interact with a wide variety of texts and tasks. We close this chapter by emphasizing a refrain that will be repeated throughout this book: To be successful learners, students must be able to monitor their comprehension and to control the four variables that interact in learning.

Teaching Students to Think Metacognitively

To understand a text, you need to split your mental focus. On the one hand, you need to focus on the material itself. At the same time, however, you need to constantly monitor your cognitive activity to make sure that you are comprehending and learning (Garner & Alexander, 1989). Unsophisticated readers are generally unsure about how to make room on their "cognitive workbench" for metacomprehension. Fortunately, teachers can successfully guide students in acquiring metacomprehension skills (Palincsar & Brown, 1984).

In discussing reading for key ideas in a preceding section, we recommended that teachers model for students what good readers do to make sense out of text. There is considerable agreement in the literature as to how good readers read (Pearson, 1985). For instance, they

- Understand their purpose for reading.
- Use their prior knowledge to help them understand what they read.
- Focus on major ideas.

- Keep tabs on their comprehension to make sure it is occurring.
- Make and test inferences.

An instructional approach that has been found to be extremely successful in helping secondary students develop these skills involves interactive or reciprocal teaching (Brown & Palincsar, 1982). In classrooms where **reciprocal teaching** takes place, the teacher and student take turns generating questions and summaries and leading a discussion over sections of a text. Initially, the teacher models questioning, summarizing, clarifying, and predicting activities while encouraging students to participate at whatever level they can manage. Gradually, students become more capable of contributing to such discussions and assume more responsibility for their own learning.

Rob teaches a freshmen reading and study skills course for the first two quarters of the school year. In the class, Rob spends many sessions interacting with students during the comprehension process. Here, we provide an excerpt of Rob and his students interacting during reciprocal teaching.

Rob began by modeling comprehension of a short segment from a biology textbook chapter about lightning. He allowed his students to eavesdrop on his thought processes as he attempted to make sense of the chapter.

Students sat in desks arranged in a horseshoe shape with their copies of the chapter as Rob commented after reading the first short paragraph:

> What I understand here is that up until very recently we haven't known much about lightning, but now things are changing. I'll probably read something about the technology we're using to figure out how lightning occurs.

During reading he shared comments such as this:

> Right now I'm staring blankly at the page trying to gather my thoughts. I'm not reading anything new. . . . I think I'm just cycling these things around to see if anything seems reasonable.
>
> I'm looking again for key words . . . like positive and negative particles . . . cumulonimbus cloud. . . . They're going to tip me off as to the big point.

When Rob finished the first major section of the chapter, he attempted to summarize:

> Okay . . . the first thing is I went over it . . . and skimmed through the section again, so I can remember where I saw the important things.
>
> It's [the passage] talking about how technology is helping us to better understand lightning so we can figure out how to protect ourselves against it.

He paused periodically and posed questions to himself ("What's the main idea here?" or "What details support my main idea?"). Often after finishing a paragraph, he stated the gist. He made predictions about where the text was going next, and his soliloquy included connecting what he was reading with his store of prior knowledge and personal experiences.

In this next excerpt, Rob and his students were reading and discussing paragraphs from their history textbooks. They took turns asking questions about the topic and summarizing. The first paragraph they discussed was about Commander Peary and his quest for the North Pole.

On finishing reading of the short text segment, students immediately responded:

Student 1:   I have a question about this. What year did Peary write his diary?

Rob: "Not a bad beginning, but I would consider that a question about details. Try to avoid the kind of question you can answer by looking word for word in the paragraph. See if next time you can ask a main idea question . . . and begin your question with a question word . . . like how, why, when. . . . Go ahead, try that.

Student 2:   What if I ask, Why is Peary's diary important?

Rob: A very good question. Notice how your question seems to be getting at the most important idea in the paragraph.

Student 3:   And you can't answer it by just looking at the words.

Rob: Right. Very good work! Now, can anyone give me a summary statement for the paragraph?

Student 4:   Well, the only way we really know if Peary got to the North Pole is from his diary.

Rob: And why is that?

Student 4:   Because there was no one else around who knew for sure where they were.

Student 5:   You can't bring back any proof you were there.

Rob: Okay, that explains why some think Peary may not have made it to the Pole first. Isn't that an important part of the summary?

(Several students agree.)

Rob: Let me try to make a summary for you. The most important thing we have learned is that we have to take Peary for his word that he reached the North Pole because we don't have any other evidence to support that he did. Does that make sense? Have I left anything important out?

This last example of reciprocal teaching in Rob's classroom demonstrates a noticeable increase in student involvement in and control over the dialogue. The class was working on a passage about beards.

Student 1:   What evidence do we have that early man thought beards were religious?

Student 2:   They used to burn some of their hair.

Student 1:   Okay, but why?

Student 2:   Because their enemies might get it . . . and they felt that their hair was connected to their personality.

Student 1:   That's correct. They felt that by burning their hair, the enemy was also affecting their personalities.

Rob: That was excellent. So, a summary for this paragraph might be. . . .

Student 1:   Mine would be that people once made a religious connection with beards.

Rob: Outstanding.

Student 1:   I have a prediction to make. . . . They mention how beards were thought of by people in ancient times; well, it might tell how people changed their attitudes about beards.

Rob: Okay, let's find out. Would you choose the next teacher please?

(Student 1, who directed the questioning and made the prediction, called on another student to lead the discussion of the next paragraph. This practice of students calling on other students to direct the discussion over a text reinforces their responsibility to work toward a meaningful interpretation without relying on the teacher to give it to them. In other words, it promotes independence.)

Student 3:   Why did people in France grow beards?

Student 4:   Because the king had one.

Student 3:   That's correct. Now I have a question that might be hard to answer. Do you think many of Queen Elizabeth's subjects grew beards?

Rob: That's a terrific question, how would someone answer that?

Student 5:   Probably not too many, because they would have to pay extra tax.

Student 3:   Right. My summary on this paragraph is about how kings and queens had a lot to do with whether people wore beards or not.

Rob: Excellent summary. Nice work.

The success of Rob's reciprocal teaching approach seems to be attributable to the fact that it forces the students to respond, which allows him to determine their competence and provide appropriate feedback. Also, by responding orally, the students are given the opportunity to self-diagnose and gradually improve through a trial-and-error process of continuous adjustment. Rob does not merely talk to his students about how to read and then tell them to open up their texts and read that way. Instead, he demonstrates how he reads and constructs meaning and, through interactions with students, gives them greater responsibility for learning from text.

Reading Comprehension in All Areas of Secondary School Learning

In Chapters 2 and 3, we deal with an array of information and practical teaching strategies related to reading comprehension and learning across the content areas. We placed these two chapters near the beginning of the book because we believe they form the foundation for all of the comprehension instruction and learning that is elucidated and demonstrated in the remaining chapters. Ideally, Chapters 2 and 3 will help form the foundation of your lessons and units of instruction. Many of the same strategies discussed in this chapter appear at other points throughout the book; many new strategies for helping students learn more effectively will also be presented. Nevertheless, all of the strategies are underpinned by the principles of developing active, independent readers and learners.

Comprehension should not—and cannot—be taught in isolation of the very material from which students are trying to learn. This is especially true in the secondary school. Consequently, in future chapters, we demonstrate that comprehension is at the heart of reading and learning in junior and senior high school. In Chapter 4, assessment and teaching comprehension are presented as integral instructional activities. You will see in Chapter 5 how schema activation and development guide readiness strategies. In Chapter 6, we show how effective vocabulary instruction develops contextual and conceptual understanding of important textual information and ideas. In Chapter 7, writing is seen as a tool for expanding comprehension and learning of text material and course content. In Chapter 8, literature is discussed as an alternative and companion to the textbook for building prior knowledge, generating interest, and expanding comprehension. The purpose of Chapter 9 is to demonstrate how students can make comprehension more permanent with text study strategies. Adapting comprehension strategies to special students is the focus of Chapter 10. Finally, we contend in Chapter 11 that secondary teachers will become more effective if they take on responsibility for teaching comprehension along with content.

Case Study Revisited

Charles, the biology teacher introduced in the beginning of this chapter, was searching for ways to engage his students in more meaningful interactions with his course content. Having read this chapter, propose strategies that may help Charles move his students toward more elaborative and meaningful processing of text material related to the topic of genetic engineering.

Charles decided to use a variety of readiness strategies to initiate his students to the new content and gain their interest.

He began by having students respond to an anticipation guide containing true or false statements related to genetic engineering, cloning, and selective breeding.

Next, Charles exposed his students to alternative source material for exploration of the topic. He ensnared his students' interest by reading aloud daily from a science fiction novel, Hayford Peirce's *Phylum Monsters,* about a genetic engineer called a "life-stylist." The novel helped motivate Charles's class to dig deeper into the content.

Charles shared examples of exciting and wild experiments done by genetic researchers. For example, he read to students about researchers at the University of California, San Diego, who in 1986 took the gene that makes fireflies glow and inserted it into the DNA of tobacco. The researchers were then able to raise tobacco plants that glowed in the dark. Charles then asked students to devise their own "wild" experiments in genetic engineering.

Charles asked his students to read articles on genetic engineering from news magazines and to generate lists of advantages and disadvantages of this technology. These lists were discussed in small groups and by the whole class.

Finally, Charles helped his students write to the FDA explaining their views on the subject of genetically engineered food.

As a result of these efforts to prepare students for and initiate them to their new learning, Charles saw his students become active learners. They read and participated with enthusiasm, and were motivated to work together in small groups and as a class to better explore the topic of genetic engineering.

Summary

This chapter has provided a range of actual classroom examples and concrete illustrations of exactly the kinds of processes we need to model for students if we want them to become active, mature readers and learners. It is organized around four important principles of building active learners. The first principle is concerned with how readers use their prior knowledge to interact with text. In relationship to this principle, we discussed strategies for activating and building prior knowledge. The second principle focuses on how active learners use text structure to guide their meaning construction. We discussed the importance of alerting students to the structures of expository and narrative text and presented a method of teaching them how to recognize and manipulate words and structures that connect ideas. The third principle concerns how active learners process text in an elaborative fashion. Strategies discussed in relation to this principle include study guides and QAR. We also emphasized the importance of deriving the main idea of what we read and demonstrated an effective method for modeling and teaching the active process of constructing main ideas. The fourth and final principle discussed in this chapter deals with how active learners possess knowledge and control of strategies. In connection with this principle, we emphasized the importance of helping students develop their metacognitive skills. We pointed out that successful comprehension depends on the reader's ability to self-monitor and self-regulate while reading. We described how students can be led to think metacognitively through a form of reciprocal or interactive teaching that exploits modeling, active questioning, and discussing. Finally, we pointed out how the principles and strategies discussed in this chapter form the basis for the reading and learning strategies that appear throughout this book.

(How well did you anticipate the answers in our anticipation guide for Chapter 3 shown in Figure 3–1? Turn back to that anticipation guide and record your agreement or disagreement with the five statements now that you have completed your reading of the chapter.)

References

Afflerbach, P. (1990). The influence of prior knowledge on expert readers' main idea construction strategies. *Reading Research Quarterly, 26,* 31–46.

Afflerbach, P. P. (1987). How are main idea statements constructed? Watch the experts. *Journal of Reading, 30,* 512–519.

Alvermann, D., & Hague, S. (1989). Comprehension of counter-intuitive science text: Effects of prior knowledge and text structure. *Journal of Educational Research, 82,* 197–202.

Alvermann, D., & Hynd, C. (1989). Study strategies for correcting misconceptions in physics: An intervention. In S. McCormick & J. Zutell (Eds.), *Cognitive and social perspectives for literacy research and instruction. Thirty-eighth yearbook of the National Reading Conference.* Chicago: National Reading Conference.

Atwell, N. (1987). *In the middle.* Portsmouth, NH: Heinemann.

Baumann, J. F., & Serra, J. K. (1984). The frequency and placement of main ideas in children's social studies textbooks: A modified replication of Braddock's research on topic sentences. *Journal of Reading Behavior, 16,* 27–40.

Brown, A., & Day, J. (1983). Macrorules for summarizing texts: The development of expertise. *Journal of Verbal Learning and Verbal Behavior, 22,* 1–16.

Brown, A., & Palincsar, A. (1982). Inducing strategic learning from texts by means of informed, self-control training. *Topics in Learning and Learning Disabilities, 2,* 1–17.

Brozo, W. G., Stahl, N. A., & Gordon, B. (1985). Training effects of summarizing, item writing, and knowledge of information sources on reading test performance. In J. Niles & R. Lalik (Eds.), *Issues in literacy: A research perspective. Thirty-fourth yearbook of the National Reading Conference.* Rochester, NY: National Reading Conference.

Calkins, L., & Harwayne, S. (1991). *Living between the lines.* Portsmouth, NH: Heinemann.

Dole, J., Duffy, G., Roehler, L., & Pearson, P. D. (1991). Moving from the old to the new: Research on reading comprehension instruction. *Review of Educational Research, 61,* 239–264.

Duffy, J. (1985). Effects of instruction in noting and using an author's pattern of writing on sixth graders' understanding and memory for expository text (Doctoral dissertation, Temple University). *Dissertation Abstracts International, 46,* 2274A.

Garner, R. (1988). *Metacognition and reading comprehension.* Norwood, NJ: Ablex.

Garner, R., & Alexander, P. (1989). Metacognition: Answered and unanswered questions. *Educational Psychologist, 24,* 143–158.

Greenberg, L. (1992). *AIDS: How it works in the body.* New York: Franklin Watts.

Graff, H. F. (1980). *The free and the brave.* Chicago: Rand McNally.

Hare, V., & Rabinowitz, M., & Schieble, K. (1989). Text effects on main idea comprehension. *Reading Research Quarterly, 24,* 72–88.

Herber, H. (1978). *Teaching reading in the content areas.* Englewood Cliffs, NJ: Prentice-Hall.

Herber, H., & Nelson-Herber, J. (1993). *Teaching in content areas with reading, writing, and reasoning.* Needham Heights, MA: Allyn & Bacon.

Hynd, C., & Alvermann, D. (1989). Overcoming misconceptions in science: An on-line study of prior knowledge activation. *Reading Research and Instruction, 28,* 12–26.

Kintsch, E. (1990). Macroprocesses and microprocesses in the development of summarization skill. *Cognition and Instruction, 7,* 161–195.

Langer, J. (1981). From theory to practice: A pre-reading plan. *Journal of Reading, 25,* 152–156.

Marshall, N. (1989). Overcoming problems with incorrect prior knowledge: An instructional study. In S. McCormick & J. Zutell (Eds.), *Cognitive and social perspectives for literacy research and instruction, Thirty-eighth yearbook of the National Reading Conference.* Chicago: National Reading Conference.

McNeil, J. (1987). *Reading comprehension: New directions for classroom practices* (2nd ed.). Glenview, IL: Scott, Foresman.

Miller, K. (1988). *Effects of expository passage organizers on sixth graders' reading and writing of text.* Unpublished doctoral dissertation, University of Missouri, Kansas City, MO.

Miller, K., & George, J. (1992). Expository passage organizers: Models for reading and writing. *Journal of Reading, 35,* 372–377.

Palincsar, A. S., & Brown, A. L. (1984). Reciprocal teaching of comprehension-fostering and comprehension-monitoring activities. *Cognition and Instruction, 1,* 117–175.

Pearson, P. D. (1985). Changing the face of reading comprehension instruction. *The Reading Teacher, 38,* 724–738.

Pickle, H., & Abrahamson, R. (1980). *Introduction to business.* Glenview, IL: Scott, Foresman.

Raphael, T. E., & Pearson, P. D. (1985). Increasing students' awareness of sources of information for answering questions. *American Educational Research Journal, 22,* 217–235.

Readence, J. E., Bean, T. W., & Baldwin, R. S. (1985). *Content area reading: An integrated approach* (2nd ed.). Dubuque, IA: Kendall/Hunt.

Romano, T. (1987). *Clearing the way.* Portsmouth, NH: Heinemann.

Santa, C., & Havens, L. (1991). Learning through writing. In C. Santa & D. Alvermann (Eds.), *Science learning: Processes and applications.* Newark, DE: International Reading Association.

Sinatra, R. (1986). *Visual literacy connections to thinking, reading and writing.* Springfield, IL: Charles C. Thomas.

Sinatra, R. (1991). Integrating whole language with the learning of text structure. *Journal of Reading, 34,* 424–433.

Slater, W., Graves, M., & Piche, G. (1985). Effects of structural organizers on ninth-grade students' comprehension and recall of four patterns of expository text. *Reading Research Quarterly, 20,* 189–202.

Thomas, K. J. (1979). Modified CLOZE: The inTRAlocking guide. *Reading World, 19,* 19–27.

Trends in academic progress. (1991). Princeton, NJ: Educational Testing Service.

Wixson, K. (1983). Questions about a text: What you ask about is what children learn. *Reading Teachers, 37,* 287–293.

4

Classroom Assessment of Literacy Growth and Content Learning

[When we assess] we are watching children as they develop personal understandings of literacy that are both socially constructed and individually situated in the practical accomplishments of their everyday lives.

—Denny Taylor (1990)

Despite nearly 20 years of theory development and research that characterizes literacy as an interactive, context-bound, purposeful process of meaning construction (Bissex, 1980; Clay, 1975; Pinnell, 1989; Sulzby, 1985); despite extensive descriptive literature providing examples of how students have grown in literacy within holistic learning environments (Graves & Hansen, 1983; Newman, 1985; Rief, 1992; Taylor, 1989; Wells, 1985); despite major paradigm shifts among teachers throughout the nation away from the kind of literacy and content-area curriculum that dwell on small language parts and isolated bits of information toward a curriculum that provides students with integrated, meaningful, and personally relevant learning experiences; despite all of what we now know about literacy teaching and learning, decontextualized measures such as formal standardized tests are still commonly used (Calfee & Hiebert, 1991). In this chapter we present the view that our knowledge about literacy processes and holistic teaching/learning environments has reached a level of development at which we can no longer rely solely on traditional reading, writing, and content knowledge testing practices (e.g., commercially prepared standardized reading tests, criterion-referenced tests, unit/chapter tests). Instead, we argue for and present approaches to assessment grounded in secondary school classroom instruction.

In this chapter, issues and strategies of assessment are presented relative to one basic guideline: The goal of literacy assessment is knowledge for teachers about how best to improve and support learning for students and self-knowledge for learners for them to become more reflective, active, and purposeful learners. Because most of you do not administer reading tests unless you are required to do so, we have focused on assessment strategies that are most relevant to you in your content classroom. We demonstrate how your assessments can reveal to you and to students important information about students' thinking and language processes as well as their content knowledge. Because assessment guides and informs instruction and can be integrated within the daily flow of instructional events in the classroom, this chapter serves as a foundation for assessment strategies that appear in later chapters. It also builds on the comprehension strategies discussed in Chapters 2 and 3 by demonstrating how assessments can be used to reveal useful information about students' literacy and learning processes.

We are also mindful, however, of the fact that standardized reading tests are being used more than ever in schools (Valencia, 1990). According to Pearson and Valencia (1986), there are now at least 40 statewide competency testing programs, leading those authors to conclude that "the influence of testing is greater now than at any time in the history of schooling." Furthermore, the Department of Education spends more on the National Assessment of Educational Progress (NAEP, briefly described in Chapter 1) than on any other initiative (Elbow, 1991). The inescapable result of all this testing is that occasionally you will be required to administer standardized reading competency tests and be asked by your students and their parents to interpret the results. What will you say to them? Do you understand the intent of such tests? To help prepare you to deal with these issues, we provide a brief primer on standardized reading tests, discuss the strengths and limitations of these tests, and suggest ways in which you can converse meaningfully with students and parents about test results.

Case Study

Terri is a ninth-grade general science teacher interested in discovering more about her students' ability to comprehend textbook information. At in-services on holistic teaching and testing, she began to recognize the need for alternative assessments to the chapter check tests in her science textbook. After 5 years of teaching, she discovered that she was relying more and more on these tests for grading purposes and less and less on other "views" of her students as learners and knowledge seekers. Moreover, the results of these tests were not providing Terri with information about why students performed the way they did. She had no way of discovering whether success or failure was tied in any way to students' study processes or to their ability to understand the prose in the science text.

The in-service presenter emphasized the need to tie content material with the processes for effectively learning it. Suggestions were made concerning ways teachers could teach and assess at the same time using the class textbook. Terri decided a good place to start was to develop an assessment strategy that would provide her with information about her students' ability to understand how text in their science book was structured. Her goal was to use this information to develop teaching strategies for improving students' thinking about text structure.

To the Reader: Think about Terri's concern as you read this chapter, and be prepared by the end of this chapter to suggest possible assessment/teaching solutions for her.

Guidelines for Literacy Assessment

Assessment Is a Process of Becoming Informed About Authentic Learning

Authentic learning refers to learning that is functional and meaningful. As we stated in Chapter 1, the extent to which students use learning beyond the boundaries of the classroom is directly related to its perceived functionality. For authentic learning to occur, assessments should be rooted in activities that have genuine purposes (Edelsky & Harman, 1988). In this way, acquiring information about student learning does not become an end in itself but is an evolving process of gathering feedback for the teacher and student so that instruction can become more engaging, more tied to real-world issues and concerns, and more personally meaningful.

So then, what do we want to know about students that requires us to assess them? We want to know under what conditions they learn best, what instructional strategies we can employ to facilitate their learning, and how to encourage independent, active reading. We also want students to discover more about themselves as learners so they can expand their capabilities as literate knowledge seekers.

Secondary school teachers want to know whether or not their students are likely to profit from textbook reading, daily instruction, process writing, research projects, and so on. The assessment tools we use for these purposes should, therefore, be designed to provide insights into students' reading, writing, and thinking strategies with the actual texts they must use on a daily basis and in the actual, authentic contexts of their use. In this way, the information gained from assessment can be immediately translated into action, such as promoting elaborative processing (Chapter 3); activating and building relevant prior knowledge (Chapter 5); teaching key concepts and vocabulary (Chapter 6); facilitating thinking and reflection through writing (Chapter 7); developing text study skills (Chapter 9); or improving other important reading, writing, and learning processes.

Assessment of Literacy and Content Learning Should Occur in Multiple Contexts

If a basketball coach desires to find out how well new recruits can play the game, the coach does not give a paper and pencil test. The players are required to perform on the court, and their ability is assessed while being directly observed. By making assessments of **situated performances** (Valencia, McGinley, & Pearson, 1990), a coach can learn the most about a player's true ability and potential. This makes perfectly good sense, doesn't it? Although we do not need to, we generally approach things differently when it comes to literacy assessment, however.

A ninth-grade science teacher may feel that she has all the information needed about a student's reading ability when given the test results of the Comprehensive Test of Basic Skills (CTBS). But what do percentiles and grade equivalents have to do with reading and learning from a science textbook? Perhaps very little, and for obvious reasons. First, the comprehension passages on a test like the CTBS may not cover science or science-related topics. Second, the kind of reading demanded by reading comprehension tests is significantly different from the way a student would read and study a science textbook. For example, on the test, a student reads one or two paragraphs and must do so under strict time limitations. In contrast, the actual reading assignment in the science class may require the student to spend an entire week reading a 20- to 30-page chapter, allowing enough time to generate study aids and learn the material. Finally, the CTBS measures reading performance with multiple-choice questions. The science teacher may require students to write out answers to short and long essay-type questions.

A science teacher needs more information about students than simply the standard scores from a survey-level reading test such as the CTBS to make meaningful instructional decisions. More useful information could be obtained by such approaches as assessing students' ability to process and understand the science textbook, or gaining insight into students' problem-solving abilities and use of experimentation through field notes and logs. The advantage of determining students' progress and understanding with the actual materials used in the science class is that the teacher would then have a much clearer idea about how to modify instruction to improve student learning.

The preceding example reinforces an important point we made in the first chapter: Literacy ability is context bound. No single test (whether the CTBS or any other paper and pencil measure) can adequately reflect the teaching/learning process. As a former student of ours expressed it, the old "clump theory" of literacy doesn't make sense any longer. Traditional views of literacy held that all of us possess a given, measurable quantity, or "clump," of literacy ability and that reading tests could accurately weigh our clumps. As our conceptions of what it means to be literate have changed to include the dynamic, generative, and idiosyncratic nature of literacy, the most commonly used formal measures of reading and writing have remained largely decontextualized (Collins, Brown, & Newman, 1989; Glazer, Searfoss, & Gentile, 1988). To assess in ways consistent with our best thinking about literacy, our assessment repertoire must be expanded to include multiple demonstrations of ability in situated contexts of authentic teaching and learning.

Assessment Is a Continuous Process

A high school teacher of learning disabled (LD) students recently complained about how she is often excluded from the decision-making process concerning student needs and placement. She said that decisions are made about students based on clinical testing in language competencies, intelligence, and behavior with virtually no input from the teacher who is working closely with and observing the students every day. One of her students, she said, is entirely capable of regular education course work, according to her observations, because he is an excellent reader and possesses some good study skills. When she talked with the clinician, she was shown the students reading test scores on the Woodcock Reading Mastery Tests (WRMT), which placed him nearly 3 years below his grade placement of 10th grade. It is unlikely, she was told, that he had improved as much as she claimed in the 1 month since he was tested. The question comes down to this: Whose assessment—the clinician's WRMT or the teacher's observations—is more reflective of the student's true ability?

Considering our point about the important influence of context on learning performance, isn't it possible that the context itself— that is, the conditions under which literacy activities and tasks are assessed—has influenced the 10th-grade LD student's reading test performance? The answer is an unequivocal "yes." Carey, Harste, and Smith (1981) discovered that students will often demonstrate much better recall and supply richer information when retelling a story or text to a friend or fellow student than to a teacher, researcher, or test giver. We also have known for some time that when a student is excessively anxious about a task because the perceived consequences of failure are threatening, generally, a concomitant decrease in performance results. The LD teacher's student could have been very threatened by the clinical setting while taking the WRMT, resulting in an artificially low estimate of his reading ability. On the other hand, the student may have perceived the LD teacher in a nonthreatening way and the classroom as a supportive environment. In this context, the student may have demonstrated his true ability. To reiterate, we believe that any test is only a small sample of behavior, and when a single test or observation occurs in isolation (i.e., by a clinician with one test at one point in time), there is insufficient grounds for drawing meaningful diagnostic conclusions.

Besides the influence of context on reading performance, there are other reasons why reading assessment should be a continuous process. Any test result or observed score is partly a reflection of the test taker's true ability, or true score, and a host of other factors we did not plan to measure, referred to as *error score*. Contextual factors, as in the preceding case with the LD student, contribute to error score, and there are many others. The reader's health, attitude, propensity toward guessing, prior knowledge, the test's ability to communicate, and the quality of the test questions, to name a few, are all factors that influence to one degree or another a test taker's observed score. Unfortunately, we can never be absolutely certain how much of an observed score is composed of error score. This critical issue should be considered before we base major decisions on one test or observation—especially if that test or observation is isolated from the conditions under which actual reading tasks are performed—because the observed score may not measure a student's true ability.

All of what we have just said can be applied to classroom teachers who rely exclusively on end-of-chapter, -unit, or -year tests for basing decisions about grading and student progress. Learning is a continuous and dynamic process that takes place over time and changes with each new instructional situation. Therefore, to obtain more useful and meaningful information of your students' literacy and learning abilities, we recommend that you base instructional decisions on long-term observations and assessments. Later in this chapter we provide guidelines and details for assessment formats that use day-to-day information gained from observing students and gathering reflections of their progress over time. Only with such important assessment data can we expect to build a supportive classroom learning environment.

Assessment Should Include Students' Interests and Attitudes

Carmen begins every new school year with an activity designed to help her eighth graders get to know one another. Using a strategy called "My Bag," Carmen and her students bring in bags filled with objects and items that represent who they are. Students form groups of three or four and share these items. Carmen asks students not to do a "show and tell" but to use an item to elicit questions. For example, Juanita took an onyx ring out of her bag and passed it around for her group members to inspect. Soon students were asking her questions such as "Where'd you get it?" "Was it your mom's?" "What kind of stone is that?" Juanita revealed that the ring belonged to her "*tia*," her aunt, with whom she had a very close and friendly relationship, and that the ring was given to her just before her aunt died. In another case, Carlos showed his group a model car and a screwdriver. Before long, he was responding to questions that allowed him to go into great detail about his interest in fixing cars with his older brother and his plans to be an auto mechanic.

While students go through the "My Bag" activity, Carmen circulates throughout the room taking note of students' interests, desires, needs, and concerns, such as Juanita's relationship with her aunt and Carlos's interest in auto repair. Armed with this knowledge, Carmen tailors certain writing, reading, and group projects to her students' needs and desires. She alludes to particular characteristics of students revealed through the "My Bag" during class activities, which helps demonstrate her interest and concern for her students and builds a caring atmosphere in the classroom. In the end, Carmen, too, shares her bag, allowing students to get to know their teacher as a real person who has goals, desires, and interests just as they do. Carmen has found that in being part of the "My Bag" activity herself, she can establish an initial foundation on which trust and cooperative problem solving can be built.

Through the use of the "My Bag" strategy, Carmen gathers invaluable assessment information about her students' interests and attitudes in a highly personal, unique, and fun way. Along with gathering information about how students process text, we should be equally concerned with discovering students' habits, interests, and attitudes to reinforce and reward students' use of reading and writing for self-development and learning, and for joy and escape. The benefits that result from bringing students in touch with books that match their interests cannot be denied.

An acquaintance recounted the story of how he had been diagnosed as a remedial reader every year from second to seventh grade. Teachers were beginning to lose hope in ever teaching Tom how to read beyond a rudimentary level. His difficulty affected his achievement in all subjects. Then, a particularly enlightened math teacher discovered that Tom's favorite thing to do was perform magic tricks. The teacher brought Tom some books on magic from the library. He read them. He began reading more and more books on magic. Soon, his ability to read and understand other books improved. Eventually, Tom graduated from high school with a good grade average and finally took a baccalaureate degree from the University of Illinois—a prominent and respected institution. The lesson here is obvious: By discovering students' interests and introducing them to books that match their interests, we stand a chance of developing enthusiastic and competent readers.

Obtaining information about students' real-world needs and interests, in other words, what they do and what concerns them when they are outside of school, can be as useful in planning ways to teach and reach your students as information about their reading/writing processes and content knowledge. Interest is one of the most potent motivators for young adults (Garner, Alexander, Gillingham, Kulikowich, & Brown, 1991; Hidi & Baird, 1988; Renninger, 1989), and teachers can take full advantage of this fact in a number of ways. One obvious strategy is to introduce students to reading material related to their interests. These materials might be tied to the topic of study in your classroom or may simply be relevant to students on a personal level. (In Chapter 8 we explain how teachers can take full advantage of trade literature to help meet students' needs.) Information about students' interests can also be used to spawn writing ideas. Another strategy is to use knowledge gained from interest assessments to create cooperative learning groups (see Chapter 8). And yet another strategy is to provide opportunities for students to pursue personally relevant learning projects that combine their interests with the concepts and information they are learning in your classroom.

Strategies for determining students' interests can take a number of forms. We're particularly fond of the "My Bag" approach because it's interactive and engaging. Another less obtrusive approach to determining students' interests is through journal writing. A sensitive reader of journal entries will be able to infer the real-world concerns of students, as well as any interests they may have related to the topics in the classroom. In the journals, you can respond with information that points students in the direction of reading material related to their concerns and interests, whether it be a self-help book for coping with divorcing parents, a popular computer magazine, or a novel about the Viet Nam war.

Another method of discovering more about students' interests and attitudes is to ask them to write autobiographies of themselves as language users and learners (Gilles et al., 1988). The idea is that students need opportunities to examine their personal histories as readers, writers, and learners both in and out of school. By exploring their pasts, students might better understand their current approaches to learning and attitudes toward literacy and its role in their lives.

To help students reflect on their past experiences as language users and learners, we recommend the following approach:

- In small groups ask students to brainstorm their pasts as readers, writers, and learners. They should try to remember about a time, person, school year, class, event, assignment, text or book, teacher, friend, relative, or the like.

- After brainstorming, students should write about that event, time, or person that had a positive or negative impact on their thinking and feeling about literacy and learning.

- Be sure students focus on the questions "What happened that influenced the way you read, write and learn now?" and "How do you feel about that influence now?"

- Students should be allowed to write as much as they need to in order to describe and reflect fully on their past influences and experiences related to how they currently think about themselves as readers, writers, and learners.

- After thinking and writing, students could be allowed to exchange their drafts with members of their brainstorm group for comment, questions, and feedback.

- Volunteers could be asked to share their autobiographies.

- We recommend that you also take part in this activity by writing and sharing your autobiography with the class.

The information gained from autobiographies of your students as language users and learners can help you make instructional decisions, deconstruct maladaptive attitudes and beliefs about literacy, target certain activities and projects to particular students, and improve and support healthy attitudes about literacy and learning.

Ann, a math teacher, asks all her students to complete a mathematics autobiography as their first entry in their journal. She uses the following directions, which can be modified to fit almost any content area.

Write your math autobiography. Think and write about the experiences you have had that relate to mathematics. These questions may be used as guides.

1. How did you feel about math in elementary school and junior high?
2. What are your experiences with effective and ineffective math teachers?

3. Is there one particular experience that stands out?

4. What were or are the attitudes of your family members towards math?

5. Was there a time you liked math? Hated it? Why did you feel the way you did?

6. Did you have any special strategies for getting through (or around) math classes?

7. Is there one particular experience you feel is responsible for your present feelings about math?

Ann tells us that she quickly learns a great deal of useful information about her students' attitudes, anxieties, and mathematical strategies from this initial journal entry. She then uses classroom observations of her students as well as their homework and test performance to validate these self-reports. One of her students, Zena, is the author of the following entry. As Ann discovered from this entry and from her interactions with Zena, Zena's self-concept related to her math ability was very low.

When I was in elementary school I had a little trouble with adding and subtracting. In seventh and eighth grade I was placed in the low track classes because I had not yet learned my multiplication tables and how to figure percentages. Story problems really bothered me so I had a tutor help me. I still am nervous about math, especially if the test is timed. In stores I always make sure they give me the correct change, but I have trouble figuring out the prices on clothes when they have sales.

If I have effective teachers I do great, but when I have ineffective teachers I do bad. I had a teacher who didn't like me and tried her hardest to make me fail her class. My parents told me to just do the best I can and not to worry about how the teacher feels about me. My father and brothers are all good in math, so I am the only math dummy in our house.

I like math when I understand it, but if I don't understand it, I don't like it. I usually am afraid to ask questions when I am lost—so please be patient with me.

Inventories and questionnaires are the simplest and most direct way of acquiring information about students' interests and attitudes related to activities and learning in school and out of school. Some inventories, like the Interest Inventory I (Figure 4–1), require only a simple check mark. Other inventories, like the Interest Inventory II (Figure 4–2), ask students to write more elaborate answers to questions regarding their interests.

Attitude inventories and questionnaires are also useful for obtaining assessment information about your students. The writing strategies questionnaire in Figure 4–3 has been used by secondary teachers to discover important past experiences their students have had with writing and how they think and feel about writing..

Although your students' actual attitudes about themselves as learners in your classroom may be difficult to uncover with one simple inventory, inventories may be a starting point for acquiring more in-depth information about your students using other direct and personal approaches. The key is that opportunities are pro-

Figure 4–1 **Interest Inventory 1**

Directions: Put a check mark (✓) on the line in front of each activity you like quite a bit.

Interests Outside of School

_____ Television	_____ Reading
_____ Movies	_____ Cooking
_____ Outdoor games	_____ Hobbies
_____ Watching sports	_____ Animals
_____ Hiking and Camping	_____ Trips
_____ Fishing	_____ Video games
_____ Music	_____ Dancing
_____ Motorcycle	_____ Being with friends
_____ Your car	_____ Your girlfriend/boyfriend

Other(s): _____

Figure 4–2 **Interest Inventory II**

Directions: Finish each sentence so that it tells something about you. You may write as much as you wish to finish each sentence.

1. After school I like to _____
   _____

2. On the weekends I like to _____
   _____

3. _____ is my favorite TV show because
   _____

4. The kind of music I like is _____
   _____

5. When I graduate from high school I want to _____
   _____

6. If I could go anywhere in the world, I'd go to _____
   because _____

7. My idea of a good adventure is _____
   _____

8. _____

9. _____

10. _____

Figure 4-3   **Writing strategies questionnaire**

1. If you knew someone was having trouble writing, what would you do to help?

2. What would a teacher do to help that student?

3. If you were told you have to write an essay due in one week, what would you do to make sure it is done on time and well written?

4. Think about someone you know who is a good writer. What makes that person a good writer?

5. What is the best advice you've ever been given about writing?

6. How did you learn to write? When? Who helped you?

7. What would help you improve your writing?

8. Do you think you're a good writer? Why or why not?

9. Why do people write? What are your purposes for writing?

10. Does the writing you do in school interest you? Why or why not?

vided on a regular basis for students to explore and share their underlying feelings and attitudes toward literacy and learning. And remember, the examples of inventories and questionnaires we have shared are merely suggestions of the kinds of issues and questions you may find relevant to your teaching situation. We urge you to use these suggestions to develop your own inventories that suit your particular need to know more about your students' attitudes and interests.

Standardized Reading Achievement Tests: What You Should Know

Question
Audrey strained to see the people who were coming through the crowd. Somewhere down there her parents were waiting to welcome her after her voyage.
A. Audrey is standing in a crowd, waiting to meet a plane.
B. Audrey is in a crowd, walking toward her parents.
C. Audrey is on a ship, looking out at a crowd waiting for the ship.
D. Audrey is looking at a ship on which her parents are arriving. (*Reading Yardsticks*, Form B, 1981, p. 11)

Does the preceding question format look familiar? It should. All of us have taken some form of a reading test that contained short passages and multiple-choice comprehension questions that were very similar to this example. Why are these tests used so extensively in schools today? How are they developed? What do they reveal about a student's reading ability? How can the results be used? These are some of the questions we'll attempt to answer in this section.

We ascribe almost magical qualities to standardized reading tests. They are "objective measurements," simple to administer and score with comprehensive tables and charts for deriving a variety of standard scores. And with more than 100 reading tests on the market, they are accessible. With the prevalence of reading testing, however, comes the very real risk that measurement instruments will eventually determine the objectives of instruction (Aronson & Farr, 1988). In fact, in many school settings today where competency testing and remedial programs are found, tests assume a very prominent place in the decision-making arena (Valencia & Pearson, 1987). In our own experience, we have found that where wide-scale testing is common, misinformation abounds. School administrators often take on faith the validity of the reading tests they use in their schools without fully understanding the technical qualities of the instrument or, more importantly, the way in which reading is operationally defined by the test passages and items. Teachers are often frustrated because they are forced to administer certain tests and, in some cases, teach to tests, and are confused about how to interpret the results meaningfully. Parents and students, who are often the least informed, may develop oversimplified notions about tests in order to make some sense of the bewildering terms and numbers.

Although reading tests have been around since the beginning of this century, it has only been since the 1930s that the question format became the most popular method of assessing comprehension and formed the basis for current standardized tests of reading achievement (Readence & Moore, 1983). Educators over the past 50 years have regarded the question-answering format as the most convenient, objective, and cost-effective means of comprehension assessment. Why is so much attention given to reading assessment? Most educators and a majority of the public agree that raising students' literacy levels is an extremely important goal of public schooling (Goodman, 1992). Since the accountability movement of the 1970s and moving toward the current glut of national reports, a prominent area of attention for educational improvement initiatives has been literacy (Liston & Zeichner, 1991). To measure the effectiveness of these initiatives, educators have come to rely on students' standardized test scores.

What is a standardized reading achievement test? The term **standardized** means that the test was administered and scored under standard and uniform testing procedures. It is typically constructed by test specialists working with curriculum experts and teachers. Before the test is made available to schools and teachers, it is given to a large number of students, who represent the group for whom the test was intended. This representative group of students is called the **norm group**. The norm group's scores on the test are statistically transformed into **standard scores**, which are usually made available in tabular form in the test's users manual. These standard scores allow teachers and schools to compare their students with a national group of students. The most common standard scores used by schools to interpret student performance on reading achievement tests are grade equivalents and percentiles. A **grade equivalent** interpretation of a student's reading achievement test score is indicated in terms of years and months; for instance, 10.6 or 10th grade, sixth month. When interpreting reading test performance in terms of a **percentile**, we describe a student's score as a point at or below which a given percentage of other scores falls. For example, a student who scored at the 80th percentile scored as well or better than 80% of the students in the norm group.

Communicating With Parents and Students About Standardized Reading Test Results. School districts have an obligation to inform students and parents of reading achievement test results. It is their right to know. While some testing experts have argued that the distribution of assessment results should be limited to those who are prepared to use them (Venezky, 1974), classroom teachers in science, math, history, and psychology are still likely to be sent printouts of their classes' reading test scores even though the scores are not applicable to their classroom decisions. Furthermore, it is not uncommon for the classroom teacher to be asked by students and parents to explain test scores. These facts point to the need for all teachers to become informed about what these scores mean and how they can be used. Following are several suggestions for reporting and explaining standardized reading test results to students and/or parents. These suggestions come from our own experience as high school teachers as well as the experience of others.

1. Put parents at ease. Welcome them and see that they are comfortable. If possible, work where there is good lighting and privacy.

2. Before presenting information to parents, find out what information they have already received from other teachers, counselors, or administrators. Failure to do so may put you in the uncomfortable position of contradicting a colleague, having to change your position, or reporting redundant information.

3. Before presenting information, determine exactly what kind of information the parent wants.

4. If assessment information is inadequate or contradictory, be willing to admit the weaknesses of evaluation based on these data.

5. Urge parents not to fixate on standard scores, but instead pay close attention to teachers' judgments.

6. If necessary, explain the limitations of grade equivalents. They are too easily misinterpreted to be given to parents indiscriminately. These norms are often **extrapolated**; that is, they are often estimates based on trends in scores established by the norm group. In other words, if a 10th grader obtains a grade equivalent of 5.5 (fifth grade, fifth month) on a reading achievement test appropriate for 10th graders, it is unlikely that students at the 5.5 grade level were actually in the norming group for the 10th grade test. Therefore, this grade equivalent is merely an estimate based on the hypothetical performance of students at the 5.5 grade level, if they had taken the 10th-grade test. As you can tell from this explanation, grade equivalents are very difficult to explain and interpret properly. Another limitation of grade equivalents is that the amount of error may be anywhere from half a year to a full year and a half. So a score of 10.0 could be as low as 8.5 or as high as 11.5—we simply do not know for sure.

7. When explaining percentile scores, make it clear that they are not to be confused with percentages of questions answered correctly. It might be best to say, "In comparison with 10th graders throughout the United States, John is in the upper 10% to 15% as measured by the Iowa Silent Reading Test when this was taken last October."

8. Take time to explain the overall limitations of standardized reading achievement tests: (a) They are only crude estimates of a student's reading ability; (b) each test measures reading in a different way, which means a student might have five different scores on five different tests; (c) they do not provide information about how students can read and learn in their content classrooms; and (d) they provide only one glimpse of a student's reading ability and should be combined with observational, anecdotal, and classroom performance records.

There is no need for classroom teachers to become test and measurement experts simply because occasionally they may be asked to administer and interpret scores from standardized reading tests. By combining some basic knowledge about these tests with common sense, you can improve your chances of communicating effectively with students and parents.

Authentic Assessment of Literacy and Content Learning

Considering the many criticisms of standardized, commercial reading tests (Brown, 1989; Brozo & Brozo, in press; Glazer et al., 1988; Johnston, 1992; Linn, 1985; Taylor, 1988), it is not surprising that an increasing number of secondary school teachers are developing their own assessments for use in the classroom.

Earlier in this chapter, we referred to authentic learning. We now use the term **authentic assessment** to differentiate between commercial instruments that test in decontextualized ways and those created by teachers and students for their own use with genuine, functional purposes. Over the past several years, we have been collecting what we consider to be some of the best examples of authentic assessment. These examples not only reflect creative methods of discovering how students read and think, but are also consistent with current perspectives of how best to teach and assess literacy and learning processes. Because these assessments are devised and/or adapted by teachers, often in collaboration with students, they invariably yield richer and more meaningful information about student learning than could be gained from traditional testing practices (Johnston, 1989). Furthermore, using authentic assessment helps you rely on your own assessment skills and individual judgment and exercise your own professional prerogative in making important instructional decisions (Valencia et al., 1990).

One of the key principles of reading assessment discussed earlier is to embed assessment within the contexts of actual literacy and learning activities so that the results of assessment will have direct and immediate instructional implications. To this end, secondary school teachers need to devise their own approaches to assessment to determine the extent to which their students can read and learn from the various materials used in the classroom and use this new learning in functional and purposeful ways. The approaches teachers have employed to accomplish this goal have taken a number of forms, but all have these four critical characteristics in common:

1. They assess literacy and learning processes with the materials used in the classroom and in the actual contexts of their use.
2. They are so related to instruction that assessment and instruction become virtually indistinguishable.
3. They reflect the essential and important role of teacher judgment in student evaluation.
4. They develop students' abilities to think metacognitively and self-reflect.

Creating a Portfolio Assessment Culture: Process and Product

As part of a year-long portfolio teaching/assessment research project in collaboration with a high school French and English teacher, we had local professionals speak to students about the importance of portfolios in their work and lives. Frank, a local architect, began his talk to a group of industrial arts, art, and foreign language students by saying "We are all walking portfolios." Students smiled. "I mean look around, each of you projects a certain image by the way you dress, wear your hair, walk, talk, and this image is open to evaluation and judgment by peers, parents, teachers, and potential employers." Frank continued, "That's why you leave the jeans and sneakers at home when you go to a job interview." Frank's points were extremely helpful because they solidified for students the idea that portfolios are more than a product, a "thing," a container of "stuff" but are a concept and a process. In our debriefing session after Frank's presentation, students made comments such as "I'm beginning to get the picture that portfolios are anything we want them to be to help someone see what we're capable of." "Like Frank said, I can evaluate my own work and then put together a portfolio that projects the image I want."

We'll return to our experiences and the results of our portfolio research project (Moje, Brozo, & Haas, in press) a bit later in this section. First, we briefly explore the definition and history of portfolios and answer some of the hows and whys of their use.

The **portfolio** for instruction and assessment has become a popular buzz word among teachers in nearly every field. We're sure most of you are already familiar with the term. The idea of using portfolios for documenting literacy growth has many advocates (Camp & Levine, 1991; DeFina, 1992; Krest, 1990; Lamme & Haysmith, 1991; Murphy & Smith, 1991; Tierney, Carter, & Desai, 1991). One of the best working definitions of a portfolio we have seen was developed at the Northwest Regional Educational Laboratory (Arter, 1990):

A portfolio is a purposeful collection of student work that exhibits to the students (and/or others) the student's efforts, progress or achievement in (a) given area(s). This collection must include: (1) student participation in selection of portfolio content; (2) the criteria for selection; (3) the criteria for judging merit; and (4) evidence of student self-reflection. (p. 2)

Portfolios are a relatively new and unique innovation in the areas of literacy and content learning (i.e., math, science, history). Although in fields such as commercial art, modeling, photography and journalism, portfolios have been used for some time to showcase artistic and professional achievement (Tierney et al., 1991), portfolio assessment in writing emerged only in the early 1980s with the work of Judy and Judy (1981) and Elbow and Belanoff (1986) in a freshmen writing course. The growth in portfolio assessment in educational circles since then has been remarkable. It's nearly impossible to pick up a reading, writing, or language arts journal these days without finding an article on portfolios; and this is expanding to applied journals in the natural and social sciences and math.

What is the allure of portfolio assessment, beyond its bandwagon appeal? Put simply, portfolios offer an assessment framework that reflects our current understanding of the process of literacy and content learning. We know, for instance, that learning takes place over time—portfolios are collections of learning demonstrations over time; that learning occurs in multiple contexts—portfolios sample work from a variety of teaching/learning situations; that effective learning occurs when learners are engaged in meaningful, purposeful learning activities—portfolio teaching/assessment promotes authentic learning; and that effective learning requires personal reflection—portfolios have self-reflection built into the process.

Vavrus (1990) suggests that the following five questions be answered when planning to establish a curriculum that includes portfolio teaching/assessment:

What Will the Portfolio Look Like?   All portfolios should have a physical structure as well as a conceptual structure. Physically, a portfolio may be structured chronologically, by subject area, or style of work. The *conceptual structure* refers to your goals for student learning. After identifying goals, you should decide the best ways to document students' work relative to the goals.

What Goes in the Portfolio?   To determine what goes in the portfolio, several related questions must be answered first: Who will evaluate the portfolios (parents, administrators, teachers)? What will these individuals want to know about student learning? Will portfolio samples document student growth that test scores cannot capture? Or, will they further support the results of test scores? What is the best evidence that can be included in the portfolio to document student progress toward goals? Will students include their best work only, or will the portfolio contain a progressive record of student growth, or both? Will the portfolio include drafts, sketches, and ideas in unfinished as well as finished form?

Because portfolio assessment is authentic in that it should represent genuine, meaningful learning activities in the classroom, then work samples should come from the variety of daily and weekly assignments and projects students are engaged in. If you are documenting the literacy progress of a ninth grader, for example, then his portfolio would likely contain samples from a writing folder; excerpts from journals and literature logs; early and final drafts of written reports, stories, and research papers; and copies of assignments from various content areas that required reading and writing.

A 10th-grade biology student's portfolio might include lab reports documenting her ability to conduct an experiment and analyze and interpret the results, actual project hardware, photographs and logs from field work, and questions and hypotheses for further scientific inquiry.

A math student in the eighth grade might include in his portfolio documentation of improving ability to understand increasingly complex story problems or algebraic equations, samples of computations, descriptions of certain mathematical properties, explanations of why certain mathematical processes work, and evidence of math being used to solve everyday problems.

In addition to work samples, portfolios should also contain reflective records. Vital to the process of learning through portfolio teaching/assessment, **reflective records** are documentation of students' personal reflections and self-evaluations. Students should study their portfolios at various points throughout the year, focusing on a single work, a set of revisions, evidence of growth in a particular area, or the portfolio materials as a whole. In reflecting on these samples, students should ask themselves questions such as

Why did I select this piece of work?
Is this a sample of my best work?
What special strengths are reflected in this work?
What was particularly important to me during the process of completing this work?
What have I learned about (math, science, history, writing, etc.) from working on this piece or project?
If I could go on working on this piece or project, what would I do?
What particular skill or area of interest would I like to try out in future works?

Self-evaluative questions concerned solely with writing might include the following:

How has my writing changed since I wrote this?
If I revised this, what would I change?
What have I learned since I wrote this report that I would include in a follow-up report?
How did drafting and revising help me develop this essay?
How have I used this process to create other essays and reports?

Answers to these questions in the form of comments and reflections then become a part of the students' portfolio. Students should also be sure to date their work and briefly comment on why it was included in the portfolio.

You should also include brief notes about why certain samples of students' work were chosen. At the same time, you should keep personal and anecdotal records of students' work and progress based on classroom observations, inspection of portfolio samples, and conferences on the portfolio with students, parents, and other teachers. These records can complement students' reflective records (Vavrus, 1990). Given most secondary school teachers' severe time constraints, record keeping of this kind can often pose the biggest challenge in portfolio assessment.

Jenny, an 11th-grade English teacher, handles record keeping by writing brief comments on adhesive name-tag size labels from rolls she can hold in her hand. She then affixes her comments to the work sample in the portfolio. Comments on each label include identification of the sample, why the activity was completed, why the sample was included, and brief notes about what the sample shows about a student's progress toward achieving instructional and personal goals. Jenny has found her system to be more manageable than others she has tried, especially because she can also hold the roll of labels during classroom activities and make observational and anecdotal records on them quickly and unobtrusively. Later, these notes, too, can be placed in students' portfolios.

Many teachers have found the use of checklists and questionnaires essential for analyzing portfolios and keeping records on them. A math teacher uses the following set of questions to assess students' math work samples:
Describe the task the student completed:

- What mathematics did the student learn?
- How does this relate to what the student has learned before?
- Of the math the student has done lately, what areas of strength and confidence are exhibited in this work?
- What aspects of this work reflect a lack of or incomplete understanding?

A history teacher uses an overall checklist such as the one shown in Figure 4–4 to keep track of his students' progress relative to portfolio criteria established in collaboration with his class.

How and When Will Samples Be Selected?   It's important to establish a clear and efficient system for selecting materials to go into and come out of the portfolio throughout the school year. Most teachers make these decisions at the end of a unit, grading period, semester, or school year. These are all good times to keep and add work samples that provide the clearest and most compelling evidence of student growth and achievement and where appropriate to eliminate other samples. Many teachers have found time lines helpful in making the entire class aware of when portfolio checks, revisions, and new entries will occur. In this way, students are brought into the decision-making process about what to include in their portfolios; thus, students further develop the ability to monitor their own progress. As stated, the more students are brought into the teaching/learning process, the more responsibility they take for their own learning.

Figure 4–4   Portfolio criteria checklist

Name	Piece/Project	Self-Evaluation	Reference Skills	Improvement

How Will Portfolios Be Evaluated?   It is essential that evaluative criteria be established relative to the goals for student learning you and your students set up beforehand. We recommend that the greater part of a student's portfolio be evaluated on the basis of growth, both in terms of academic achievement and self-knowledge, instead of on the basis of comparisons with other students' work.

The evaluation process typical in most secondary classrooms or schools where portfolio assessment/teaching occurs looks like this:

1. Teacher discusses and negotiates goals of portfolios with students.
2. Teacher and students develop guidelines and procedures for showcasing portfolios.
3. Showcase portfolio is developed by students with assistance and feedback from peers.
4. Students develop self-evaluation comments and present their portfolio.
5. Students evaluate their portfolio according to criteria they help develop with the teacher (i.e., evidence of improvement, evidence of effort, quality of self-evaluation, range of projects, presentation, future goals).
6. Student submits portfolio to the teacher, who reviews it along with student self-evaluations and peer criteria scores. A grade is awarded.
7. The portfolio is returned to the student.

Figure 4–5 shows a **portfolio grade sheet** (Krest, 1990) that can be used to record individual grades for each writing sample and portfolio grades for students' progress.

Figure 4–5   **Portfolio grade sheet**

	Date	Portfolio Grade	Sample	Comments

Due Dates: _____
_____
_____

Name: _____

HP:*
MP:
LP:

HP:
MP:
LP:

HP:
MP:
LP:

HP:
MP:
LP:

*HP = high priority; MP = middle priority; LP = low priority

How Can Portfolios Be Passed On?   As many teachers have noted, one of the special advantages of portfolio assessment is that the records of student progress can be passed on to succeeding teachers. In this way, the portfolio process promotes continuity in a student's education and collaboration among teachers at various grade levels. We suggest that as the school year draws to a close, you get together with other teachers at the next grade level to discuss their expectations and to find out what kind of information from portfolios would be most helpful to them in determining student accomplishment. In this process, you can make decisions about what to include or exclude before passing on portfolios. This is also a good time to have a conference with students about their portfolios in terms of the kind of work they believe would best reflect their growth and achievement for next year's teacher.

A Study of Portfolio Assessment: What We Learned   In this section, we discuss the findings of our own research about the benefits of portfolio teaching and assessment. We are vitally concerned about the extent to which the strategies and ideas we offer are implemented in real classroom settings by real teachers. Given this concern, much of our own research over the course of our careers has been devoted to discovering how teachers implement instructional innovations.

We conducted one research project about strategy implementation during the 1990 to 1991 school year. For 6 months, we worked with and observed an experienced senior high school French teacher, Jayne, as she implemented portfolio instruction and assessment. Our goal was to gain insights into the potential effectiveness of the strategy and the teacher change process itself. Furthermore, we hoped to develop a better understanding of the realities of using portfolios in a secondary school classroom where an individual teacher was attempting to put ideas from the literature into practice.

Our findings suggest that students—their input and voices—are often omitted in reports on the effectiveness of portfolios. Similarly, a factor not often accounted for in the rhetoric of educational change is the response and cooperation of students themselves. Yet, we discovered that without student cooperation and involvement, portfolio teaching and assessment is as vulnerable to failure as any other highly touted instructional innovation that has come before it. Perhaps the most important insight we gained from our experience in Jayne's classroom was that *students, like teachers, need scaffolding for change.* In other words, we can't always expect students to take advantage of new strategies simply because we think they should. The change process must include them as well; therefore, we need to prepare students for change, support them as they move through the change process, and provide them with ample opportunities for reflection on and critique of the change process.

With these general findings in mind, and based on our numerous conversations and interviews with several students from Jayne's classroom, we (Moje et al., in press) offer the following guidelines for implementing portfolios with secondary school students:

1. Start with simple activities.
2. Negotiate firm deadlines.
3. Encourage students to set concrete goals.
4. Provide initial resources.
5. Integrate other classroom activities with the portfolios.

Start With Simple Activities.   We suggest that you begin to use portfolios by asking students to complete simple and short writing activities. The activities can take any form. For example, in an advanced algebra class, students could make journal entries that ask them to reflect on their reasons for taking the advanced class; or they could prepare goal statements or biographies that link the class to their needs and interests. Starting with simple activities with foreseeable deadlines will allow students to slowly work up to more comprehensive projects.

Negotiate Firm Deadlines.   When students are not used to the cognitive ambiguity and uncertainty of the portfolio process, it is important to help them set deadlines to keep them focused on their work. Despite the fact that the portfolio is designed to be an ongoing activity, as opposed to a finite project, students who are accustomed to "due dates" may require your guidance in setting deadlines to get work completed and to meet project goals.

Encourage Students to Set Concrete Goals.   Rather than expecting all students to be able to generate their own projects and samples for the portfolios, we suggest that you conduct conferences with students to create plans of action. Such a plan would provide students with short-range goals that could be accomplished according to agreed-on deadlines, giving students a clearer view of their progress toward long-range goals. Plans of action can also provide students with a means of self-assessment, because students would be able to evaluate both their progress at meeting steps in the plan and the wisdom of the steps they chose.

Provide Initial Resources.   Providing initial resources is especially critical in classrooms where portfolios will comprise project materials and samples. Students who are not used to conducting extended research that might require finding contacts, following up leads, making phone calls, and the like will need an initial source of specific information to get them started. These sources can help students sustain their research efforts, while helping them learn valuable reference skills in the process.

Integrate Other Classroom Activities With the Portfolios.   Many content teachers feel the necessity of covering certain concepts that are integral to their content area by means of direct instruction to ensure that the concepts are learned. Jayne, for example, felt it was necessary to continue using the French text and to provide direct instruction in grammar and vocabulary. She understood that students might be unprepared for complete immersion in the portfolio project and consequently moved back and forth between the two types of teaching. The stark contrast, however, between the teacher-led instruction and the student-led portfolios created tension and ambiguity among students.

Although Jayne meant for the portfolio writings to be applications of the book lessons, students didn't readily make the connections on their own. On reflection, Jayne decided she could have tied activities together in a variety of ways. For example, she could have demonstrated the grammar rules the students read about in the textbook by pointing out the uses of grammatical structures in their portfolios writing samples. Integration helps students see the utility and value of portfolios as an integral part of the learning process in content classrooms.

Perhaps the most outstanding benefit of portfolio assessment is that it invites students and teachers to be allies in the assessment process. When a portfolio culture is established, there is a good chance that students will become more concerned, thoughtful, and energetic learners. At the same time, teachers will find a renewed enthusiasm for providing support and guidance of others' learning while growing as learners themselves.

Assessment by Observation

Suggesting to teachers that they assess through observation is like asking them to breathe or walk; it comes so naturally to most of them that its importance and power as an assessment strategy is often overlooked (Brown, 1987). For instance, teachers make minute by minute decisions and lesson adjustments during classroom learning as they discover that students lack appropriate prior knowledge, fail to understand key vocabulary, or need further concept development (Johnston, 1989). Unfortunately, these days, assessments based on teacher intuition about, interaction with, and systematic observations of students has been devalued (Johnston, 1990; Lucas, 1988). Now, when classrooms seem to be virtually inundated by tests (e.g., standardized tests, state-mandated tests, end of unit tests, departmental tests), many teachers have become more trustworthy of test data from formal assessments than the data they collect in their normal, everyday teaching and interactions with students.

Observational assessment is superior to formal assessment for providing the classroom teacher the critical information needed to make important instructional decisions. Assessing through observation requires that teachers become more sensitive to the entire instructional situation: the reader, the text, the tasks required of the reader, the processes needed to complete the tasks, and the environment in which tasks occur. Assessments conducted as students interact with text and complete daily assignments, engage in class discussions, or work cooperatively to solve problems can provide a rich source of information about students' relative strengths and weaknesses as well as how instruction can be modified to better facilitate learning (Readence & Martin, 1988).

Observations are likely to be highly valid and reliable measures of students' reading and learning ability (Moore, 1983). Observing students over time in a variety of classroom situations can provide teachers an objective, unbiased view of students. Earlier, we discussed the limitations of making instructional decisions based on a single assessment at one point in time; specifically, that single assessments are not very reliable measures of a student's true reading and learning ability. The nature of observational assessment, however, requires that teachers base decisions on numerous observations over an extended period. The observed patterns of students' behaviors that lead to instructional decisions have occurred frequently in genuine reading and learning situations—not in artificial or contrived testing situations (Johnston, 1992).

The virtue of observational assessment is that it is ongoing and occurs within the context of normal classroom activities while students are engaged in genuine literacy events. What is more, teachers can learn to plan, structure, and systematize their observations.

Finally, as indicated earlier, observation records can become an integral part of student portfolios.

To discover the learning needs of their students, teachers can structure observations within the context of "real" learning to systematically evaluate students. For example, a science teacher put together the observation checklist shown in Figure 4–6 based on classroom behaviors exhibited by her poor readers/learners. With each new class she uses the checklist, over the course of a few weeks, to note similar behaviors exhibited by her new students. In this way, she accurately and reliably determines which individuals need special assistance.

Another teacher put together his observation checklist (Figure 4–7) based on characteristics of good readers (Pearson & Valencia, 1986). With the knowledge he gains about his students' strategies for processing their textbook and other reading material, he determines the relative need for reading and study skills instruction for the group, and for individuals.

Because these observations occur as a natural part of the content-area lesson, students can demonstrate their true ability. Teachers can obtain highly relevant and useful data by measuring what they choose to measure in the classroom context where students perform actual reading, writing, and learning tasks. The checklists shown in Figures 4–6 and 4–7 are examples of more systematic attempts to assess through observation. They can and should be modified to fit your particular assessment needs.

Figure 4–6   Behavioral clues to students needing special assistance

Student: _____

_____ 1. Avoids eye contact with me, especially when I'm asking questions of the class over the reading assignment.

_____ 2. May create the "impression" that he or she knows the answer to my question by looking intently and flagging his or her hand.

_____ 3. During oral reading of the textbook, tries to be the first one to read to get it over with.

_____ 4. During oral reading, tries to be the last one to read or tries to avoid being called on to read.

_____ 5. Frequently forgets to bring to class books and other materials that may be used for oral reading or needed to do in-class work.

_____ 6. Twists and turns restlessly in seat, often talking with neighbor.

_____ 7. Attempts to disrupt class.

_____ 8. Uses manipulative techniques within and outside of class to try to gain my positive perceptions of his or her ability in spite of poor performance.

_____ 9. Uses neighbor for information about assignments and answers to questions.

Figure 4–7   Characteristics of good readers

Student: _____

____ 1. Uses prior knowledge to help construct meaning from text.

____ 2. Draws inferences at the word, sentence, paragraph, and text levels.

____ 3. Provides many plausible responses to questions about text.

____ 4. Varies reading strategies to fit the text and the reading situation.

____ 5. Synthesizes information within and across text.

____ 6. Asks good questions about text.

____ 7. Exhibits positive attitudes toward reading.

____ 8. Integrates many skills to produce an understanding of text.

____ 9. Uses knowledge flexibly.

Source: Adapted from P. D. Pearson & S. Valencia, "Assessment, Accountability, and Professional Prerogative," in J. Readence & R. S. Baldwin (Eds.), *Research in Literacy: Merging Perspectives.* © Copyright 1986, National Reading Conference.

Verbal Reporting

As early as 1917, E. L. Thorndike was focusing on the reasoning processes involved in reading. Today, most researchers and thinkers in the field would agree that to understand the basic processes of reading is to understand the very nature of comprehension itself. Most of our current models of reading, which are rooted in sound theory and research and are compelling on a commonsense level, attempt to describe the processes involved in constructing meaningful interpretations of text. This attention to reading process marks a significant shift in thinking from traditional conceptions of reading ability as a static entity or a collection of skills.

Process is the mental work involved in comprehending. Just as teachers of mathematics have for some time recognized the importance of process and have credited students' work (in spite of a right or wrong answer to a math question), so, too, are our reading assessments moving toward learning about how students create interpretations of what they read and away from merely checking their answers to questions. We are learning that the better the process, the better the products or results of our reading. To continue the math analogy: For math teachers to credit a student's work, they must see it. Therefore, students are asked to write out all the computations they make in working out a math problem and to hand those in along with the answers. Obviously, most students cannot compute mathematical operations in their heads and, therefore, must make visual records to put together all the steps in solving a problem. The purpose of asking students to write out their work is so that teachers can determine if the students' process is sound. In the private act of reading, the mental operations involved in constructing meaning also need to be "observed" to determine if a student's reading processes are sound. One way to accomplish this is through the use of verbal reports.

Verbal reports require a student to "think aloud" while reading or writing to allow the teacher to eavesdrop on the student's thought processes. Researchers and practitioners have discovered that students can be trained to become "tuned in" to their reading processes through teacher modeling and demonstrations, as in the reciprocal teaching strategy discussed in Chapter 3. The major advantage of verbal reports is that they allow access to reasoning processes underlying cognitive activity during reading (Afflerbach & Johnston, 1984, 1986). Once this information is obtained, the teacher can determine whether or not students need to develop more effective comprehension strategies.

With these ideas in mind, let us consider a freshmen science classroom in which the teacher was attempting to gather verbal reports on her students' reading processes. She talked about the reading process and modeled how she would attend to process while reading. For example, as she read a passage, she stopped after each sentence and made comments such as these:

> Now, at this point, I would describe what the sentence meant, how it fit in with what came before and how I figured all of that out . . . in other words, what I have to think about in order to make sense out of these sentences.
>
> Here is a word I had to think about, I would try to tell you how I figured out what it meant or how it fits in with the rest of the sentence or passage.
>
> Okay, now I'm finished with this paragraph and I should tell you how I'm going about coming up with a gist for it.

She tried to show her class the difference between talking about process and talking about the content of the passage by statements such as these:

> By saying "this word means such and such, and such and such" doesn't tell me anything about how you figured out the meaning for the word . . . so you should tell me how you figured it out.
>
> I could say "the main idea of this paragraph is . . ." but that doesn't explain how I figured out the main idea.

The following transcript is an example of the science class's interactions and verbal reporting as they interpreted a passage about a praying mantis from their science textbooks.

Student: "What is a praying mantis? Although it is really no more than an insect, it is the only insect that can turn its head and look over its shoulder like a man, wash its face like a cat, and bend over and drink water like a horse." This is just describing the praying mantis . . . but I already knew about this. . . . I used to collect insects when I was a kid, and I learned a lot about them from books.

Teacher: Okay. Remember, I'm interested in your process . . . what you're doing to make sense out of the sentences.

Student: Well, I understand all the words, and like I said I'm thinking about what I already know about praying mantises . . . "Yet, this unusual insect is considered to be a valuable garden helper." . . . I guess they're going to tell how the mantis is helpful in the garden. . . . They eat other insects, I know that . . . I'm thinking about how the author used this sentence as a way of getting into the main part of the passage . . . I know it's the main part because the title says "Garden Helper."

Teacher: Okay, now read some more.

Student: "The body of the adult female mantis is three to four inches long and is usually a light-brown color. The male is an inch or so shorter and brilliant green. He develops a pair of wings that are soft green underneath with a bright green band down the sides. . . ."

Teacher: What are you thinking about now, Bill?

Student: Well, I was expecting it to start to mention why the mantis is helpful in gardens, but it's just describing the mantis. . . . I'll have to keep reading to see why the author is doing this. "Thus, as the insect hangs in a ver-ver-ti-cal . . . position along the stem of a flower or shrub, it blends perfectly into its background."

Teacher: What about "v-e-r-t-i-c-a-l"? Do you know what this word means?

Student: I've seen it before. . . . I'm not sure.

Teacher: How would you figure out what it meant? What are you going to do with this word?

Student: Well, sometimes I just keep reading past words, and if I don't think they're too important, I won't spend a lot of time on them. . . . I think this word is important because the sentence starts out with "thus" so the author was trying to relate the stuff about the mantis's body and wings to this sentence. I need to look at the sentence again to see how the word fits in. . . . It says it "hangs . . . along the stem of a flower or shrub, it blends into its background" . . . stems grow up, sorta straight up, so vertical probably means that the mantis hangs onto the stem and looks like a leaf or something. Now I'll read the last sentence: "A person can come very close to one and never see it." I'm thinking about all the times I've probably never even noticed one even if I was looking right at it.

This dialogue enables the teacher to learn quite a bit about her student's strategies for comprehending words and paragraphs. The student demonstrated in his verbal reports how he anticipates what is likely to come next in a passage based on the organization of the passage, a sensitivity to signal words used by the author, and how he uses context to figure out the meanings of words.

In another example, a high school history teacher asked his students to write summaries to short sections from their textbook and try to explain the thoughts and decision making that went into creating the summaries. Student's summary writing ability can be a very useful indicator of their overall comprehension of a text (Afflerbach & Johnston, 1986). Summary writing requires the reader to think metacognitively, make inferences, select important ideas, and form gists (Brozo & Curtis, 1987). The teacher set up a hypothetical situation that required his eleventh graders to think about what he would tell a fifth grader who was trying to write a summary. In the example in Figure 4–8, students were summarizing a section on the history of beards.

Gathering verbal reports such as these from students can provide a teacher with a great deal of rich, useful information about how they think while they read and the strategies they use for comprehending passages. Traditional, formal methods of reading assessment cannot uncover information about these underlying processes.

The verbal report examples demonstrate that teachers can gather valuable information about students' text processing strategies in a class question/discussion format. Nevertheless, it is impossible to obtain a detailed understanding of each student's particular reading strengths and weaknesses unless more time is devoted to working individually with each student. Obviously, most teachers do not have the time to collect verbal reports on all students, and it is not absolutely necessary to do so. Rather, a more realistic plan of action would be to ask one or two students who show signs of failing to understand critical information from text to meet with you and provide additional verbal reports while the rest of the class is engaged in study guide or cooperative learning activities.

Verbal report data, as with all test data, should be used to aid instructional decision making. Instructional modifications based on assessments are often made after testing. Another way of thinking about assessment is that testing and teaching are integral events. Within this kind of assessment context, information about how students learn and how those learning conditions can be improved occur together. Testing actually *informs* teaching. At other points in this book, we demonstrate how verbal reporting can be used to assess and teach important comprehension processes.

Written Retellings: Using Writing to Assess Comprehension

How well students understand a text can be determined by asking them to **retell in writing** what they have read, thus creating a record, or protocol of their comprehension (Smith & Jackson, 1985). The following letter from P. T. Barnum to General Ulysses S. Grant (*Sequential Tests of Educational Progress,* 1957) was given to 10th-grade American history students at the beginning of a unit on entrepreneurs of the late 19th century. The teacher asked his students to read the letter and then, without looking back, write everything they could remember about the letter, the main idea, and any other relevant information or ideas.

Figure 4–8   Verbal reporting during summarizing

Student: Okay, I'd say take each paragraph separately because the reason that you have paragraphs is because there's usually a key idea or key bit of information in each paragraph they want to get across. That's why paragraphs are broken up. And I'd say read the paragraph through, then think of what the paragraph is mostly about—not the most interesting part of the paragraph necessarily, but the main idea in the paragraph. You need to think of the paragraph as almost like a little story. There's usually an idea they're trying to get across, like, it'll usually be in the first or last sentence of the paragraph. When you've read the paragraph, think to yourself, Do you have the main idea? Are there things in the paragraph talking about that main idea you've come up with? And if there are, you can be pretty sure that that is the main idea of the paragraph. And if there aren't, go back and see if you can come up with another main idea. For instance, if you were to come up here with the main idea being "the burning of hair clippings," you could figure out that that was wrong because the rest of the paragraph really doesn't have anything to do with that. Everything kind of points to that central idea of the paragraph. And when you get your main idea of the paragraph, just make it into a one-sentence statement of the paragraph, and then put them all together. Do this with each paragraph, and then put all of the sentences together so they flow smoothly.

Teacher: Okay, what if I ask you this question: What do I do with all these particular examples, all these specific examples, how do I deal with them? For instance, in this second paragraph, it's talking about "tongs," "curling irons," "dyes," "gold dust" . . .

Student: Okay, try to put those into one category of, like, what are all those things? They're hair instruments. Or, they're all used for the same type of job. And just try to group them into one word, like tools. I don't know . . . is that what they call "hair stuff?"

Teacher: So if I encounter lists of things in any text, I should do this?

Student: Right, right. Like if it was about building machines or something, and it listed cogs and cams and nuts and bolts, you could say "hardware of the machine."

Teacher: How about this problem? When the teacher asks me to make a summary. I can't reproduce the page, I can't include every word of the text in my summary. How do I make decisions about what to keep and what not to keep?

Student: If there are paragraphs that don't have much information in them and it's not really that pertinent . . . disregard them . . . don't worry about them if you want to shorten up your summary. But don't necessarily think that a paragraph that's short isn't important. Because sometimes you'll have a big paragraph and it will just take a lot of explanation to get the point across, where a short paragraph might have a lot of information in one or two sentences. You need to take an overall view of the whole story that you've read, and there's an underlying idea there, like "beards," the whole thing's on beards, and then this kinda breaks down into an outline of very early man, just moving forward in time, early civilizations, all the way up through the middle ages, and how each of these people treated beards.

Teacher: Okay, so now can you summarize how you would summarize?

Student: Sure. Go through and read the whole passage, take the main idea of the passage out, and then go back and paragraph by paragraph take the main idea out of each paragraph and summarize it, putting those main ideas from each paragraph into a summary, and that should do it.

Honored Sir:

The whole world honors and respects you. All are anxious that you should live happy and free from care. While they admire your manliness in declining the large sum recently tendered you by friends, they still desire to see you achieve financial independence in an honorable manner. Of the unique and valuable trophies with which you have been honored we all have read, and all have a laudable desire to see these evidences of love and respect bestowed upon you by monarchs, princes, and people throughout the globe.

While you would confer a great and enduring favor on your fellow men and women by permitting them to see these trophies, you could also remove existing embarrassments in a most satisfactory and honorable manner. I will give you one hundred thousand dollars cash, besides a proportion of the profits, if I may be permitted to exhibit these relics to a grateful and appreciative public, and I will give satisfactory bonds of half a million dollars for their safe-keeping and return.

These precious trophies of which all your friends are so proud, would be placed before the eyes of your millions of admirers in a manner and style at once pleasing to yourself and satisfactory to the best elements of the entire community. Remembering that the momentoes [sic] of Washington, Napoleon, Frederick the Great, and many other distinguished men have given immense pleasure to millions who have been permitted to see them, I trust you will in the honorable manner proposed, gratify the public and thus inculcate the lesson of honesty, perseverance, and true patriotism so admirably illustrated in your career.

I have the honor to be truly your friend and admirer,

P. T. Barnum
("A Letter From the 1870s," 1957)

The teacher asked his students to read the letter and then, without looking back, write everything they could remember about it; the main idea and any other relevant information or ideas. The three types of written protocols produced by the students are representative of the responses obtained by the history teacher. Here is one example:

Honored sir: The whole world respects you with honor. All are anxious that you should live happily with care. While the whole world worries about the manliness in declining the money tendered you by friends, they respect you to manage with honorable manner.

This response revealed to the teacher a couple of possibilities. First, because the student apparently tried to simply rewrite the letter, the student may have misunderstood the directions. If not a problem of understanding directions, this response could also reflect a reader who, being incapable of understanding the surface logic of the letter (let alone the implied ideas), may have resorted to a strategy intended to disguise this possible serious lack of comprehension by simply writing down the words of the letter. In any case, the history teacher had what he believed to be a student who needed definite follow-up, and he immediately got together with the student for further assessment and discussion.

Another student submitted this protocol:

The passage was a letter sent to Ulysses S. Grant from P. T. Barnum. The letter outlined how Barnum wanted to bring his attractions before millions of admirers with the permission of Ulysses Grant. Barnum was willing to pay $100,000 and a portion of the profits if he was so permitted to be allowed to show his trophies to the American public. Barnum promised $500,000 in satisfactory bonds to Ulysses Grant for safekeeping and return to demonstrate how serious Barnum was in bringing his trophies to the people.

Barnum started his letter to Ulysses Grant that the people as well as himself respected his position of President and wished him the best of health. Barnum also finished his letter in the same fashion, comparing Grant with other great men such as Frederick the Great, Washington, and Napoleon.

What appeared obvious to the history teacher in this response was that the student had a good grasp of the basic information in the letter. The student recalled the significant details and followed the surface logic of Barnum's proposal to Grant. What is not reflected in this response, however, is any indication that the student appreciated the subtlety and irony in Barnum's letter. Also, this reader apparently had little prior knowledge for the topic because no additional ideas or information, beyond those included in the text, were provided.

A third student turned in this record:

The letter from P. T. Barnum to Grant was first a letter honoring and showing Grant how much his public loved him. In other words, a real snow job. Because in the latter part of the letter, Barnum gives Grant a proposal of, first, paying Grant one-hundred thousand dollars to let Barnum exhibit his oddities, or as Barnum puts it, his trophies. Second, Barnum pledged to pay a half a million dollars in bonds for Grant's protection of his trophies. The whole letter came out to be a bribe on Barnum's part. But in real life it worked in favor of Barnum. The reason that one can tell this letter was a real snow job is because Grant wasn't everything Barnum said he was.

The teacher felt this was an impressive response. Not only did it reflect a basic understanding of the facts of Barnum's proposal, but also an understanding of Barnum's power of persuasion by heaping, what history perhaps has proven unfounded, lofty praise on Grant. This student's ability to pick up on the underlying themes and rhetorical devices in the letter indicates a good deal of relevant prior knowledge for the topic and the skill to bring that prior knowledge to bear in constructing a multilevel understanding of the text.

Students who show signs of lacking relevant prior knowledge or the literacy skills to interpret meaningfully the assessment passage may be given special assistance. You can provide these students additional or alternative reading opportunities from books that are content related, including some that are easier and more enjoyable to read than the textbook, to help build prior knowledge. Cooperative learning experiences are helpful for improving students' interpretive powers. Beyond the revelation of your students' reading performance with the texts used in your classrooms, the written recall protocol approach to assessment has another advantage in that an entire class can be assessed at one time. This advantage in efficiency, however, can be a disadvantage for students who are poor writers. An alternative to written recalls is to assess students' comprehension of text by having students orally retell what they remember and learned from the text.

Oral Retellings

Asking students to put into their own words what they just read or to tell all the details they can remember after reading is certainly not a new assessment innovation. What is new, however, is a slightly more formalized approach to this kind of assessment that attempts to measure the number and kind of ideas recalled by the reader. Although **oral retellings** can reveal a great deal about a particular reader's content-based literacy skills, this strategy is designed to be administered individually. Therefore, retellings can be obtained most feasibly from those few students who show clear signs of needing personal assessments and extra assistance.

Within any text, within any paragraph, some ideas are more important, more central to the overall meaning than other ideas. It is possible, therefore, to rank these ideas on a scale of importance (Winograd, 1984); for instance, an idea of great importance might have a ranking of 3, while an idea of little importance might have a ranking of 1. Suppose you and I are going to read a passage about pollution. The author of the passage makes a few major points about the global consequences of pollution and also presents several specific examples of pollution. After reading, in my retelling I mention three specific examples of pollution, while your retelling includes two of the author's major points and one specific example. Although we both recalled three ideas, your retelling would receive a higher rating because you recalled two major ideas.

A senior psychology teacher put the retelling method into practice by designing a short assessment with paragraphs from the course textbook. First, he read the textbook and additional readings used in the class and identified segments, paragraphs that were relatively intact, that is, they could stand alone and did not require the pages of text before and after to be understood. Next, he rated the ideas, the sentences in the passage, by deciding those that were major points and those that were minor points. He then devised a simple form for recording a student's retelling. Figure 4–9 includes one of the paragraphs he used and the retelling form. Notice that the retellings the teacher looks for not only include specifically recalled textual information but also ideas that link information to prior knowledge and other insights into a student's ability to think about text (Kalmbach, 1986).

Early in each new year, while the rest of the class is occupied with reading and personal research, the psychology teacher will pull aside certain students he suspects might be having difficulty with the reading material and has them retell the selected passages he has rated. He can then combine this information with their behaviors and performance he observes during regular class meetings to develop a better understanding of needed modifications to his general instructional

Figure 4-9 Sample passage and record sheet for oral retelling

The attitudes of today's children, regardless of age, are quite different from what they were in "the good old days." Children no longer accept parents' judgments as absolute, and in many cases they pay little attention to them at all. Parents are called on to justify their actions in ways that were not expected of them in the past. In addition, defiance and even outright rebellion are becoming more characteristic of even very small children. Fifty or even 30 years ago, no child would dream of "getting the law" on his parents after he had been beaten by his father. Today this is a relatively commonplace occurrence. In more than one instance, we have read that children have shot and killed their parents for some real or imagined grievance. Far more frequent are the hidden forms of rebellion, the unwillingness rather than the inability of children to learn and cooperate in the school and at home.

Retelling Record

Idea	Importance	Text
_____	1	The attitudes of today's children, regardless of age, are quite different from what they were in "the good old days."
_____	2	Children no longer accept parents' judgments as absolute,
_____	2	and in many cases they pay little attention to them at all.
_____	2	Parents are called on to justify their actions in ways that were not expected of them in the past.
_____	2	In addition, defiance and even outright rebellion are becoming more characteristic of even very small children.
_____	1	Fifty or even thirty years ago, no child would dream of "getting the law" on his parents after he had been beaten by his father.
_____	1	Today this is a relatively commonplace occurrence.
_____	1	In more than one instance, we have read that children have shot and killed their parents for some real or imagined grievance.
_____	3	Far more frequent are the hidden forms of rebellion, the unwillingness rather than the inability of children to learn and cooperate in the school and at home.

Overall rating _____
Total recalled _____
Average importance _____
Additional background information:

Tone of retelling:

Other observations:

Source: Adapted from R. Dreikurs & L. Grey, *A Parents' Guide to Child Discipline.* © Copyright 1970 by Hawthorn Books.

approach. For instance, for students who seem to have especially large gaps in prior knowledge for the broad topic of psychology, he has discovered that he can offer them additional selected articles and stories that are more readily understood and enjoyed than the textbook. For specific topics, he has found that linking these students with more competent students in cooperative learning activities has helped build their confidence and expand their understanding of the content.

A more holistic evaluation of student retellings was developed by an English teacher (Figure 4–10). The questions include many aspects of reading such as comprehension, metacognitive awareness, strategy use, level of text involvement, and facility with language.

Group Informal Reading Inventory

Another effective assessment strategy that can be used efficiently with the whole class is the **group informal reading inventory (GIRI)**, which asks students to demonstrate thinking and study processes with the content-area textbook the teacher plans to use for instruction. The results of this type of assessment are far

Figure 4–10   Retelling check sheet

Directions: Indicate with a check mark the extent to which the student's retelling includes evidence of the following:

	No Evidence	Some Evidence	A Great Deal of Evidence
1. Includes verbatim information.	_____	_____	_____
2. Includes inferred information.	_____	_____	_____
3. Includes most important ideas.	_____	_____	_____
4. Connects prior knowledge with text information.	_____	_____	_____
5. Makes summary statements and generalizations.	_____	_____	_____
6. Indicates affective involvement with text.	_____	_____	_____
7. Demonstrates appropriate use of language.	_____	_____	_____
8. Demonstrates sense of audience or purpose.	_____	_____	_____
9. Indicates control of mechanics of speaking.	_____	_____	_____
10. Indicates creative impressions/reactions to text.	_____	_____	_____

more informative than commercially prepared tests, we believe, because the assessment is based on material that students will be using throughout the year (Dishner & Readence, 1977; Shepherd, 1982). In addition, the results point to specific and general reading and study needs of students, which the teacher can take into account during each content lesson.

The GIRI can be designed to assess whatever processes you desire students to possess and that you wish to promote in your classroom. The following GIRI (Figure 4–11) was developed by a driver's education teacher from his class textbook.

The driver's education teacher administered this assessment during the first week of classes at the beginning of the school year. With the results, he was able to determine to what extent students could use their text as a resource and comprehend and process the textual information at a meaningful level. This knowledge led to specific instructional approaches such as cooperative grouping, direct process instruction in comprehension and concept knowledge, and training in designing and using study aids based on text and lecture information.

The GIRI as well as all of the assessment approaches offered in this chapter can help secondary school teachers replace the standardized test mind-set with the idea that they can create and use approaches to reading assessment that are understandable and instructionally meaningful.

Case Study Revisited

Terri, the ninth-grade science teacher introduced in the case study in the beginning of the chapter, wanted to find a classroom-based assessment strategy of her students' ability to understand their science text. Now that you have read about and explored a variety of assessment approaches in this chapter, reflect again on Terri's concerns and generate a few suggestions for meeting her assessment needs. Afterward, read about what she actually did to assess her students' knowledge and understanding of the structure of science prose.

In our discussion of schema theory in Chapter 2, we pointed out that for students to be successful in high school they need to have a well-developed sense about how authors structure ideas in narrative and especially in expository texts. These schemata for text structure help readers predict, assimilate, and retrieve text information—three critical reading processes. As we discovered, junior and senior high students may have a very good sense of how stories are structured but a relatively poor sense about the structures of complex expository texts they are likely to find in their social science and science books.

Mindful of the problems students have "thinking like writers," Terri has developed an extremely useful assessment strategy for gathering information about her ninth graders' understanding and use of expository text structure. It combines observations of text structure understanding with performance on text reconstruction activities (Bean, 1988). Putting together suggestions she obtained from an in-

Figure 4–11   Group informal reading inventory (GIRI) for a driver's education textbook

---

Using Book Parts

1. On what page does the unit (section) entitled "When You Are the Driver" begin?
2. On what pages can you find information on smoking and driving?
3. In what part of the book can you find the meaning of *kinetic energy*?

Understanding Graphs and Charts

1. According to the chart on page 61, what is the second-largest cause of rural fatal accidents?
2. What does the chart on page 334 imply about the relationship between speed and fuel consumption?
3. Using the chart on page 302 and your own weight, determine how much alcohol concentration in your blood would make you legally drunk.

Vocabulary in Context

1. What does the word *converse* mean in the following sentence?

   Do not take your eyes off the road to *converse* with a passenger.

2. What does the word *distracting* mean in the following sentence?

   He should avoid *distracting* the driver.

3. What does the word *enables* mean in the following sentence?

   It *enables* you to carry out your decisions promptly and in just the way you planned.

Summarizing and Sensing Key Ideas

1. Write a one-paragraph summary for the section entitled "A Defensive Driver's Decision Steps" on page 101. Be sure to include in your summary the key ideas and any other pertinent information. Use your own words as you write the summary.

2. Using your own words, state the key idea of the following paragraph.

   Not only does a defensive driver have to see all hazards and decide on his defense—he also has to act in time. A defensive driver's thinking shows in his actions as he drives. He anticipates hazards and covers the brake in case a stop is needed. He has both hands on the wheel, so he will be ready to act.

3. Write one or two sentences stating the key idea(s) of Chapter 18, "Controlling Your Emotions and Attitudes."

Creating Study Aids

1. Imagine that you will have a multiple-choice and short-answer test on Chapter 18. Organize the material in that chapter by taking notes over it or by creating some form of study aid.

---

service workshop with her own ideas, Terri discovered that her assessments provide rich information about students' text structure knowledge. By using the class text and other reading material from which students are expected to read and learn, her authentic assessments look like and function as teaching strategies as well.

Terri is constantly on the lookout for signs that her students are using the author's text structure to their advantage. She pays special attention to the following signals of text structure awareness:

- As students are retelling or discussing a selection, she determines whether they are using the author's organizational structures as their retellings or comments unfold.
- When students are writing responses to text reading, she looks for indications that they are using text structure knowledge as a framework for developing their writing.
- When students are taking notes, outlining, or mapping text ideas, she looks for patterns that show they are using text structure cues to organize the concepts in the text.

Terri gives her students articles that have been cut up at paragraph boundaries and scrambled. She tells them that they will be reading a text that is mixed up. Working in pairs, students are asked to put the article back together in the author's original fashion. While doing so, they are asked to "think out loud" and explain their decisions during the text reconstruction process to their partners. Terri sits in with each pair of students to monitor their progress and provide assistance through modeling and questioning.

An example of one of the passages Terri uses in her text-structure assessment activity appears in Figure 4–12. It is presented in scrambled form, as Terri would present it to her students. As you can see, the paragraphs are numbered to make it easier for students to reference them in the reconstruction process. Their correct sequence is provided at the end of the passage.

With this and other similar activities, Terri can discover the extent to which her students can perceive and use text structure to organize their thinking and improve their understanding. For instance, with the passage shown in Figure 4–12, Terri looks for evidence that her students grasp the problem–solution pattern employed by the author. Her evidence comes from students' comments and statements such as these:

Number 5 has to go near the end because it sounds like a summary of the problems with deforestation in developing countries.

I'm going to put paragraph 6 after all this stuff that says there's more planting of trees in developing countries than people thought. . . . Still, the problem is really bad there.

I counted up about five different paragraphs that talk about the history of the problem, and the rest talk about the problem today . . . so I'm going to put the history paragraphs first.

Figure 4–12 Scrambled passage for assessing students' text-reconstruction process

---

The Relentless March of Deforestation

(1) Efforts to slow deforestation certainly deserve redoubled support. But even if forest clearing miraculously ceased today, millions of acres of trees would still have to be planted to meet future fuelwood needs, stabilize soil and water resources, and satisfy rising demands for paper, lumber, and other industrial wood products. Expanding forest cover for all these reasons will reduce pressures on remaining virgin forests. At the same time it will slow the build-up of atmospheric carbon dioxide.

(2) For centuries, this reduction in the Earth's biological stock hindered human progress little, if at all. Indeed, the clearing of trees to expand food production and the harvesting of forest products were vital aspects of economic and social development. But the relentless loss of tree cover has recently begun to affect the economic and environmental health of numerous nations, mostly in the developing world. Large-scale reforestation, combined with concerted efforts to protect remaining forests, now appears essential to improving the human prospect.

(3) Before the dawn of agriculture, some 10,000 years ago, the Earth boasted a rich mantle of forest and open woodland covering some 15,300 million acres. Over the centuries, a combination of land clearing for crop production, commercial timber harvesting, cattle ranching, and fuelwood gathering has shrunk the Earth's forests to some 10,300 million acres—a third less than existed in pre-agriculture times.

(4) Despite the growing recognition of the importance of forests to the economic and ecological health of nations, surprisingly little is known with certainty about the state of forest resources today. Many countries have not fully inventoried their forests, and the data that do exist vary widely in quality. Nevertheless, recent data for individual countries suggest that forest cover trends in some regions are very bleak. Satellite imagery of five States in Brazil, for example, shows that deforestation in parts of the Amazon has proceeded much faster than estimates for the entire region suggest.

(Note: The correct sequence is 3, 2, 8, 1, 7, 4, 6, 5.) Source: Adapted from S. Postel & L. Heise, "The Fragile Forest," *The Courier,* January 1988–1989, pp. 25–30.

Combining text reconstruction activities with observations of students' oral and written responses to text reading, Terri can assess her students and build into her assessments instructional strategies that help familiarize them with expository text structures. Furthermore, she has found what researchers before her have found (Meyer & Rice, 1984; Pearson & Camperell, 1985; Richgels, McGee, Lomax, & Sheard, 1987)—that familiarity with expository text structure enhances comprehension and that knowledge of text structure can be directly taught.

(5) In the developing countries, the prospect that forest cover will stabilize any time soon is doubtful. The forces behind deforestation remain strong, and planting efforts are woefully inadequate to reverse the loss of tree cover.

(6) The loss of forest cover in developing countries in tropical regions remains rampant. Conversion of forest to cropland is by far the leading direct cause. Population growth, inequitable land distribution, and the expansion of agricultural exports have greatly reduced the area of cropland available for subsistence farming, forcing many peasants to clear virgin forest to grow food. These peasant farmers often use continuous cropping that is ill suited to fragile forest soils. Eventually, the soils become so depleted that new forests must be cleared for peasants to survive.

(7) Successfully reforesting large areas of degraded lands, however, will require much more than financial commitments from governments and international lending agencies. It will take a shift in emphasis from government foresters and commercial plantations to the much more complex tasks of starting nurseries in thousands of villages and encouraging the planting of multipurpose trees along roads, on farms, and around houses. Only by gaining the support and human energy of rural people themselves is there any hope of success.

(8) Most tree-planting efforts over the last several decades have aimed at increasing supplies of marketable timber, pulp, and fuelwood for cities—forest products that yield obvious economic benefit. By contrast, reforestation has been vastly underattended. Yet trees quite literally form the roots of many natural systems. With the steady march of deforestation, the ecology of many areas is disintegrating—causing severe soil loss, aggravating droughts and floods, disrupting water supplies, and reducing land productivity.

Summary

Assessment of literacy and content learning is a process of becoming informed about teaching and learning in order to improve instruction for the teacher and to increase self-knowledge for students. Merely administering and scoring a reading test does not ensure that classroom teachers will obtain useful information about their students' literacy skills as they relate to the learning of the course content.

Because formal, standardized tests have limited utility for most secondary school teachers, we emphasized the importance of authentic assessments that are designed to reveal important content-specific literacy and content-learning processes. A portfolio approach was presented as an exciting form of classroom authentic assessment for documenting student growth and achievement in all areas of secondary school learning. We also urged that teachers continue to use the most obvious data collection opportunity—observation—for determining students' acquisition and application of literacy/learning behaviors. We pointed out how literacy assessment in content areas can be made more meaningful when it is tied to the teacher's goals of instruction and the underlying processes needed to understand the material.

Finally, we have demonstrated that when process assessment of literacy is integrated within the content classroom, the result is that assessment and teaching become nearly indistinguishable. Therefore, throughout this book we discuss strategies in relation to how they can be used to assess and teach particular literacy/learning processes. For example, in the next chapter, our discussion of effective strategies for preparing students for content-area assignments includes how assessment of prior knowledge and building prior knowledge can be complementary. In Chapter 6, we describe vocabulary strategies that have built-in assessments not only for the teacher but also in the form of self-assessment for the student. This holds true for Chapter 7, in which we demonstrate how students' writing can be used in assessment and development of comprehension. Many of the strategies for teaching with trade literature, developed in Chapter 8, can be used to reveal what students are learning. And in Chapter 9, strategies for developing text study processes are interwoven with teacher assessment and self-assessments of these strategies. Assessment and teaching of important comprehension and literacy processes is at the heart of our chapter dealing with special needs students. Finally, in the last chapter, we discuss the role of assessment as a tool of reflection in improving teaching effectiveness.

References

Afflerbach, P., & Johnston, P. (1984). On the use of verbal reports in reading research. *Journal of Reading Behavior, 16*, 307–322.

Afflerbach, P., & Johnston, P. (1986). What do expert readers do when the main idea is not explicit? In J. Bauman (Ed.), *Teaching main idea comprehension*. Newark, DE: International Reading Association.

Aronson, E., & Farr, R. (1988). Issues in assessment. *Journal of Reading, 32*, 174–177.

Arter, J. (1990). *Using portfolios in instruction and assessment*. Portland, OR: Northwest Regional Educational Laboratory.

Bean, T. W. (1988). Organizing and retaining information by thinking like an author. In S. Glazer, L. Searfoss, & L. Gentile (Eds.), *Reexamining*

reading diagnosis: New trends and procedures. Newark, DE: International Reading Association.

Bissex, G. (1980). *GYNS AT WORK: A child learns to write and read*. Cambridge, MA: Harvard University Press.

Brown, R. (1987). Who is accountable for thoughtfulness? *Phi Delta Kappan, 69*, 49–52.

Brown, R. (1989). Testing and thoughtfulness. *Educational Leadership, 46*, 31–33.

Brozo, W. G., & Brozo, C. L. (in press). Literacy assessment in standardized and zero-failure contexts. *Reading and Writing Quarterly*.

Brozo, W. G., & Curtis, C. L. (1987). Coping strategies of four successful learning disabled college students: A case study approach. In J.

Readence & R. S. Baldwin (Eds.), *Research in literacy: Merging perspectives. Thirty-sixth yearbook of The National Reading Conference.* Rochester, NY: National Reading Conference.

Calfee, R., & Hiebert, E. (1991). Classroom assessment of reading. In R. Barr, M. Kamil, P. Mosenthal, & P. D. Pearson (Eds.), *Handbook of reading research* (Vol. 2). New York: Longman.

Camp, R., & Levine, D. (1991). Portfolios evolving: Background and variations in sixth- through twelfth-grade classrooms. In P. Belanoof & M. Dixon (Eds.), *Portfolios: Process and product.* Portsmouth, NH: Boynton/Cook.

Carey, R. F., Harste, J. C., & Smith, S. L. (1981). Contextual constraints and discourse processes: A replication study. *Reading Research Quarterly, 16,* 201–212.

Clay, M. (1975). *What did I write?* Aukland, New Zealand: Heinemann.

Collins, A., Brown., J., & Newman, S. (1989). Cognitive apprenticeship: Teaching the craft of reading, writing, and mathematics. In L. Resnick (Ed.), *Knowing, learning and instruction: Essays in honor of Robert Glaser.* Hillsdale, NJ: Lawrence Erlbaum.

DeFina, A. (1992). *Portfolio assessment: Getting started.* New York: Scholastic.

Dishner, E. K., & Readence, J. E. (1977). Getting started: Using the textbook diagnostically. *Reading World, 17,* 36–43.

Edelsky, C., & Harman, S. (1988). One more critique of reading tests—with two differences. *English Education, 20,* 157–171.

Elbow, P. (1991). Foreword. In P. Belanoff & M. Dixon (Eds.), *Portfolios: Process and product.* Portsmouth, NH: Heinemann.

Elbow, P., & Belanoff, P. (1986). Portfolios as a substitute for proficiency examinations. *College Composition and Communication, 37,* 336–339.

Garner, R., Alexander, P., Gillinghan, M., Kulikowich, J., & Brown, R. (1991). Interest and learning from text. *American Educational Research Journal, 28,* 643–659.

Gilles, C., Bixby, M., Crowley, P., Crenshaw, S., Henrich, M., Reynolds, F., & Pyle, D. (1988). *Whole language strategies for secondary students.* New York: Richard C. Owen.

Glazer, S. M., Searfoss, L. W., & Gentile, L. M. (1988). *Reexamining reading diagnosis: New trends and procedures.* Newark, DE: International Reading Association.

Goodman, J. (1992). *Elementary schooling for critical democracy.* Albany, NY: SUNY Press.

Graves, D., & Hansen, J. (1983). The author's chair. *Language Arts, 60,* 176–183.

Hidi, S., & Baird, W. (1988). Strategies for increasing text-based interest and students' recall of expository texts. *Reading Research Quarterly, 23,* 465–483.

Johnston, P. (1989). Constructive evaluation and the improvement of teaching and learning. *Teachers College Record, 90,* 509–528.

Johnston, P. (1992). *Constructive evaluation of literate activity.* New York: Longman.

Johnston, P. (1990). Steps toward a more naturalistic approach to the assessment of the reading process. In S. Legg & J. Algina (Eds.), *Cognitive assessment of language and mathematics outcomes.* Norwood, NJ: Ablex.

Judy, S., & Judy, S. (1981). *An introduction to the teaching of writing.* New York: Wiley.

Kalmbach, J. R. (1986). Evaluating informal method for the assessment of retellings. *Journal of Reading, 30,* 119–129.

Krest, M. (1990). Adapting the portfolio to meet student needs. *English Journal, 79,* 29–34.

Lamme, L., & Haysmith, C. (1991). One school's adventure into portfolio assessment. *Language Arts, 68,* 629–640.

Linn, R. (1985). Standards and expectations: The role of testing (summary). *Proceedings of the National Forum on Educational Reform* (pp. 88–95). New York: The College Board.

Liston, D., & Zeichner, K. (1991). *Teacher education and the social conditions of schooling.* New York: Routledge.

Lucas, C. (1988). Toward ecological evaluation. *Quarterly of the National Writing Project & Center for the Study of Writing, 10,* 1.

Meyer, B. J. F., & Rice, E. (1984). The structure of text. In P. D. Pearson (Ed.), *Handbook of reading research.* New York: Longman.

Moje, W., Brozo, W. G., & Haas, J. (in press). Portfolios in a high school classroom: Challenges to change. *Reading Research and Instruction.*

Moore, D. W. (1983). A case for naturalistic assessment of reading comprehension. *Language Arts, 60,* 957–969.

Murphy, S., & Smith, M. (1991). *Writing portfolios: A bridge from teaching to assessment.* Markham, Ontario: Pippin Publishing.

Newman, J. (1985). *Whole language: Theory and use.* Portsmouth, NH: Heinemann.

Pearson, P. D., & Camperell, K. (1985). Comprehension of text structure. In H. Singer & R. B. Rudell (Eds.), *Theoretical models and processes of reading* (3rd ed.). Newark, DE: International Reading Association.

Pearson, P. D., & Valencia, S. (1986). Assessment, accountability, and professional prerogative. In J. Readence & R. S. Baldwin (Eds.), *Research in literacy: Merging perspectives. Thirty-six Yearbook of the National Reading Conference.* Rochester, NY: The National Reading Conference.

Pinnell, G. S. (1989). Reading recovery: Helping at-risk children learn to read. *Elementary School Journal, 90,* 161–183.

Readence, J. E., & Martin, M. A. (1988). Comprehension assessment: Alternatives to standardized tests. In S. Glazer, L. Searfoss, & L. Gentile (Eds.), *Reexamining reading diagnosis: New trends and procedures.* Newark, DE: International Reading Association.

Readence, J. E., & Moore, D. W. (1983). Why questions? A historical perspective on standardized reading comprehension tests. *Journal of Reading, 26,* 306–313.

Reading yardsticks. (1981). Level 14—Grade 8. Chicago: Riverside. Renninger, K. (1989, March). *Interests and noninterests as contexts in reading comprehension and mathematical word problem solving.* Paper presented at the annual meeting of the American Educational Research Association, San Francisco.

Richgels, D. J., McGee, L. M., Lomax, R. G., & Sheard, C. (1987). Awareness of four text structures: Effects on recall of expository text. *Reading Research Quarterly, 22,* 177–196.

Rief, L. (1992). *Seeking diversity: Language arts with adolescents.* Portsmouth, NH: Heinemann.

Sequential Tests of Educational Progress, (1957). Princeton, NJ: Educational Testing Service; CTB/McGraw-Hill.

Shepherd, D. L. (1982). *Comprehensive high school reading methods.* Columbus, OH: Charles E. Merrill.

Smith, S. P., & Jackson, J. H. (1985). Assessing reading/learning skills with written retellings. *Journal of Reading, 28,* 622–630.

Sulzby, E. (1985). Kindergartners as writers and readers. In M. Farr (Ed.), *Advances in writing research: Vol. 1. Children's early writing development.* Norwood, NJ: Ablex.

Taylor, D. (1988). Ethnographic educational evaluation for children, families, and school. *Theory Into Practice, 27,* 67–76.

Taylor, D. (1989). Toward a unified theory of literacy learning and instructional practices: A critical response to Chall and Carbo. *Phi Delta Kappan, 71,* 184–193.

Taylor, D. (1990). Teaching without testing. *English Education, 22,* 4–74.

Thorndike, E. L. (1917). Reading as reasoning: A study of mistakes in paragraph reading. *Journal of Educational Psychology, 8,* 323–332.

Tierney, R., Carter, M., & Desai, L. (1991). *Portfolio assessment in the reading-writing classroom.* Norwood, MA: Christopher Gordon.

Valencia, S. (1990). National survey of the use of reading test data for educational decision-making. In P. Afflerbach (Ed.), *Issues in statewide reading assessment.* Washington, DC: American Institutes for Research.

Valencia, S. W., McGinley, W., & Pearson, P. D. (1990). Assessing reading and writing. In G. Duffy (Ed.), *Reading in the middle school.* Newark, DE: International Reading Association.

Valencia, S., & Pearson, P. D. (1987). Reading assessment: Time for a change. *The Reading Teacher, 40,* 726–732.

Vavrus, L. (1990, August). Put portfolios to the test. *Instructor,* 48–53.

Venezky, R. L. (1974). *Testing in reading: Assessment and instructional decision making.* Urbana, IL: NCTE.

Wells, G. (1985). *The meaning makers: Children learning language and using language to learn.* Portsmouth, NH: Heinemann.

Winograd, P. (1984). Strategic difficulties in summarizing texts. *Reading Research Quarterly, 19,* 404–425.

5

Initiating Students to New Learning

*It is clear that very little improvement may be expected from formal drill . . .
unless at the same time provision is made for the enrichment of experience, the
development of language abilities, and the improvement of thinking.*

—Ernest Horn (1937)

When Ernest Horn made these comments in 1937, workbooks and skills kits
were beginning to flood the reading materials market. These materials were
designed to drill students on reading skills and were based on the assumption
that drill alone would develop competent readers. Horn's insights into the complex interactions between readers' experiences, language abilities, and cognitive
strategies on the one hand and the extent to which the context supports meaningful learning during literacy events on the other have only recently been confirmed through scholarly research (c.f., Harste, 1989). Today, teachers and
researchers agree that to create the best conditions for learning, students need to
be **prepared** to learn.

In Chapters 2 and 3 we discussed several important principles of active learning and demonstrated how many useful strategies can be employed by secondary
classroom teachers to promote literacy growth and increase content learning. In

this chapter, we explain the important role the preparation phase plays in learning in the content classroom. We argue that when students are adequately prepared for and actively engaged in literacy and content learning activities, their enthusiasm for learning increases, and their comprehension of the material actually improves.

Our primary focus in this chapter is on strategies, ideas, and guidelines for preparing students for learning information and concepts in secondary school classrooms through reading and writing. We also describe class discussion and prediction strategies that teachers have used to help students prepare for listening to lectures. We hope that the principles of effective readiness instruction and numerous classroom examples described in this chapter will stimulate your own innovative approaches to setting the stage for and engaging students in new learning.

Case Study

Theresa is an eighth-grade social studies teacher. She has noticed how her students appear to have become increasingly disinterested and passive over the past 10 years. Although she has typically taught units from the textbook, her efforts to enlist students in learning social studies content have been moving further and further from the text—with encouraging results. For instance, early in the school year she employed some new strategies to help students develop a broader sense of community responsibility. To her delight, the class took off with the strategy, exhibiting a level of enthusiasm Theresa hadn't seen for some time.

Theresa is in the process of planning a unit on early Native Americans. Last year was the first year she deviated from the textbook approach to teaching about native peoples by having a local Huron tribesman talk to the class about history and customs. He also shared costumes and artifacts. This year she would like to do more to help students develop a better understanding of what we know about the early Native American cultures and how we learn about these cultures. She wants to devise active, hands-on approaches to engaging her class in the study of this important topic.

To the Reader: As you read and work through this chapter, think about possible strategies and teaching approaches Theresa might use to engage her students in learning about early American cultures. Be prepared to offer your suggestions when we revisit this case study at the conclusion of the chapter.

Guidelines for Effective Readiness Instruction

Generate Interest in the Topic

A self-evident and empirically grounded truth about learning is that students will expend the energy necessary to learn if they are interested in the material to be learned (Hidi & Baird, 1988; Mathison, 1989; Renninger, Hidi, & Krapp, 1992). This is certainly not a recent revelation. Eighty years ago, John Dewey promoted the idea that when students are interested in a topic or activity they will learn "in a whole-hearted way" (1913, p. 65). Unfortunately, although we all pay lip service to this principle, we fail to put it into practice often enough. If you spend any time at all working with textbooks, you will soon notice that the prose is abstract, formal, and lifeless (Tyson-Bernstein, 1988). To expect students to relish textbook reading is, we believe, unrealistic. Therefore, every effort needs to be made to get students interested in the textbook topic (Wade, Schraw, Buxton, & Hayes, 1993). This can be accomplished with language experiences, films, games, role playing, guest speakers, field trips, writing, reading-related texts, and fictional works to name just a few ways. Interest-promoting strategies such as disrupting learner's expectations, challenging learners to resolve a paradox, and introducing novel and conflicting information or situations have also been shown to be effective (Mathison, 1989). The unexpected benefit of your efforts to develop imaginative, unique, interest-engendering activities is that you will become more interested in the content as well. And as you know, the more enthusiastic you can be about learning, the greater chance you have of awakening interest in your students.

Activate and Build Relevant Prior Knowledge

Pearson and Johnson (1978) describe the process of activating and building **relevant prior knowledge** as one of "building bridges between the new and the known." It is a simple yet elegant concept that is neglected far too often in instructional plans.

To demonstrate the importance of being prepared for reading and learning, we have a "reading assignment" for you. Read the following passage, and be prepared to discuss the main points, supporting details, and the relationships between the themes in the passage and other related passages you have read.

> It is highly unsettling for some to come into close contact with them. Far worse to gain control over them and to deliberately inflict pain on them. The revulsion caused by this punishment is so strong that many will not take part in it at all. Thus there exists a group of people who seem to revel in the contact and the punishment as well as the rewards associated with both. Then there is another group of people who shun the whole enterprise: contact, punishment, and rewards alike.

Members of the first group share modes of talk, dress, and deportment. Members of the second group, however, are as varied as all humanity.

Then there is a group of others, not previously mentioned, for the sake of whose attention all this activity is undertaken. They too harm the victims, though they do it without intention of cruelty. They simply follow their own necessities. And though they may inflict the cruelest punishment of all, sometimes—but not always—they themselves suffer as a result. (Gillet & Temple, 1986, p. 4)

Do you have any idea what this passage is about? Every time we ask our students to read this passage, they first try desperately to impose a sensible interpretation on the words, offer possibilities that leave them uncomfortable, and finally give up, resorting to protests that sound all too familiar to any classroom teacher: "This is too hard." Most complain that this reading exercise is unfair because the passage has too many unclear referents, which makes it impossible to understand with any certainty. The typical guesses we get include parents and children, concentration camps, corporal punishment, teachers and students.

With this exercise, we have been able to simulate for you how many students must feel when given reading assignments without any direction, warm-up, or any of the relevant background knowledge necessary for interpreting the statements in the passage. We know that secondary students often finish textbook readings and come away as bewildered as you probably were about the preceding passage.

By the way, the title of the passage is "Fishing Worms." Does that help? Go back and reread it now, and notice as you read how all the ideas seem to fit together, how meaning jumps automatically into consciousness. The title acts as an organizer, a unifying theme, and brings to mind a schema for fishing and worms, which, as discussed in Chapter 2, provides a slot in memory for filing the information presented in this text. Now imagine a ninth grader trying to grapple with the ideas and facts in the following text segment. Without any preparation for this text, the student might find it as unintelligible as our passage above, sans title, was for you.

A systematic examination of all known rock types shows that two principal kinds predominate. The first are *igneous rocks,* formed by the cooling and crystallization of liquids from deep in the crust or upper part of the mantle, called *magmas.* The second are *sedimentary rocks,* formed by compaction and cementation of sediment derived from the continuous erosion of the continents by water, atmosphere, ice, and wind. Most of the sediments are deposited in the sea along the margins of continents. As the marginal piles of sediment grow larger and are buried deeper, increasing pressure and rising temperature produce physical and chemical changes in them. The resulting *metamorphic rocks,* however, generally show whether they were originally sedimentary or igneous rocks. When a sedimentary pile becomes thick enough, material near the bottom may melt to form *magma.* The newly formed magma, being less dense than the rock from which it was derived, will tend to rise up, intruding its parents, and as it cools and crystallizes it will form a new igneous rock.*

What can a teacher do to build schema and thereby prepare students for reading and learning about rocks within a unit on geology? The possibilities are many and are limited only by the teacher's imagination. The teacher could provide students direct experience with rock types by bringing actual examples to class to hold and study. An expert on local geology might give a class demonstration. A field trip to observe natural rock formations could be planned. Students could be asked to find and bring to class examples of rock types. The teacher might prepare a graphic representation of the key vocabulary in the passage depicting the relationships among the ideas. Other high-interest, topically related materials such as Lauber's *Volcano* (1986), a brief but superbly written account of the Mt. St. Helen eruption and its aftermath, could be read before tackling the text. And these are only a few suggestions.

For some topics, students will already possess a great deal of background knowledge but simply need to be reminded of what they know. For instance, a class of sophomore history students fails to comprehend the full significance of Julius Caesar's move to publish the activities of the Roman senate. The teacher writes on the board "Jay picks his ears." "Myra sniffs glue." Jay and Myra, students in the class, begin protesting vehemently as the others roar. "The point," she says, "is how many of you would like to have your foolish acts made public?" Caesar felt that the senators were behaving without decorum, she goes on to explain, and believed that having their behavior posted for all to read would pressure them into changing their ways. She then apologizes to Myra and Jay for libeling them. The teacher, in this example, using information gained from what we might call, on-the-spot assessment, modified her instruction to include a concrete example to make her point clearer.

With other topics, students will have great gaps in knowledge that will need to be bridged before they can be expected to profit from their reading and learning (McKeown, Beck, Sinatra, & Loxterman, 1992). We often take too much for granted when we assign readings or begin lectures or lab activities. We assume students have all the prerequisite knowledge for easy assimilation of the new ideas and facts they will encounter. For instance, in spite of the popularity of a topic such as baseball, many students do not possess sophisticated baseball schema. Two early studies on the role of prior knowledge in comprehension demonstrated that students who were similar in reading ability performed differently on a comprehension exercise over a passage about baseball, depending on their levels of prior knowledge for that topic (Spilich, Vesonder, Chiesi, & Voss, 1979). Similarly, Hayes and Tierney (1980) found that high school students who had difficulty reading and recalling newspaper reports of cricket matches improved their performance dramatically when they received instruction on the

*Source: Adapted from Stokes/Judson/Picard, INTRODUCTION TO GEOLOGY: Physical and Historical, 2e, © 1978, pp. 73–75. Adapted by permission of Prentice Hall, Inc. Englewood Cliffs, New Jersey.

nature of the game of cricket before reading the newspaper reports. Findings such as these have been replicated in numerous studies over the past decade (Pressley, Johnson, Symons, McGoldrick, & Kurita, 1989).

Help Set Meaningful Purposes for Learning

Over 20 years ago, Illich advocated a curriculum that engendered "self-motivated learning instead of employing teachers to bribe or compel the student to find the time and the will to learn" (1970, p. 104). Students become independent knowledge seekers when they perceive what they are learning to be personally meaningful and relevant to their lives and futures. So on one level, we are suggesting that meaningful purposes for learning can be established only when the learning itself is meaningful.

On a practical level, setting meaningful purposes for learning is essential to remaining focused on an activity. For example, consider this often-repeated scenario. You are assigned a textbook chapter to read as homework. As you are reading, you realize your eyes just seem to be moving over words; you're not sure what to concentrate on or what to gloss over. You decide to try to remember facts, but you're not sure why. You realize that you have not been given any direction for *how* you should read. In other words, you have not been provided a *purpose* for reading, and to figure out what you are expected to recall as a result of your reading becomes a matter of guesswork. Unfortunately, by studying the facts of the chapter, you guessed incorrectly. Your examination about the chapter is an essay-type test with conceptual questions. There is a bright spot in this story, however. At least you attempted to set your own purpose for reading, even though you were not provided one. Many students have not learned to establish a reason for reading before they begin a reading assignment. We have a responsibility for setting clear expectations for students when making reading assignments, and for showing students how to read to meet those expectations. Furthermore, we all need to provide instruction in helping students learn how to set their own purposes for reading.

This guideline applies equally to lectures, labs, and other learning experiences in addition to reading. Students should be made aware of what they are about to learn and, more importantly, why the content is being discussed and studied. To tell students "You must learn this because I say so," is not a meaningful purpose for learning. Instead, try to make students aware of real-world purposes for learning. That is, by linking the learning of course content to students' own needs, issues, concerns, and interests inside and outside of school, we can show them the function and meaningfulness of learning: for instance, demonstrating for the athletes in a math class how math can be used to compile sports statistics.

Preteach Critical Concepts and Vocabulary

With some content, particularly content for which students have limited schema, deciding how much to preteach can seem overwhelming. Obviously, all new concepts and all unfamiliar terms cannot be taught. Some researchers (Nagy, Anderson, & Herman, 1987) have speculated that if teachers concentrated on teaching students unfamiliar words, that is all they would have time to do, every day! We recommend here, as we recommend throughout this book, that when deciding what to preteach, or for that matter when deciding on any content to teach, emphasize the *most important* ideas and information to be learned. Not all information is vital; not all of it needs to be taught directly, nor should it be. Normally, students are under the impression that every idea and each bit of information in a chapter is of equal importance. The ways in which you prepare students for their learning can help dispel this misconception.

Use Writing to Prepare Students for Reading and Learning

Writing is especially well suited for preparing students for reading and learning (Hamann, Schultz, Smith, & White, 1991). Writing before learning from text or a lecture allows students to explore what they already know about a topic, thereby building a bridge from their prior knowledge and experiences to the new information. It also is an effective medium for self-reflection. Students can decide where they possess sufficient knowledge and where gaps in knowledge exist. Based on this information, they can seek people and resources to expand their knowledge base. (See Chapter 7 for an in-depth discussion of effective writing to learn strategies.)

Assess Prior Knowledge

As stated earlier, teachers often take for granted that students possess appropriate prior knowledge for the topics at hand. One way to determine whether students have the relevant foundational information in memory is to assess background knowledge (Frager, 1993). We recommend that you employ procedures such as the Pre-Reading Plan (PReP), discussed in Chapter 3, as well as adaptations of the authentic assessment strategies we have outlined in Chapter 4. Designing short inventories that ask students to report what they know about a topic and its important concepts is a simple yet effective strategy for deciding how much background building will be necessary. A great deal of useful information for you and your students can be uncovered in the process of assessing prior knowledge. For instance, many students believe they accurately understand certain concepts when in fact their knowledge is based on faulty assumptions (Alvermann, Smith, & Readence, 1985). Students themselves can discover that they know more or less than they thought they knew.

Activate Schema With Cooperative Learning Groups

Students often need to be reminded of what they know about a topic because they will not automatically bring relevant information to bear (Pearson & Spiro, 1982). A highly effective strategy for activating available schema is through the use of

cooperative learning groups. As we explained in Chapter 3, there are many benefits to using cooperative groups as an integral part of classroom instruction. In
small groups with their peers, students can share what they know about a topic
without feeling the stress and self-restraint that often accompany responding to
the teacher before the entire class. Furthermore, as we have already pointed out,
students will often provide rich and elaborate responses to their peers. Perhaps
the most important aspect of using cooperative learning in the preparation phase
of reading and learning is that students can contribute to one another's schema
development (Radebaugh & Kazemek, 1989; Wood, 1987).

Channeling Knowledge and Interest

Reading Young Adult Literature to Build Prior Knowledge and Generate Interest

Teachers often ask how they can get their students interested in units about
which they themselves are not especially excited. Take a unit on Australia, for
example. In such a case, many teachers would be inclined to simply assign the
textbook reading and then lecture, although they know that students' interest will
be minimal. As an alternative, we suggest that they consider reading aloud or asking students to read one of the many outstanding trade books from Australia such
as Maire Clark's *The Min Min* (1969), Colin Thiele's *The Fire in the Stone*
(1974), and Ivan Southall's *Hills End* (1963), *Ash Road* (1966), and *About Tomorrow* (1977). In addition to galvanizing the students with their narrative, these stories indirectly provide readers with an accurate, living context in which to place
the facts and details in the text.

Students can also be introduced to topics with nonfiction books. Many teens,
especially boys, prefer nonfiction to fiction (Reed, 1988). Unfortunately, their
experiences with nonfiction in school are limited usually to textbooks (Clary,
1991), which may contribute to their lack of interest in the first place. Many
junior and senior high students are never exposed to nonfiction books that have
been written specifically for them. The numbers of nonfiction titles for adolescents grows annually, making it easier for classroom teachers to identify appropriate books to incorporate into their content lessons.

Christine Arnothy's *I Am Fifteen—and I Don't Want to Die* (1950) could be
offered as a prelude to the study of the Nazis and the Jews during World War II.
An autobiography, this gripping account of a young woman who survived the
Hungarian Holocaust is filled with facts and details that help students better
understand that tragic period in world history. Relevant prior knowledge for
boreal ecosystems could be acquired by reading *Dance of the Wolves* (Peters,
1985), the story of a young researcher's study of wolves in Northern Michigan.
For students about to begin a creative writing unit, *Chapters: My Growth as a
Writer* (Duncan, 1982) is a splendid prelude. This autobiography of a popular
young adult writer appeals to adolescents who aspire to a career in writing. With

nonfiction books such as these, students develop schema while reading an interesting and palatable alternative to the textbook. (See Chapter 8 for a comprehensive discussion of strategies for using trade books in the classroom.)

Activating Schema With Discussion

With simple and effective whole-class discussions as students are about to begin the exploration of a new topic, teachers can assess how much students already know about the topic to be studied and vary the degree or emphasis of preteaching relative to what they discover. In addition, teachers who use discussion create a learning environment that fosters a free exchange of different viewpoints, which helps students actively shape their own knowledge and enrich and refine their understandings of a topic (Alvermann, Dillon, & O'Brien, 1988; Alvermann & Hayes, 1989).

Teachers who desire to exploit the learning potential of class discussion often tend to undermine it by doing most of the talking and asking most of the questions (Alvermann, O'Brien, & Dillon, 1990). These practices will inhibit rather than foster the enrichment of understanding through the exchange of viewpoints. Dillon's (1984) seven alternatives to questioning and teacher-dominated discussions provide teachers strategies for gaining greater student involvement in class discussion:

- Make a declarative or factual statement.
- Make a reflective statement.
- Describe the student's state of mind.
- Invite the student to elaborate on a statement.
- Encourage the student to ask a question.
- Encourage students to ask questions of one another.
- Maintain a deliberate silence.

The following example demonstrates how a teacher can employ effective student-centered discussion strategies in preparation for reading and learning.

An economics class preparing to read and learn about the effects of a recession on the economy watched as the teacher wrote the word *recession* in large letters on the board. Without saying anything, he waited for students to react, question, and elaborate. In no time, students began to make associations with the word. As they responded, the teacher jotted down responses on the board. This initial association with the concept provided students the opportunity to find associations with their prior knowledge. As students responded, the teacher wrote them on the board while purposely avoiding reacting to every response. Responses such as "inflation" and "higher gas prices" were typical, but everyone was surprised to hear the word "grounded" shouted out by a student in the corner. Instead of asking a question himself, the teacher asked if anyone had a question for the student who said "grounded." Students were eager to find out what "grounded" had to do with recession and pressed the student for an explanation. The young woman explained that she had once made significant contributions to her parents' whopping phone bill during a financially tight period that she said was caused by the recession. Her parents punished her by taking away her phone privileges and restricting her after-school activity for a couple of weeks. By using discussion as a readiness to learn activity, the teacher helped students develop an awareness of their network of associations and allowed them to listen to one another, weigh, reject, revise, and integrate ideas in their own minds. The young woman's contribution turned out to be very profitable because the textbook chapter they were assigned to read devoted a major section to the everyday, personal effects of a recession.

After the discussion, the teacher restated students' initial associations with the concept. In this way, students were able to reflect on their own thinking and offer any new ideas about *recession.* This allowed students to verbalize associations that had been elaborated or changed through the discussion and to probe their memories to expand on their prior knowledge. Interestingly, several other personal connections with the topic were discovered. A fellow talked about having to limit his "cruising" because he couldn't afford to waste gas. Another mentioned that his brother had to put off buying a house because interest rates were so high. When the class ended, the students had a better idea about how much they knew about the topic, and the teacher, who encouraged student-centered discussion, had a good picture of his students' existing knowledge. With this information, adjustment in the preparatory phase of instruction can be made.

Purpose-Setting Strategies

Many highly effective classroom strategies have been designed to help secondary students set purposes for their reading and develop an anticipatory set for their reading and learning. In this section we demonstrate how three particularly useful strategies—prediction, KWL, and anticipation guides—can be used to help students set meaningful purposes for and encourage higher level thinking about class topics. Furthermore, these strategies induce students to attend to text more closely, interact with text in more meaningful ways, and combine their world knowledge with text information, resulting in new understandings.

Prediction.   One excellent way of helping students set their own purposes for reading is with prediction activities (Hennings, 1991). Anderson (1984) has proposed that this technique is consistent with a schema-theoretic perspective of optimal reading because it helps students meaningfully integrate what they already know with what is presented on the printed page. Using a **prediction** technique, students either simply generate some form of prediction in advance of reading, or they read titles, headings, subheadings, or a short segment of text and, based on this limited information, predict what they expect to read in the passage. In this way, they become aware of their prior knowledge and begin to organize what they already know about the subject at hand. By making predictions, they anticipate what they will find in the text, leading them to read for the purpose of finding out if their predictions are corroborated. Countless methods can be used to help students anticipate the content of their reading.

A wonderful example of the effectiveness of using prediction as purpose setting was provided to us by a senior high journalism teacher. He was instructing students in editorial writing by sharing examples of editorials and analyzing them. He handed out a sheet of paper with the title, "A No-Lose Proposition," by Stanley J. Lieberman, and the first paragraph, which read:

> America is the most litigious society in the world. We are suing each other at an alarming and increasing rate, and we have more lawyers per capita than any other nation. Since 1950 the number of lawyers in America has increased 250 percent. We have well over half a million lawyers—one for every 450 people. In New York state the ratio is one lawyer per 18. By contrast, the ratio in West Germany is one lawyer per 2,000.

After reading, the students worked in small groups and were asked to discuss the possible directions the editorial might take, given the title and first paragraph. Each group was to make two predictions. The teacher moved around the room, listening in on each group, assisting when asked. Next, each group's predictions were presented to the whole class, while the teacher wrote them on the board. A lengthy and immensely beneficial discussion then ensued, which included a class-derived definition of *litigious* and an impassioned defense of lawyers by a student whose father and mother were attorneys. An impressive amount of background and related knowledge poured out, as did the exchange and exploration of biases, opinions, and beliefs. The teacher played a facilitative role during the discussion. He prodded when necessary, refocused the conversation when it seemed to stray too far from the task of determining what the author was likely to say in the passage, and clarified points and details. When the debate over which predictions were likely to be verified by the text wound down, the students were eager to finish reading the editorial. Three class-agreed-on predictions remained on the board, and the students were reminded to read and discover to what extent, if any, the text supported them. After reading, the class discussed the accuracy of their predictions. No one had foreseen that the author would make a pitch for mediation as a way out of a clogged court system, although one prediction anticipated some kind of workable solution to this problem based on the editorial's title.

Reflect for a moment about how the preceding scene differs from the way a typical reading assignment is given students—with little or no preparation or direction. By the time these students were ready to read the editorial, they had activated and elaborated their schema for "lawyer" and related legal issues, they had developed an interest in the topic through small-group and whole-class discussions that challenged beliefs and biases and piqued curiosities, and they had developed their own purposes for reading. As a result, attention to the text and comprehension cannot help but improve.

Schema theorists say that reading comprehension involves constant hypothesis testing. Predictions are like hypotheses that can be confirmed, refined, extended, or rejected using evidence from the text. In this process, original predictions give way to new predictions as new information from the text is encountered, thus setting further purposes for reading.

Many variations on the prediction theme can help students develop an anticipatory set for the text information. In a 12th-grade sociology class preparing to read about the benefits and limitations of day-care centers, the teacher posed this problem:

> If you were a parent who needed to work to keep the family going, yet you desperately wanted to spend more time with your children, what would you do?

In cooperative learning groups, the students talked among themselves, proposing solutions to the problem. After the entire class discussed possible solutions, their strengths, and limitations, the teacher invited them to read the essay and find out how a working parent handled this dilemma. The students now had a purpose for reading.

A ninth-grade science class preparing to read a chapter on genetic engineering was given this statement:

> Making exact replicas of dogs, cats, and even human beings through the process of cloning may be possible within this century.

The students were then asked to generate five questions based on this statement that they were likely to have answered as a result of reading the chapter. After reading, they told which, if any, of their questions were answered. These students also had a purpose for reading.

In a seventh-grade health class, students working in cooperative groups were asked to generate as many words as they could within 3 minutes related to the concept "necessities to sustain life." At the end of 3 minutes, students were asked to arrange their words into subcategories and to be prepared to explain the logic behind them. One group clustered their words around "necessities for the body" (oxygen, food, water); "necessities for the heart" (relationships, religion); and "necessities for the mind" (books, music, art). Another group categorized their words with *work* and *fun*. After this exploration of what they already knew about the topic, students were asked to use their words and categories to predict what the reading assignment would be about. Once again, we see how this prediction strategy helped students develop purposes for reading.

Remember, prediction strategies can work equally as well before lectures and experiential, hands-on activities such as labs and field trips.

From these examples, you can see that the list of ways of helping students set purposes for reading is limited only by a teacher's imagination. Other variations on the prediction strategy include KWL, and anticipation guides.

KWL.   **KWL** focuses on the student as a strategic learner and is based on three principal components: (a) recalling what is **known**, (b) determining what students **want** to learn, and (c) identifying what is **learned** (Carr & Ogle, 1987; Ogle, 1986). We strongly endorse this strategy because it can be carried out before, during, and after reading. Before reading, the student activates background knowledge and sets a purpose for reading; during reading, the student thinks critically about information and monitors learning; and after reading, the student integrates and consolidates information read. Here, we focus on the before-reading benefits of the strategy.

To give you a better idea of the kind of thinking involved in the KWL strategy, let us assume you were asked by the professor using the book to employ the strategy for Chapter 5, the chapter you are reading now. First, you would be directed to read the title, "Initiating Students to New Learning," and in small cooperative groups or as a whole class, you would brainstorm and discuss ideas and information you already hold in prior knowledge about the topic. Through discussion, a good deal of known information will be generated, and unresolved points and unanswered questions also will likely emerge. These will be saved and referred to later as information about which you desire further information. So after brainstorming and discussing, you would have a collection of ideas and facts about the chapter topic listed on a chart in the *K* (what is *known*) column.

In the next phase before reading, you would be asked to generate questions based on unresolved information you would like answered by the text. Questions come from the brainstorming and discussion, as well as anticipated information you think will be encountered in the text. These questions comprise the entries in the second column on the chart: *W* (what you *want* to learn). By developing questions in this way, you will tend to define for yourself your purpose for reading. The result is that your reading and self-monitoring during reading will be more focused. As you read, you will pause periodically to monitor your comprehension by checking the questions from the *W* column that can be answered by what you have read. As new information is encountered, additional questions can be added to the list. Thus, purposes are refined and extended throughout reading.

Figure 5–1 depicts what you might have generated for the first two columns of the KWL chart. As you read, you would note in the *L* column new information and information that helps answer the questions you posed in the *W* column. After reading, you would be asked to discuss what you have learned from your reading. You would review the questions asked before and during reading to determine if and how they were resolved. For example, in the chart in Figure 5–1, the first three questions in the *W* column can be answered fairly thoroughly with the information in this chapter. For the last question, which would remain unresolved because this chapter does not specifically discuss the DRTA (Directed-Reading-Thinking-Activity) strategy, you would be encouraged to conduct some personal research to gather further information about this aspect of the topic. Perhaps the professor would direct you to additional secondary reading methods textbooks or to journal articles that deal with the topic of using DRTA as a prereading strategy.

Figure 5–1   KWL chart for Chapter 5

K (Known)	W (Want to Know)	L (Learned)
Reading readiness is important for beginning readers.	What can the classroom teacher do to prepare students for reading assignments?	
Schema theory says prior knowledge for a topic makes it easier to read about that topic.	Why is readiness important for secondary school reading?	
One strategy is to read the introduction and conclusion before reading the chapter.	What are all the things that should be done during readiness?	
	Is Directed-Reading-Thinking-Activity a good readiness strategy?	

The KWL strategy can be applied in a variety of content areas with a range of text material. Figure 5–2, for example, is a KWL chart created by an eighth grader reading about the formation of mountains. In this example, you will note that the student did not appear to have a great deal of prior knowledge for the topic. As a result of a liberal exchange of ideas in small groups and with the whole class, she asked some excellent questions (in the W column) that were resolved by the reading. In cases in which students' questions cannot be answered by the text, many teachers will ask students to pursue answers to these unresolved questions through research and present their findings to the class.

Students will develop the ability to use the KWL strategy on their own through instruction that gradually shifts responsibility for initiating the strategy from you to your students (Carr & Ogle, 1987). After you introduce the strategy with a textbook example and model KWL thinking by talking through how you would develop a chart, you should ask students to implement it on their own. Cooperative groups are ideal for helping learn and extend expertise with the strategy. Your role should gradually become one of providing feedback, informally observing, discussing, and reinforcing independence and transfer. As with most content-area reading/writing/learning strategies, you can improve the likelihood that students will use this strategy on their own if you demonstrate how using KWL for activating prior knowledge and setting purposes for reading facilitates their class performance and helps meet your expectations for learning.

Anticipation Guides.   Another highly regarded strategy for activating prior knowledge for text topics and helping students set purposes for reading is the **anticipation guide**. Introduced in Chapter 3, this strategy involves giving students a list

Figure 5-2   An eighth grader's KWL chart for the formation of mountains

K	W	L
Volcanoes help form mountains.	Do mountains grow?	Mountains form when heat within the earth pushes bedrock up.
The Rocky mountains are very tall.	How do they erode?	Lava forces its way up and hardens into rock, causing mountains to grow bigger.
	Why are the Rockies taller than the Smokies?	Rain and wind wear them down.
		Mountains are part of a cycle—ocean sediment to solid rock pushed up to form mountains, then worn down into the sea again.
		Mountains in the eastern U.S. are very old.
		Mountains in the West are not as old.

of statements about the topic to be studied and asking students to respond to them before reading. Guides are particularly useful when they provoke disagreement and challenge students' beliefs about a topic. They should serve the function of reinforcing relevant prior knowledge for and modifying misconceptions about the topic (Irwin & Baker, 1989). The functions seem especially important given recent research findings indicating that students' existing prior knowledge and biases will superimpose themselves on text information when the two are at odds (Marshall, 1989). In other words, if misconceptions about a topic are not cleared up before reading, they may still be around after reading.

Anticipation guides should contain statements that are text and reader based. In addition, Duffelmeyer, Baum, and Merkley (1987) recommend the inclusion of certain statements that force students to reconsider existing beliefs. They suggest that two kinds of statements have the potential to do this: (a) those that appear "correct" but are incompatible with the text and (b) those that seem "incorrect" yet are compatible with the text.

The response format for anticipation guides should follow criteria similar to those of study guides. Students should not be asked to write extended answers to questions that resemble discussion or essay questions. Instead, have students respond with simple check marks or brief statements. But make sure the guide includes a feature that tests and confronts students' beliefs.

Figure 5–3   Anticipation guide for diet and nutrition: Part I

Directions: Read each statement. If you believe that a statement is true, place a *check* in the *Agree* column. If you believe the statement is false, place a check in the *Disagree* column. Be ready to explain your choices.

Agree   Disagree

____   ____   1. About 45% of the total food dollar is spent on food away from home.

____   ____   2. More cookbooks are being purchased today than ever before.

____   ____   3. Soft drinks are essentially sugar.

____   ____   4. The average person's diet consists of between 60% and 70% fat and sugar.

____   ____   5. People are eating fewer fruits today than in the 1940s.

____   ____   6. Many so-called primitive cultures have more nutritious diets than many affluent Americans.

____   ____   7. Vitamin C has been used effectively to treat mental diseases.

Look at the anticipation guide designed for a health class shown in Figure 5–3. We would like you to respond to this guide so you will have a better understanding of the points we have just made.

If we had assigned you to use this anticipation guide for an upcoming reading assignment or lecture on diet and nutrition, we would ask you first to meet in small groups, then with the entire class, to discuss your viewpoints and share information and ideas. As you and other students debate and defend your responses, we would remain neutral by not giving away answers or taking over the discussion. Periodically, we would restate points of view or try to clarify ideas.

A second part to this guide (Figure 5–4) adds additional learning potential to the activity by forcing you to self-interrogate and interact more elaboratively with text. Part II requires you to find ideas and information from text or lecture that either reinforce and verify your existing beliefs, force them to be altered or modified, or require you to completely reject them. During reading, as you encounter information related to the statements in the first part of the guide, you are asked to indicate whether the text or lecture material supports or does not support what you had previously asserted.

As you can see, the anticipation guide takes advantage of prediction as a powerful prereading tool. It forces students to think about what they already know and believe about a topic, then confirm, modify, or disconfirm existing beliefs. Working with anticipation guides helps create the urge in students to know more. They confront the topic ideas and information purposefully and enthusiastically (Nessel, 1988).

Figure 5–4   Anticipation for diet and nutrition: Part II

> *Directions:* Now you will be reading and listening to information related to each of the statements in Part I of this guide. If the information you read supports your choices in Part I, place a *check* in the *Support* column. If the information does not support your choices, place a check in the *No Support* column. Write in your own words the relevant text and/or lecture information for your answer.
>
> | | Support | No Support | Text/Lecture Information |
> |---|---|---|---|
> | 1. | ___ | ___ | _____ |
> | 2. | ___ | ___ | _____ |
> | 3. | ___ | ___ | _____ |
> | 4. | ___ | ___ | _____ |
> | 5. | ___ | ___ | _____ |
> | 6. | ___ | ___ | _____ |
> | 7. | ___ | ___ | _____ |

Like study guides, discussed in Chapter 3, anticipation guides can take on a number of different forms, depending on the nature of the content and your specific intent with the guides. The guide in Figure 5–5, for example, was given to students by a senior government teacher to stimulate prior knowledge about the U.S. Constitution. In this guide, students first guess answers to the questions about the Constitution. Guesses, in this case, serve as predictions. Then, as they read the Constitution, they try to answer the questions with information from text. The questions are both text and reader based to encourage various levels of thinking and to focus on the key issues and points in the Constitution.

Anticipation guides require time to prepare, but we think you will agree that it is time well spent. By forcing students to make and defend predictions, guides can help sustain interest in topics, promote active involvement with text and in discussion, and facilitate assimilation of new information into existing schemata.

Preteaching Critical Vocabulary and Concepts

Graphic Organizers and Word Webs.   Schema theory informs us that it is best to preteach the overarching concepts and terms that provide the mental framework for building new knowledge structures. One excellent way to teach terms and concepts directly is with **graphic organizers** and **word webs**. These are diagrams of the relationships among the key concepts and terms. The key difference between the two is that the graphic organizer is a teacher-provided structured overview, whereas the word map is developed by students with teacher guidance.

The graphic organizer in Figure 5–6 was given to eighth graders in a history class before they began reading in their texts about the Industrial Revolution. An

Figure 5–5   Anticipation guide for a government chapter about the U.S. Constitution

Directions: Read the following questions and try to answer them. Put your answers in the column marked *Guess*. After we share the guesses in class, you will read the chapter to compare your guesses against information in the text. Put the answers you find in the chapter in the column marked *Text Answer*.

	Guess	Text Answer
1. What kind of government did the Founding Fathers prefer?		
2. What is rule by one person called?		
3. What is an advantage and a disadvantage of rule by one?		
4. What does the executive branch do?		
5. Why is separation of powers a good thing?		
6. What are *checks and balances?*		
7. What does *impeach* mean?		
8. How is the Constitution changed?		
9. Is the Constitution flexible?		
10. What is the most important part of the Constitution?		

organizer such as this enables students to see the structure of the text material and anchors in memory the big ideas to which details and facts can be attached.

Word webs are created by branching off from a major concept the related terms and concepts, much like a planet ringed with clustering satellites. The result is a graphic representation of the relationships among concepts and related terminology that approximates a cognitive network of related ideas, or a schema. These semantic networks help students explore and expand their associations with a central concept, thereby building schemata. Figure 5–7 provides a glimpse of a classroom teacher's effective use of a word-web strategy to preteach the critical concept of *prejudice.*

Both graphic organizers and word webs help students focus on the information you deem most important in the text. At the same time, they assist students in the assimilation and clustering of additional details. (Chapter 6 provides a detailed explanation of how to design and use graphic organizers as well as many other effective vocabulary strategies.)

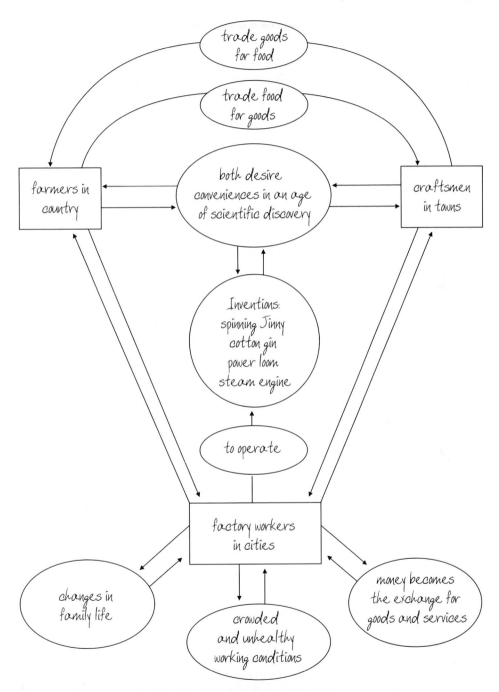

Figure 5–6   Graphic organizer for the Industrial Revolution

Figure 5–7   Classroom example of students' creation of word webs to prepare for a unit on prejudice

Margaret teaches 11th-grade gifted English. In planning a unit around the concept of *prejudice,* she had selected a trade book to use with her students that told a story of racism and prejudice in recent United States history. The book was *Farewell to Manzanar* (Houston & Houston, 1974), a true account of Jeanne Wakat-suki and her family, who spent the World War II years in an internment camp off the West Coast of the United States. Before assigning any reading of the book, Margaret wanted to remind her students of examples of prejudice they were already familiar with to sensitize them to the issues of prejudice and to engage them in a lengthy discussion of the concept.

Margaret first worked with the whole class to create a word web for the broad concept *racial prejudice.* She wrote the words on the board, circled them, and then helped the class come up with an array of related ideas, examples, and terminology. At the conclusion of this activity, the class was divided into groups of four or five, and each group was asked to develop its own word web for one major case of racial prejudice, such as "Naziism," "South African Apartheid," "Southern Blacks in the 1950s," and "Japanese Americans during WWII." Groups were asked to put their webs on transparencies to share them with the class. After working for several minutes, spokespersons from the various groups were asked to share their group's web and explain the rationale for its terms and groupings.

The group working with "Southern Blacks in the 1950s" presented the following word web:

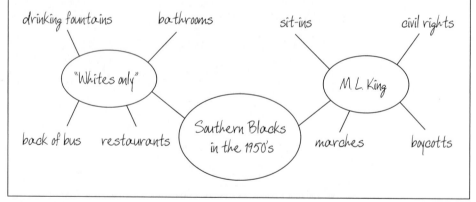

Writing to Prepare for Reading and Learning

Writing Solutions to Problems Posed Before Reading.   Many of the purpose-setting activities discussed earlier can be easily adapted to include a writing component. For instance, a seventh-grade geography class preparing to study the Kalahari bushmen was asked to write a solution to this problem:

The men have gone to work the big farms for harvest season. The women and children have not eaten meat in several weeks. One morning a herd of giraffe are spotted in

Figure 5-7 *(continued)*   **Classroom example of students' creation of word webs to prepare for a unit on prejudice**

"Well, we knew there were lots of places where blacks couldn't go," said one spokesperson, "and there were signs that said 'Whites only,' or something like that, so we used it as one of our subcategories. Then we listed some of the places where blacks couldn't go . . . like they couldn't use certain bathrooms and drinking fountains . . . and they had to sit in the back of the bus . . . and they couldn't eat in certain restaurants . . . we could have listed more places. We also thought about Martin Luther King, because he was trying to change all that back then, so we listed some of the things he did to try to get rights for blacks. We couldn't remember much about the boycotts and marches, so we just said that."

"Didn't they also go to restaurants that we supposed to be for whites and just take up all the seats and stay there?" a student asked.

"I guess they did, so we could include . . . what would you call that?"

Margaret helped out, "They were called 'sit-ins.' That's an excellent word map."

After each group's spokesperson had an opportunity to present and explain its word web, answer questions, and gather feedback and additional ideas from the class, Margaret then focused the discussion on the commonalities among the major cases of racial prejudice that were depicted in the word maps. The class derived three: (a) one group feels superior to another group, often based on physical characteristics, (b) the superior group denies the rights of the other group, and (c) the superior group often uses violence to gain an advantage over the other group. Students were then asked to pay close attention to the novel they were about to read, *Farewell to Manzanar,* and to be prepared to discuss how the case of prejudice in the story shares common characteristics with the other forms of prejudice discussed in the class that day.

the bush nearby. Because you are the most experienced hunter, you are asked to kill a giraffe. You are sent off alone with only a spear. How will you succeed?

In small groups, the students were given the chance to discuss ideas for solving the problem before writing. After composing their answers, several volunteers shared them with the class. The gists of some of the more inventive solutions follow: Dig a big hole, cover it with grass and leaves so that the giraffe will fall in it; wait hidden in a tree that has the giraffe's most irresistible leaves, and when the giraffe comes by to eat, lasso it. Other solutions anticipated the way it really happens: Put poison on a spear tip, sneak up on a giraffe, and spear it. Many students imbedded their solution within stories. The teacher then asked the class to read the text, which explained bushmen hunting strategies and included a description of a giraffe hunt. As they read, students compared their solutions with the text's.

Cheng, a ninth-grade teacher, used writing, cooperative learning, and class discussion to garner students' interest in the topic of equal rights and opportunities in their American citizenship class. Cheng introduced students to the topic by having them form two groups. First students read about laws and regulations developed in the United States to promote equal opportunity. Then he distributed a written scenario of discrimination to Group 1 and an alternative version of the same scenario to Group 2.

Group 1: You are the lawyers representing the Jackson family in a court case. Mr. and Mrs. Jackson wanted to buy a large house in an upper-middle class suburb of a major urban center. They found a house for sale "by owner" that was just the right size for themselves and their two children. The Jacksons called in advance to set up an appointment to see the house. The owner, Mr. Simon, was uncourteous when the Jacksons arrived and only let them in his house after he told them he was convinced it would be sold soon to another party.

The Jacksons were very impressed with Mr. Simon's house. They were told by their bank that if they chose to buy the house they would be approved for a loan. When the Jacksons contacted Mr. Simon the next day to make an offer to buy his house, he told them he was not going to sell it to them. When asked why, he said flatly that he "preferred not to."

Mr. and Mrs. Jackson were very upset. They felt that they were being denied the house because they were African-American.

As the lawyers for the Jacksons, your job is to convince the judge that Mr. Simon was discriminating against the Jacksons on the basis of their race. In your group:

1. Write as many reasons as you can why the Jackson family should be allowed to buy Mr. Simon's house. Make sure your arguments make sense and seem fair.
2. Choose a spokesperson who will present your case to the judge.

Group 2: You are the lawyers representing Mr. Simon in a court case. Mr. Simon is a hard-working, law-abiding citizen who has owned his large suburban home for 17 years.

A couple of months ago, he came home from work late in the evening. As he attempted to unlock his front door, he was accosted by two men, who forced him inside at gunpoint. For the next hour, one of the thieves held a gun to his head, while the other raced through the house, taking valuables and money. Before leaving, the men took Mr. Simon's wallet, watch, and jewelry, then knocked him unconscious. The two robbers were African-American.

Word of Mr. Simon's incident swept through the all-white residence of the suburb, where fear mixed with disgust.

Mr. Simon decided to sell his house and move to a more rural part of the state to get away from the crime influence of a nearby large city. An African-American family, the Jacksons, looked through his house and wanted to buy it, but Mr. Simon chose not to sell to them.

Mr. Simon is now being sued by the Jacksons because they feel they were unfairly discriminated against because of their race.

As the lawyers for Mr. Simon, your job is to convince the judge that he, as owner of the property, has the right to decide who may or may not purchase his home. In your group:

1. Write as many reasons as you can why Mr. Simon has the right to make the decision he made. Make sure your arguments make sense and seem fair.

2. Choose a spokesperson who will present your case to the judge.

Cheng gave each group enough time to generate arguments and formulate defenses of their respective clients. He then identified himself as the "judge" and asked for the spokesperson for Mr. and Mrs. Jackson and Mr. Simon to present their cases. After the spokespersons presented their cases, Cheng invited further comment form the rest of the class. He thanked the groups for their fine work and said the next step would be to do more research on how similar cases have been resolved in the past. At this point, Cheng directed students to a section in their textbook that discussed several similar discrimination court cases and asked them to read the pages carefully for homework.

By having his students work together to think about, write, and present their ideas and beliefs, Cheng used conflicting perspectives to generate arguments and discussion about the topic of equal rights. After this activity, students brought a heightened level of enthusiasm and interest to their textbook reading assignment because they were anxious to discover how discrimination cases similar to theirs had been resolved in the past.

Learning Logs.   Another outstanding way of using writing to help students prepare for learning by thinking about new knowledge in terms of preexisting knowledge is with **learning logs** (Newkirk, 1986). Students can keep notebooks in content classrooms to record what they already know about a topic; what they desire to know about the topic; and then, after reading, lecture, and class discussion, an amalgamation of these two aspects with what they have learned. The amalgamation is in essence a revision of first interpretations of the content. Cassie kept a learning log in sophomore history. In preparing to read and study a unit on the American Revolution, which she felt she had gone over 20 times before, she wrote at length about how the war started, some of the battles, Washington's role, the effect of losing on the British and victory on the Colonies, and so on. She had little to ask of herself in terms of what she further desired to learn; she thought she had the Revolutionary War down cold. She wrote in her log, "I want to refresh my memory." But then, her teacher gave the class a trade book to read as a prelude to reading the text—*My Brother Sam is Dead* by Collier and Collier (1974). Cassie had never read a fictionalized account of the Revolutionary War and was doubtful about whether she could discover any new fact or detail that had been overlooked by her present or past texts. As she read the book, though, a change began taking place as reflected in the entries in her log.

> I didn't know families were split about how they felt about the war. I didn't realize there were so many colonists who were against the war and for the British. I wonder how these people were treated during the war?

Further into the book, she found an answer to her question.

> I can't believe how cruel the colonists who supported the war were to those who didn't support the war. They were treated like enemies. Sam's father was not helping the British he was just minding his own business and for that he gets captured and his family isn't even told where he is or whether he's alive. I wonder what's going to happen to Mr. Meeker now, and Tim and his mom, and Sam for that matter.

The trade book forced Cassie to reconsider her beliefs about the Revolutionary War in light of some new and, to her, startling information. The learning log facilitated this process of reinterpretation. When Cassie completed the book, she wrote another extended entry in her log, where she recorded the same facts she had written before reading the book but this time qualifying each with new information and ideas she had gleaned from the trade book.

Students will be more enthusiastic learners and you will be a more enthusiastic teacher when you create a context that is supportive of learning using the following:

- Demonstrate that the content your students are about to read and study is meaningful and interesting.
- Make provisions to garner interest in and motivation for the topic.
- Activate and build relevant prior knowledge.
- Preteach the most important concepts and terminology.
- Help students set purposes for reading.

Role Playing and Simulations

Martin teaches history to 10th-grade learning disabled students in a self-contained classroom. One of his principle objectives for a unit about how the American colonies gain their freedom is to develop a thorough understanding of the concept "taxation without representation." Martin knew that in the past his students were reasonably excited about the topic, but he found in his assessments that they failed to grasp the significance of the essential concepts leading to a full understanding of the antecedents and consequences of the American Revolution. Martin also knew that the more he could transform lifeless textual information into something tangible and personal, the greater the level of involvement on the part of his students and the more they seemed to learn.

As a motivator and as a way of personalizing the concept, Martin had his class participate in a **simulation activity**. He called it a "government experiment" as he handed out written directions and guided the class through them. The students were divided into two groups: one was called the "Oros" and the other, the "Bindus." Martin appointed himself the king of the Oros. Each group was given a set of directions for electing representatives to make laws or rules. The Bindus were told they could only make rules that applied to themselves, while the Oros could impose rules on the Bindus if they chose. Each group also was given a lump sum of a thousand play-dollars for their treasuries.

Martin, as king of the Oros, immediately began imposing laws on the Bindus that roughly paralleled the Stamp Act and the Tea Act. The "Paper and Pencil Rule" taxed every Bindu 5 cents for every pencil, pen, and piece of paper used; the "Pop Rule" taxed the Bindu's 10 cents for having a soda or any other drink in class (Martin permitted his students to have soft drinks in the classroom). Interestingly, the turn of events in Martin's classroom resembled what had happened between the British and American colonies. Complaining fell on deaf ears, so at first, the Bindus gave in to the Oros's rules. Soon, however, the Bindus began to protest—first, by not bringing paper or pencils to class, then, by simply ignoring the rule and disdainfully using as many sheets of paper and pencils they wished. The same thing happened with their soda drinking. Soon, the Bindus were challenging the Oros's authority by drinking without paying taxes. By week's end, the Oros were debating among themselves as to whether they should take back the taxes or impose penalties and stiffer taxes, while the Bindus were prepared to resist at all costs.

At this point, Martin asked the class to analyze their situation. The Bindus argued that it was extremely unfair for a separate group of people to tell them what to do. They said that they wanted and were able to take care of themselves. One student put it succinctly to the Oros, "What gives you the right to tax us?" The Oros had never really considered this question. They behaved as though that was the only way to behave. Martin took advantage of the students' self-discovery about what can happen when one group imposes rules on another group against their will by having the students draw parallels to the conditions that led to war between the British and the colonies. He asked students to divide a sheet of paper in half and list on one side the rules imposed by the Oros and the Bindus's reactions to those rules and then, as they read and studied the chapter, to list on the other side of their sheets the events that took place in colonial America just before the Revolutionary War.

This section described several effective strategies for preparing students for reading and learning experiences. These strategies should be viewed as mere representations of the countless possibilities for activating and building relevant prior knowledge, engendering interest and motivation, setting meaningful purposes, and engaging students in the reading and learning process.

Case Study Revisited

Remember Theresa, the eighth-grade social studies teacher? She was preparing for a unit on the early Americans. Take a moment to write your ideas for Theresa to help her students prepare to study this content and become engaged in learning.

Theresa introduced students to a prereading activity on the first day that we thought was exceptional. She began by involving the class in a discussion of the role of archaeologists in understanding the relationship of artifacts to past societies. She then explained that one way to understand the past is to relate it to the present, and one way they could do that was by making a time capsule. After defining a time capsule, she asked students to think of objects they felt would be important to include in one that would be buried today and excavated in 2994, a thousand years later. Theresa jotted down ideas on the board and asked students to explain why their particular object would help people living in 2994 to understand what life was like in the year 1994. Clearly, the purpose of exploring the idea of a time capsule was to motivate students to learn about the past by making it relevant to their own lives. The students were genuinely enjoying this activity, as reflected in interchanges such as this:

Student 1:   Did you see that Coke commercial where this class sometime way in the future is walking through a 20th-century ruin and they find a Coke bottle?

Class: Yeah, I've seen that.

Theresa: What does a bottle of Coke say to these future people about ourselves and our culture?

Student 1:   That we like to drink Coke.

Theresa: Would it? How could you be sure? Let's say people aren't drinking Coke a thousand years from now, and let's say these people you're talking about also found a tattered T-shirt with "Madonna" written on it, and . . . a broken television? How would they piece together the way we lived if this is all they found?

Student 2:   They might think Madonna was our President or something. . . .

Student 3:   They might not even know what a television was. I read a science fiction story about these people who could put this machine on their heads, like a headset, and see images in their heads and feel what you would feel if you were there.

Theresa: That's interesting. So they might not even be able to recognize that it was a television or exactly what it was used for, especially if it was really badly broken up. Do you see now how hard it would be for future people to describe who we were and how we behaved from the few things they might find?

Student 4:	Maybe if we put a Coke can in our time capsule, we should tape a piece of paper to it that tells what it is and all about it.
Theresa:	If the paper didn't crumble and rot away, that would be very helpful for future people. Good idea. Unfortunately for archaeologists, the original inhabitants of North America didn't leave written directions and explanations with all of their artifacts. . . .
Student 5:	Didn't they draw pictures in caves of hunting buffalo and stuff like that?
Theresa:	That's right, and those wall paintings help us quite a bit, but they don't tell the whole story. For instance, the wall pictures don't tell whether men and women married like they do today, or whether one man could have several wives. They don't tell us if the Indians were nomadic or whether they lived in one place for long periods of time. Did these people have music or play games, etc.?

Eventually, the class formulated a list of things to put in their time capsule. It was fascinating to listen to the students rationalize why certain items would be appropriate to include. For instance, one young man wanted to contribute his tennis shoes—one was green, the other orange, and both were untied. He argued that they would reflect what young people were like in 1994. The class concluded that his mismatched tennis shoes would give a misleading impression because only a small minority dressed that way. Instead, it was decided that pictures from magazines depicting many different fashions would be better. Another student said the time capsule should have a record album or compact disc of contemporary music. This didn't seem feasible, the class agreed, because in a thousand years, probably no means of playing the record or disc would exist.

The final list included a Coke can, accompanied by a picture of someone drinking from a can of Coke, a copy of *Time* magazine, several photographs of cars, fashions, stereos, TVs, and houses, lyrics and sheet music to a couple of popular songs, and a class portrait. The activity culminated at week's end with a ceremonial burial on a section of school grounds of a time capsule (actually a large plastic canister) containing the items the class had decided on.

Theresa conducted a couple of other readiness activities during the week, including a word scavenger hunt, which involves students in a game for learning key words from their readings (see Chapter 6 for details), and viewing a film that traced the journey of the first people to emigrate from Europe into the area we now call Iowa. Students were also provided a structured overview depicting the migration patterns, names, and terms associated with the first Americans.

This case study makes clear how varied and yet how effective creative and meaningful activities before reading about and studying class topics can be. It demonstrates how a talented teacher takes her students far beyond the traditional boundaries of a content-area lesson in preparing them for learning by generating interest in the topic and activating and building appropriate prior knowledge for the content to be learned.

Summary

Because we believe that the degree of success with a topic of study in the content areas depends on how well students are prepared for learning about the topic, we have devoted most of this chapter to presenting a range of classroom practices that teachers in secondary schools have used to hook their students into the topic. The examples included here represent only a few of the potentially endless possibilities for getting students excited about the content to be read and studied. We hope these guidelines and examples help you become more sensitive to the importance of providing preparation activities for all reading and learning experiences and inspire you to expand your notions about what is possible in your classroom before telling students, "Open your books and begin reading Chapter 7."

In the next chapter you will read more about some of the vocabulary strategies briefly discussed in this chapter. You will also discover a range of additional word-learning strategies designed to expand students' understanding of course concepts.

References

Alvermann, D., Dillon, D., & O'Brien, D. (1988). *Using discussion to promote reading comprehension.* Newark, DE: International Reading Association.

Alvermann, D., & Hayes, D. (1989). Classroom discussion of content area reading assignments: An intervention study. *Reading Research Quarterly, 24,* 305–335.

Alvermann, D., O'Brien, D., & Dillon, D. (1990). What teachers do when they say they're having discussions of content area reading assignments: A qualitative analysis. *Reading Research Quarterly, 25,* 296–322.

Alvermann, D., Smith, L., & Readence, J. (1985). Prior knowledge activation and the comprehension of compatible and incompatible text. *Reading Research Quarterly, 20,* 420–436.

Anderson, R. (1984). Role of the reader's schema in comprehension, learning, and memory. In R. Anderson, J. Osborn, & R. Tierney (Eds.), *Learning to read in American Schools: Basal readers and content texts.* Hillsdale, NJ: Lawrence Erlbaum.

Carr, E., & Ogle, D. (1987). K-W-L Plus: A strategy for comprehension and summarization. *Journal of Reading, 30,* 626–631.

Clary, L. (1991). Getting adolescents to read. *Journal of Reading, 34,* 340–345.

Dewey, J. (1913). *Interest and effort in education.* Boston: Houghton Mifflin.

Dillon, J. T. (1984). Research on questioning and discussion. *Educational Leadership, 42,* 50–56.

Duffelmeyer, R., Baum, D., & Merkley, D. (1987). Maximizing reader-text confrontation with an extended anticipation guide. *Journal of Reading, 31,* 146–150.

Frager, A. (1993). Affective dimension of content area reading. *Journal of Reading, 36,* 616–623.

Gillet, J., & Temple, C. (1986). *Understanding reading problems: Assessment and instruction: Instructor's manual* (2nd ed.). Boston: Little, Brown.

Hamann, L., Schultz, L., Smith, M., & White, B. (1991). Making connections: The power of autobiographical writing before reading. *Journal of Reading, 35,* 24–28.

Harste, J. (1989). *New policy guidelines for reading: Connecting research and practice.* Urbana, IL: National Council of Teachers of English.

Hayes, D. A., & Tierney, R. J. (1980). *Increasing background knowledge through analogy: Its effects upon comprehension and learning* (Technical Report No. 186). Urbana: University of Illinois, Center for the Study of Reading.

Hennings, D. (1991). Essential reading: Targeting, tracking, and thinking about main ideas. *Journal of Reading, 34,* 346–353.

Hidi, S., & Baird, W. (1988). Strategies for increasing text-based interest and students' recall of expository texts. *Reading Research Quarterly, 23,* 465–483.

Horn, E. (1937). *Methods of instruction in social studies.* New York: Charles Scribner's Sons.

Illich, I. (1970). *Deschooling society.* New York: Harper & Row.

Irwin, J., & Baker, I. (1989). *Promoting active reading comprehension strategies: A resource book for teachers.* Englewood Cliffs, NJ: Prentice-Hall.

Marshall, N. (1989). Overcoming problems with incorrect prior knowledge: An instructional study. In S. McCormick & J. Zutell (Eds.), *Cognitive and social perspectives for literacy research and instruction.* Chicago: National Reading Conference.

Mathison, C. (1989). Activating student interest in content area reading. *Journal of Reading, 33,* 170–177.

McKeown, M., Beck, I., Sinatra, G., & Loxterman, J. (1992). The contribution of prior knowledge and coherent text to comprehension. *Reading Research Quarterly, 27,* 78–93.

Nagy, W., Anderson, R., & Herman, P. (1987). Learning word meanings from context during normal reading. *American Educational Research Journal, 24,* 237–270.

Nessel, D. (1988). Channeling knowledge for reading expository text. *Journal of Reading, 32,* 231–235.

Newkirk, T. (1986). *To compose: Teaching writing in the high school.* Portsmouth, NH: Heinemann.

Ogle, D. (1986). K-W-L: A teaching model that develops active reading of expository text. *The Reading Teacher, 39,* 564–570.

Pearson, P. D., & Johnson, D. D. (1978). *Teaching reading comprehension.* New York: Holt, Rinehart & Winston.

Pearson, P. D., & Spiro, R. (1982). The new buzz word in reading as schema. *Instructor, 89,* 46–48.

Pressley, M., Johnson, C., Symons, S., McGoldrick, J., & Kurita, J. (1989). Strategies that improve children's memory and comprehension of text. *The Elementary School Journal, 90,* 3–32.

Radebaugh, M., & Kazemek, F. (1989). Cooperative learning in college reading and study skills classes. *Journal of Reading, 32,* 414–418.

Reed, A. (1988). *Comics to classics: A parent's guide to books for teens and preteens.* Newark, DE: International Reading Association.

Renninger, K., Hidi, S., & Krapp, A. (1992). *The role of interest in learning and development.* Hillsdale, NJ: Lawrence Erlbaum.

Spilich, G. J., Vesonder, G. T., Chiesi, H. L., & Voss, J. F. (1979). Text processing of domain-related information for individuals with high and low domain knowledge. *Journal of Verbal Learning and Verbal Behavior, 18,* 275–290.

Tyson-Bernstein, H. (1988). *A conspiracy of good intentions.* Washington, DC: Council for Basic Education.

Wade, S., Schraw, G., Buxton, W., & Hayes, M. (1993). Seduction of the strategic reader: Effects of interest on strategy and recall. *Reading Research Quarterly, 28,* 92–115.

Wood, K. (1987). Fostering cooperative learning in middle and secondary level classrooms. *Journal of Reading, 31,* 10–19.

Young Adult Books

Arnothy, C. (1950). *I am fifteen—and I don't want to die.* New York: Dutton.

Collier, J. L., & Collier, C. (1974). *My brother Sam is dead.* New York: Scholastic.

Clark, M. (1969). *The min min.* New York: Collier.

Duncan, L. (1982). *Chapters: My growth as a writer.* Boston: Little, Brown.

Houston, J. W., & Houston, J. (1974). *Farewell to Manzanar.* New York: Bantam Books.

Lauber, P. (1986). *Volcano.* New York: Bradbury Press.

Peters, R. (1985). *Dance of the wolves.* New York: McGraw-Hill.

Southall, I. (1963). *Hills end.* New York: St. Martin's Press.

Southall, I. (1966). *Ash road.* New York: St. Martin's Press.

Southall, I. (1977). *About tomorrow.* New York: Macmillan.

Thiele, C. (1974). *The fire in the stone.* New York: Harper & Row.

6

Expanding Vocabulary and Developing Concepts

The goal for vocabulary development is to insure that students are able to apply their knowledge of words to appropriate situations and are able to increase and enrich their knowledge through independent encounter with words. . . . [T]he best way to reach this goal is to help students add to their repertoires both specific words and skills that promote independent learning of words, and also to provide opportunities from which words can be learned.

—Beck and McKeown (1991)

What does it mean to "know" a word? That question has been debated for about 50 years, starting with Cronbach (1942), who suggested that word knowledge existed in dimensions. In the vernacular, to know a word means to be able to give a definition for it. But is this an adequate measure of one's word knowledge? When asked what the word *light* meant, 4-year-old Ryan's reply was "It comes from the sun and helps us see things." However, he had no idea what "light as a feather" meant, nor did he know the meaning of light in the sentence, "I saw the birds light on the tree." Does Ryan really know the word *light*?

One of the primary goals of vocabulary development in the secondary school is not simply to increase the breadth of students' vocabularies (i.e., the number of words for which students have a definition) but to increase the depth and precision of their word knowledge. In other words, the goal is to help students develop a full and complete understanding of words to expand their abilities to comprehend the texts they read. This is especially important in the secondary school because most students are expected to read and listen to content packed with concepts and technical vocabulary that they need to understand fully if meaning is to be gained (Jenkins, Matlock, & Slocum, 1989).

In this chapter we present a variety of methods for teaching key vocabulary and for developing students' strategies for acquiring and studying new vocabulary independently. You will notice that certain vocabulary strategies can also serve an excellent readiness or assessment function, but all the strategies discussed are intended to expand students' comprehension of class texts. We believe the best way to develop word knowledge is by capitalizing on the same effective teaching strategies discussed in previous chapters and throughout this book. Teacher demonstrations and modeling, small-group interactions, class discussions, and reciprocal teaching are all powerful teaching tools. As you read this chapter, you will see how these teaching strategies can be effectively applied to word learning.

Case Study

Liz Yates, The Curriculum Director of the Parkview School, District analyzed the results of the competency-based reading test that was given to high school sophomores in the spring. Much to her dismay, the vocabulary scores for Parkview High School were again low. She called the principal to highlight her concerns and to recommend that a committee be formed to investigate the problem and offer some specific solutions. Consequently, a committee was formed of teachers who taught sophomores. They met regularly during the school year to discuss the problem in more depth, but they could not agree on what should be done. Several committee members thought the English department should be responsible for improving the vocabulary scores. Other members complained that the additional burden of teaching vocabulary words would rob them of precious instructional time. And three members wanted the school to purchase a computer program promising to teach students 50 words a week. Patience was wearing thin as the school year drew to a close.

To the Reader: As you read and work through this chapter on expanding vocabulary and concepts across the content areas, consider ways in which this committee could solve their problem. Think about the characteristics of effective vocabulary instruction, what it means to know a word, and possible strategies that this school district might incorporate into the curricula.

Definitional Versus Conceptual Understanding of Words

One of the underlying themes of this chapter is that word-learning strategies should require students to combine new text information with their prior knowledge to yield conceptual understanding of words. The admonitions of our best vocabulary writers and researchers are entirely consistent with this theme (e.g., Beck & McKeown, 1991; Konopak, 1988). Earlier in this chapter, we mentioned 4-year-old Ryan who had partial definitional understanding of the word *light*. But Ryan did not have a conceptual understanding of light that would have allowed him to interpret its meaning in a variety of contexts.

Steven Stahl (1985) has made the distinction between definitional and contextual word knowledge. **Definitional knowledge** is essentially knowing a dictionary-like definition for a word. It is important word knowledge, but it limits understanding of the word to restricted contexts. **Contextual understanding,** on the other hand, means that the reader has a sophisticated schema for the word that facilitates meaningful interpretations in a variety of contexts.

To help you understand the important distinction between definitional and contextual word knowledge, we have prepared an exercise for you. For the following sentence, two key words have been defined. Write in the space provided what the statement means in your own words.

Surrogate: judge or magistrate
Testator: on making a claim on a will

The learned Surrogate has held that an intent to have an apportionment will be imputed to the testator.

In your own words:

_____

_____

_____

For this next sentence, the topic area is provided. Given the topic, write in your own words the special definition of the two italicized words in the sentence:

Topic: commodities futures

Live hogs *found* November *unchanged*.

Your definition of *found*:

_____

_____

Your definition of *unchanged*:

_____

_____

Now that you have finished the exercise, some explanation is in order. In the first sentence, you undoubtedly discovered that even with a couple of the key terms defined, you were still unable to make sense of it. Why? Because the meaning of the sentence is larger than the sum of the definitions of each of its words. To state it another way, to understand this sentence, you must connect individual definitions to a broad context of meaning. You must possess the schema for these words, for without schema, the sentence is an unintelligible collection of fragments of definitions. If, however, you were a lawyer of contracts and estate settlements, this sentence would be perfectly understandable.

What about the second sentence? Were you able to supply the appropriate special definitions for the commonly understood words found and unchanged? If not, it is likely due to the fact that your schema for the language of commodities futures is not especially well developed. Once again, without the necessary schema, or relevant prior knowledge, the sentence is as oblique as a line from a surrealistic poem. Of course, if you are a member of the Chicago Board of Trade familiar with hog futures in the commodities market, the expression would make perfect sense to you.

The difficulty you probably experienced in completing the definitions in this exercise is not unlike the problems many students in junior and senior high school often encounter when trying to read their content textbooks. When students are not given adequate preparation for dealing with the critical terms and concepts in the text, or strategies for discovering word meaning while reading, comprehension can proceed only haltingly or may break down altogether (Schwartz, 1988). For the two sentences you were given, knowledge of the words and, most importantly, of the concepts they represent is essential if they are to be understood. It is how students acquire this important prior knowledge and how they can use strategies for elaborative understanding of words and concepts that comprise the major themes in this chapter.

As you have now seen in your own experience, definitional word knowledge does not imply a conceptual understanding of a word. It is, however, an aspect of word knowledge that allows readers to bring to mind appropriate schema to aid them in interpreting word meanings in various contexts (Schwartz & Raphael, 1985). Therefore, the principles and strategies of effective vocabulary instruction discussed in this chapter are not meant to make students experts at writing or reciting definitions. If a strategy or program focuses only on correctly matching a word to a definition, then what is obtained is limited in vision and probably has a low chance of being transferred to students' actual reading tasks (Beck & McKeown, 1991).

Guidelines for Effective Vocabulary Instruction

After reviewing the literature pertaining to vocabulary instruction, S. A. Stahl and Fairbanks (1986) and Mezynski (1983) agreed that no single method appears to be consistently superior. Therefore, it appears advantageous for teachers to select a variety of techniques or approaches for increasing their students' vocabulary knowledge. In addition, the following five guidelines, gleaned from research studies, should be considered when planning vocabulary lessons:

1. Teach vocabulary in context.
2. Emphasize students' active role in the learning process.
3. Give students tools to expand word knowledge independently.
4. Reinforce word learning with repeated exposures over time.
5. Be an enthusiastic model of vocabulary use.

Teach Vocabulary in Context

The findings from numerous research studies suggest that vocabulary knowledge is best taught from a unifying context (Jenkins & Dixon, 1983; Mezynski, 1983). Words taught in a context of a content area such as biology will be learned more effectively than words taught in isolation because context allows students to integrate words with previously acquired knowledge. The implication, of course, is that students will not improve long-term vocabulary knowledge and understanding by memorizing definitions for a list of essential words that high school students should know.

Thus, content-area teachers need to select or have students select the targeted words for study from textbooks, newspapers, magazines, or novels. For example, if students are reading a short selection from a speech textbook on words and their meaning, words such as *arbitrary, connotation, denotation,* or *syntax* could be studied. Another alternative is to group targeted words into semantic categories (Beck, Perfetti, & McKeown, 1982). One such category could be adjectives that negatively describe a person's actions: *lax, infantile, obsequious, narcissistic.* Whatever approach is used to provide a context and organizing schema, remember that lists of words that are introduced on Monday and tested on Friday will probably be forgotten on Saturday.

Emphasize Students' Active Role in the Learning Process

Researchers who required their subjects to be actively involved in their own vocabulary development (Carr, 1985; Diekhoff, Brown, & Dansereau, 1982; Mc-

Keown, Beck, Omanson, & Pople, 1985) have found that such learners performed significantly better than other subjects on measures designed to evaluate vocabulary knowledge. From their reviews, S. A. Stahl and Fairbanks (1986) and Mezynski (1983) likewise concluded that active processing and involvement is critical for students to improve their vocabulary knowledge.

S. A. Stahl (1985) described active involvement of the learner as "generative processing." Generative or elaborative processing engages students in activities such as (a) sensing and inferring relationships between targeted vocabulary and their own background knowledge, (b) recognizing and applying vocabulary words to a variety of contexts, (c) recognizing examples and nonexamples, and (d) generating novel contexts for the targeted word. In contrast, an example of passive involvement related to vocabulary instruction would be worksheet-type activities asking students to select definitions, whether in multiple-choice or matching formats.

Give Students Tools to Expand Word Knowledge Independently

Stahl (1987) has differentiated between additive and generative approaches to teaching word knowledge. **Additive approaches** are word specific and emphasize the learning of a predetermined set of words. **Generative approaches,** on the other hand, emphasize vocabulary-learning strategies that permit students to increase vocabulary independently, beyond the instruction context. Think about it this way: If you teach students some words, they will be able to recognize and read those particular words; but if you teach students some word-learning strategies, they will be able to continually expand their vocabulary and read and understand many more texts.

We are not arguing generative over additive approaches. Instead, we make the point that classroom teachers should strike a balance between these two approaches. Students should be exposed to and actively involved in the learning of key terms and concepts related to text topics. In this case, developing broad understanding of a set of critical vocabulary is relevant and purposeful, as it will contribute to greater comprehension of the text. Indeed, we provide many strategies for this purpose in this chapter. Too often, however, word-specific methods for teaching vocabulary involve handing students a list of arbitrarily selected words without demonstrating a clear connection between remembering definitions and meaningful learning (N. A. Stahl, Brozo, & Simpson, 1987). Teachers should also move students toward becoming independent word gatherers by helping them develop ownership of effective generative strategies (Schwartz, 1988).

Reinforce Word Learning With Repeated Exposures Over Time

To really own a word, not only must we possess an elaborative understanding of it, but we must also be able to use it freely in appropriate contexts. Nagy, Anderson, and Herman (1987) discovered that word ownership is reinforced when students receive multiple exposures to targeted words in multiple contexts. A history and current events teacher puts this principle into practice by building vocabulary through (a) extensive discussions of key terms, exploring what students already know about them; (b) previewing how the words are used in context; (c) asking students to record the words and original sentences in a vocabulary notebook; (d) finding and creating new texts with the targeted words; (e) and practicing the words with a variety of activities that require students to think and write rather than circle answers. These approaches to reinforcing vocabulary ensure students' elaborative understanding and hasten their spontaneous use of the words in spoken and written contexts.

Be an Enthusiastic Model of Vocabulary Use

We can hardly expect our students to become sensitive to words and interested in expanding word knowledge if we cannot demonstrate interest in words ourselves. Manzo and Sherk have stated that "the single most significant factor in improving vocabulary is the excitement about words which teachers can generate" (1971, p. 78). As we emphasized in previous chapters, modeling is a powerful teaching tool. If you desire students to learn certain words, then model their use. Show students that you use the dictionary to look up words you do not understand or for definitions you need to clarify so they realize that vocabulary acquisition is a lifelong goal. During class discussion, in conversation with students, or when responding to journal or other student writing, use words you want them to integrate into their written and spoken vocabularies. Above all, be playful with words and exhibit enthusiasm for the strategies you are teaching students.

Build a Language-Rich Environment

Word learning should occur within a context that supports literacy and language development. According to Auten (1985), teachers can best promote vocabulary growth by working with students to create an environment where learning new words and strategies can be done through genuine communication processes. Students should be involved in using all of the language systems for learning concepts and expanding comprehension. For example, they should be given opportunities to experiment with using words in low-risk situations, to discuss new ideas daily, to talk freely and openly about how text concepts relate to their real-world concerns, to read a variety of text genres related to concepts, and to write purposeful and meaningful texts that employ key words and demonstrate understanding of important concepts.

We know teachers, for example, who allow vocabulary learning to occur naturally by making writing an integral part of the daily classroom activities. They provide regular writing and review experiences to help their students become more aware of contextual meanings as well as their lack of specific vocabulary. In addition, the revision and editing stages of the writing process become excellent opportunities to engage students in searches for "that one perfect word" that conveys the precise meaning they have in mind.

In the next section, we will discuss the types of vocabulary students encounter in their reading and criteria for selecting the ones that should be taught.

Selecting Key Terms and Concepts

Types of Vocabulary

If you were to skim a chapter in this textbook, you would probably discover that the vocabulary words could be classified in two ways. The first type of words are those **general words** that are not particularly associated with any single content area and could be found in any newspaper or weekly magazine. For example, a science teacher who asked his ninth-grade students to read a brief excerpt from Rachel Carson's book *The Silent Spring* identified the following general words that he thought should be taught: (a) maladies, (b) blight, (c) moribund, (d) specter, (e) stark, and (f) droned. A British journalist could have easily used some of these same words to describe a winter day in London because they are common to many communication situations.

The second type are the **technical vocabulary words** that are unique to a particular content area or take on a specialized meaning when used in that content area. As Konopak and Mealey (1992) point out, technical words include general words that are used in a specialized way and technical words that have only one distinct meaning and application. Examples of the former are words such as *table, matter, set,* or *drive,* which take on specialized meanings, depending on the content area. Examples of the latter include words such as *alveoli* in science, *sonority* in music, or *matte effect* in art.

A Process for Selecting Words to Teach

Because it is impossible to teach all the general and technical words from a content-area chapter, an important first step in teaching vocabulary is to decide which terms and concepts should be taught. Traditionally, teachers have used the textbook as a guide, focusing on the words that have been highlighted in the text. Basing vocabulary instruction on these words alone, however, may not meet your overall goals for teaching the content or unit. Researchers (e.g., Duffy, Roehler, & Mason, 1984) have made clear the fact that students will learn what is emphasized. If instruction focuses on the important and meaningful details, concepts, and issues, those things will be what students learn and remember. Vocabulary instruction, then, should focus on words related to those important ideas. Sometimes the words the textbook author has chosen to highlight will match with the concepts you chose to emphasize; sometimes they will not. It is important, therefore, that you have a system for selecting the appropriate vocabulary terms that help students better understand the key ideas of the unit.

Another related issue to selecting words to teach is that it is impossible to teach students every word that they may not fully understand in their texts. Time constraints alone preclude our doing so (Nagy et al., 1987). Any of you who have tried to identify and teach all the words in a text you think might cause your students difficulty have discovered that your entire lesson can be taken up with vocabulary instruction. It is simply not feasible to attempt to teach every word that might potentially pose trouble for your students. We submit that a far more efficient and effective approach is to select the salient terms and concepts, those that carry and represent the most important ideas, and teach them well. A thorough and elaborative understanding of those vocabulary terms will, in turn, contribute to your students' enhanced understanding of the text itself.

The following process should help in determining what vocabulary words should be taught as a part of a unit of study:

1.   Determine what you want your students to learn as a result of reading and studying the content. We might call this the **theme** of the unit. For instance, a music teacher may want students to develop a sense of musical interpretation as a result of a unit on opera; an art teacher may wish that students develop a sense of character as a result of reading stories with well-developed characters for a unit on portrait painting; a history teacher covering the Vietnam Conflict may stress the danger of foreign intervention in civil strife.

2.   Identify **key terms** that are related to the unit's theme. For example, considering the theme of Sparta and its unique political structure, the teacher would likely select technical terms such as *euphors, assembly, council of elders,* and *helots,* because they are important words related to the theme.

3.   Decide on appropriate strategies to introduce and reinforce the words. For example, the words related to Sparta could be arranged into a graphic organizer, a strategy introduced in Chapter 5 and discussed in more detail later in this chapter.

4.   Identify the general words that are not necessarily central to the theme of the unit but that lend themselves to various word-learning strategies that promote independence, such as modeling words in context.

You should not underestimate the importance of these first steps in teaching key terms and concepts related to a unit of study. The more discretionary you are in selecting vocabulary that potentially has the highest payoff regarding comprehension, the greater the likelihood that students will learn the designated content-area material.

Traditional Approaches to Vocabulary Instruction

In this section we examine two traditional approaches to teaching vocabulary—context clues and the dictionary. This section could have also been titled "Caveats to Vocabulary Instruction," in that we directly discuss the limitations of using context clues and the dictionary, two very traditional and prevalent approaches (N. A. Stahl et al., 1987). Though we offer several caveats to each approach, we also outline ways in which teachers can constructively encourage students to use context clues and the dictionary as methods of vocabulary development.

Using Contextual Analysis

Contextual analysis refers to our attempt to understand the meaning of a word by analyzing the meaning of the words that surround it. Put another way, contextual analysis is figuring out a word by the way in which it is used in a textbook, novel, or magazine. For example, one way in which we figure out the meaning of words is by using extended descriptions or appositives such as the following:

> There was a strange sound *emanating* from the hood of my car. When I opened the hood, I found a stray cat huddling to keep warm and meowing in fear.

> The *decadent,* or overindulgent, society in which we live spoils children by buying them whatever they see on television.

On the surface, the idea of learning words from context makes a lot of sense. As logical as it may seem, the research that has investigated students' incidental learning from context seems to indicate that "some learning from context does exist, but that effect is not very powerful" (Beck & McKeown, 1991, p. 800).

One reason why the utility of contextual analysis is challenged is that previous research studies have used contrived, unnatural texts as their materials of study and high-frequency words as their target of study (Nist, 1993). The following examples illustrate the type of oversimplified exercises that have been used in studies and in workbooks designed to teach students how to use context clues. Can you figure out the meaning of the italicized nonsense words?

> The boys brought their tickets for the brand new outer space movie and entered the theater with mystic expectation all over their *whitors.*

> Some even looked alive, though no *fome* flowed beneath the skin.

> A little later as he sped southward along a Florida *uwurt,* he was stopped by a state police officer.

If you were able to figure out the *whitors* means "faces," *fome* means "blood," and *uwurt* means "highway," congratulations. But is your performance on these sentences indicative of your genuine ability to use contextual analysis? Imagine high school students who correctly complete 20 sentences similar to those you have just tried. The students may be left with the impression that they have mastered the use of context for determining word meanings. Then imagine their enthusiastic attempt to apply their new skills with a real passage from the history textbook.

To understand the possible frustrations students encounter when told to "use the cues around the word to find its meaning," read the following passage about the Andersonville prison. As you read, think about the difficulty a ninth grader might have in trying to determine the meanings for the italicized general words using contextual analysis.

> Prisoners from the North during the Civil War who found themselves in Andersonville had to contend with unhealthful, *debilitating* conditions as well as *depredations* by their fellow inmates, who frequently stole food, clothing, and whatever other necessities for survival they could lay their hands on. The Andersonville Raiders were a large, organized group of thieves and murderers. For nearly four months these *notorious predators* controlled what went on inside the prison, committing robbery and murder on a daily basis. Finally, after six leaders were captured and a quick trial by fellow inmates, they were hanged on July 11, 1864.
>
> When the war ended, the *emaciated* survivors of Andersonville returned to their homes amidst *strident* demands in the North for swift *retribution*. It was claimed that prison commanders were responsible for deliberately planned *atrocities*.*

As you undoubtedly discovered, trying to figure out the meaning of such words as *emaciated* and *atrocities* using context alone is very difficult. Schatz and Baldwin's (1986) research concurs. In this study, instead of using high-frequency words and researcher-made passages, they chose to use low-frequency words and passages from history and science textbooks. They found the use of context clues ineffective in helping students determine the meanings of those targeted low-frequency words. This is a critical aspect of contextual analysis, because students' textbooks are typically lean on clues, and students need to learn how to cope with those contexts.

If very few meaning clues are provided for textbook vocabulary, how do we teach our students to use context clues? Despite the fact that real text is not always as generous in providing clues to the meanings of unknown words, several approaches can be used to help students become more aware of the importance of contextual analysis. In addition, these teaching approaches can help students develop a habit of using context in conjunction with others strategies to establish or verify word meanings.

Previewing in Context.   **Previewing in context** is teacher-directed activity that relies on modeling and demonstrating to students how word meanings can sometimes be inferred from context. Modeling how you go about finding clues to word

---

*Adapted from B. Bowles, "Prison Site in Georgia Marks Civil War Horror," *Detroit News,* December 11, 1988, p. 11–H.)

meanings with actual content reading materials allows students to see the practical application of this skill. As an example of how modeling can be used to help students understand some of the key vocabulary in the passage about the Andersonville Raiders, consider these previewing-in-context strategies employed by a ninth-grade teacher.

First, she read the text carefully and identified general and specific key vocabulary and all the words and terms likely to pose difficulty for her students. Her list included the following words:

debilitating	predators
strident	inhumane
depredations	emaciated
retributions	notorious
atrocities	expired

She next considered the list and pared it down to those words she felt were essential to the overall understanding of the material and consistent with her unit objectives. She included those words that could be used most instructively for teaching contextual analysis. The reason for this step was both to avoid spending too much valuable class time on teaching vocabulary and to leave several unfamiliar words for the students to analyze independently. Through this process, her list was limited to the following:

debilitating

predator

inhumane

emaciated

expired

When she directed students to each word and its surrounding context, she "thought out loud," modeling using the context to determine word meanings. She questioned students to help them discover a word's probable meaning in the existing context. Some of her specific strategies follow:

1. She spent a considerable amount of time activating students' prior knowledge for the topic. She knew that most of her ninth graders had some information about prison conditions in general. Perhaps they had seen TV documentaries of World War II concentration camps or had read about what it is like to be in prison. Using what her students already knew about the topic, she made it easier for them to figure out many difficult words in this passage, especially the word *emaciated*.

2. She reminded students of what they already knew about syntax and word order in sentences. This clue helped in narrowing the contextual definition of debilitating because it appeared between a modifier (*unhealthy*) and a noun (*conditions*).

3.   She activated students' prior knowledge acquired in other subjects. She thought it likely that the students had encountered the word *predator* in science class as a technical vocabulary word. They were shown how to apply their understanding of the word in science to this context.

4.   She impressed on the students the importance of taking advantage of obvious clues when they are provided. For instance, in the last sentence, the students were provided an obvious clue for the meaning of *expired—died*, which was used earlier in the sentence.

5.   She alerted students to clues within words; for example, the *in* in the word inhumane.

6.   She made students aware of the idea that context is more than just the few words surrounding an unknown word or the sentence in which the unknown word appears. She helped expand their notion of context to include information and ideas within, before, and after the passage.

7.   She demonstrated checking the dictionary to validate her hunches about the meaning of a word.

Previewing in context is an honest way of demonstrating how challenging it is for readers to employ contextual analysis for determining word meanings in genuine text. Although students' attempts to use context clues may not always produce precise meanings, the use of contextual analysis in conjunction with other sources and approaches should increase their comprehension and understanding.

Possible Sentences.   **Possible Sentences** is a teacher-directed prereading activity that prepares students for the technical and general vocabulary they will encounter in a reading assignment (Moore & Moore, 1986). During this activity, students make predictions about content, establish connections between words and concepts, write, discuss, and read their assignments carefully to verify their predictions. S. A. Stahl and Kapinus's (1990) research with fifth graders indicated that the Possible Sentences Activity could improve students' written recall and long-term understanding of word meanings.

The Possible Sentences Activity requires minimal advance material preparation but a considerable amount of teacher time in thinking and planning. First, the teacher identifies the general or technical vocabulary that are key to the theme of the unit and are adequately defined by the context. For this activity to succeed, at least five to eight words should be taken from a subsection of a chapter rather than three or four words dispersed across an entire chapter. For example, in the Andersonville Prison excerpt, the following words could be used for part of the lesson:

debilitating   predators   inhumane   expired

Teachers need to carefully select the targeted words because students must be able to verify their predictions by reading the text during the third step.

During the second step, the teacher asks students to select at least two words from the list and generate one sentence that they think might possibly be in the text. Students can either write their sentence before sharing or dictate their sentences to the teacher spontaneously. As students share their predicted sentences, the teacher should write them on the overhead transparency or chalkboard. Moore and Moore (1986) stress that it is important for the teacher to write the sentences just as they were dictated, even if students provide inaccurate information or use the word incorrectly. With the Andersonville Prison excerpt, students might pair the following words in this manner:

In the Andersonville Prison the *predators expired.*

During the Civil War the *inhumane* generals were *debilitating.*

Please note that the second example uses the word *debilitating* in a syntactically incorrect manner, but the teacher recorded it. This sharing of predicted sentences should continue until all the words on the list have been included in at least one sentence.

In step three, the teacher asks the students to read their text to verify the accuracy of the sentences the class created. Once students have finished their reading, during step four they evaluate the predicted sentences. Moore and Moore (1986) recommend that students ask these type of questions to evaluate the sentences: (a) Which sentences are accurate? (b) Which need further elaboration? (c) Which cannot be validated because the passage did not deal specifically with them? For example, with the first possible sentence cited previously, the teacher would want the students to realize that the predators did die, but not of a natural death. The possible sentence merely needed more elaboration (i.e., "The predators were caught, tried, and expired as a result of hanging"). With the second possible sentence, students will need to discuss the meaning and usage of the word *debilitating*, but the context should provide them an adequate model for making their evaluations and revisions.

With the fifth and final step of Possible Sentences, students are asked to create new sentences using the targeted words. This activity can be a homework assignment for the next class period, or it can occur during class as students work in pairs or share in large group discussion. As students share these sentences, everyone should be involved in checking the text as well as checking the agreed on definitions generated during class discussion.

On the plus side, the Possible Sentences Activity involves students in the elaborative thinking processes that characterize active learning. However, as with any teacher-directed activity, it will not work with all units of study. This is especially true for units containing a lot of technical vocabulary for which students may not have any prior knowledge.

Previewing in context and Possible Sentences are two teacher-directed strategies for helping students become more comfortable in using contextual analysis as a means of unlocking the meaning to difficult words. If students can learn how to use context clues in conjunction with other word-meaning approaches, they will increase their chances of understanding content-area vocabulary.

Using the Dictionary

If you have ever asked someone the meaning of a word, you were probably told to "look it up in the dictionary." You probably can also recall the frustration you felt as you tried to make sense of the entry once you found the word. Often, you were given a definition that would help only someone who already knew the meaning of the word. For example, look up the meaning of the word *conservative* in your dictionary. Did you find a definition similar to this one?

> "of or relating to a philosophy of conservatism" (*Webster's Ninth New Collegiate Dictionary*).

Did that definition help you? More importantly, would that definition help your students understand the word *conservative*? Dictionaries are not a panacea for learning the meanings of unknown words.

Interpreting a dictionary entry and identifying an appropriate and useful definition requires sophisticated thinking skills (Miller & Gildea, 1987). Thus, if students are not taught how to use a dictionary, they will have several predictable problems. One such problem is that many students target only a part of the definition, ignoring the rest of the entry (Miller & Gildea, 1987). In fact, many students do not read beyond the first definition, even though some dictionaries place the oldest and least used definition first. For example, the first meaning of *excoriate* is to "tear or wear off the skin." Imagine the difficulty students might have in comprehending text if they had only that definition for *excoriate*. A recent magazine article described how Washington officials were about to *excoriate* the FBI for the way in which they conducted their investigation. With only the first definition, students would have a rather grisly interpretation of what the FBI was about to endure. However, had students read the second definition, they would have discovered that the word also means to "denounce or censure strongly."

A second common problem students have with interpreting entries is that they find a familiar word in the definition and attempt to substitute the unknown word with the familiar word. Nist (1993) cites a good example of this with the word *liaison*. She points out the dictionary definition of the word *liaison* is "a close relationship, connection, or link." One of her students who read that definition substituted the familiar word *connection* for *liaison* and wrote the following sentence: "The storm caused a *liaison* between the two islands."

A third problem students have in using the dictionary is that they cannot construct an adequate and precise meaning from the vague and disjointed fragments provided in the entries. As McKeown (1990) points out, dictionaries give "multiple pieces of information but offer no guidance in how they should be integrated" (p. 6). Nist (1993) provides an excellent illustration of this problem with the word *vacuous.* The dictionary entry for *vacuous* is "devoid of matter, empty, stupid, lacking serious purpose." Unable to synthesize the vague parts of this definition for *vacuous,* one of Nist's students wrote this sentence: "The glass was *vacuous* because I was thirsty and drank all the Gatorade."

Do these problems that students have with dictionaries mean that we, as teachers, should avoid the dictionary in our classroom? Of course not. What we want to stress is that the dictionary, with all its limitations, can be a tool in building word knowledge. The dictionary, however, should be used in conjunction with personal experiences and textual context if students are to learn the meanings of unknown words. In short, dictionaries can validate students' hunches about words.

From our experiences as secondary teachers, we believe that students must be taught how to use and interpret the dictionary if we want them to construct useful and precise definitions. How can we help students use the dictionary? Perhaps the most important thing we can do is to avoid assignments in which we provide students lists of words to look up in the dictionary. Without the context of a sentence or paragraph, students will not be able to construct an appropriate definition for the general or technical word and consequently will not be able to apply the word correctly.

We can also help students if we point out and reinforce the following ideas about dictionaries:

1. The format and organization of a dictionary entry: For example, each dictionary has its own system or hierarchy for arranging definitions. Many dictionaries such as *Webster's Ninth New Collegiate Dictionary* list definitions in order of historical usage, thus making their last definition the most current or widely used definition. However, some list the most current or widely used definition first. Students need to know that this information can be found by reading the user's guide or introduction.

2. The abbreviations and symbols in an entry: Dictionary entries contain numerous abbreviations and symbols that initially confuse students. They need to master those abbreviations and symbols so they can decipher the entries. For example, it is important for students to know that "n, pl" stands for the plural noun form of a word.

Teacher-Directed Approaches for Building Vocabulary Knowledge

In this section we outline several different ways in which teachers can introduce and reinforce the general and technical vocabulary words that are important to students' understanding of content-area concepts. Using the principle that students will understand and remember more when they experience concepts in a direct and meaningful fashion, we begin by explaining firsthand concept development and word scavenger hunts. The next two approaches, semantic-feature analysis and graphic organizers, emphasize the importance of students' elaborative understanding of key content area vocabulary.

Firsthand Concept Development

The terminology in content textbooks is often sterile, abstract, and lifeless, which makes this content especially difficult to understand and retain and leaves students unmotivated to read. Standing before the class and stating glossary-type definitions of textbook vocabulary merely reinforces students' passivity. We need to find ways of making key terms and concepts come alive to draw students into the word-learning process and make their learning more permanent.

Firsthand concept development refers to any number of approaches that provide students ways of experiencing words (Sartain & Stahl, 1982). The premise underlying this vocabulary strategy is that information stored in long-term memory is undoubtedly a direct result of a great deal of mental, emotional, and physical involvement with the content.

In planning for the strategy, begin by identifying the most critical terms and concepts from the content. **Critical terms** are those that are essential to the overall understanding of the material, those that match your goals and themes for the unit.

After selecting these key terms and concepts, determine ways in which students can experience them. The possibilities are limitless here, but they require some careful preplanning. Ideally, students should be given opportunities to come in direct contact with the words. For instance, students about to study a unit about meteorology could be allowed to hold and inspect a barometer or a rain gauge. Unfortunately, many technical vocabulary words are too abstract to be easily represented by a physical object brought into the classroom. Therefore, you must invent ways in which abstract terminology can become tangible for students.

Bernard, a senior high psychology teacher used an inventive activity to help his students experience and understand a key concept they were preparing to read about in their textbooks. The topic was *human memory,* and the class was asked to write 10 things they did the first day of second grade. Over the initial moans and groans, Bernard insisted that each student list 10 items within a couple of minutes to "play the game" properly. Eventually, all students were busy working on their lists. When all the students were finished, Bernard asked them to read the items on their lists and to talk about how they produced the items they could not recall with certainty. Students read off such things as "met the teacher," "talked with my friends from first grade," "took my seat," "received my books," and so on. Most said they could not remember all the details about what they did the first day of second grade, but they put on their list the things they assumed they had done. Afterward, Bernard explained that the students had been "confabulating" by creating their lists of 10 things on the basis of related experience rather than on definite memory.

Defined in the traditional way, with a textbook definition, *confabulation* is a sterile term. When students were allowed to experience confabulation firsthand, however, they then had an experience to which they could affix the meaning of the concept in memory. In turn, the textbook chapter on memory should be easier to understand. Bernard said that his students remembered the meaning of confabulation and other concepts long after the unit in which they appeared had been completed, if he tied an experience to the process of learning the terms. Firsthand concept development allows for greater student involvement in the learning of new terminology and concepts, which then encourages deeper understanding of the concepts and improves the likelihood that the textual information you are stressing will be easier to comprehend.

Word Scavenger Hunts

All of us have been participants in a real scavenger hunt at some time in our lives. Remember the thrill and excitement of competing with other teams in trying to be the first to gather assorted items in a limited time? Scavenger hunts for helping students build word meanings by collecting real items and pictures are valuable because they are fun, develop cooperative learning skills, and require active involvement. These elements of the strategy ensure that vocabulary learning will be more memorable (Moore, Moore, Cunningham, & Cunningham, 1986).

An eighth-grade science class developed a genuine "learning frenzy" when given the opportunity to work in cooperative groups and compete with other groups in a **word scavenger hunt**. The teacher, Margo, had selected vocabulary words from a textbook chapter on astronomy, words for which she thought students could find actual objects, models, or pictures. She included the key terms that the students needed to learn to gain a full understanding of the important content of the astronomy unit. In compiling her master list, which follows, she included technical words she knew would be easy to collect as well as difficult words:

comet	meteor	pulsar	nova	cosmic dust
red giant	sextant	black hole	radiation	big bang
telescope	asteroid	gravity	radar	crater

Margo divided her class into teams of four students and explained the scavenger hunt to be sure that all of them understood the rules and purpose. She accomplished this by asking students to share their experiences with scavenger hunting. She then specified the conditions of the competition.

- Students must bring in objects and pictures by a certain date
- Each team should not reveal to any other team which items they collected and where they found the items until the hunt is over.

As she handed out the master list of content vocabulary words to each team, Margo explained that teams earn 3 points for an actual object, 2 points for a model or facsimile, and 1 point for a picture. A few students asked if they were allowed to draw or trace, and Margo said that such art would be admissible; however, the drawing should reflect genuine effort and should not be something put together minutes before the conclusion of the hunt. She went on to explain that an object or picture cannot count for more than one word. Teams were then given the opportunity to assign specific roles for each of their members and to discuss strategies for finding words. Teams were allowed 1 week to complete the hunt.

During the week, teams met a couple of times to update their progress in finding words and to revise strategy, if necessary. Periodically, they were reminded to maintain secrecy about the status of the hunts, which heightened the suspense of the competition. By midweek, some students were complaining that they could not find an object or picture for certain words. Margo told them that it might be impossible to collect objects or pictures for every word. Statements of this kind inevitably push teams to search out difficult words with renewed vigor just to prove the teacher wrong.

At week's end, the teams were allowed to go over their findings and tally points. Margo double-checked the teams' figures and looked over the drawings to make sure they clearly represented the words and were not thrown together haphazardly. Finally, the team with the most points was declared the winner. They were allowed to gloat over their victory only briefly, however, because Margo rewarded each team for its efforts with an opportunity to display and publish its work.

Giving them the following options, Margo asked the groups to select what they wished to do with their findings and provided the necessary materials to get them started:

- Collages with the words on cards appropriately arranged
- Slide shows developed by photographing the objects and pictures and writing a brief text
- Picture books with photographs and illustrations accompanied by a brief text
- Newspapers or comic books with pictures and illustrations accompanied by stories
- An exhibit table with objects labeled and briefly described

Not only are word scavenger hunts fun, but they also go a long way toward building relevant prior knowledge for the chapter or unit. Hunts allow students to explore the topic by collecting and reading about key vocabulary words taken from the content. Students gather a great deal of information about the topic and develop an interest in it. The benefits of the hunt last throughout and beyond the unit. For instance, in the classroom just described, students were surrounded during the unit with reminders of the topic's key terms in the form of collages on the wall, a display corner in the back of the room, and class books featured on the classroom library shelves.

The hands-on approach to gathering pictures and objects for words makes scavenger hunting a sound instructional strategy for developing vocabulary and improving comprehension (Cunningham, 1992).

Semantic-Feature Analysis

As stated throughout this chapter, to succeed with reading materials in the content areas, students must have a deep, elaborative understanding of important concepts. Semantic-feature analysis (Johnson & Pearson, 1984) is a highly effective technique for reinforcing the vocabulary essential to understanding important concepts.

Semantic-feature analysis involves building a grid in which essential vocabulary is listed along one dimension of the grid, and major features, characteristics, or important ideas are listed along the other dimension. Students fill in the grid, indicating the extent to which the key words possess the features or are related to important ideas. Once the grid is completed, students are led to discover both the shared and unique characteristics of the vocabulary words.

Figure 6–1 is a word grid created for a study of polygons. Notice that the vertical dimension contains the names of geometric figures, whereas the horizontal dimension contains important features or characteristics of these various figures. The extra spaces are there for students to add more vocabulary and features as they work through the reading material.

	opposite sides parallel	equilateral	equiangular	4-sided	3-sided	
square						
rectangle						
triangle						
rhombus						
trapezoid						

Figure 6–1   **Word grid for *polygons***

Another example of the use of word grids is provided by Aaron, a 10th-grade government teacher, who is particularly effective in teaching key terms and concepts with semantic-feature analysis. He begins by asking his class for the names of fruit, writing them on the blackboard in a vertical column as students call them out. After several fruits are listed, he writes a couple of general features of fruit along the top horizontal dimension of the grid, such as "tree grown" and "edible skin"; then he asks for additional features. Finally, he asks the class to consider each type of fruit and whether it possesses any of the features. As they go down the list of fruit, they discuss each one relative to the characteristics listed across the top, and Aaron puts a 0, 1, or 2 in the box where the fruit and feature meet on the grid. A 0 indicates that the fruit possesses none of that feature, a 1 indicates that it possesses some of that feature, and a 2 means that the fruit possesses all of the feature. When the grid is entirely filled in (Figure 6–2), Aaron explains to the students how they can, at a glance, determine the key characteristics of a particular fruit and how the fruits' similarities and differences can be determined as well.

By involving students in the construction of a simple word grid, Aaron initiates students to the semantic-feature analysis process. He goes on to explain how to build word grids for the key vocabulary in their textbook. To help students dis-

	edible skin	tree grown	bunches	citrus	fleshy
banana	0	2	2	0	2
peach	2	2	0	0	2
orange	1	2	0	2	0
apple	2	2	0	0	2
grapes	2	0	2	0	2
grapefruit	0	2	0	2	0

Figure 6–2 **Word grid for fruit**

Figure 6–3   Key vocabulary for a word grid for the Fifth Amendment

The Fifth Amendment			
*Citizens' right to remain silent Capital crime Infamous crime Indictment	Double-jeopardy *Private property cannot be taken Due process	Just compensation Deprived Compelled Offense	*Doesn't apply to military cases *Citizens' right to avoid self-incrimination

cover how the grid-building process can be applied to the content vocabulary in their texts, he presents them with a grid based on a section of a recently completed chapter that covered the Fifth Amendment. Aaron tells them that in building the grid, he first thoroughly read the selection and identified the major ideas. Next, he listed in a phrase or a single word the vocabulary that represented or was related to each idea. This step, he tells them, was followed by an examination of the list to determine which words represent the biggest ideas (indicated by asterisks in Figure 6–3).

Then, Aaron identified the words representing the important details related to the major ideas. At this point, he says, he now had enough information to organize the vocabulary and major ideas into a grid, with the major ideas across the top and the related vocabulary listed on the side (Figure 6–4).

Aaron then walks students through the process of deciding on components of the grid, discussing with them the relationship between each major idea and each vocabulary word as they fill in the grid together.

Later, as his students improve their ability to design word grids, Aaron gives them increasing responsibility to complete grids on their own. This is accomplished by providing them with partially filled-in grids containing a few key vocabulary words and major ideas or essential features. As students move through the chapter or unit of study, they expand the grid work to include additional vocabulary and features.

These students are also allowed plenty of time for class discussion and for review of the vocabulary and major ideas. They are given the opportunity to work in cooperative groups where they share their entries on the grids and review each vocabulary word, noting the pattern of numbers (0, 1, 2).

We recommend semantic-feature analysis for three reasons: (a) It is supported by solid theory and research (Baldwin, Peleg-Bruckner, & McClintock, 1985; Johnson, Toms-Bronowski, & Pittelman, 1981; Osako & Anders, 1983), (b) it is relatively easy for classroom teachers to implement and for student to use, and (c) it enables students to learn the relationships between and among the key vocabulary and major concepts in the text, thus enhancing both vocabulary development and reading comprehension (Anders & Bos, 1986).

The Fifth Amendment

	citizen's right to remain silent	private property cannot be taken	doesn't apply to military cases	citizen's right to avoid self-incrimination
capital crime				
infamous crime				
indictment				
double–jeopardy				
due process				
just compensation				
deprived				
compelled				
offense				

Figure 6–4   Word grid for the Fifth Amendment

Graphic Organizers

As we discussed in Chapter 2, schema theorists have made significant contributions to a better understanding of the reading process. One of the principle features of a schematic-theoretic perspective of reading is that the reader needs anchor points in memory for new information and ideas if they are to be assimilated and retained. For example, if you already have a firm general understanding of the earth's rotation and track around the sun, it is likely that you would find cognitive linkages for new information about the rising and receding of ice sheets relative to the earth's spin and distance from the sun. **Graphic organizers**, which structure the relationship of key vocabulary words in a visual format, can provide students the necessary anchor points for easier assimilation of textual information and ideas.

We initiated a discussion of graphic organizers in the preceding chapter as a strategy for introducing students to critical vocabulary and concepts before reading. By visually representing key vocabulary and their relationships, graphic organizers can activate and build schemata for relevant vocabulary as well as serve as a bridge between existing and new knowledge related to the topic.

Perhaps the most common organizational structure of graphic organizers is hierarchical. This is because nearly any group of vocabulary words pertaining to a

Figure 6–5   Graphic organizer for the periodic table

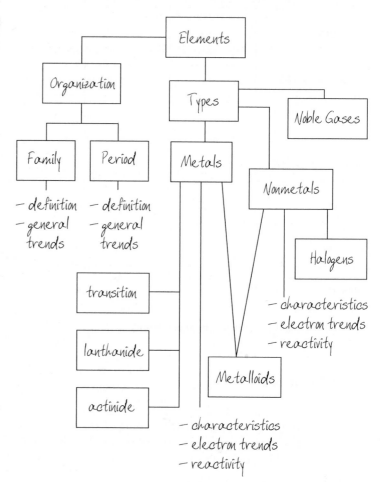

topic can be presented in a hierarchy. Hierarchies are organized with the most general information at the top and the most specific information at the bottom, as in the example of a graphic organizer for a unit on understanding the periodic table in a chemistry class (Figure 6–5).

You should, nonetheless, look for clues from the text on the best way to organize the vocabulary into a logical and interesting scheme. For example, an eighth-grade science teacher designing a graphic organizer for a chapter on rock formations noticed that the author used words such as *begins with, the next stage, it then becomes,* and *forms into again;* this led to the realization that the process was cyclical. She decided that the best way to organize vocabulary related to the formation of rock types was in a cycle (Figure 6–6). In another example of creating a visually interesting graphic organizer, a literature teacher arranged key terms used to describe the development of a story in the form of a ski slope (Figure 6–7).

The following is a description of the process that Andy, a ninth-grade health teacher, went through in designing and implementing a graphic organizer for a chapter on cigarette smoking from the health textbook. The process of constructing the organizer began with Andy's specifying what he thought were the most important ideas students should learn from a study on cigarette smoking. He decided that by emphasizing the dangers of smoking he could discourage students from taking up or continuing the habit. After establishing his theme for the unit, Andy began an analysis of the vocabulary in the chapter. He listed all the words

Figure 6–6   Graphic organizer for the formation of rocks

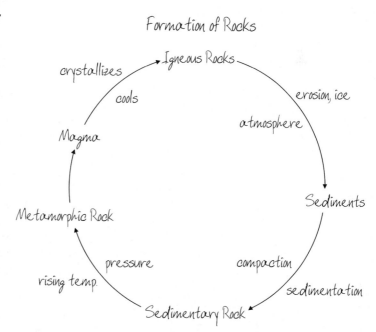

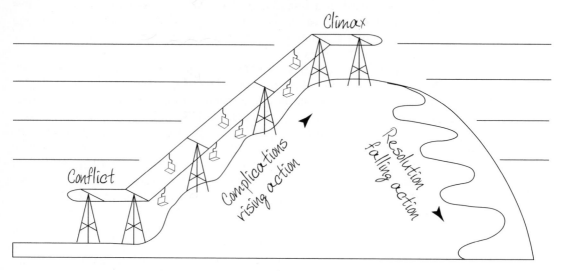

Figure 6–7   Graphic organizer for the development of a story

he felt were important relative to the theme, resulting in the following list of general and technical vocabulary terms:

cancer	nicotine
bronchitis	addiction
carbon monoxide	emphysema
hazardous	tars
heart disease	carcinogens

Next, using the text as a guide, Andy arranged the words until he had a general scheme that depicted the interrelationships among these key terms. He then added to the scheme vocabulary terms that he believed his students already understood, to reinforce the relationships between the key terms. With the initial word list and additional vocabulary words, Andy created the interesting graphic organizer in Figure 6–8, entitled "Up in Smoke."

In evaluating the organizer before giving it to his students, Andy made sure that he (a) included vocabulary appropriate to his theme, (b) depicted clearly the major relationships among the critical terms and concepts, (c) checked whether the organizer could be simplified and still effectively communicate the ideas he considered to be crucial to the topic, and (d) determined whether a good balance was struck between an organizer that was too busy, with too much information, and one that was too general or sparse.

At this point, Andy was now ready to introduce his students to the chapter by presenting the graphic organizer and informing them of his reasoning for arranging the terms as he did. He encouraged his students to contribute as much addi-

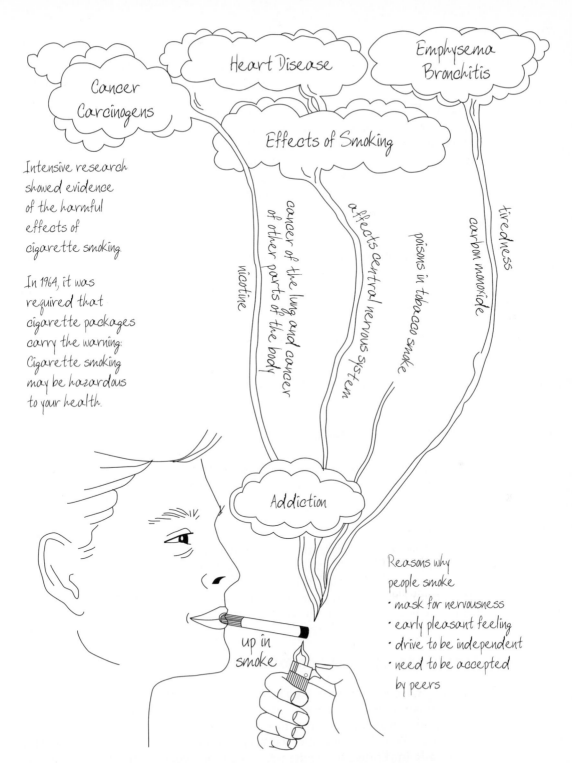

Figure 6–8   Graphic organizer for the effects of cigarette smoking on the body

tional information as possible, and he helped to focus the ensuing discussion on how each key term fit into students' prior knowledge about cigarette smoking and related health problems. Also, he pronounced each new difficult word for students. As they worked through the chapter, Andy capitalized on every opportunity to relate new information to the organizer.

Graphic organizers offer an excellent way of teaching essential vocabulary. Students can use organizers to remind themselves of what they already know about the topic, to help organize their own thinking as they move through the specific textual information, to focus their attention on important information and ideas, and to aid in long-term recall of key terms and concepts in the text. Although we have focused on the use of the graphic organizer as a vocabulary strategy for text, it should also be noted that many teachers have used graphic organizers as excellent word and concept development strategies for lectures, demonstrations, and films. Regardless of its application, the graphic organizer provides students with a conceptual framework in memory, which enhances comprehension of content material (Anderson, 1984).

These four approaches to vocabulary development—firsthand concept development, word scavenger hunts, semantic-feature analysis, and graphic organizers—are typically initiated by the content-area teacher to improve conceptual understanding.

Promoting Independent Word Learning

As we made clear earlier in this chapter, secondary classroom teachers should be concerned about two vitally important aspects of vocabulary development. One is to teach key vocabulary and concepts that students need to understand the important content, whether in a listening or reading situation. The previous section demonstrated several effective ways in which classroom teachers can help their students develop elaborative understandings of critical terms and concepts. Another equally important aspect of vocabulary development is to teach students a variety of strategies for independently gathering and learning new words. This section describes and exemplifies generative methods of vocabulary development that can be used in a variety of content areas.

Conceptual Understanding of Content-Area Vocabulary

Not every general or technical vocabulary word must be learned at the conceptual level. Without a well-developed conceptual language of a content area, however, students often become outsiders to the learning process (Moore, Readence, & Rickelman, 1982). Assuming that a conceptual understanding of key terminology is frequently imperative for content-area learning, what are the critical thinking processes involved?

Tennyson and Park (1980), in their extensive review of the research relating to concept development, proposed a four-step teaching procedure. Using their work and a review of recent vocabulary studies, Simpson (1987) suggested that conceptual understanding of content area vocabulary words should involve students in the following:

1. Recognize and generate the critical attributes, characteristics, examples, and nonexamples of a concept.
2. Sense and infer relationships between concepts and their own background information or prior knowledge.
3. Discover comparisons and contrasts between different concepts to determine meaningful similarities and differences.
4. Determine superordinate concepts and subordinate concepts related to the targeted concept.
5. Apply the concept to a variety of situations.
6. Create new examples and applications for the targeted concept.

Concept-learning strategies based on these processes will promote elaboration of key concepts and vocabulary for greater understanding and long-term retention. Many of the teacher-directed vocabulary approaches discussed earlier in this chapter, such as semantic-feature analysis, emphasize some of these processes. We discuss two more of these vocabulary strategies in the next section—word maps and concept cards. Later, we return to these six processes when we share activities that teachers have used to reinforce and evaluate students' understanding of key terminology.

Word Maps

Students will become more independent in their vocabulary learning if we provide instruction that gradually shifts the responsibility for generating word meanings for new words from us to them. One effective way of encouraging this successful transition is with word maps. Schwartz and Raphael (1985) developed this strategy for helping students establish a concept of definition for content-area words. The strategy stresses the importance of teaching students how to use context clues independently, how to determine if they know what a word means, and how to use prior knowledge to enhance their understanding of words.

To build a **word map**, students write the concept being studied, or the word they would like to define, in the center box of a map, as, for instance *quark* in Figure 6–9. Next, in the top box they write a brief answer to the question "What is it?" This question seeks a name for the class or category that includes the concept. In defining *quark*, the category is a "subatomic particle." In responding to the question to the right,"What is it like?" students write critical attributes, characteristics, or properties of the concept or word. In the example, three critical properties of quarks are listed. The question along the bottom, "What are some examples?" can be answered by supplying examples of different kinds of quarks, such as *top* and *charmed.*

Teaching students the process of creating word maps not only gives them a strategy for generating word meanings independently but also, because of the checking process they go through in asking questions of the context, fosters self-monitoring and metacognitive thinking (Schwartz, 1988). The goal, therefore, is to help students internalize this test-questioning process for all of the important words they must learn. All of us ask similar questions when we encounter unfamiliar words in context, though we rarely, if ever, draw (as in the form of a word map) the information we are seeking about the words. Think of the word map as a visual representation of students' thought processes while trying to figure out word meanings in context. Eventually, after they have demonstrated an understanding of the process by creating appropriate word maps, students should be shown that they do not have to create a map for every word they do not know. Instead, they should go through the questioning process in their heads, similar to mature readers.

To help you understand how the process of teaching students to use word maps can be accomplished in a classroom setting, the experiences of Tonya, an eighth-grade science teacher, are described. She began her vocabulary lesson by displaying the structure of the word map and introducing it as a visual guide to remind her students of what they needed to know to really understand a new, important word or concept. As the components of the map were discussed, she supplied a concept and filled in answers to the questions on the map with information from a recently studied chapter in their science textbook.

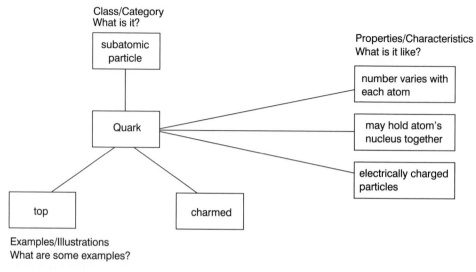

Figure 6–9 Word map for *quark*

Tonya then directed students to the chapter they were about to read and, with their help, identified a key concept found within the first few pages: *conifer.* She asked the students to work in cooperative groups to find information in their texts and in their heads to answer the questions on the word map. As they read about conifers, they discussed the relevant information that helped define the concept and inserted it into the appropriate spaces on the map they were creating. When they completed their maps, Tonya modeled how information about class/category, properties/characteristics, and examples related to the concept could be pulled from context. She talked about how contexts vary from **complete** (containing rich information) to **partial** (containing scanty information). She encouraged students to include their own information and ideas, especially with stingy contexts, to further their understanding of the word. Drawing on the input from groups, the whole class then worked together to create a word map for conifer (Figure 6–10).

At this point, Tonya asked her students to write a definition for *conifer* based on the word-map activity. Afterward, she asked students to work in their cooperative groups and evaluate each other's definitions to determine if they were complete and, if not, to write whatever additional information was needed. Definitions were then returned to their owners, who responded to the group's feedback. With their maps and definitions completed, students were shown that their work can serve as excellent study aids for long-term retention of the concept.

Tonya ended the day's lesson by assigning the students to create word maps for three other key concepts in the chapter. Before leaving, students began their assignment by identifying the possible concepts in the chapter. This procedure of modeling and assigning continued throughout the semester until Tonya felt secure that students knew how to independently employ the word-map strategy

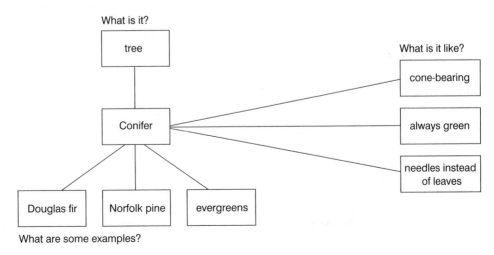

Figure 6–10   Word map for *conifer*

to their science vocabulary. She also encouraged students to try applying the strategy to their other courses.

Using word maps can help students guide their search for new information, monitor their learning of vocabulary, and improve understanding and recall of content area concepts.

Concept Cards

As with the word-map strategy, concept cards are another strategy students can use to learn difficult general or technical vocabulary (Nist & Diehl, 1990). You may have used these in your study but probably called them "flashcards." Even though **concept cards** share a common format with flashcards in that they allow students to test themselves, we prefer the term *concept cards* because they involve students in learning more than just definitions for difficult terminology. As illustrated in Figure 6–11, on the front of the concept card, students write the targeted word and the superordinate idea that the word belongs to. On the back of the card, students are to include the following information, when appropriate: (a) definition(s), (b) characteristics or features, (c) examples from the text and/or personal experiences, and (d) personal sentences. The card in Figure 6–12 illustrates how one 12th grader used concept cards to study the technical terms in her business course. Notice how she adapted the card to fit her purposes.

Students can use either 4 x 6 or 3 x 5 index cards, but it is important that they use cards rather than pieces of notebook paper because the cards encourage students to test themselves rather than to look at the terminology passively. Cards are also more durable and portable, thus permitting students the opportunity to study them when they are standing in line, riding the bus, or waiting for class to begin.

Hector, a 10th-grade English teacher, assigns students to create concept cards for the general words he must teach during the year. The words he selects for the students' study come from their literature anthology. Because he wants his students to understand the original context and to apply the word to new situations, he asks students to write the original sentence on the front of the card and at least one original sentence on the back. Hector omits the characteristics and personal examples components from the back of the card because they are not typically appropriate. However, he requires students to include antonyms of the targeted word and information as to whether the word has a positive or negative connotation. Figure 6–13 shows a concept card a student made for the word *turgid* that came from a short story.

To determine the students' accuracy in finding the most appropriate dictionary definition and for precision in writing a sentence that uses the words correctly, Hector usually checks the cards while students are working in groups on another activity. By doing these quick checks of the cards, he knows what words need to be emphasized the next day during discussion. Hector is a big believer in taking time to discuss words so students can hear the various definitions and sentences that their classmates have written. He tells us that the nuances and connotations

Figure 6–11 Content of a concept card

SUPERORDINATE IDEA

TARGETED WORD

[FRONT OF THE CARD]

---

1. Definitions

2. Characteristics: features

3. Examples (text or personal)

4. Personal sentences

[BACK OF CARD]

of words are not learned from the dictionary, but rather, they are learned from "trying on the words and playing with the words" in an environment that invites experimentation.

Hector models for the students how they should study their concept cards because he has discovered that many of them merely look at the front of their cards and then the back without testing themselves or reciting aloud. In this modeling he makes sure that students realize the importance of saying aloud the definitions and sentences. Moreover, he stresses the importance of practicing from front to back and back to front on the cards and the usefulness of making piles of cards that represent the words that are known and the words that need further study. Hector has been requiring students to make concept cards for about

Figure 6–12   A concept card by a 12th grader for technical terms in a business course

There are 2 types

FORMAL ORGANIZATION

1. Clearly defined relationships, channels of communication, and delegation of authority.

2. Characteristics: clearly defined authority relationships, well-developed communication systems, stable/permanent, capable of expansion.

3. Tools of formal organizations include charts, policy manuals, organization manuals.

4. Example: where my father works (IBM).

5 years and has noticed a substantial improvement in his students' retention of the words, and more importantly, their ultimate use of the words in their written work.

Word Sorts Using Concept Cards.   A **word sort** is an excellent reinforcement activity that students can use with their concept cards. During a word sort students group their cards into different categories that share common features. There are two types of word sorts: the closed sort and the open sort (Gillet & Kita, 1979).

With the **closed sort**, students know in advance the categories for which they must place their cards. For example, in Hector's English class, he has asked students to sort their concept cards into positive adjectives and negative adjectives.

Figure 6–13   Concept card for the word *turgid*

adjective

TURGID

The 13-page text includes a poem, an introduction, and a *turgid* opening chapter interpreting the First Seal.

1. Excessively ornate, flashy, wordy, and pompous in style or language

2. Synonym: *bombastic*   Antonym: *plain, simple language*

The minister's turgid sermon put everyone to sleep on the warm Sunday evening.

Thus, students sorted words such as *turgid, pretentious, neurotic,* and *condescending* into the negative adjectives category and placed words such as *charismatic* and *diligent* into their positive adjectives category. Hector assigns students to do this activity in small groups and then asks each group to explain and justify their groupings. Being able to manipulate the concept cards certainly makes the word-sort activity more interesting and flexible for students.

Open sorts require students to determine ways in which their general or technical vocabulary can be grouped. Therefore, students search for relationships that might exist among the words rather than depending on the teacher for that structure. In a ninth-grade science class, students were studying pollution and were asked to group their concept cards into one or more categories. The following words represent some of those words:

biodegradable

leaching

incineration

silting

photosynthesis

surface mining

acid mine drainage

reclamation projects

Can you group the words into some categories? With open sorts there are no correct categories or sorts for the cards. Instead, what is important is that students can explain and justify how they grouped the words. Possible sorts or categories with the preceding words include the broad category of land pollution. On a more specific level of sorting, categories might include causes of land pollution (i.e., silting, acid mine drainage, leaching) and solutions (i.e., biodegradable, reclamation projects). Because open sorts demand more elaborative thinking from students, they probably should be preceded by several closed sorts activities. Students, however enjoy both types of activities. More importantly, teacher preparation for this activity is minimal.

In this section we have discussed two generative strategies for helping students independently learn the meanings of technical and general vocabulary in their content-area courses. Other formats emphasizing the processes involved in conceptual understanding are certainly available. For example, Diekhoff, Brown, and Dansereau (1982) have studied the Node Acquisition and Integration Technique, and Carr (1985) has studied the vocabulary overview guide. Both of these vocabulary strategies emphasize processes similar to word maps and concept cards but with a different appearance. Teachers can create an appropriate format once they understand the processes involved in knowing a word at a conceptual level and the ways in which students can be taught to independently employ strategies. In the next section we examine how content-area teachers can reinforce and evaluate students' understanding of words with activities similar to the word sorts.

Activities for Reinforcing and Evaluating Word Knowledge

As mentioned earlier in this chapter, one characteristic of effective vocabulary instruction is that teachers reinforce students' word learning over time. That is, once targeted vocabulary words have been introduced and discussed, students need to interact with those words in a variety of new situations. Therefore, fewer words will be taught, and more instructional time will be provided for meaningful reinforcement activities and cumulative review if we want to make a difference in students' understanding of content-area textbooks.

The first vocabulary review strategies discussed, imagery and keywords, can be used across the content areas to help students learn technical and general words.

Imagery and Keywords

Have you ever created a mental picture in your mind to remember a difficult word or procedure? Many of us do this on a routine basis because we know that images can be powerful reminders. For example, if the targeted word you need to learn is *acrophobia*, what mental picture could you use to remember that the word means someone who is afraid of high places? One option would be to focus on the first part of the word, *acro* and develop the image of an acrobat who is afraid of heights walking on a tightrope high in the sky. You could follow up your image or picture with a sentence such as this, "The acrobat, who has always been afraid of high places, suffered from acrophobia." Hence, when we make pictures in our mind to help us remember what a word means or how a word relates to another word or superordinate concept, we are using the strategy of **imagery**. Research suggests that imagery can be a powerful strategy for reinforcing vocabulary knowledge (e.g., Smith, Stahl, & Neel, 1987).

The **keyword strategy** differs slightly from imagery, in that we think of catchy phrases or sentences that are related to the word we want to remember. For example, if you were having trouble remembering *amorous*, you might think about a phrase such as "more love for us," which sounds like amorous but has a synonym for the word in it. Though the research findings on the keyword and imagery strategies are positive and promising, they will not work for every vocabulary word or for every student. In addition, it is important to remember that students' personal images or catchy phrases will always be more powerful than the images or phrases provided by their teacher.

Dale, a 10th-grade biology teacher, uses a combination of imagery and keywords to help his students remember difficult definitions and relationships between concepts. During his unit on the endocrine system, he modeled the procedures he used in creating images and keywords to remember the functions of the glands and hormones in the endocrine system. One of his students, Lara, had difficulty applying the strategies, so Dale met with her during homeroom to help her. The lesson follows:

Dale: Lara, let's start with the pituitary gland and the thyrotrophic hormone. To remember the definition, we need to think of something memorable from part of the word *thyrotropic*. I'll start first, and then I'll have you help me. When I hear the word *tropic*, I think of the jungles where rain stimulates extreme growth. Thyrotropic hormones stimulate growth in the thyroid, the other part of the word.

Do you see what I did, Lara? I took parts of the word that I could remember because they were already familiar to me. Then I made up a sentence to help me remember the definition. Which word would you like to try next?

Lara: I missed *prolactin* on the pop quiz. Can we try this one?

Dale: Okay, Lara. Lets look at the word carefully—each letter and the parts. Can you divide the word into familiar parts?

Lara: Well, there is the word *pro,* which means a professional in the word *prolactin.* There is also the word *tin.*

Dale: Okay, Lara. Will either of them help you remember the definition of *prolactin*—a hormone that stimulates milk production?

Lara: No, I don't see how.

Dale: Okay. Let's see if we can play with the middle part of the word, *lac.* This part of the word sounds like what word in our language, Lara?

Lara: Lack?

Dale: That's right! Has your mother ever told you that you lack milk—that you should drink more milk if you hope to be healthy?

Lara: Yes! And I hate the stuff.

Dale: Could we use the letters *lac* to remind us of milk? Many people *lack* the correct amount of milk.

Lara: Yes, but what about the *pro* part of the word?

Dale: Good question. Could we use *pro* to remind us in some way that prolactin is a hormone that stimulates milk? Think about this for a moment, Lara.

Lara: (a few seconds later) Yes! Professional athletes should not suffer from a lack of milk. Will that work?

Dale: Will it work for you, Lara? That is what makes the difference.

Lara: Hmm. Yes, I can use that—it makes sense. Professional athletes should not suffer from a lack of milk. Prolactin stimulates milk production.

Dale: Let's review before we go to the next word, Lara. Give me the definitions of *thyrotropic* and *prolactin.*

Lara: Prolactin stimulates the production of milk, and the thyrotropic hormone stimulates the thyroid. This is easy.

Dale: The next hormone you missed on the quiz is *thyroxine.* Lara, what are the steps to this process of remembering a definition to a difficult word?

Notice how Dale encourages Lara to state the steps of this vocabulary strategy before she independently applies the strategy to another word. Had Lara not been able to use the strategy after this individual lesson, Dale would have shown her another strategy to help her keep straight the definitions and functions for the 47 different technical terms in this unit. He tries to present a variety of choices for his students because he knows that not every student will feel comfortable with concept maps or imagery. With Lara, however, imagery and key words worked once she realized the processes involved in them.

Activities and Test Formats that Reinforce and Evaluate Word Learning

If students are to learn their targeted words at a full and conceptual level of understanding, then the activities and test formats we select for reinforcement and evaluation should also match that level of thinking. Evidence suggests, however, that a mismatch often exists. For example, N. A. Stahl et al. (1987) found in their content analysis of 60 vocabulary textbooks that multiple-choice and matching formats were the predominate ways in which words were reinforced and tested. Kameenui, Dixon, and Carnine have argued that multiple-choice vocabulary tasks are "useless at best and dangerous at worst" because they cannot reveal the full dimensions of students' conceptual knowledge (1987, p. 15). Even asking students to write a definition of a word from memory does not stimulate students into conceptual understanding. Therefore, alternative reinforcement and evaluation activities are needed.

Constructing creative and appropriate reinforcement and evaluative activities can be challenging. However, several activities and formats can be incorporated into any classroom routine, homework assignment, or exam. These activities and formats involve students in a variety of elaborative thinking processes. Some of these activities and test formats follow.

Statement Plus a Request.   With the **statement plus a request** activity, students read two related statements, each containing the same targeted word. The second statement, however, asks students to demonstrate their knowledge of the underlined word by exceeding the usual simplistic definition. In a sophomore history class, a teacher included this question on her unit test:

Directions: Read the first statement carefully. Then read the second statement and answer it. Pay close attention to the italicized word.

1. Statement: Robert LaFollette was a *Progressive* with many ideas on what he wanted changed in Wisconsin.

2. Request: What are some of the *Progressive* ideas that Robert LaFollette had?

Exclusion.   Henry (1974) states that excluding is one of the basic operations involved in concept development. When students practice **exclusion**, they discriminate between, negate, and recognize examples and nonexamples. The following example is a sample from an algebra teacher's homework assignment.

Directions: Choose the one equation in each group that does not relate to the others and should be excluded. Write the letter of it in the blank after "Exclude." In the blank labeled "General Concept," write the concept that describes the remaining words.

1. a. $x^2 - y^2 = (x + y)(x - y)$
   b. $x^2 + 5x + 6 = (x + 3)(x+2)$
   c. $ax^2 + a^2x = ax(x - a)$
   d. $3x^2 + 4x^2 + 1 = 7x^2 + 1$

   Exclude: _____

   General Concept: _____

The following example of an exclusion item is from a French teacher's unit test.

1. la glace   la moutarde   le gâteau   la tarte
   Exclude: _____
   General concept: _____

Paired Word Questions.   The long-term vocabulary study by Beck et al. (1982) employed a question-asking activity that paired two targeted words. To answer these **paired word questions**, students must understand the underlined concepts or words and then determine if any relationships exist between them. The following example is one of several items that an art teacher uses during class when he pairs students for a review. Notice that he tests both technical (*avant-garde*) and general vocabulary word knowledge (*incoherent*).

Directions: Answer the following questions as completely as possible, making sure you demonstrate your full knowledge of the underlined words.

1. Would an *avant-garde* painting be *incoherent*? Why or why not?

The next example is from a review activity that a ninth-grade science teacher included in a homework assignment.

1. Why is *deterioration* by *corrosion* greater in cities than in the country?
2. What part of *flora* is particularly *vulnerable* to pollutants in the air such as SO_2?

Seeing the Big Picture.   With the format called **seeing the big picture**, students are asked to select the word or phrase that subsumes all the other words. By completing such an item, students demonstrate that they can discriminate the difference between a major concept and a detail or supporting idea. The following example illustrates how a mathematics teacher used the format in one of her review activities.

Directions: Look at the group of words below and select the one word or phrase which subsumes the other four. Circle it.

1. Distributive properties, axiom, multiplicative inverse, cancellation law, additive identities

Analogies.   **Analogies** are multifaceted in that they can involve students in knowing the synonyms or antonyms of targeted words or can encourage students in sensing the relationships between words. In fact, there are probably 50 different formats to the analogy. The following example is from a French teacher's homework assignment.

Directions: Fill in the blanks with the appropriate vocabulary word. You may use each word only once.

1. beau: mauvais :: froid: _____

The next analogy is from an 11th-grade art class. The teacher had just finished a unit on film and used items such as this for a review activity.

1. celluloid: film :: matte effect: _____

Paired Word Sentence Generation.   Traditional sentence-writing activities have never been considered particularly creative or productive. However, **paired word sentence generation** forces students to demonstrate their conceptual understanding of both words and to seek out their implied relationship to write a sentence that uses the words correctly. The following example illustrates how a history teacher incorporated sentence writing into his exam.

Directions: You will find two words below which I have purposely paired because they have some relationship to each other. Your task is to write one sentence which correctly uses both of the words and clearly demonstrates your understanding of them and their relationship to each other. The first item has been done for you as an example.

1. muckrakers, *McClure's Magazine*

The muckrakers included journalists and novelists who wrote magazines such as *McClure's Magazine* and books such as *The Jungle* to expose the evils and corruption in business and politics.

2. Wisconsin idea, referendum

Because these alternative activities and formats may initially confuse or surprise the students, a few important guidelines about their use should be remembered (Simpson, 1987). First, match the reinforcement or evaluation activity to the unit objectives or goals. Students can only demonstrate the level of conceptual understanding that they have been involved in during the unit. Second, vary the activities and formats across the school year and within the units of study. For example, a history teacher might include five exclusions, five analogies, and five paired word sentence-generation activities into a unit test to represent the different thinking processes underlying conceptual understanding. Finally, inform, practice, and discuss the differing activities and formats with students, especially before they see them on a test. If students are not accustomed to a new activity or test format, their response or score could mask their real understanding. In fact, it is always a good idea to provide a sample item, as did the history teacher for the paired word activity.

Case Study Revisited

We now return to the Parkview School District where teachers have been meeting throughout the school year to solve the problem of low vocabulary scores in their high school. After reading this chapter, you probably have some ideas on how the committee could solve this problem. Take a moment now to write your suggestions.

By the end of the school year, Liz, the Curriculum Director, and the teachers on the committee had reached only one decision. The 10th-grade biology teacher had shared an article he had read on the characteristics of effective vocabulary instruction, prompting the committee to decide that there were no "quick fixes" and that no single type of commercial materials would fully address their school's problems. Perhaps that decision was the most important, because it removed as an option the vocabulary computer program that several members were urging the school to adopt. The committee members realized that the computer program was expecting students to learn the targeted words in lists with no context and that only rote-level definitional knowledge was emphasized on the activities and quizzes. Hence, they were concerned whether or not students would learn the words well enough to be able to apply them to new situations.

Although the committee did reach agreement on the use of commercial materials for Parkview High School, they still disagreed about the English teachers' role in improving students' vocabulary. Some teachers saw the teaching of vocabulary as a time-consuming intrusion into an already very hectic teaching schedule. Moreover, they viewed vocabulary instruction as a natural and logical part of an English curriculum. Consequently, the Curriculum Director suggested that the issue be tabled for a while, at least until they had finished their intensive study of vocabulary acquisition.

During the summer the committee members were provided a stipend to read and plan further. The Curriculum Director had the money for their study because expensive commercial materials had not been purchased from the school budget.

At their first meeting, she suggested that the committee begin with some general goals rather than adopting commercial materials or another school's approach. With the focus of establishing specific goals for vocabulary instruction at their school, the teachers read intensively about vocabulary development and kept personal learning logs. They chose articles from journals in their own content area, articles from the *Journal of Reading,* and recent books on the topic. A major breakthrough occurred when one of the more vocal and negative teachers read a review of the literature explaining how vocabulary knowledge was closely related to students' understanding of what they read. She shared that information with the rest of the committee and made a rather compelling case for the importance of vocabulary knowledge to content-area learning. From that point on, very few committee members wanted only the English teachers to assume the responsibility of vocabulary development.

After considerable reading and discussion, the committee developed the following goals for Parkview High School:

1. The students should develop a long-term interest and enjoyment in developing and refining their vocabulary.
2. The students should learn some independent strategies for learning new technical and general vocabulary words.
3. The students should become skilled in the use of the dictionary, and when appropriate, contextual analysis.

Pleased with their goals, the committee members decided that their next step was to specifically outline how each of those goals could be incorporated into their own curriculum and how each department could reinforce each other.

The English teacher decided that she would teach one interesting word history a day to build her students' interest in words. She demonstrated to the committee the word *berserk* and how it originated from Norse mythology. Berserk was a fierce man who used no armor and assumed the form of a wild beast in battle. Supposedly, no enemy could touch him. Her source for these stories was Wilfred Funk's *Word Origins and Their Romantic Stories.* The biology and history teachers decided to implement "The Word of the Week," which they would choose together from something they had heard on the news or read in the newspapers. This word would be placed on the bulletin board and discussed on Mondays and reinforced throughout the week. The home economics teacher incorporated that idea with a slightly different twist. Modifying Haggard's (1982) vocabulary self-collection strategy, she had her students select the word of the week.

The committee members decided that they also needed to identify the technical vocabulary they would teach their students for each of their units, making sure that they did not try to teach too many words. They had read about the importance of teaching words intensively rather than extensively. The biology teacher recommended that they should share these words with each other so they could gain a big picture perspective of the words students were being asked to learn.

Of course, the committee did not agree on everything. By the end of the summer, they were still debating who should be responsible for teaching the fundamentals of how to use the dictionary. In addition, some teachers wanted everyone to agree that they would assign students to complete concept cards for all the new vocabulary. The others, while conceding the importance of teaching students a vocabulary strategy, wanted more flexibility in selecting the strategies. They all agreed, however, on the importance of selecting and teaching vocabulary strategies that would encourage students' conceptual understanding of important new words.

Because the school year was about to begin, the committee decided to implement the first two goals and to evaluate the impact of their unified effort at the end of the school year. They concluded, however, that students' scores on the competency-based reading test would probably not suddenly increase as a result of these small steps toward their unified effort to improve word knowledge and reading comprehension. From their readings and discussions, they realized that their goals to improve students' vocabulary knowledge would be a long-term commitment across the content areas.

Summary

In this chapter we stressed the importance of students having an elaborative understanding of technical and general vocabulary to learn in a content area. Because simple definitional knowledge of a word is not sufficient for students' textbook comprehension, teachers will need to stress the context links from what students know to what they will learn. This contextual understanding of content-area terms and concepts can be facilitated via teacher-directed approaches such as firsthand concept development, word scavenger hunts, semantic-feature analysis, and graphic organizers.

Teachers not only should stress the vocabulary of their content area but should also encourage students to become independent word learners. We therefore discussed generative vocabulary strategies such as word maps and concept cards that students can use as they read and study their assignments. Whether they are teacher-directed or student-initiated, these vocabulary strategies become even more powerful and useful when anchored in content-area lessons that emphasize teachers' demonstrations, modeling, small-group interactions, class discussion, and reciprocal teaching. None of these strategies is mutually exclusive, but they can and should be used together. For instance, combining strategies such as firsthand concept development and word scavenger hunts with previewing in context will have a stronger and more long-lasting effect than any of these strategies alone.

As with nearly all methods presented in this book, the vocabulary strategies discussed here will not always engender immediate enthusiasm for learning words or produce an immediate impact on reading comprehension. Teachers must take time to warm students up to these methods and must allow their students to develop expertise in using the vocabulary strategies.

Finally, remember that any method, regardless of its novelty, will eventually become ineffective if overused. Therefore, it is wise to vary the vocabulary strategies and reinforcement activities often to sustain students' excitement. In the end, however, any vocabulary development strategies that require students to process terms and concepts in elaborative, meaningful, and unique ways will help them understand words and text more fully and retain important concepts and ideas much longer.

References

Anders, P. L., & Bos, C. S. (1986). Semantic feature analysis: An interactive strategy for vocabulary development. *Journal of Reading, 29,* 610–616.

Anderson, R. C. (1984). The role of the reader's schema in comprehension, learning, and memory. In R. Anderson, J. Osborn, & E. R. Tierney (Eds.), *Learning to read in American schools: Basal readers and content texts.* Hillsdale, NJ: Lawrence Erlbaum.

Auten, A. (1985). Building a language-rich environment. *Language Arts, 62,* 95–99.

Baldwin, R. S., Peleg-Bruckner, Z., & McClintock, A. H. (1985). Effects of topic interest and prior knowledge on reading comprehension. *Reading Research Quarterly, 20,* 497–504.

Beck, I., & McKeown, M. (1991). Conditions of vocabulary acquisition. In R. Barr, M. Kamill, P. Mosenthal, & P. D. Pearson (Eds.), *Handbook of reading research* (Vol. 2, pp. 789–814). New York: Longman.

Beck, I., Perfetti, C. A., & McKeown, M. (1982). The effects of long-term vocabulary instruction on lexical access and reading comprehension. *Journal of Educational Psychology, 74,* 506–521.

Bowles, B. (1988, December 11). Prison site in Georgia marks Civil War horror. *Detroit News,* p. 11–H.

Carr, E. (1985). The vocabulary overview guide: A metacognitive strategy to improve vocabulary comprehension and retention. *Journal of Reading, 21,* 684–689.

Cronbach, L. J. (1942). An analysis of techniques for systematic vocabulary testing. *Journal of Educational Research, 36,* 206–217.

Cunningham, P. (1992). Content area vocabulary: Building and connecting meaning. In E. K. Dishner, T. W. Bean, J. E. Readence, & D. W. Moore (Eds.), *Reading in the content areas: Improving classroom instruction* (3rd ed., pp. 182–189). Dubuque, IA: Kendall/Hunt.

Diekhoff, G. M., Brown, P. J., & Dansereau, D. F. (1982). A prose learning strategy training program based on network and depth-of-processing models. *Journal of Experimental Education, 50,* 180–184.

Duffy, G. G., Roehler, L. R., & Mason, J. (1984). *Comprehension instruction: Perspectives and suggestions.* New York: Longman.

Gillet, J., & Kita, M. J. (1979). Words, kids, and categories. *The Reading Teacher, 32,* 538–542.

Haggard, M. R. (1982). The vocabulary self-collection strategy: An active approach to word learning. *Journal of Reading, 26,* 203–207.

Henry, G. H. (1974). *Teach reading as concept development: Emphasis on affective thinking.* Newark, DE: International Reading Association.

Jenkins, J. R., & Dixon, R. (1983). Vocabulary learning. *Contemporary Educational Psychology, 8,* 237–260.

Jenkins, J. R., Matlock, B., & Slocum, T. A. (1989). Two approaches to vocabulary instruction: The teaching of individual word meanings and practice in deriving meaning from context. *Reading Research Quarterly, 24,* 215–235.

Johnson, D. D., & Pearson, P. D. (1984). *Teaching reading vocabulary.* New York: Holt, Rinehart & Winston.

Johnson, D. D., Toms-Bronowski, S., & Pittelman, S. (1981). *A review of trends in vocabulary research and the effects of prior knowledge on instructional strategies for vocabulary acquisition.* (Theoretical Paper No. 95). Madison: Wisconsin Center for Education Research.

Kameenui, E. J., Dixon, R. C., & Carnine, D. W. (1987). Issues in the design of vocabulary instruction. In M. G. McKeown & M. B. Curtis (Eds.), *The nature of vocabulary acquisition* (pp. 129–145). Hillsdale, NJ: Erlbaum.

Konopak, B. C. (1988). Using contextual information for word learning. *Journal of Reading, 31,* 334–338.

Konopak, B. C., & Mealey, D. L. (1992). Vocabulary learning in the content areas. In E. K. Dishner, T. W. Bean, J. E. Readence, & D. W. Moore (Eds.), *Reading in the content areas: Improving classroom instruction* (3rd ed., pp. 174–182). Dubuque, IA: Kendall/Hunt.

McKeown, M. G. (1990, April). *Making dictionary definitions more effective.* Paper presented at the annual meeting of the American Educational Research Association, Boston.

McKeown, M. G., Beck, I. L., Omanson, R. C., & Pople, M. T. (1985). Some effects of the nature and frequency of vocabulary instruction on the knowledge and use of words. *Reading Research Quarterly, 20,* 522–535.

Manzo, A., & Sherk, J. (1971). Some generalizations and strategies to guide vocabulary acquisition. *Journal of Reading Behavior, 4,* 78–89.

Mezynski, K. (1983). Issues concerning the acquisition of knowledge: Effects of vocabulary training on reading comprehension. *Review of Educational Research, 53,* 253–279.

Miller, G. A., & Gildea, P. M. (1987). How children learn words: *Scientific America, 257,* 94–99.

Moore, D. W., & Moore, S. A. (1986). Possible sentences. In E. K. Dishner, T. W. Bean, J. E. Readence, & D. W. Moore (Eds.), *Reading in the content areas* (2nd ed., pp. 174–179). Dubuque, IA: Kendall/Hunt.

Moore, D. W., Moore, S. A., Cunningham, P. M., & Cunningham, J. W. (1986). *Developing readers and writers in the content areas.* New York: Longman.

Moore, D. W., Readence, J. E., & Rickelman, R. J. (1982). *Prereading activities for content area reading and learning.* Newark, DE: International Reading Association.

Nagy, W. E., Anderson, R. C., & Herman, P. A. (1987). Learning word meanings from context during normal reading. *American Educational Research Journal, 24,* 237–270.

Nagy, W. E., & Herman, P. A. (1987). Breadth and depth of vocabulary knowledge: Implications for acquisition and instruction. In M. G. McKeown, & M. E. Curtis (Eds.), *The nature of vocabulary acquisition* (pp. 19–35). Hillsdale, NJ: Lawrence Erlbaum.

Nist, S. L. (1993). *The role of context and dictionary definitions on varying levels of word knowledge.* Unpublished manuscript, University of Georgia, Athens, GA.

Nist, S. L., & Diehl, W. (1990). *Developing textbook thinking* (2nd ed.). Lexington, MA: D. C. Heath.

Osako, G. N., & Anders, P. L. (1983). The effect of reading interest on comprehension of expository materials with controls for prior knowledge. In J. Niles & L. Harris (Eds.), *In search for meaning in reading language processing and instruction.* Rochester, NY: National Reading Conference.

Sartain, H., & Stahl, N. A. (1982). *Techniques for teaching language of the disciplines.* Pittsburgh: University of Pittsburgh Press.

Schatz, E. K., & Baldwin, R. S. (1986). Context clues are unreliable predictors of word meanings. *Reading Research Quarterly, 21,* 439–453.

Schwartz, R. M. (1988). Learning to learn vocabulary in textbooks. *Journal of Reading, 32,* 108–118.

Schwartz, R. M., & Raphael, T. E. (1985). Concept of definition: A key to improving students' vocabulary. *The Reading Teacher, 39,* 198–205.

Simpson, M. L. (1987). Alternative formats for evaluating content area vocabulary understanding. *Journal of Reading, 31,* 20–27.

Smith, B. D., Stahl, N. A., & Neel, J. H. (1987). The effect of imagery instruction on vocabulary development. *Journal of College Reading and Learning, 22,* 131–137.

Stahl, N. A., Brozo, W. G., & Simpson, M. L. (1987). Developing college vocabulary: A content analysis of instructional materials. *Reading Research and Instruction, 26,* 203–221.

Stahl, S. A. (1985). To teach a word well: A framework for vocabulary instruction. *Reading World, 24,* 16–27.

Stahl, S. A. (1987). Three principles of effective vocabulary instruction. *Journal of Reading, 29,* 662–668.

Stahl, S. A., & Fairbanks, M. M. (1986). The effects of vocabulary instruction: A model-based meta-analysis. *Review of Educational Research, 56,* 72–110.

Stahl, S. A., & Kapinus, B. (1990, April). *Possible sentences: Predicting word meanings to teach content area vocabulary.* Paper presented at the meeting of the American Educational Research Association, Boston.

Tennyson, R. D., & Park, O. (1980). The teaching of concepts: A review of instructional design literature. *Review of Educational Research, 50,* 55–70.

7

The Active Learner and Writing in the Secondary Classroom

Students can write on the first day of class and on the last: they can write during and outside of class. They should recognize that writing is one extremely valuable way of learning, and of finding out what one knows and thinks, as well as showing what one knows. Writing is a way to explore and question, as well as to gain control over and exhibit knowledge of subject matter.

—Draper (1982)

Because secondary-level teachers have traditionally used textbooks as the backbone or "safety nets" to their curricula, reading has become the primary means of student learning, and the other communication processes have been virtually ignored. This situation has been especially true for writing. Langer and Applebee (1987) explained that "American children do not write frequently enough, and the reading and writing tasks they are given do not require them to think deeply enough" (p. 4). Although writing has been historically viewed as a skill reserved only for the English classroom, recent research has demonstrated that the integration of writing and reading into content-area lesson plans can greatly facilitate students' learning and thinking (Konopak, Martin, & Martin, 1992; Simpson, Hayes, Stahl, Conner, & Weaver, 1988).

In this chapter we explain why the writing process should be included across the curricula. Reading and writing are parallel processes that actively involve learners in the construction and monitoring of conceptual understanding. Many of the concepts presented in this chapter should remind you of ideas and strategies discussed in Chapters 2, 3, 5, and 6.

Case Study

Dave, a first-year teacher, is a member of the biology department at an urban high school. His students are those who plan to not attend college, and thus they differ from the students he experienced during his practice teaching. Dave is a bit frustrated because his first unit did not go well. The students appeared to be very bored with the chapters he assigned, and many did not complete any of the homework. In fact, out of his five classes, only 10 students received an "A" or "B" on the first unit exam. Dave's department chairperson has urged him to be stricter with the students. Another new teacher in the English department with whom he shares lunch duty has suggested that he incorporate more relevant reading materials and assignments into his units. Dave considers the English teacher's recommendation more intriguing than the chairperson's but does not know where to begin. He knows he wants to motivate his students into seeing biology as relevant to their lives, but he needs direction in planning his next unit. As you read this chapter, think about how Dave might incorporate writing and any other strategies into his next unit on the environment.

Reading and Writing as Constructive and Parallel Processes

If your friend observed you reading this book and asked for a synopsis, you probably could provide one with a quick glance at the table of contents. What if, however, you were asked to write a summary? Could you complete this task as quickly and easily? Find out by writing a five-sentence summary of the key ideas of the first six chapters.

Did you think about the ideas before you began to write your summary? Did you revise your ideas several times? Are your thoughts about the key ideas presented in this book more focused than when you first started to think about the task? Did you learn anything as a result of your writing? If you answered yes to any of these questions, you have experienced the power and permanence of writing. Just as reading is more than moving your eyes across the page, writing is more than "putting ideas" on paper. In fact, reading and writing are very similar activities for the active learner.

Recent research and theory suggest that reading and writing are not mirror images of each other but parallel processes in that they are both constructive (Tierney & Shanahan, 1991). By constructive, we mean that students construct meaning; it does not reside in their textbooks or in any written material. Meaning emerges from an interaction among student, text, and context or situation (i.e., the assignment, the classroom, the teacher, the audience). When students read an assignment from a textbook or write a paper, they are involved in the active process of building their own "text world" or internal configuration of meaning (Kucer, 1985). Simply put, when students grapple with questions such as "How can I factor a polynomial?" or "How can I explain in my own words the relationship between time, velocity, and distance?" they are beginning to construct meaning and create their own text.

The writing process, not unlike the reading process, has overlapping and recursive stages (Tierney & Pearson, 1983). Although the labeling of these stages is considerably diverse, the motif common to all appears to be a concern for prewriting, writing, and postwriting. Just as active learners use what they already know and set purposes before they begin to read, they also spend extended periods of time before the actual writing to plan, to discover ways of approaching the task to self-question and to identify purposes. This stage of the composing process is often ignored because of an inordinate concern for a written product that will be evaluated by the teacher (Florio-Ruane & Dunn, 1987). If students could be provided more time in class to brainstorm ideas and to discuss writing plans with their peers and their teachers, the quality of their writing would significantly increase.

The second phase of the writing process focuses on the initial draft. At this point the writer is engaged in the enormous struggle to get words onto paper and into sentences, paragraphs, and sections. As with the reading process, the writer works to make things cohere and fit between the whole and parts and among the parts (Tierney & Pearson, 1983). Most writers, however, do not follow an orderly process in this initial drafting. In fact, research suggests that mature writers engage in extensive revision of their prewriting plans so that thinking and writing shape each other (Florio-Ruane & Dunn, 1987). This stage is often misconstrued by many teachers, causing them to collect the initial draft as if it were the final product and to look for perfection in spelling, punctuation, and other mechanics. Often, teachers do not allow enough time in class for this initial drafting, or they allow no time at all. Instead, they assign the writing to be done outside of class, where other classmates and the teacher are not available for support and coaching. If students could write their initial drafts during class, teachers would then gain the timely opportunity to meet with their students to discus their problems in getting ideas down on paper. Moreover, these mini debriefing sessions can often save teachers considerable evaluation time on the subsequent final product.

The third phase of the writing process involves the revising, editing, proofreading, and polishing for readability and interest so that the text is ready for sharing with an audience. Just as active readers pause to reflect on their ideas and then reread to verify, elaborate, or evaluate, mature writers take time to read, reflect on, and evaluate their writing as another would. By taking the role of the reader during this third phase of the writing process, students begin to see their "writing" as a piece of "reading" that must make sense to another individual.

The intensity and willingness that students devote to any of these phases depend on the two conditions that we, as teachers, can control. First, most students have a very naive idea of what it takes to be a "good writer," just as they do of what it takes to be a "good reader." To them, good writing has correct spelling and grammar, whereas good reading is the accurate pronunciation of words. When teachers share with them the processes of their own writing tasks, students are surprised to discover that professionals or mature writers must evaluate and revise extensively before they concern themselves with the surface features of spelling and grammar. Second, students who have never written for anyone but the teacher often feel that their ideas are not worthy of extended writing and revision or that the teacher already understands the ideas, so there is no urgency to be explicit and clear. They also have difficulty believing in a real audience, because the writing task to them is no more than an occasion for a grade (Shaughnessy, 1977). Teachers can change this misconception by providing their students real and intriguing audiences for their writing so the urgency of communicating ideas becomes a passion and a drive.

In short, teachers can help their students understand these recursive and overlapping stages by reserving time in class for brainstorming, planning, drafting, revising, editing, and proofreading. Most importantly, teachers need to be writers, too.

How Can the Writing Process Help the Content-Area Teacher?

Content-area teachers rely heavily on their textbooks, lectures, and question–answer sessions as means of transmitting information to students (Ratekin, Simpson, Alvermann, & Dishner, 1985). Unfortunately, many students begin to expect teachers to tell them the important information so they do not have to think about ideas. Often, textbook assignments are not read, or at best, the ideas are quickly memorized for examinations and then forgotten. In short, students become passive learners, sponges soaking up details to pass exams.

The following example from a high school government class demonstrates how the sponge theory operates:

Ernesto assigns his 11th graders the first part of Chapter 2, which describes the characteristics of public opinion, and to come to class prepared for discussion. In their reading, the students come across one of the characteristics of public opinion, latency, and its corresponding definition—an opinion not yet crystallized or formed.

Marty, an especially diligent student, repeats that definition several times before coming to class, confident that he is prepared for discussion or an unannounced quiz (for which Ernesto is infamous). Ernesto lives up to his reputation. He asks the students to list and define the five characteristics of public opinion and to give an example of each. Marty, confident of the latency definition, writes the words "not yet crystallized" but gives no example. In fact, none of the students give examples, and they complain loudly about this aspect of the exam. "There were no examples in the textbook! You are not being fair! We really did read the assignment."

Was Ernesto unfair? Did Marty really understand the concept *latency* or the words "not yet crystallized"? Should Ernesto's students be expected to create examples of concepts? Although we believe Ernesto was justified in not accepting rote memorization by his students, we also believe that he could have prevented this minor student revolt by integrating the processes of reading and writing into his lesson plans. The combined use of reading and writing in this government class would have provided the students with more opportunities to construct their own definitions of the key concepts (e.g., latency) and to discover whether or not they understood. Writing is a potent means of learning that can help passive memorizers become active learners and thinkers.

Writing is a powerful means for learning because the more students manipulate content, the more they are likely to remember and understand that content (Langer & Applebee, 1987). In fact, Langer and Applebee's 3-year study of 326 students and their 23 teachers found that "any kind of written response leads to better performance than does reading without writing" (p. 130).

When students are asked to write about content-area concepts, they must select and then organize words to represent their understanding of what they have read. To accomplish this, they must relate, connect, and organize ideas from the text to one another. They must establish systematic connections and relationships between words and sentences, the sentences in paragraphs, the paragraphs in texts, and the paragraphs across texts. They must also build interrelationships between the ideas stated in the texts and their own prior knowledge, background, and purposes for reading. These are active processes. In contrast are the passive process that the students probably employed when they read about the characteristics of public opinion: calling out the words, locating definitions or details, and memorizing word-for-word those definitions or details. Had they been required to write in some manner about the reading assignment, they would have better prepared for Ernesto's exam.

Ernesto could have incorporated writing into his classroom routine in three basic ways. Perhaps the most common use of writing is to help students consolidate and review key ideas and experiences once they have finished reading. Ernesto's students could have been assigned to write a brief summary of the chapter's key ideas. In giving the assignment, he could have emphasized the importance of translating ideas into "your own words" and of creating examples. The students could have compared their summaries at the beginning of the class before the "infamous" and expected quiz.

Writing activities can also be used before students read in order to motivate, to focus their attention, and to help them draw on relevant knowledge and experience. This is the stage at which Ernesto could have capitalized on the power of writing. He could have introduced the chapter and unit by asking the students to take 5 minutes to describe in their journals the typical American's opinion about capital punishment for mass murderers. Then he could have asked them to describe their own opinions. After several students had shared their journal entries with the class, Ernesto could have asked the students to brainstorm reasons why there were so many differences in opinions across the classroom. His students would have then been better prepared to read about the five characteristics that influence political opinion, having brainstormed several of them already.

Finally, writing can be used in the content-area classroom to help students extend and reformulate knowledge. As described by Langer and Applebee (1987), this type of writing asks students to explore relationships among concepts, develop classification systems, trace causes and effects, and speculate about future developments—all higher level and elaborative thinking processes. For the chapter on public opinion, Ernesto could have asked his students to poll a representative sample of 25 individuals about an important issue and then to summarize and explain these findings in light of what they have learned thus far about public opinion.

In short, writing is valuable to you because students cannot remain passive if they are asked to put their ideas on paper. Writing activities demand participation by every student, not just those who volunteer. More importantly, writing activities can quickly inform you as to which students understand and to where the understanding breaks down, so reteaching can be planned. In the next section we discuss several important principles to guide you in the use of the writing process as a tool for learning.

Principles Guiding the Use of Writing

You can maximize the potential of writing in your classroom if you remember that writing is a process, not a product. The following principles more specifically describe the implications of the process approach to writing.

- Keep content at the center of the writing process (Tchudi & Huerta, 1983).

- Before designing a writing activity, ask yourself what you want your students to learn about your content area. Then select the activity that will best accomplish the objective: It may or may not involve writing.

- Design writing assignments that encourage active learning. Avoid asking students to do little more than passively regurgitate information. Remember that students learn more when they are required to actively manipulate concepts.

- Teach the process of writing by providing sufficient class time for students as they prewrite, write, and revise. Ample time and opportunities for prewriting discussions and brainstorming are especially important. This is not wasted class time, because you will ensure quality work by being there with your students to troubleshoot and to support and assist their efforts.

● Design writing assignments that have a real and immediate audience, whether it be other students in the class, other students in the school, community members, or imaginary individuals. If students only write for you, they will see their audience as someone who "knows it all" already and whose primary reason for reading their work is to give a grade.

● Vary the assignments and the discourse modes, moving from simple to complex. Allow students to master the narrative form before assigning the expository essay. An overreliance on the expository essay can discourage and frustrate many students. The options in Figure 7–1 emphasize many exciting possibilities for your writing assignments.

● Include publication of your students' writing in the final phase of the writing process. You can display their work on the bulletin board, in booklets, or in school newspapers. Students can also share their work

Figure 7–1   **Possible discourse modes**

Abstracts	Inquiries
Advice columns	Jokes and riddles
Advertisements	Journals, diaries
Announcements	Letters (personal, public)
Applications	Limericks
Biographical sketches	Mottoes, slogans
Brochures	News stories
Coloring books with text	Parodies
Cartoons	Petitions
Case studies	Posters
Character sketches	Proposals
Children's books	Protests
Commercials	Oral histories
Complaints	Rebuttals
Correspondence	Recipes
Demonstrations	Requests for information
Dramatic scripts	Reviews
Editorials	Songs, ballads
Eulogies	Scripts, skits, puppet shows
Feature stories	Stories
Forms	Technical reports
Games and puzzles	Tall tales
Guess who/what descriptions	Telegrams
Historical "you are there" scenes	Time capsule lists
Instructional manuals	Word problems

by reading it aloud to their classmates; you too should share your writing with your students. When students publish their work, they know they have an audience and thus, a reason for the hard work of revising, editing, and proofing their work.

Connelly and Irving (1976) once said that the single most important cause for bad writing is bad assignments. Even though bad writing assignments are never intentional, their effect is still the same. Bad writing assignments can become good assignments when certain information is communicated to the students orally and in writing. When you communicate your writing assignment to your students, they will first need to know the **purpose of the assignment**, the **topic**, the **audience**, and the **options for discourse modes**. A specific statement of purpose (e.g., "to understand the impact of words on interpersonal communication") will help students understand just why this writing is being done. The topic for the writing assignment usually originates from content and course objectives, but you will need to specify how you want the students to narrow that focus without dictating their thesis. The audience will determine the background knowledge, vocabulary, and opinions of the individual who will read the writing, whether that is you, the teacher, or another student, or a small child in the community. Ideally, writing assignments should provide students several suggestions as to possible discourse modes, rather than just a single option such as the essay. Even the most reluctant student will become intrigued by writing a letter to the editor of a local newspaper or an imaginary diary.

An effective writing assignment should also include information on the recommended process, steps, or strategies that a student might use to complete the assignment. In addition, your writing assignment should include information on your expectations for (a) length; (b) level of polish; (c) format; (d) grammar, mechanics, and spelling; and (e) how the paper will be evaluated. The following writing assignment was used by Jill, an 11th-grade American history teacher, for the unit on the Progressives. Note that she specifies the discourse mode that she wants the students to use, but she gives them choices within that mode.

We have been studying the Progressive Era for the past week. This assignment will help you summarize the key issues and assess the impact of this intriguing period in our history. I want you to imagine that you are either Dan Rather or Connie Chung and you will be interviewing Robert LaFollette or Alice Paul—who have briefly returned from the dead. What would Rather and Chung want to ask these individuals? What would the television viewers want to know about these people and this time in history? You are to write out Rather's or Chung's questions and LaFollette's or Paul's replies. Then close the interview with a written commentary by Rather or Chung that evaluates the impact of LaFollette or Paul and the Progressive Era. Your audience will be television viewers unfamiliar with this historical period.

Your first step in doing this assignment will be to review the relevant readings that we have done this week. You should also watch several news shows so you can get an idea of the range of questions that could be asked. In class on Wednesday you will have time to brainstorm and role play with a partner. By Thursday I want you to be prepared for the first draft, which we will write in class.

In grading this assignment I will use these criteria:

1. Your understanding of the Progressive Era and its impact on history.
2. Your creativity and imagination, as demonstrated by your ability to write meaningful and interesting questions, responses, and a commentary.
3. Your quality of writing: It should be clear and free of gross mechanical and spelling errors.

The final draft, which is worth 50 points, will be due at the beginning of class on Tuesday. Please use ink and write every other line. As for length, the bare minimum is 3 pages of normal handwriting. These papers will be shared in class.

After assigning this writing activity, Jill also shared some examples of interviews and commentaries from a unit on the Vietnam Era so that her students could visualize the finished product. She told us that the time she spends "frontloading" a writing assignment really pays off in the quality of work she receives from the students.

We have discussed some general principles to help ensure the success of a writing assignment in the content area. In the next section, we will describe some specific writing activities that can be adapted to any secondary classroom to improve content-area learning.

Writing Activities That Prepare Students for Learning

As discussed in Chapter 5, one way to stimulate students to process and think more elaboratively about content-area concepts is to help them make connections between what they already know or want to know and what they are about to read and study. Remember the ease of reading a difficult Russian novel like *War and Peace* after you had viewed the movie? The ease of remembering a fact-filled history chapter on the Civil War after you had visited the Shiloh and Gettysburg battlefields during your summer vacation? The same advantage can be gained by your students if you provide them relevant and concrete classroom activities such as discussing, brainstorming, organizing, and writing responses before they read their test assignments. The Guided-Writing Activity and the academic journal are two such activities.

Guided-Writing Activity

The **Guided-Writing Activity** (Smith & Bean, 1980), an instructional strategy that uses all four of the communication arts, has been researched by Konopak,

Martin, and Martin (1987). Using 11th-grade students in a history course, they found that the experimental group who used a modification of the Guided-Writing Activity generated higher quality ideas and better synthesized information on the written post-test. The steps of this strategy follow:

1. On the first day activate the students' prior knowledge on the topic of study by brainstorming and listing ideas on an overhead or chalkboard.
2. Ask the class to collectively organize and label the ideas.
3. Then ask the students to individually write on the topic using this information.
4. In preparation for the second day, assign the class to read the text and revise their explanatory writing.
5. In class on the second day, give a follow-up multiple-choice and essay exam on the text's key ideas.

To visualize how the guided-writing procedure could be incorporated into a secondary classroom, let's examine Lila's ninth-grade health class. Lila began the lesson by asking her students to write any ideas, definitions, or emotions that came to mind when they heard the words *stress* or *stressful.* She then circulated around the room and asked the class to share what they had written while a student wrote these ideas on the chalkboard. The students' reactions were varied. Some mentioned how their parents complained of too much stress in their executive-level jobs, and others commented on the stress their mothers felt trying to raise a family alone and work a full-time job at the same time. Some students pointed out that newspapers and television shows constantly focus on how to control stress to prevent serious illnesses. A few students discussed the stress they felt over trying to be accepted by the best college. When Lila was sure that everyone had contributed, she asked the students to help her categorize the list of ideas and emotions on the board. The categories that emerged from this discussion were (a) the causes of stress, (b) the feelings associated with stress, (c) the dangers of stress, and (d) the cures for stress. She next asked the students to preview (see Chapter 9) their chapter to discover which of these ideas would be included in their next assignment. The students quickly pointed out that all four ideas were included in the chapter's boldface headings. Lila then asked them to determine the headings in the textbook that were not included in their list. One student suggested that the dangers of stress were subdivided into the physical and mental effects of unrelieved stress, a differentiation they had not made in their own list. Another student pointed out that there was a separate section on adolescent stress in the chapter—a comment that generated considerable discussion and excitement.

Lila closed the class period by assigning the students to read the chapter, to focus on gathering information on those four areas, and to be prepared for discussing and writing during the next class period. On the second day, Lila began her lesson by asking the students to take out the entry they had written about stress the day before and to reread it for possible revisions. Her directions were, "Imagine that you are explaining the concept of stress to a younger brother or sister. What would you add to your original entry? Jot these ideas down." After a few minutes, she asked the students to share and discuss their ideas. As she recorded their ideas on the board, she was surprised by the number of students who volunteered and eagerly participated in the discussion. In fact, the discussion took longer than she had expected. Thus, on the third day of class, Lila returned to the writing task and asked the students to revise their original entry on stress, keeping in mind their audience, a younger brother or sister. Although this activity was not the end of her unit on stress and health, it does capsulize how one teacher used writing as a means by of helping students make connections between what is to be learned and what is already known.

Academic Journals

As Fulwiler has explained, the **academic journal** "stimulates classroom discussion, starts small group activity, clarifies hazy issues, reinforces learning, and stimulates imaginations" (1987, p. 15). Most importantly, journal writing makes it difficult for passive students to remain passive. Journals, logs, and idea books can be used in class in many different ways. In this section we examine how they can be used to start class and to stimulate passive students into thinking actively about ideas.

Have you ever begun a class by asking the infamous question "Are there any questions about the assigned reading?" If your students are like most teachers' students, the result is an uncomfortable silence. Rather than asking a question that rarely will be answered, ask your students to take our their journals and spend 5 minutes responding to what they have read. They can summarize key ideas, ask questions, or merely list pages where they become lost. A more focused approach is to write on the board an interesting quotation from the reading assignment or a statement of opinion (e.g., "The pituitary gland is the most important gland in the endocrine system") and ask the students to respond in writing. After 5 minutes you can ask student volunteers to read their entries. To help students feel more comfortable, read your entry first and then ask students to share. This brief writing activity helps the students to focus on the topic of discussion and to identify ideas that they do and do not understand.

The same procedure can be used before a lecture or lecture-discussion to stimulate students to think about a certain topic. Although we all have used a question at the beginning of class to pique our students' interest, only a few really respond. Writing in a journal for 5 minutes is one way to guarantee that all students are reacting and thinking about the course's objectives. For example, in a ninth-grade English class about to start a mythology unit, the teacher could begin the lesson by asking the students to define their concept of a myth or legend in their journals. The teacher could either have the students share their entries or merely use the writing as a way to establish mood. As discussed in the next section, these academic journals can also be used at the end of the lesson for summarizing and reacting.

Writing Activities That Encourage Students to Summarize and React

As mentioned in Chapter 2, active learners can state in their own words the key ideas of what they read, and they can synthesize, evaluate, and apply those ideas to other contexts. Most secondary-level students are not active learners but are memorizers who can regurgitate textbook or teacher statements with minimal levels of understanding and involvement. Even though it is admittedly difficult to move a student from memorization to application, this transition can be facilitated through the use of strategically planned writing assignments. The writing activities, however, must require students to do more than merely answer teacher- or text-posed questions (Langer, 1986). In this section, we will share three activities to help students summarize and interpret concepts. All of the activities can be easily integrated into the classroom routine and require minimal teacher preparation and response.

Reader Response Applied to Expository Text

As we said earlier, meaning does not reside in any written text. Rather, meaning or comprehension emerges from an interaction among the reader, the text, and the context. This concept puts into perspective your reaction to the reading assignments you had in your educational methods courses. When you first read those seemingly dry and boring textbook chapters, you almost certainly had no students of your own and no specific problems to solve (e.g., How do I motivate adolescents?). Hence, you probably remember little or nothing from them, even though you were a fluent and highly competent reader. This phenomenon also happens for your students as they read unless they are provided opportunities to explore the connections between what they already know, feel, and want to know, and the information contained in their textbooks.

One way to help students make those connections is through the **reader-response heuristic**. A heuristic is a method of inquiry, and the reader-response heuristic is a method of self-inquiry in which readers write about their own responses to certain aspects of the text. The reader-response heuristic asks readers to first write what they perceive in the text, then explain how they feel about what they see, and finally discuss the thoughts and feelings emanating from their perceptions (Petrosky, 1982). This is a personal type of writing, which is very much different from summary-type writing. Summaries are often audience-oriented tasks in that they are written exclusively for other individuals to read. On the other hand, reader-response tasks exist for the learner and the reader. Summaries and brief essays require writers to support stances and assertions with public-based information. Conversely, reader-response tasks value the examples, beliefs, and assumptions of the students.

Brozo (1988) has suggested these three generic questions to guide students in making connections to expository text:

1. What aspect of the text excited or interested you the most?
2. What are your feelings and attitudes about this aspect of text?
3. What experiences have you had that help others understand why you feel the way you do?

To visualize how the reader-response journal entry would work in a content-area classroom, consider Bob's 11th-grade history and current events class. He introduced the activity by presenting model answers he had created, talking his students through while paying special attention to how they attempted to answer these three main questions of the self-inquiry process. Bob's essay was a response to an article in *Newsweek* about the former system of apartheid in South Africa. He emphasized how this statement of feeling—that the United States should be doing more to abolish racial segregation in South Africa—was explained and supported by his personal experience of witnessing racial prejudice when he was in the Navy in South Carolina during the early 1960s. He then assigned students to go through the same process of discovering personal connections with several different articles from *Newsweek*. One student, Eric, read an article about Arab–Israeli relations. His ideas blossomed as he moved from brief responses to the three questions to a multiple-page essay. Eric's first response follows:

> Whenever I read that there might be peace among Arabs and Israelis I get real excited. I believe that when they can figure out how to solve the problem for the Palestinians, the entire Middle East will become peaceful. I know Arabs and Jews can live in peace and happiness. I'm part Lebanese and I have friends who are Jewish. If we can get along why can't they? Instead, they fight and every day more people die. My mom told me Lebanon used to be a beautiful country. Now its people and its economy are ruined. (Brozo, 1988, p. 3)

Eric's writing partner thought he had a good start and suggested he find an experience to give his feelings and ideas some authority. Together, they brainstormed possible personal connections, which helped Eric explore the roots of his feelings. Bob worked with them too, encouraging and probing Eric to be more specific about why he felt that way. In this third draft, which follows, Eric created an essay that demonstrated a genuine sensitivity to his readers by linking the text to his strong feeling and attitudes and by explaining his feelings with a vivid experience.

> Whenever I read that there might be peace among Arabs and Israelis I get real excited. I believe that when they can figure out how to solve the problem of the Palestinians, the entire Middle East will become peaceful. It seems like all the problems exist

because of the Palestinian issue. I can just think of a time when Israelis and Arabs will work, play, and grow together. I know Arabs and Jews can live in peace and happiness. I hope it happens in my lifetime. [Eric's answer to question one].

I feel so deeply about this issue for two reasons. First, I hate war and how it ruins a country's economy and most importantly, its people. And second, I'm part Lebanese, yet I have real good friends who are Jewish. [Eric's feelings].

Last year I rode twice a week to basketball practice with a Jewish guy named David. I felt close to David right away. We shared ideas and feelings about basketball and our girlfriends and geometry. We talked very personally. We became close even though we didn't get together that often outside of basketball practice.

One day David asked about my ethnic background. He was Jewish and proud of it. But who was I? An American who happens to be part Lebanese (I'm also part Italian and Irish) only by chance. I mean I could have just as easily been born an African bushman or an Alaskan Indian. My nationality is not a big deal to me. So I didn't know what to say at first to David. I was afraid to tell the whole truth. Then I thought, I like and trust this guy as a friend—he has told me many things about his Jewishness expecting me to accept and respect him, so why should I feel different?

"I'm half Lebanese," I said.

David smiled, "We're cousins. I knew there was something special about us. Salam ah likum," he said.

"Shalom," I replied. [Eric's personal experience]

(Brozo, 1988, pp. 14–15)

With the response heuristic and the assistance of both his writing partner and Bob, Eric was helped to see how his interpretations of the text on Arab–Israeli relations were mediated by his feelings and experiences. His moving responses also created a good, solid essay that supports assertions with an excellent example derived from personal experience.

The next step in the process is the sharing of essays. Bob found it to be a particularly exciting phase of the lesson because multiple viewpoints were exchanged, questioned, and debated. This sharing also gave his students a wider audience and extended feedback for the revision process.

The reader-response heuristic can be easily modified to any content area. Because Brozo's three questions were intended only to be generic stimuli, you can create content-specific questions relevant to your course objectives and your students. Remember, not every student-response entry must be turned into an essay like Eric's. Your students will profit immensely just from the processes of summarizing, interpreting, questioning, and reacting. The summary microtheme and academic journal discussed in the next section provide you with two more formats for these important processes.

Summary Microthemes and Journals

Microthemes are essays so short that they can be written or typed on a single 5 x 8-inch note card and evaluated within a matter of minutes (Bean, Drenk, & Lee,

1982). They are productive in the content areas because they ask the students to do a small amount of writing preceded by a great deal of summarizing, interpreting, synthesizing, applying, and planning. Microthemes can also be designed to emphasize different content-area objectives. The most common microtheme asks students to summarize key ideas from a reading assignment or lecture in their own words. The advantage of a student's summary recorded on an index card rather than in a journal is that the cards are much easier to handle and carry home for grading. On the other hand, the journal can provide students with an ongoing chronicle of their summaries, which they can use for test review and self-evaluation.

The following example illustrates how Ann, a 10th-grade math teacher, uses a journal assignment to encourage students to state in their own words their conceptual understanding of exponents. Notice also that the same entry could have been done on an index card.

Integral Exponents

Rule 7 is in addition to previous ones you have worked with in other chapters. In your words explain what this rule means and how you might use it to simplify 2^{-4} and $1/4^{-3}$.

Rational Exponents

1. Define radical, radicand, index, and principal root. Identify each in an example you supply.
2. The cube root of a number means _____.

The summary microtheme, as well as the academic journal, can be used in the following ways:

- To emphasize a new and important technique that has just been introduced in science, industrial arts, or home economics class, stop the class and ask students to write for 5 minutes to describe the technique to another student who was absent from class.
- To focus a class discussion that becomes rambling or dominated by just a few students, stop and ask the class to write for 5 minutes. They could respond to these questions: "What are we trying to explain?" or "Restate the key points that have been made thus far."
- To help students reflect on the key ideas of a specific unit, ask the students to review their notes and assigned readings and then to write. This activity works best when announced in advance so students can think and plan for a while. Such a synthesis is also especially advantageous for the students as a means of preparing for an examination.

Whether the students' entries are in the format of an index card or an academic journal entry, the next step is for you to decide what you will do with their written work. Walvoord (1986) suggests several options. First, you could simply go on with the lesson and hope that the writing has served its purpose in helping students summarize and focus on key concepts. Second, you could give the students an immediate chance to ask questions and clear up any confusions they may have discovered while they were writing. They could pose questions or difficulties for you to answer, or they could turn to a neighbor to share their answers and resolve their questions on their own. As the students work, you could circulate around the room to eavesdrop and troubleshoot. Finally, you could collect the cards or journals and read them for your own information. The students' writing becomes excellent feedback as to whether they learned what you had tried to teach that day. Some teachers grade this type of writing by awarding several points for each entry. Other teachers prefer to wait until the end of the quarter or unit and ask the students to hand in their five best entries. Regardless of the evaluating procedure or question posed for the students' writing, these forms of writing activities can facilitate student learning as well as provide you immediate feedback on your teaching effectiveness.

Writing Activities That Encourage Students to Extend and Reformulate

Langer and Applebee (1987) concluded from their 3-year study of 23 high school teachers that review- or summary-type writing assignments were the predominant choice in most classrooms. Although these forms of writing assignments are especially useful in courses where students must memorize large quantities of material, they will do little to develop students' higher levels of thinking. In Chapter 1 we described the recent surveys that have suggested that American schools are doing a good job of teaching the lower level skills, such as reading for details; however, those same surveys have told us that our students are deficient in higher-order thinking skills (Applebee, Langer, & Mullis, 1986). One way we can increase our students' experiences with such thinking is by providing writing assignments that ask students to extend and reformulate ideas, to think analytically. Analytical writing assignments require students to manipulate a smaller number of concepts in more complex ways, which, in turn, promotes deeper reasoning, thinking, and remembering.

So which type of writing assignment should you emphasize in your content-area classroom? Langer and Applebee suggest that a balance is healthy because each type of writing has its "place in school, particularly when writing is used selectively for particular purposes" (1987, p. 136). We have shared several writing activities that encourage students to react, connect, review, and summarize. In this section we examine other variations of the microtheme and present the SPAWN mnemonic to help teachers create analytical writing assignments.

Variations of the Microtheme

The **thesis-support microtheme** can help students discover issues and develop arguments and stances that are supported with empirical evidence. When writing a thesis-support microtheme, students must often go beyond the textbook to build a logical, cohesive argument. When students think about and research a particular issue, they actively master the unit's objectives. Most importantly, they begin to realize that their textbook presents only one point of view and that all content areas are in a constant state of controversy and flux.

An example of a thesis-support microtheme developed by an 11th-grade teacher follows:

> Directions: The purpose of this assignment is to provide you an opportunity to examine an issue in depth by taking a stand and developing a logical argument for that stand. Choose one of the following issues and select one side. You cannot take both sides— no fence sitters allowed! For the side you have selected, write a microtheme that defends that position. Use evidence and reasoning from your textbook, our discussion in class, or from your library research. Write your final draft on the index card you have been given. Class time will be provided for brainstorming, planning, and prewriting. You will be graded on your clarity of support, logic, and quantity and quality of support. HAVE FUN WITH THIS!

> 1. The media (does/does not) have an irresistible influence on public opinions.
> 2. Polling (is/is not) a scientific means of discovering what people feel on a particular issue.
> 3. The family (is/is not) the greatest influence on a young person's development of political opinions.

The teacher discussed and distributed several examples of thesis-support microthemes after announcing the assignment. Following a discussion of the assignment, he invited the class to help him do a task analysis of this seemingly simple assignment so they could plan appropriately. In addition, he provided one class period for the students who had selected the same issues to meet, debate, and brainstorm. Several days later, he set aside a class period for the students to write their initial draft so that he could be available while they wrote. The teacher reported that the students did have fun with this assignment and, more importantly, did better than usual on their unit exam.

Another variation of the microtheme, **the data-provided microtheme**, helps students with inductive reasoning and the subsequent arrangement of words, sentences, and paragraphs that signal this type of thinking. Students are provided data in a list of sentences or in a graph, table, or chart. They then must arrange the data in a logical order, connect the parts with appropriate transitions, and write general statements that demonstrate the meaning they have induced. This type of microtheme is especially useful for students who ignore or who cannot accurately interpret important visual aids, especially from math or science classes.

The secret to the microtheme is in the format of the card. Students must carefully plan what they will say and how they will say it, because they receive only one index card to record their ideas. They also learn that more is not always better. Just as a poet carefully chooses words for each poem, so will the students as they write a microtheme. What they write depends on your course objectives and content, because these variations are only a beginning.

SPAWN-ing Writing Assignments

Creating unusual and challenging assignments to stimulate students into higher levels of thinking is not always an easy task. To help in the creation of these assignments, the SPAWN acronym (Martin, Martin, & O'Brien, 1984) is very useful. **SPAWN** stands for **special powers, *problem solving, *alternative viewpoints, *what if, and *next**; each is a category of writing assignments that can encourage students to move beyond the memorization of facts. What you can do to construct such an assignment is to select one of the categories from SPAWN and to combine it with the most appropriate writing form. Refer to Figure 7–1 for some examples of writing forms that are creative and nontraditional.

Beth is a 10th-grade English teacher who decided to use the SPAWN mnemonic to help her construct possible writing topics for the book *Farewell to Manzanar* (Houston & Houston, 1974). The book fit perfectly into the sophomores' unit on prejudice and injustice, because it describes the internment of a Japanese girl in an American camp on the West Coast during World War II. Although Beth likes to give her students wide choices for their writing, she also knows that they appreciate some suggestions. Thus, she distributed the following ideas:

Option 1: Special Powers

You have the power to change any event in *Farewell to Manzanar*. You must write and tell what event you changed, how you changed it, why you changed it, and what could happen as a result of the change. For instance, what if Rodine's mother had welcomed Jeanne into the Girl Scouts? Would that affect just that part of the story, or might Jeanne's life have been totally different if she had been accepted right from the first?

After you have completed the written section of this assignment, I will meet in a group with all who elected to do this assignment. We will discuss the changes that have been made and the possible consequences.

Option 2: Alternative Viewpoints

We heard Jeanne's viewpoint of her friendship with Rodine. We were told of their experiences as their friendship began to grow through their years at Cabrillo Homes and during junior high school. After entering high school, they began to drift apart. What is Rodine's viewpoint? What happened according to her perspective? How did she feel?

Pretend that you are Rodine. Write several journal entries in which you discuss the beginning of the friendship, a few of the high points, and finally when you realized that you were no longer special friends to each other. You will have the chance to share this with others who do this same assignment.

Option 3: What If?

What if this story took place in Japan after World War II. Rodine's father was in the army as an officer in the occupational forces. He wanted her to become familiar with the Japanese culture, so she attended a Japanese school, where she was the only white person. Jeanne was in her class. Starting with Rodine's first day in class, write a story of the experiences Jeanne and Rodine had. How would life be different now that Rodine is the minority and Jeanne is the majority? You may tell your story from either Jeanne's or Rodine's point of view. You will have the opportunity to meet with others in the class to share your story and to discuss the approach that they followed for the same assignment.

Beth reported that the students enjoyed these writing options and that several of them used the SPAWN mnemonic to create their own assignments. More importantly, this writing assignment more completely measured her students' achievement of unit objectives than any multiple-choice exam she could have created.

Diverse writing tasks are available for secondary students—assignments that effectively smuggle oral and written language into the curriculum, assignments that motivate and intrigue, and assignments that can maximize students' learning and thinking. Several issues that must be resolved, however, before teachers and students feel comfortable in using writing as a way of learning. In the next section we discuss four of these.

Critical Issues Concerning the Use of Writing as a Means of Learning

The decision to use writing as a means of encouraging students' active learning changes the way many teachers view their content area, the writing process, and their responsibilities negotiating the two. As a result, numerous questions and issues are posed that need to be addressed. We deal with four of the more urgent and far-reaching of these:

1. Grading and responding to students' writing
2. Student involvement in evaluation
3. The use of writing in a testing situation to evaluate students' mastery of concepts
4. The ubiquitous research paper

Sane Methods for Grading and Responding

Pearce (1983) found in his interviews with teachers that many were hesitant to incorporate writing into their units of study because of the overwhelming amount of work that would be generated by the 100 or more students they see each day. Over the years, we have collected specific techniques from other teachers and from our own experiences that have made it feasible for students to write and teachers to survive. These techniques acknowledge that teachers have personal lives and thus, would prefer not to spend the weekend glued to the kitchen table writing comments to students about their written work. All of the techniques are based on the premise that responding is more important than grading in the writing process and in students' mastery of content-area concepts. The following are some general guidelines to expedite the process of responding and grading:

1. Remember the purpose of each writing assignment and keep content the center of your focus. If students write a journal entry, the purpose is to help them construct meaning and to learn content-area concepts. Hence, the evaluation process should reflect that and not focus on mechanics and spelling. If, however, the students have worked their way through the processes of writing, and class time has been provided for feedback at each stage, evaluate the writing as a final draft. Students should be told, in advance, the importance of their spelling, grammar, and mechanical errors in the total evaluation process. As discussed earlier, the assignment-making process should be thorough to inform students of your expectations and purposes.

2. Avoid zealous error detection as you respond to your students' writing because this type of response can consume huge amounts of your time and energy. Remember that students are more likely to make mechanical errors when they first begin to write on a topic that is unfamiliar or new to them (Shaughnessy, 1977).

3. Write at least one positive comment or reaction: Sometimes a large "yes!" does the trick.

4. Use green, purple, or orange pen, or better yet, use a pencil—any color but red, which connotes a highly punitive message.

5. Use abbreviations for comments you frequently use. For example, instead of writing Be More Specific countless times, write BP. Provide students a list of your abbreviations.

6. Troubleshoot many of the errors that students commonly make by providing them class time, in advance of the due date, to read and edit their assigned partner's rough draft. This will save you time and provide them with more sensitivity and appreciation for the writing and thinking processes.

7. Consider the possibility of not evaluating every assignment, especially journal entries or reader-response entries. Many teachers put a check in the upper corner after quickly skimming to make sure the assignment was complete. On other occasions, especially with multiple journal entries or summaries, some teachers determine in advance the one that they will grade thoroughly or ask the students to select their best papers to be graded.

8.   Severely limit the length of some assignments, as with the microthemes, which are written entirely on an index card. The important criteria should not be length, but rather the student's effectiveness in judiciously selecting the words they will explain or defend. Space limitation not only will save you time, but it will also educate your students so they will not always equate length with quality.

9.   Stagger your writing assignments across your classes so you do not require all your students to hand in their work at the same time. For example, your first- and second-period classes could hand in their writing on Mondays, your third- and fourth-period classes on Tuesdays, and your fifth- and sixth-period classes on Wednesdays.

10.   Perhaps the most important thing to remember about grading is to carefully think and plan before assigning. Writing tasks do not facilitate all types of course objectives and all types of students.

Often teacher- or text-posed questions are more effective than writing tasks when you want your students to simply memorize a large body of information (Langer & Applebee, 1987). On those rare occasions when your students are already familiar with the content and understand the relationships between concepts, writing assignments may have no major effect at all (Langer & Applebee, 1987). Nevertheless, when you want your students to move beyond memorization, writing can be a very useful tool to maximize learning.

In addition to these general guidelines, you can develop some forms (checklists, primary trait evaluation guides, and rubrics) to help decrease the amount of time devoted to providing students quality comments and responses to their written work (Pearce, 1983). These forms, which can be adapted to any content area and any assignment, are discussed next.

Checklists.   Checklists contain the general criteria that you wish to focus on when you read students' writing, whether their thesis statements or their use of support to defend a position. Rather than writing the same comment over and over again (e.g., "be more specific," "support your statements"), you merely circle the item on the checklist. In addition, the checklist allows you to indicate the level of competence the student displayed on the checklist's criteria. Figure 7–2 illustrates a type of checklist that Mary, a health teacher, used when she evaluated her students' papers about heart disease. Notice that it concentrates on content development and organization. You could easily modify such a checklist by adding different criteria.

Primary Trait Evaluations.   Much like the checklist, with **primary trait evaluations** teachers focus on the desired traits they want in their students' writing. For example, if Mary would have done a primary trait evaluation on her students' essays, it probably would resemble Figure 7–3. You have probably constructed something similar and called it your "grading template." Byers and Brostoff (1979) suggest that teachers write brief comments on students' papers and focus on one or two primary traits, especially with students' first efforts in writing about a concept. In addition, those authors recommend that content-area teach-

Figure 7–2   **Checklist for grading a health essay**

	Below Average	Average	Above Average
1. The essay has an introduction.	————	————	————
2. The essay answers the question and provides key ideas from the text or lecture.	————	————	————
3. The essay provides support for each of the key ideas.	————	————	————
4. The essay personalizes the information by relating it to situations beyond the text and lecture.	————	————	————
5. The writing is clear and organized.	————	————	————
6. The essay summarizes the findings.	————	————	————

ers write students questions rather than comments such as "be specific." Questions, they believe, force students into solving problems and interacting with the material. For example, instead of writing the comment "Be specific," Mary could write a question such as this: "Can you convince me that fitness relates to general health?"

Rubrics.   A **rubric** provides content-area teachers more structure for their responses, because it summarizes the traits or criteria as well as the characteristics of high-quality and low-quality papers (Pearce, 1983). Using the rubric as a

Figure 7–3   **Primary trait evaluation of health essay**

1. The essay lists five of the nine factors impacting heart disease. (age, sex, race, genetic factors; cholesterol and triglycerides; hypertension; diabetes; obesity; smoking; type A behavior; stress; inactivity)	5 points
2. The essay explains these five factors with statistics, examples, support.	15 points
3. The essay relates these factors to personal situations (i.e., the author assesses his/her own risks for heart disease).	15 points
4. The essay is clear and organized.	5 points
TOTAL	40 points

Figure 7–4   Scoring rubric for a health essay

An "A" Essay Would Contain

1. An introduction or thesis statement
2. A list of the factors (five minimum) impacting heart disease
3. Explanations, examples, statistics for each of the five factors
4. A personal application or assessment (i.e., the author would assess himself/herself as to the risks of heart disease)
5. An implication statement discussing solutions
6. Very good organization, few mechanical errors

A "B" Essay Would Contain

1. An introduction or thesis statement
2. A list of the factors (5 minimum) impacting heart disease
3. Explanations, examples, statistics for four of the factors
4. An attempt of a personal application
5. A summary statement
6. Good organization, few mechanical errors

A "C" Essay Would Contain

1. A list of the factors (five minimum) impacting heart disease
2. Explanations, examples, statistics for three of the factors
3. A conclusion or summary
4. Fair organization, some mechanical errors

A "D" Essay Would Contain

1. A list of the factors (three or four) impacting heart disease
2. Explanations, examples, statistics for two of the factors
3. Below-average organization and many mechanical errors

A "F" Essay Would Contain

1. A list of the factors (less than three) impacting heart disease
2. Explanations, examples, statistics for one factor
3. A list of points, poor organization, many mechanical errors

---

guide, the teacher can quickly read the students' work and respond specifically and appropriately. For Mary's assignment, the rubric might resemble Figure 7–4.

Regardless of the form you select, it is a good idea to introduce it with the assignment and ask the students to attach it to their writing assignment. In that way, the form becomes a concrete reminder for students of what the criteria will be for your responses and eventual evaluation. In the next section, we will discuss how students can participate and assist in the evaluation of their writing.

Effective Activities for Involving Students in Evaluation

Students should be involved in evaluating their writing and other students' writing if we hope for them to gain independence as learners and consumers of print.

Figure 7–5   "The Good, the Bad, and the Ugly" exercise

EXAMPLE Number 1

We employ categories for the purpose of classifying the stimuli. We note the similarities and the differences. Like the English bulldog and Labrador.

The abstraction process could be termed a stereotyping process. Rather than do that, we employ abstractions and stereotypes. Like doctors.

Abstractions can cause some real problems in interpersonal communication. General semanticists have suggested that the abstraction process causes us to overlook the differences in people and things, simply because they are all in the same category.

Always try to check with them to make sure that our responses to words are compatible with theirs.

EXAMPLE Number 2

The abstraction process is of interest to interpersonal communication. When we use the abstraction process, we employ categories for the purpose of classifying the stimuli we perceive. To conceive of the category *dog,* it is necessary for us to abstract from each of these furry creatures those characteristics they all have in common. To do this we note the similarities, but also overlook the differences.

When we categorize we obviously overlook some significant differences. An English bulldog is short, bowlegged, and waddles. On the other hand, a Lab is incredibly graceful, can jump, and has long silky hair. Yet these two dogs have much in common. Both are interested in chasing birds, barking at strangers, and playing with balls and sticks.

Abstractions can be good in that they help us deal with the incoming stimuli in our day-to-day world and provide us some predictive ability. However, the abstraction process can also cause some real problems. We often assume that the characteristics of a category will hold true for every member. General semanticists have suggested that the abstraction process causes us to overlook the differences in people and things, simply because they are all in the same category.

One way to avoid these kinds of errors with the abstraction process is to use indexing, dating, and quotation marks. What it involves is marking a word by the use of numbers or quotes or dates to indicate that dog 1 is different from dog 2. This should remind us that all dogs are not necessarily friendly, and that we must test this assumption with each dog.

Because many students have been conditioned to respond on only a mechanical level (i.e., "Did I misspell any words?") to their writing, this self-evaluation or peer evaluation takes time to develop. The advantages far outweigh the disadvantages, however, especially in terms of lightening your responsibilities as the sole responder and evaluator. In addition, if students can identify or troubleshoot some common writing problems during class, they then can use that information once they begin to revise their final product.

Over the years we have discovered several activities that help students learn how to evaluate and respond to writing. We have found it best to begin with a

Figure 7–5 *(continued)* "The Good, the Bad, and the Ugly" exercise

---

EXAMPLE Number 3

When we use the abstraction process, we employ categories for the purpose of classifying the stimuli we perceive. To conceive of the category *dog,* it is necessary for us to abstract from each of these furry creatures those characteristics they all have in common. An English bulldog is short, bowlegged, and waddles. On the other hand, a Lab is incredibly graceful, can jump, and has long silky hair. Yet these two dogs have much in common. Both are interested in chasing birds, barking at strangers, and playing with balls and sticks.

Abstractions provide us some predictive ability. The abstraction process could also be termed a stereotyping process. Although the abstraction process is useful, there are some real problems it can create in interpersonal communication. General semanticists have suggested that the abstraction process causes us to overlook the differences in people and things, simply because they are all in the same category.

One way to avoid these kinds of errors is to use indexing and dating. Like dog1, dog2 and dog3.

---

whole-class activity that involves students in judging optimal and nonoptimal written models. Another name for this activity is "The Good, the Bad, and the Ugly," because good writing samples as well as bad are shared with the students. It is best not to use actual student work but to create samples of student writing that typify what "past students" have written. Usually, these samples are combinations of student work and teacher concerns about common writing problems. The three essays in Figure 7–5 illustrate what one English teacher developed to help students objectively evaluate short essays. The essays were on the abstraction process and fit nicely into her unit on language. See if you can determine the "good", the "bad," and the "ugly" with these essays.

Students are assigned to read the samples and then assign a grade for each. After grading each, they are to rank the writing samples from best to worst. Once they have completed these tasks, the teacher then leads a discussion on the grades, ranks, and students' rationales. From our experiences with this activity, students become highly motivated to participate and defend their judgments.

When students feel comfortable with the concept of evaluating and responding to their classmates' writing, it is a good idea to pair them for peer evaluation of a writing assignment they have recently completed. One student begins by reading her paper while the other student listens, using a set of questions to guide his eventual response. The questions should vary according to the content area and assignment, but the following typify some that can be used:

1. What did you like best about your partner's paper?
2. What could be added to make the paper more interesting?
3. What facts, ideas, and evidence could be added to strengthen your partner's paper?

4. What parts are not clear?

5. What two parts should be changed or revised?

To help students remember what their partner has recommended, it is a good idea to provide students a form, such as the one in Figure 7–6. After the student read her paper, the partner shares his ideas and responses to the questions as they talk. It is important that they talk to each other about the writing rather than just exchange forms. After the talking and responding, they then switch roles. If the activity is difficult for the students or if they feel uncomfortable initially, you can model the procedure for the class by becoming the partner who responds.

A third activity can be done in small groups (Pearce, 1983). A volunteer in each group reads his paper. Then the other members of the group state ideas from their papers that either were or were not present in the paper just read. According to Pearce, each member of the group must respond. Because all students are required to participate, they profit from hearing how others have interacted with the targeted concepts. This information should assist students in revising their papers once they leave class. Moreover, this activity can also serve as an excellent review for an examination.

Figure 7–6   Student evaluation form for working in pairs

Author's Name: Peer Reviewer's Name:

Authors: Read your paper aloud to your reviewer.

Reviewer: Answer the questions below so the author has a written copy of the comments you will give them orally.

1. This paper is mainly about _____

2. The best part of the author's paper was _____
_____

3. These parts of the author's paper were not clear to me:
   a.
   b.
   c.

4. I think the author's paper could be strengthened by:
   a.
   b.
   c.

5. I think the author's paper could be even more interesting if he/she would _____
_____
_____

Reviewer and Author: Talk to each other about your ideas.

Using Writing to Test Learning

If you have ever used an essay examination in your class as a means of measuring student learning, you probably have made the same exclamations that most teachers have: "No more essays!" "These students can't write, so why should I waste my time grading these pitiful excuses for essay answers!" or "Did these students even study?" Although the most judicious use of writing is not for testing or evaluating, essay examinations should not be avoided just because students initially are inept with them. As stated in Chapter 4, writing is one of the best means, next to an individual conference with each student, to assess how well students can analytically think about content. If we expect our students to synthesize, evaluate, and apply course objectives to new contexts, we should design evaluation measures that are sensitive to those objectives. In short, true–false and multiple-choice questions should not be the only examinations that students take.

How then do we prepare students to be adept at taking essay examinations? One way to help students through their first essay test is by teaching them the processes involved in **PORPE** (**predict, organize, rehearse, practice, evaluate**), an essay preparation strategy built on research and theory in writing and metacognition (Simpson, 1986). In the initial validation study, the high-risk college freshmen trained in PORPE as a means of preparing for a psychology exam performed significantly better than an equivalent group answering short-answer questions (Simpson et al., 1988). Not only were these students' essays superior in content, organization, and cohesion, but their scores on the multiple-choice exam were also significantly superior to the control students. This study demonstrated that any student, with assistance from the teacher, can learn how to apply the steps of PORPE to improve in essay and multiple-choice test performance.

PORPE's first step, **predict**, asks students to generate some potential questions that would make good essays. To help students at this point, teachers should introduce the language used for writing essay examinations by providing them with a glossary of commonly used essay-question words such as *explain, discuss, criticize, compare,* and *contrast.* Once students understand the meaning of these essay-word starters, teachers can involve students in brainstorming possible essay questions from a specific chapter. Often, the main difficulty students have with essay prediction is that they focus on minute details rather than key ideas. Thus, try telling them to check the boldface headings and summaries for possible essay topics. Essay prediction is not easy, but all students can learn this very important step if given considerable guidance. The following questions illustrate some of the questions students predicted for their history unit on the 1950s:

1. Compare and contrast Eisenhower's term of office to Truman's term. Include in your discussion their economic and social goals, achievements, and failures.
2. Discuss the affluence and anxiety that occurred during the 1950s.
3. Discuss the Red Scare that took place during the 1950s. Include in your discussion the individuals responsible, the possible causes, and the impact of the Red Scare on our country.

The second step in PORPE, **organize**, involves students in gathering and arranging the information that will answer the self-predicted essay question. This step is very much like brainstorming and prewriting in that students map or outline answers in their own words. Content-area teachers can help students with this step by sharing their own maps or outlines that answer a predicted essay question. Students can also work in pairs to brainstorm their own organizational structure for another predicted essay question. Representatives from each pair could then share and discuss their structure and rationale on the chalkboard. The final step could be for the students to develop their own map or outline for a different essay question and to receive brief written or oral feedback from the teacher. This step encourages students to build connections among ideas so that the course content becomes reorganized into a coherent structure instead of memorized as a list of unrelated bits of information.

The third step of PORPE, **rehearse**, engages students in the active self-recitation and self-testing of the key ideas from their maps or outlines. At this point, teachers should stress the difference between the processes of *recall* and *recognition* so that students will accept and internalize the need for a rehearsal step in their study. Most of the students we have worked with think that studying is the same as "looking" at the information, and they see no differential demands between essays and multiple-choice exams. One of the major reasons why secondary students have difficulty writing essay answers is that they have not spent the concentrated time rehearsing information to transfer it to long-term memory.

To help students rehearse, we have found it useful to incorporate the talk-through strategy (see Chapter 9) at this stage. During class, students meet with their partners and practice talk-throughs for a specified amount of time. After discussing and evaluating each other's talk-through, students then write, from memory, an answer to one of their self-predicted essay questions.

The fourth step, **practice**, is the validation step of learning because students must write from recall the answers to their self-predicted essay questions in preparation for the "real" examination. Before students begin their practice, content-area teachers should provide them many examples of essay answers, good and bad, and discuss their relative merits. Teachers can also reduce students' anxiety by outlining the procedures for writing an effective answer in an actual testing situation. For example, students should be taught to read each question carefully before they begin to write, underlining key words. Next, they should be encouraged to sketch their outline or map in the margin of their test paper before they begin writing. Once they begin answering the question, they should make sure that their opening sentence rephrases the essay question and/or takes a position. Finally, students should reread the essay question to ensure that they have directly answered the given question.

The final step of PORPE, **evaluate**, requires students to evaluate the quality of their practice answers. To facilitate this process, students are given a checklist that requires them to read and evaluate their text as would a teacher. The checklist in Figure 7–7 helps students to completely and objectively evaluate their essay answer and their own readiness for the real examination that follows in a few days. Content-area teachers can introduce this final step of PORPE by arranging brief sessions when students read, discuss, and evaluate the merits of various essay answers. Once students become more accustomed to evaluating writing with a checklist, they can work in pairs to evaluate each other's essays and independently evaluate their own answers.

Even though the steps of PORPE will take some additional class time, it is important to remember that students not only will learn how to prepare for and take an essay exam, but they also will learn important course concepts. In addition, the PORPE strategy can help students prepare for multiple-choice exams, especially when the questions ask them to draw conclusions and apply information to new contexts. Thus, the essay test should not be feared by students or teachers but used when appropriate and when students have been taught the *how*.

The Research Paper

At the college level, the most common writing assignment that students encounter across the curriculum is the **research paper** or **written report** (Bridgeman & Carlson, 1985). The research paper or report is also a common assign-

Figure 7–7   Student checklist for self-evaluation

Directions: Evaluate the quality of your answer by using this checklist. If you score *above average* on the six questions, you are probably ready for the exam. If, however, you find some of your answers to the predicted essay questions to be *below average* or *average*, go back to your notes, annotation, and recitation strategies. Examine your organization (STEP TWO) again—did you leave out some key ideas or details? Repair and then go through the steps again—ORGANIZE, REHEARSE, PRACTICE, AND EVALUATE.

EVALUATING PRACTICE ESSAY ANSWERS

	Below Average	Average	Above Average
1. I directly answered the question that was asked.	1	2	3
2. I had an introductory sentence which restated the essay question and/or took a position on the question.	1	2	3
3. I organized the essay answer with key ideas or points which were made obvious.	1	2	3
4. I included in the answer *relevant* details or examples to prove and clarify each idea.	1	2	3
5. I used transitions in the answer to cue the reader. (e.g., First, Finally)	1	2	3
6. My answer made sense and demonstrated a knowledge of the content.	1	2	3

Source: From Simpson, M. L. (1986), "PORPE: A Writing Strategy for Studying and Learning in the Content Areas," *Journal of Reading, 29*, p. 411. Reprinted by permission of the publisher and the author.

ment in the secondary schools. These assignments, as Nelson and Hayes (1988) point out, require sophisticated reading and thinking skills because students must be able to identify a focused topic, locate appropriate sources, summarize key ideas, and then synthesize these ideas from the multiple sources into a coherent written product. Because of these sophisticated demands, students and teachers often become frustrated and disillusioned. Students are frustrated because they do not understand the intricate and time-consuming processes involved in writing from multiple sources. Teachers are frustrated because the products students hand in are not what they have anticipated. So what is the solution? Should content-area teachers avoid research papers or written reports? We think a better solution is to define clearly the goals of such assignments and to provide specific interventions that will help students during the processes of researching, reading, planning, and writing.

The goals of a research paper can vary along a continuum, with one type of goal emphasizing knowledge telling and the other, knowledge transformation (Nelson & Hayes, 1988). Knowledge telling requires students to locate and summarize what other individuals have stated about a certain topic. For example, a student in a history course might select to do a research paper on blacklisting or the Red Scare. Knowledge transformation involves students in reading and evaluating information in terms of a specific question or goal that they have personally established for themselves. A student doing a research paper of this type would selectively read, evaluate, and synthesize information from the sources with the goal of answering a question such as whether or not the activities and behaviors of people during the Red Scare are in any way characteristic of the present era. Knowledge telling differs significantly from knowledge transformation in that students must plan, evaluate, and synthesize more with the latter. If teachers want students to do the type of critical thinking and writing involved in knowledge transformation, then they should inform students of that when giving the assignment. Otherwise, students typically will reinterpret the research report as an assignment in which they gather information and then record that information into a paper (Nelson & Hayes, 1988).

In addition to informing students of the goals of a paper, content-area teachers can assist students by sharing with them the processes or stages involved in writing a research paper:

1. Selecting a topic or issue that is of high interest.
2. Getting started and narrowing the focus of the topic or issue by doing some initial reading and thinking.
3. Searching for more relevant sources and taking notes using your own organizational system rather than the author's.
4. Thinking and planning the organizational structure of the paper.
5. Returning to the library if necessary for additional sources to fill out your organizational structure.
6. Writing the first draft.

7. Evaluating, revising, and editing with a sense of audience.

8. Writing the final version of the paper.

Students can also profit if they are told about the time necessary to move from stage 1 and stage 8. Our experiences have suggested that students often miscalculate the time necessary to find the appropriate sources in the library. More importantly, they underestimate the time that must be devoted to the stages that follow the actual research, thinking that the actual paper can be written the night before.

Content-area teachers can facilitate students in progressing through the stages of writing a research paper in several ways. First, they can provide a reading list or key words that students can use in their library searches. Second, teachers can ask students for progress reports in the form of journal entries where students discuss what they have done and list their concerns or questions. These entries can be shared with the teacher as well as other students in group problem-solving sessions during class. Some teachers ask students to hand in writing products as a way of ensuring that students are progressing. For example, students can hand in their initial reference list, outline, or notes to demonstrate that they are on task. Such work, handed in early, also allows teachers an opportunity for providing students specific feedback. Third, teachers can require students to present to the class an oral report of their paper 1 week before the written report is due. In this way, students are forced to think about and organize their ideas for an audience other than the teacher. When students realize that they will be presenting for a "real audience," they tend to adapt and transform the information they have gathered to meet the needs of their uninformed listeners (Nelson & Hayes, 1988).

Finally, content-area teachers can help students with the research report by providing them in advance the specific criteria that will be used to grade or evaluate their work. As mentioned earlier in this chapter, explicitly describing writing assignments can prevent bad writing. Students should understand the role of mechanics, organization, content, and writing style in the grading process of their research papers. Some teachers we know use a checklist and ask students to attach it to the first page of their paper. The checklist incorporates the grading criteria and also helps students evaluate their work before handing it in. We think this is a good idea that can make the grading process somewhat easier.

The Role of Computers During the Writing Process

The use of computers is more fully addressed in Chapter 11, but it is appropriate to outline briefly how the computer could be used during the writing and learning process. Specifically, we discuss word-processing programs and their supplemental software because they seem highly compatible with the recursive nature of the writing process.

As you undoubtedly have already discovered, computer technology can be initially intoxicating for students. They hope that computers can think for them and miraculously generate quality text with little or no effort in a short amount of time. We must remind students that this technology is not inherently advantageous to the writing process. When used correctly and insightfully, however, a word-processing program can develop students' understanding of and sensitivity to how they write and can thus increase their control over their writing process (Elder, Bowen, Schwartz, & Goswami, 1989). That is, a "user-friendly" word-processing program can facilitate the recursive stages of prewriting, writing, and postwriting so that your students will take more risks in the meaning-making processes of writing and learning. In the next sections examine the role of the computer during each of these three stages.

Prewriting Stages

A word-processing program can be advantageous at the prewriting stage, because it can reduce the anxiety that some students feel about writing, especially those who will tell you that they know nothing about the topic or are unsure where to begin. With a word-processing program, students can freely and quickly brainstorm ideas, especially if they know the keyboard. They can then delete, add, and rearrange those ideas into groups, and those ideas can then be labeled and ordered. If students suffer from the "fuzzy-thinking" syndrome during their planning, they can stop and practice what Flower (1985) describes as nutshelling. Nutshelling is helpful to students who have brainstormed many ideas, but who lack a focus or precise direction. To **nutshell** on the computer, students must compress into a sentence the key idea they would like to write about and then teach that idea to someone else before they move any further in the composing process. The following example of nutshelling came from a student who was writing an essay about the novel *The Contender.*

> Through boxing and his interactions with several different people, Alfred learned that he could be a contender in life.

By taking the time to nutshell, this student began to understand what he wanted to say about the book he had just read.

In addition to brainstorming and nutshelling, **invention programs** will encourage students to "generate, expand, and make connections among their ideas" (Elder et al., 1989, p. 167). These invention programs provide students with questions or prompts (e.g., "What are the good consequences of your topic? Whom do you consider an authority on your topic?"), which help students consider what they already know about a topic and what they still need to research or explore. Some credible invention programs are SEEN (1992, Conduit), PreWrite (Boynton/Cook), Organize (Wadsworth), and Writer's Helper (1993, Conduit).

Writing Stages

Some of your students will be able to compose at the computer, but the majority will use the computer only to type their first draft, which they probably have already handwritten. Word-processing programs have many advantages at this stage of the writing process. If students know the keyboard, they can be more effective and efficient because their thoughts are almost always ahead of their finger when they write by hand. With the computer, students are more likely to experiment by trying out ideas, erasing ones they do not like, and skipping ahead and then returning to difficult introductions or transition sentences. They even can write two different versions for a sentence or paragraph, marking one by parentheses or capitals, either of which can easily be deleted later. In short, word-processing programs encourage flexibility and efficiency during the drafting stages of writing.

Postwriting Stages

The postwriting stages of the writing process include revising, editing, and proofing. After the draft has been saved and copied on the computer, students will be able to read and revise and/or share copies with their peers or teachers for feedback. This typed, double-spaced draft is far more readable, and gross mistakes, such as misspellings and punctuation omissions, are extremely obvious. Moreover, students are more likely to accept the suggestions for major revisions given by teachers and peers because the computer makes draft writing so easy. Instead of saying "Do I have to do this whole thing over?" students are more likely to say "How else can I make this draft better?" The word-processing program allows them to insert new text, combine paragraphs, move entire paragraphs or pages to different places, or delete unnecessary text.

Several word-processing commands and software packages can help students with their editing. Some word-processing programs have search commands that can identify a character or string of characters, such as a word or a mark or punctuation. The computer will then scan the entire text, stopping each time to highlight the designated character so the students can change or correct it. The search and replace command locates a character and then automatically replaces it with another (e.g., *effect* for *affect*). Many word-processing programs have spelling checkers, and some have thesauruses to help students with word choices. Some popular programs are Sensible Speller (Sensible Software), Microspell (Trigram Systems), and Webster's New World Spelling Checker (Simon & Schuster). Finally, there are software programs called *text analyzers* that provide your students with information about their word choices, wordiness, jargon, weak verbs, long sentences, and other aspects of style and diction. As with any adjunct aid, these programs must be used cautiously by informed students. You may wish to review the text analyzers entitled Writer's Workbench (AT&T), and Writer's Helper (Conduit).

As you can see, the computer, word-processing programs, and software packages have the potential for helping your students while they complete extensive written assignments for you. We realize that every teacher does not have access to 30 computers, but not all students are ready or eager to use the computer. You may wish to arrange your assignments so students can elect to use the computer at any stage of the writing process.

Case Study Revisited

At the beginning of this chapter, we shared with you the problems that Dave was experiencing in his first year teaching biology to non-college-bound students. After reading this chapter, you probably have some suggestions on how he could motivate his students into more active participating and learning. Write your suggestions now.

After talking to the English teacher and doing some of his own research and planning, Dave decided to activate his students' interest in the environment unit in several ways. Because the unit was to last approximately 9 weeks, he felt he had the time to assign students to read some literature and expository pieces other than just the textbook. In addition, he decided to actively involve his students by asking them to write about their concerns and questions rather than having them merely answer questions at the end of the textbook chapter.

Dave began the unit with an activity designed to assess his students' present attitudes toward the environment. The students were prepared for a lecture and textbook assignment when they entered class on the second day of the unit. Instead, they were greeted with Dave's slides of beautiful outdoor scenes and Jethro Tull's "Songs From the Woods" playing in the background. As the song faded, Dave shifted the slides to scenes of human filth and flotsam. Slides of dumps, incinerators, and cities were now shown, and the background music was John Prine's "Paradise." When the slides and song were finished, Dave handed out the following questionnaire:

Directions: Answer as completely as possible. There are no right or wrong answers, so feel free to express yourself.

1. Briefly, tell me how the slide presentation made you feel?
2. What was the message of the second song, "Paradise?"
3. Is there a place outdoors that you especially like to go? Where? Why?
4. Have you ever thought or read or heard about the ideas presented today? If so, tell me about them in more detail. What was the source for those ideas?

Dave read his students' responses before he assigned the next activity, which was designed to provoke them into comparing their personal feelings about the environment with society's attitudes. When his students entered the classroom on the third day, he handed them "a letter from archy," excerpted *from the life-times of archy and mehitabel* by Don Marquis (1950), and asked them to read it. The English teacher had suggested this particular piece to Dave, and he found it especially relevant.

Dave then broke the students into groups of five and gave them a study guide to provide a focus for their discussions. He circulated around the room as they discussed the questions; he joined in on groups and provoked them into thinking beyond the obvious. One of the statements on the study guide required them to estimate the date of the letter. As Dave interacted with each of the groups, they were shocked to learn that the letter had been written in 1935.

Dave then brought the class together to brainstorm all the actions and decisions people have made that have ignored archy's warnings. Because of recent media coverage, the students were able to quickly list things like the greenhouse effect, acid rain, deforestation, and the loss of wildlife. At the end of the hour, he told his students that they were going to focus on one issue, specifically the loss of wildlife.

On the next day of class, Dave handed out copies of Farley Mowatt's (1963) *Never Cry Wolf* and told them they would be reading the book for the next few days. To establish an overall purpose for their reading, he asked the students to focus on three questions: (a) Why was the wolf endangered? (b) What was the likely future of the wolf? (c) What must we do to prevent its extinction? He then read aloud the first few pages to elicit their interest and assigned the first 30 pages. Each day the students gathered in their groups to discuss and then write a group response to the "Question for the Day" that Dave had written on the board (e.g., "What were the reasons for Farley's boss giving him this assignment?" "What do you think Farley is going to find out about the wolf?"). When the students finished the book, Dave gave each of them an index card and asked them to respond to the three focus questions he had established the first day. After reading the students' microthemes, Dave led a class discussion of the book and the three questions. He was pleased with this activity because most of his students had actually read the book and some reported that it was their first.

Because Dave's next unit objective was to have his students localize and personalize the issue of endangered species, he obtained a list of locally endangered animal and plant species from the Department of Natural Resources and asked each student to select a species from the list. The librarian and English teacher suggested that he provide his students a lot of structure for the assignment, so Dave distributed a handout outlining his expectations:

You are to select one of the species from the list and gather information about its problem of survival. Specifically, I want you to include the following information in your paper: (1) past and present range and population, (2) length of time it has been endangered, (3) reasons for its being endangered, (4) why it is important that this species survive, and (5) actions currently being taken to improve its chances for survival.

You will have 2 weeks to complete this assignment. Your first step in doing the assignment will be to use the classroom library and any resources I have listed for you on the accompanying page. Read extensively and take notes for about 4 days. On the fifth day, begin organizing your ideas into an outline or map, making sure you have answered all five questions. On the sixth day, you will deliver a 3-minute presentation to the class on what you have learned thus far about your endangered species. Rough drafts of your written paper will be due on October 15. I will read them and provide you feedback. The final paper will be due October 30.

In grading this assignment, I will use these criteria:

1. How well you answered the five questions concerning your species. Were you complete? Accurate? Did you explain yourself so your best friend could understand? This part is worth 35 points.

2. Your spelling, mechanics, and grammar. This part is worth 15 points. As to length—there are five questions, so I expect 3 pages as a minimum.

Most of Dave's students attempted the assignment, so he was pleased. He realized, however, that he probably should have started on a smaller scale with a less intimidating discourse mode. After chatting with the English teacher during lunch, he decided to try letter writing because it was a less formal type of writing and was closer to talking, something his students were good at.

The next week, Dave began his final activity for the unit. The class brainstormed what could be done to stop or slow down the process of environmental degradation. When Dave asked his students what they could do, he received many blank stares. He then suggested to them that education was one answer and that they could be a part of that education process by becoming informed and involved. Dave explained that involvement can occur in many forms, but that letter writing was one powerful and permanent means of disseminating ideas. With that introduction, he assigned the students each to write a letter to his or her Senator or Representative asking for support of legislation they considered important for the protection of wildlife. After discussing proper form and decorum for a letter to a government official, the students were given time to begin their rough drafts. Dave provided feedback on all rough drafts, and by the end of the week, he held 24 letters to mail to Washington, D.C. Many students doubted whether they would receive a response, but within a month, all of Dave's students had received replies from the Senators and Representatives. Copies of the 24 letters were placed on Dave's bulletin board and shared with group members. Even after 4 months and several other units of study, the students still gathered at the bulletin board to read those letters and to discuss the status of their environment.

Dave is still struggling with ways to involve his students with the biology curriculum. He has some good days and some bad, but he feels that his students are certainly more involved than they were before, when he taught only from the textbook.

Summary

We have tried to demonstrate in this chapter that the writing process can be a powerful tool for helping students learn content-area concepts. Writing, just like reading, is a constructive process that can stimulate passive learners into becoming active learners as they grapple with the task of putting their own words on paper. Although writing can be extremely useful in teaching content, teachers must also remember that writing is not a product, but a process with overlapping and recursive stages. Sufficient instructional attention and time must be allotted to these stages so that students plan, draft, revise, edit, proofread, and polish their writing before the possibility of grading is even considered. For those teachers wondering how to evaluate students' writing, we offered some practical grading guidelines and suggestions to make the task easier and more reasonable.

This chapter was organized on the assumptions that writing can be used to help students (a) prepare for their reading assignments, lectures, demonstrations, and class discussions; (b) summarize and react to concepts; and (c) think analytically. Using those three assumptions, we presented a variety of activities: the Guided-Writing Activity, the academic journal, the reader-response heuristic, and the microtheme, as well as the SPAWNing method for creating assignments to stimulate students into higher levels of thinking and PORPE. For those teachers interested in computers or who have access to computers in their classroom, we also recommended some materials and activities for word-processing programs. Any of these writing activities could easily be incorporated into content-area lesson plans to challenge and motivate even the most reluctant learner.

References

Applebee, A. N., Langer, J. A., & Mullis, I. V. S. (1986). *The writing report card: Writing achievement in American school National Assessment of Educational Progress.* Princeton, NJ: Educational Testing Service.

Bean, J. C., Drenk, D., & Lee, F. D. (1982). Microtheme strategies for developing cognitive skills. In C. W. Griffin (Ed.), *New directions for teaching and learning* (pp. 27–38). San Francisco: Jossey-Bass.

Bridgeman, B., & Carlson, S. B. (1985). Survey of academic writing tasks. *Written Communication, 2,* 247–280.

Brozo, W. (1988). Applying the reader-response heuristic to expository texts. *Journal of Reading, 32,* 140–145.

Byers, B. K., & Brostoff, A. (1979). The time it takes managing/evaluating writing and social studies. *Social Education, 43,* 194–197.

Connelly, P. J., & Irving, D. C. (1976). Composition in the liberal arts: A shared responsibility. *College English, 37,* 670–674.

Draper, V. (1982). Writing to assist learning in all subject areas. In G. Camp (Ed.), *Teaching writing: Essays from the Bay Area Project* (pp. 147–184). Upper Montclair, NJ: Boynton/Cook.

Elder, J., Bowen, B., Schwartz, J., & Goswami, D. (1989). *Word processing in a community of writers.* New York: Garland.

Florio-Ruane, S., & Dunn, S. (1987). Teaching writing: Some perennial questions and some possible answers. In V. Richardson-Koehler (Ed.), *Educator's handbook: A research perspective* (pp. 50–83). New York: Longman.

Flower, L. (1985). *Problem solving strategies for writing.* New York: Harcourt Brace Jovanovich.

Fulwiler, T. (1987). *Teaching with writing.* Upper Montclair, NJ: Boynton/Cook.

Houston, J. W., & Houston, J. (1974). *Farewell to Manzanar.* New York: Bantam.

Konopak, B. C., Martin, M. A., & Martin, S. H. (1992). Reading and writing: Aids to learning in the content areas. In E. K. Dishner, T. W. Bean, J. E. Readence, & D. W. Moore (Eds.), *Reading in the content areas: Improving classroom instruction,* (3rd ed., pp. 296–302). Dubuque, IA: Kendall Hunt.

Konopak, B. C., Martin, S. H., Martin, M. A. (1987). An integrated communication arts approach for enhancing students' learning in the content areas. *Reading Research and Instruction, 26,* 275–289.

Kucer, S. L. (1985). The making of meaning: Reading and writing as parallel processes. *Written Communication, 2,* 319–336.

Langer, J. A. (1986). Learning through writing: Study skills in the content areas. *Journal of Reading, 29,* 400–406.

Langer, J. A., & Applebee, A. N. (1987). *How writing shapes thinking: A study of teaching and learning.* Urbana, IL: National Council of Teachers of English.

Marquis, D. (1950). *from the lifetimes of archy and mehitabel.* Garden City, NY: Doubleday.

Martin, C. E., Martin, M. A., & O'Brien, D. G. (1984). Spawning ideas for writing in the content areas. *Reading World, 11,* 11–15.

Microspell. [Computer program.] Trigram Systems.

Mowatt, F. (1963). *Never cry wolf.* Boston: Little, Brown.

Nelson, J., & Hayes, J. R. (1988). *How the writing context shapes college students' strategies for writing from sources* (Tech. Rep. No. 16). Berkeley: Center for the Study of Writing, University of California at Berkeley.

Organize. [Computer program.] Wadsworth.

Pearce, D. L. (1983). Guidelines for the use and evaluation of writing in content classrooms. *Journal of Reading, 27,* 212–218.

Petrosky, A. R. (1982). From story to essay: Reading and writing. *College Composition and Communication, 33,* 19–36.

PreWrite. [Computer program.] Upper Montclair, NJ: Boynton/Cook.

Ratekin, N., Simpson, M. L., Alvermann, S., & Dishner, E. (1985). Why teachers resist content area reading instruction. *Journal of Reading, 28,* 432–437.

SEEN. (1992). [Computer program.] Iowa City, IA: Conduit.

Sensible speller. [Computer program.] Sensible Software.

Shaughnessy, M. P. (1977). *Errors and expectations.* New York: Oxford University Press.

Simpson, M. L. (1986). PORPE: A writing strategy for studying and learning in the content areas. *Journal of Reading, 29,* 407–414.

Simpson, M. L., Hayes, C., Stahl, N., Conner, R., & Weaver, D. (1988). An initial validation of a study strategy system. *Journal of Reading Behavior, 20,* 149–180.

Smith, C. C., & Bean, T. W. (1980). The guided writing procedure: Integrating content reading and writing improvement. *Reading World, 19,* 290–294.

Tchudi, S. N., & Huerta, M. C. (1983). *Teaching writing in the content areas.* Washington, DC: National Education Association.

Tierney, R. J., & Pearson, P. D. (1983). Toward a composing model of reading. *Language Arts, 60,* 568–580.

Tierney, R. J., & Shanahan, T. (1991). Research on the reading/writing relationships: Interactions, transactions, and outcomes. In M. Kamill, P. Mosenthal, P. D. Pearson (Eds.), *Handbook of reading research* (Vol. 2, pp. 246–280). White Plains, NY: Longman.

Walvoord, B. E. F. (1986). *Helping students write well: A guide for teachers in all disciplines.* New York: Modern Language Association.

Webster's new world spelling checker. New York: Simon & Schuster.

Writer's helper. (1993). [Computer program.] Iowa City, IA: Conduit.

Writer's workbench. [Computer program.] AT&T.

Literature Across the Curriculum and Throughout Life

Real books are wonderful. These are the books you find in public places like libraries, bookmobiles, bookstores, and sometimes even in supermarkets. Real books rest beside your bed, clutter the coffee table, and stand on shelves at the ready—waiting to be lifted, opened and brought to life by your reading. Real books—each one with its own individual binding, each one sized just right for the story it houses—are written by authors who know how to unlock the world with words and to open our eyes and our hearts. Each real book has its own voice—a singular, clear voice—and each speaks words that move us toward increased consciousness.

—Peterson and Eeds (1990)

Many junior and senior high school students receive their first serious look at different cultures, historical eras and events, politics, and scientific advances of the human race through content-area textbooks. As we stated earlier, because of the demands of limited space, adoption committees, and readability constraints, textbook publishers often present a distilled version of content-area information. Emphasis is on important facts, broad views, pivotal characters, and general effects on whole populations, resulting, inevitably, in a detached tone and dry material.

But we must not forget that within each of these cultures, social movements, historical eras, and scientific advances lie richly detailed stories about the people who made them or who watched them being made and were affected by them. The narrative element—the stories that lie within all human interactions—is often left out of many content-area lessons. Yet, it is narrative that can bring the content to life.

One of the most instructive precedents for bringing content material to life is Selma Lagerlof's book *The Wonderful Adventures of Nils* (1912), written for and adopted by the public schools of Sweden in 1907 and a rare example of textbook and trade book successfully written as one. In this adventure-filled story, Nils, a boy-turned-to-elf, sails back and forth across Sweden astride a barnyard goose as the author subtly acquaints the reader with an encyclopedia of knowledge about that country. Lagerlof recognized the value of story and exploited it fully by stringing dry, educational subjects on the thread of exciting adventures and the engaging character of Nils Holgersson.

Children learn to read with stories. In fact, their early reading experiences include story reading exclusively. So it is not surprising that for many children the transition to content textbooks employing expository structures leads to their first difficulties with reading (Atwell, 1987; Frew, 1990). We believe that one very effective response to the difficulties students may experience with reading textbooks, not only in the transitional middle grades but in secondary school as well, is for the content-area teacher to continue to exploit students' past successes with literature by using narratives in conjunction with textbooks.

In Chapter 2, we described some important instructional requisites for developing the higher levels of literacy many secondary students seem to lack. Literature, when used appropriately with textbooks, can become a powerful teaching tool for expanding literacy. This approach builds relevant prior knowledge, capitalizes on the student's skill in reading narrative, engenders interest and motivation and, consequently, promotes a deeper understanding and appreciation of the content in both trade books and textbooks.

This chapter has two main thrusts. It is devoted primarily to ways in which young adult literature can be skillfully integrated into the content curriculum to make it more palatable, comprehensible, and memorable. Additionally, we discuss ways in which teachers can encourage students to make reading an integral part of their lives outside the classroom.

Case Study

Linda is a high school teacher who has two junior-level American history classes. In planning a unit, "Immigration to the United States," she established three primary goals. First, she wanted her students to recognize and appreciate that the United States is made up of immigrants from virtually every country of the world and they have played a role in the creation of our country and our culture. Second, she wanted her students to be able to recognize, explain, and describe the concept of *cultural diversity* and be able to determine the advantages and challenges that cultural diversity has brought to this country. Finally, she wanted her students to be able to recognize and appreciate both the specific contributions and the specific problems associated with Jews and African-Americans in the United States.

During the year, the class discussed immigration several times as it related to various eras of our country's history. For example, they studied Spanish, French, English, German, and Swedish immigration during colonial times; Irish immigration in the 1820s and 1840s; and the forced immigration of blacks into slavery.

To the Reader: As you read and work through this chapter on the use of literature to improve content learning and develop the reading habit, consider ways that Linda could incorporate young adult books and other literature sources into her unit in order to meet her goals. Think about how the strategies described and those from your own experience and imagination could be applied to the teaching of a unit on immigration.

What Is Young Adult Literature?

According to Carlsen and Sherrill (1988), any literature read by young adults is considered young adult literature. Although we know that adolescents read a great variety of texts, there is a type of literature that is especially relevant to their interests and needs. For our purposes, **young adult literature**, **adolescent literature** and **trade books for young adults** all refer to books (a) written or marketed primarily for teenagers; (b) with main characters similar in age to the teenage readership (young adults between the ages of approximately 12 and 25) and to which teenagers can personally relate; (c) with relatively uncomplicated plot lines; (d) that match the interests, needs, and concerns of teenagers; and (e) not specifically targeted to young adults but that attract a young adult readership.

There are several major genres or types of young adult books. Indeed, the world of young adult literature is wonderfully rich, with countless high-quality books of fiction and nonfiction that cover a wide range of topics. The best of these books (a) develop honest, credible characters, (b) avoid condescending or preachy tones, and (c) allow readers to leave themselves and enter a new world only to return to oneself a changed person (Huck, 1982).

- Historical fiction: Historical fiction allows adolescents to appreciate important historical events on human terms, from the eyes of individuals of adolescent age who experienced history.
- Coming of age: Most young adults enjoy reading books about characters who are grappling with the transition from childhood to adulthood. These books are capable of moving young adults toward maturity.

- Science fiction: Young adults who are interested in science are often great fans of science fiction. By the same token, quality science fiction books can play an important role in gaining students' interest in science.

- Fantasy: Reed (1988) points out that fantasy may be the most appropriate genre to meet the needs of adolescents who are on a quest to discover where they fit into world. The dominant theme of fantasy books is the quest for good and for truth.

- Mystery and suspense: This genre has been a timeless favorite among young adults, going back to the Nancy Drew and Hardy Boys books. Today, many excellent tales of mystery and suspense are available to adolescents.

- Nonfiction: A very important genre of adolescent literature, nonfiction books written for teens draw them into the reading and learning process like no textbook ever could. Nonfiction books are typically written by authorities who cover topics from dinosaurs to dating using engaging and informative writing styles and from the perspectives of young adults. According to some (Ellis, 1987), nonfiction is the most frequently read literature among adolescents.

Guidelines for Integrating Literature in Content Classrooms

The contributions that young adult literature can make to the teaching of subject matter are limited only by your own sensibilities, because the union of trade book and textbook seems to rest on firm theoretical underpinnings. Researchers (Dillon, 1989; Eccles & Wigfield, 1985) have shown that attitudinal and motivational factors have a direct influence on students' literacy development and content learning. Reed (1988) has observed that teenagers will quickly turn off to reading if they find texts difficult or boring. On the other hand, Mathewson (1985), in reviewing research on the influence of affect in the reading process, observed that when students find reading pleasurable and interesting, their positive attitudes toward reading rapidly become generalized to most other subjects, which leads to a deeper love of reading as a primary source of information and enjoyment. Furthermore, students' reading comprehension has been shown to be greater with high-interest materials, because interesting material better maintains their attention and is motivating (Frager, 1993; Maria, 1990).

Although literature can be a powerful motivator for reading and writing, combining its use with content-area textbooks is compelling also from a schema-building perspective. In earlier chapters you learned that schema theorists posit that the more developed the knowledge structures readers possess about a particular topic, the greater the likelihood they will have successful experiences in dealing with new information related to that topic. The most important instructional implication of schema theory is for teachers to build bridges between new information, the material from which our students are expected to learn, and students' prior knowledge (McNeil, 1987). Stories written in familiar narrative style, can provide the background information and call to mind related ideas, building the foundation for easier assimilation of textual information.

Vye, Rowe, Kinzer, and Risko (1990) point to another major advantage of combining textbooks with trade books. When literacy instruction is kept separate from mathematics, science, and social studies, students learn the message that math knowledge is relevant only in math class, that science knowledge is relevant only in science class, and that social studies knowledge is relevant only in social studies class. Identifying this compartmentalized approach to teaching and learning as "inert" knowledge (Brandsford & Vye, 1989), Vye and her associates demonstrated in their research that using literature in social studies helps to circumvent problems of inert knowledge. By integrating literature in the social studies classroom, the teacher in their research project was able to help students use the cross-curricular content as a tool to better understand the social studies information and the functionality of their learning.

The union of trade book and textbook can be supported theoretically, as we have shown, and has been recommended by numerous scholars, researchers, and teachers (Brozo & Tomlinson, 1986; Fuhler, 1991; Guzzetti, Kowalinski, & McGowan, 1992; Huck, 1986; Levstik, 1990; McGowan & Guzzetti, 1991; Reed, 1985; Renner & Carter, 1991; Sanacore, 1990; J. Smith, 1993; V. Smith, Scott, & Coskrey, 1990; Stover, 1988; Swiebold, 1984).

The duration and scope of any lesson or series of lessons that integrates trade book and textbook will depend on the topic and on your judgments and preferences. Throughout this book we have noted the benefits of planning and teaching in units, whereby students experience a series of lessons often lasting up to several weeks that revolve around a unifying theme with related subtopics. The primary benefit of this approach to both you and your students is time—sufficient time to investigate a topic thoroughly through reading, discussion, writing, and research and, therefore, time to get interested in and excited about learning while producing considered responses. The following guidelines and methods are most applicable to unit-based teaching.

Identify Salient Themes and Concepts

The process of identifying important themes and concepts for a unit of study is essential for integrating appropriate trade literature. Trade books and textbooks should be bridged by overarching themes and concepts related to the most important information and ideas of the unit. The process involves first deciding what it is you want your students to know as a result of the unit and then using this theme as a guide, identifying the related concepts and subtopics.

Textbooks are usually organized by units, which make them helpful in identifying broad themes for unit plans. As we have recommended before, however, you should develop unit themes that are meaningful to you and your students, regardless of the extent to which the topics are dealt with in the textbook. In this way, you can take advantage of your own and your students' special skills or interests. We have stressed the importance of this step many times throughout this book. It involves deciding what students should take away from their study of the content so that instruction can focus on the ideas and information that are most important to you and your students.

Unfortunately, while they are excellent dispensers of facts, textbooks often lack explicit development of important themes. Therefore, you must infer essential ideas and information from texts. Try asking yourself the following questions as you look over a textbook unit:

- What are the driving human forces behind the events?
- What phenomena described in the textbook have affected ordinary people (including me and my students) or may do so in the future?
- What universal patterns of behavior related to this reading should be explained?

Answers to these questions will go a long way toward helping you decide what students should know as a result of the unit and thereby will provide direction for selecting appropriate trade books to tie in with the theme. For example, when Debbie, a seventh-grade social studies teacher, applied these questions to the textbook's unit on Australia, she inferred that the geography of a place affects the lives of its inhabitants. Because this theme seemed particularly apparent in the case of Australia with its curiously evolved wildlife and bush country life-styles, Debbie believed that this would be an advantageous context in which to teach it.

To further illustrate the process of establishing important themes related to textbook topics, consider the following excerpt about the Nazis, the Jews, and the Holocaust taken from an eighth-grade history/social studies book. Indeed, the quoted paragraphs are the extent of text related to the Holocaust in this history book. As you read the excerpt, ask yourself the three questions just posed. Then write down a theme you believe would be important to teach related to this content.

> As Allied forces were advancing, they found prison camps called *concentration camps* in various parts of Germany. The Nazis had herded millions of people into these camps. The largest group of prisoners was made up of Jews, both from Germany itself and from the conquered countries. Other prisoners included thousands of non-Jews who had opposed the Nazis.
>
> Many people had died of disease and starvation in the camps. Thousands of others had been put to death, most commmonly in gas chambers. This was part of Hitler's plan to kill off all the people he considered "unacceptable." No one was spared—not even the young and the very old. Six million Jews and perhaps as many non-Jews were murdered in what is now known as the Holocaust (that is, the terrible destruction). (Graff, 1980, p. 660)

You probably found that the preceding text is like most textbook prose. It covers the details, but offers little specific direction for identifying the underlying critical themes and concepts. By asking our three recommended questions, however, we believe you can identify one of the most important themes of this content—*the dangers of prejudice*—only hinted at in the sweeping, factual account of Nazism and the Holocaust.

After establishing a theme for a unit of study, we recommend that you explore the content further to identify important concepts and subtopics related to the unit's theme. To accomplish this, we recommend a highly useful process known as **webbing** (Huck, Hepler, & Hickman, 1987). Beginning with the unit topic or theme written in the center of a large piece of paper, you, with help from your students, generate related subtopics and write them around the main topic. These ideas may come directly from the text or prior knowledge. Figure 8–1 is an example of a web constructed by Debbie and her seventh-grade social studies class for their unit on Australia.

The connections between subtopics (indicated by broken lines in Figure 8–1) are indicative of another important benefit of unit teaching: The scope of a unit is broad enough to reveal relationships between different aspects of a topic, thereby helping students knit information together, expand schemata, and improve overall understanding of the topic. With the completed web, Debbie then decided which subtopics were most relevant to the theme of the unit. Rarely is there time to cover every aspect of a topic generated in the webbing process, and some subtopics must be deemphasized or omitted entirely—even though the information may be covered in the text. Finally, under the subtopic headings to be included in the unit, she listed related literature and activities (Figure 8–2). We

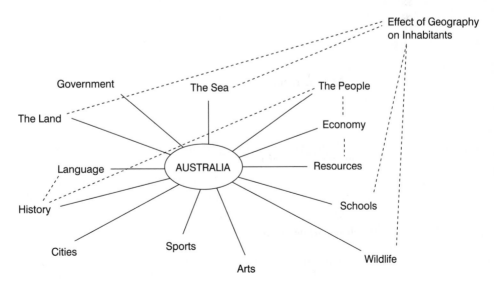

Figure 8–1   Web for a unit on Australia

Figure 8–2 Web for a unit on Australia, including appropriate young adult books

will talk more about how Debbie organized instruction with multiple trade books later in this chapter.

Identify Appropriate Literature to Help Teach Concepts

Once an important theme for the unit is established and related subtopics and concepts have been identified, the next step is to find trade books that are thematically and conceptually related.

Obviously, this approach to content-area instruction requires you to be familiar with a great variety of young adult books. To make selection easier, many bibliographies, reference guides, lists, and reviews of current young adult literature are available. In most cases, the selections in these guides are based on quality, and reading levels are often included. Some of the most helpful of these references can be found in Figure 8–3.

Figure 8–3   A list of useful guides to young adult books

Abrahamson, R. F., & Carter, B. (1988). *Books for you: A booklist for senior high students*. Urbana, IL: National Council of Teachers of English. This is a comprehensive annotated guide to literature appropriate for teenagers. Books are grouped by topics.

American Library Association. (1990). *Selecting materials for children and young adults: A bibliography of bibliographies and review sources*. Chicago: Author. This extremely useful guide contains annotations of over 300 books and review sources of children's and young adult literature.

Bogart, G. L., & Carlson, K. R. (1988). *Senior high school library catalog*. New York: Wilson. An annotated bibliography of fiction and nonfiction, updated every five years and supplemented annually.

Carlsen, G. R. (1988). *Books for young adults*. Iowa City: Books for Young Adults, University of Iowa. This list is based on a poll conducted by Robert Carlsen of the University of Iowa of readers between age 16 and 19 reacting to some 300 new books. The list contains 30 fiction and nonfiction titles and a special list of titles that are especially useful for classroom study. The list usually appears in the January issue of the *English Journal*.

Children's Science Book Review Committee. (1994). *Appraisal: Science books for young people*. Arlington, VA: National Science Teachers Association. This source (published triannually), rates books and provides grade levels of primarily nonfiction science books. A very useful guide for selecting literature to use in science classrooms.

Christensen, J. (1984). *Your reading: A booklist for junior high and middle school students*. Urbana, IL: National Council of Teachers of English. This list comprises annotations of 3,100 books of fiction and nonfiction.

Donelson, K., & Nilsen, A. P. (1989). *Literature for today's young adults*. Glenview, IL: Scott, Foresman. A textbook with many ideas and strategies for teaching with adolescent literature.

Dreyer, S. S. (1981). *The book finder: A guide to children's literature about the needs and problems of youth aged 2–15*. Washington, DC: American Guidance Service. This very useful guide includes an index cross-referenced by subject, author, and book title and a book of summaries that are organized thematically with indications of age-level appropriateness.

Gillespie, J. T. (1977). *Paperback books for young people: An annotated guide to publishers and distributors*. Chicago: American Library Association. An especially useful guide to discount distributors of hard-to-find paperback books.

Regarding our topic of Jews in Europe during World War II, we find a wealth of related young adult books listed in these references including *Friedrich* (Richter, 1970), *The Winter When Time Was Frozen* (Pelgrom, 1980), *Three Children of the Holocaust* (Chaneles, 1974), *The Book of Alfred Kantor* (Kantor, 1971), *Never to Forget: The Jews of the Holocaust* (Meltzer, 1976), *The Cage* (Sender-Minsky, 1986), *Number the Stars* (Lowry, 1989), *Refugee* (Rose, 1977), and *The Terezin Requiem* (Bor, 1963).

Figure 8–3 *(continued)* **A list of useful guides to young adult books**

Jane Addams Peace Association and the Women's International League for Peace and Freedom. (annually). *Jane Addams children's book award.* This award is given to honor books that promote peace and social justice. Works of adolescent literature are frequent award winners. For instance, Meltzer's nonfiction account of the Holocaust, *Never to forget: The Jews of the Holocaust,* was awarded in 1977.

International Reading Association. Books for adolescents. *Journal of Reading.* 800 Barksdale Road, P. O. Box 8139, Newark, DE 19711. Reviews of current young adult literature appear in all nine issues of the volume year.

International Reading Association. Children's choices. *The Reading Teacher.* This is a similar list to Carlsen's for younger readers but contains many titles that can be used profitably with secondary students. The list appears in the October issue of each volume year.

Kobrin, B. (1988). *Eye openers. How to choose and use children's books about real people, places and things.* New York: Viking Penguin. A helpful guide to selecting and teaching with books for students in the middle grades.

Mathews, D. (1988). *High interest easy reading for junior and senior high school students.* Urbana, IL: National Council of Teachers of English. An annotated bibliography of the best adolescent literature for reluctant readers.

New York Times Book Review, 299 W. 43rd St., New York, NY 10036. The weekly edition of book reviews includes reviews of new books for teens and preteens.

Scales, P. (n.d.). *Communicating through young adult books.* New York: Bantam. This book has plenty of useful strategies for teaching with adolescent literature.

Schecter, I. R., & Bogart, G. L. (1985). *Junior high school library catalog.* New York: Wilson. An annotated bibliography of fiction and nonfiction, updated every five years and supplemented annually.

School Library Journal. R. R. Bowker Co., 1180 Ave. of the Americas, New York, NY 10036. In the nine issues published annually are reviews of current young adult literature.

Young Adult Services Division of the American Library Association. *Best books for young adults.* Chicago: Author. This annual list contains approximately 50 books published in the previous year that are recommended reading for young adults.

Obviously, teachers need to read these books before using them in class. We have found that as teachers begin a reading program of their own, they rediscover their love of good literature, they develop fresh perspectives on the topic, and their enthusiasm for teaching grows. In *Friedrich* (Richter, 1970), the reader meets a German boy and his Jewish playmate and learns how both are gradually victimized by Nazi propaganda and pogrom during the years 1925 to 1942. Pelgrom's (1980) story, *The Winter When Time Was Frozen,* tells of the Dutch girl

Noortje and her life as an evacuee on the Everingen's farm in German-occupied Holland. *Three Children of the Holocaust* (Chaneles, 1974) tells of three young survivors who are adopted by wealthy American Jews. The reader comes face to face with life in a Nazi prison camp in former inmate Alfred Kantor's (1971) personal story and sketches of Terezin, *The Book of Alfred Kantor*. In Meltzer's (1976) nonfiction work, *Never to Forget: The Jews of the Holocaust*, the reader learns about the history of the Jews and the Nazis, the destruction of the Jews, and the hope a brighter future for Jews. *The Cage* (Sender-Minsky, 1986) is a compelling story about a young girl's survival, first in a Polish ghetto and then in a Nazi concentration camp. The award-winning *Number the Stars* (Lowry, 1989) captures the fear and strength of a young Jewish girl and her family as they cope with their community's Nazi occupiers. *Refugee* (Rose, 1977) traces a 12-year-old Jewish girl's flight from Belgium to New York after Hitler's invasion. In a moving story about musicians in a Nazi prison camp, *The Terezin Requiem* (Bor, 1963) tells how Jews held onto their pride through music.

On reading these stories, you will note that they and others like them are, first of all, human. You will understand that the effects of distant, large-scale events such as war will become real to students only when translated into terms of what they mean to characters such as Friedrich, Noortje, and their parents, friends, and neighbors. After hearing her teacher read *The Winter When Time Was Frozen* (Pelgrom, 1980), for example, a ninth-grade student commented, "This book describes the life of these people so well you'd think the Everingens and the other people were a part of your own family." Were it not for works of literature like these, most historical events of national and international scope and most notable human achievements and tragedies would remain for many young adults distant or even mythical notions with no emotional connections to their own lives and experiences.

A second notable characteristic of quality young adult literature is that the authors take time to describe the effects of large-scale events on ordinary people. Within the narration of realistic human interaction, concepts can be made understandable and real to young readers. Earlier, we referred to *prejudice* as an important concept to be explored in the study of Naziism and World War II. Excellent passages exploring the nature of this concept can be found in all of the previously mentioned books. Consider, for example, the following passage from Richter's *Friedrich*. In it, the 13-year-old Jewish boy is trying to retrieve his clothes from a swimming pool attendant in Germany in 1938.

> "Just take a look at this!" the attendant said. "You won't get to see many more of them." Everyone could hear his explanation: "This is one of the Jewish identification cards. The scoundrel lied to me. He claims his name's Friedrich Schneider—it's Friedrich *Israel* Schneider, that's what it is—a Jew that's what he is! A Jew in our swimming pool!" He looked disgusted.
>
> All those still waiting for their clothes stared at Friedrich.
>
> As if he could no longer bear to touch it, the attendant threw Friedrich's identification card and its case across the counter. "Think of it! Jewish things among the clothes of respectable human beings!" he screamed, flinging the coat hanger holding Friedrich's clothes on the ground so they scattered in all directions. (Richter, 1970, pp. 76–77)

When reading passages such as this, students cannot help but be affected by the injustice and humiliation suffered by this character they come to know as decent, likeable, and intelligent. Furthermore, the theme of the dangers of prejudice—its meaning, its effect on people, and its often terrible results—is made startlingly clear. After reading *Friedrich,* a ninth-grade history student wrote:

> The book made you feel how you would have felt if you were Jewish or German at the time. I learned how brave the Jewish family was in the book. I also learned how cruel and unthinking people can be and not caring and thinking that these people are the same as we are—human. Another thing I learned is that war is horrible. I hope, even though I doubt it, that there will be no more wars and discrimination in this world. The book really touched me.

Organize the Content and the Classroom for Literature

Clearly, good literature affects young adults deeply; even so, teachers who have never used trade books often ask us questions such as "How can I find the time to work literature into my daily plans when I barely have enough time to cover the chapters?" or "I have 20 to 25 students per class. How can I manage my classroom if I use literature, the textbook, and other sources?"

The first concern is easy enough to understand when you consider the fragmented, fact-laden curricula that so many content-area teachers try to operate within. Not only is each content area taught as a separate entity, but each subject is broken down into bits of information that students are required to memorize (Brown, Collins, & Duguid, 1989). Almost invariably, so much time is spent learning the small details that no time is left to experience holistic treatments of the topic and to understand the big picture. As a result, many students rarely enjoy or see the point in studying history or science facts, forget them, and often have to relearn them the next year. In contrast, time spent reading good literature can be both efficient and effective because it gets students interested in learning the content and, when the books are chosen appropriately, can serve as a source for content instruction (Brandsford & Vye, 1989). For example, one of the trade books used in Debbie's unit on Australia was Colin Thiele's (1974) *Fire in the Stone.* From this book, students learned accurate information about the country's geography, industries, schools, and social structure and, at the same time, benefited from the experience of reading whole, well-written language with an exciting message.

We believe the best way to approach the problem of finding time for trade literature is by deciding the most important themes and overarching concepts to be taught and then placing instructional emphasis on this information. Naturally, some of the textbook content is not as pertinent to the important themes as other content and, consequently, should be given less attention; deciding on a deliberate focus thus frees up time that can be spent on relevant, important information. For example, in his unit on the American Revolution, Frank decided to emphasize three important themes: (a) freedom, both for countries and for people, has a price (the heavy toll of war, even on the victor; the responsibilities that accompany self-government and personal independence); (b) war affects all citizens of a country; and (c) alternatives to war exist. Frank then selected several possible trade books that would help to reinforce these themes, finally deciding to use one primary book, *Johnny Tremain* (Forbes, 1945), and suggest others for students' independent reading. Next, he went through the 12 chapters in the text unit and, keeping his salient themes in mind, made decisions about how to teach each chapter (Figure 8–4) and listed potential writing activities for many of the chapters (Figure 8–5).

We can address the second concern about how to manage the content classroom with literature by sharing the experiences of three different teachers whose approaches represent three management systems.

Don uses the simplest of systems. He reads to his ninth graders literature that is thematically linked to the science topics under consideration. When studying the topic of genetics and genetic engineering, for instance, Don read *The Boys*

Figure 8–4   American Revolution teaching ideas

Chapter	Suggested Activity
1. Life in New England	Students read; compare w/trade book; write (see writing suggestions).
2. Work, Church, & School	Same as Chapter 1.
3. Life in Southern Colonies	Teacher lecture—brief.
4. Life in Middle Colonies	Teacher lecture—brief.
5. Life in the Wilderness	Teacher lecture; book talk: *Tree of Freedom* (Caudill).
6. Government in the English Colonies	Teacher lecture; debates (see writing suggestions).
7. Furs and Farming in New France	Teacher lecture—brief.
8. French & English Fight	Students read; map study; develop time line, write (see suggestions); book talk and sharing: *The Matchlock Gun* (Edmonds).
9. England Tightens Its Grip	Students read.
10. Colonists Become Angry	Students read; prioritize value of ways to cause change; compare text & trade book; write (see suggestions); book talk and sharing: *My Brother Sam is Dead* (Collier & Collier).
11. Liberty or Death	Students read; list causes of war, rank order & defend rankings.
12. New Nation is Born	Students read; discuss Johnny Tremain's change of mind.

Figure 8–5   **American Revolution: Suggested composition assignments**

Chapters 1 & 2

Let Johnny Tremain have a dialogue with a person of today about the living conditions in the 1700s. Make comparisons.

Write a position paper for living in the 18th century or today.

Compare & contrast women's roles in the 18th century and today, based on reading in Johnny Tremain.

Chapter 6

Debate: Develop arguments explaining the points of view of British and Colonists. Placards and posters can support either side.

Chapter 8

Thumbnail sketches of important Revolutionary War personalities.

Newspaper articles for "Colonial Times."

Editorial about British taxation.

Dialogue between a colonist and King George II.

List personal freedoms you have and value today. Which of these can be traced to the events of 1770s? Which were actually fought for in the Revolutionary War?

Chapter 10

Prioritize relative value of a variety of means of gaining one's ends and producing change.

1. Voting
2. Physical force
3. Vigilante (scare) tactics
4. Terrorism
5. Diplomacy

Chapter 12

You have just read *Johnny Tremain*. What part of this story did you react to most strongly? Do you see any connection to this part of the story and your own life?

From Brazil (Levin, 1977), the plot of which surrounds the genetic development of a race of neo-Nazis. Don made other books available to students that were related to the topic of genetic alteration including, *Prophecy* (Seltzer, 1979), *The Wanting Seed* (Burgess, 1962), and *The Island of Dr. Moreau* (Wells, 1966). Farley Mowat's *Never Cry Wolf* (1979), about a scientist's struggle to survive and study wolves within the Arctic circle, was read during the study of scientific explorations of the Arctic. Along with Mowat's narrative, Don used *Buried in Ice: The Mystery of a Lost Arctic Expedition* (Beattie & Geiger, 1992), with its vivid, gripping photographs of mummified explorers found in the arctic permafrost to grab his students' interest in the topic. Isaac Asimov's *Fantastic Voyage* (1966) was used in conjunction with a unit on the systems of the body. His students also used Schultz's light and informative *Looking Inside the Brain* (1992) during this unit. As Don reads, he asks his students to be active listeners, paying attention not only to plot developments but to how the ideas in the story relate to those in the text. With this approach, only a single trade book is needed. Don reads 15 to 20 minutes daily and is able to complete a book of average length in 2½ weeks. Over 9 months, he often reads as many as 15 books to his classes. Over the same period, he exposes his students to countless other novels, picture books, and informational books.

An alternative management plan to the teacher reading aloud is the whole class reading a single book. Jeri's eighth-grade social studies classes read Irene Hunt's *Across Five Aprils* (1965) during a unit on the Civil War. This trade book dovetailed nicely into her textbook instruction, which focused on the theme of how the war affected all citizens of our country. Historical fiction, Hunt's book spans the 5 years of the Civil War by telling the story of the Crieghtons, a southern Illinois family split by Northern and Southern sentiments. Students read the trade book and textbook as homework, then engaged in classroom activities designed to help tie the two texts together. For example, students built a chart that described each major battle as well as its effects on the Crieghtons and their community.

A more complex but exciting and powerful management system involves student-directed, **cooperative learning groups** for reading and sharing multiple novels. Earlier, we described how Debbie, a seventh-grade social studies teacher, builds webs for her units to identify salient concepts and subtopics and appropriate literature. The subtopics on Australia she decided to focus on included schools, the land, the people, and history. She secured sets of four of the following trade books: *The Min Min* (Clark, 1969), *Devil's Hill* (Chauncey, 1960), *Fire in the Stone* (Thiele, 1974), and *The Valley Between* (Thiele, 1982). Debbie then gave personal introductions to the books through book talks and allowed students to form into their own cooperative groups based on self-selection of these four books. Independent reading schedules were set for each book, and each group member was given a particular assignment that relates daily.

Figures 8–6 to 8–9 provide a more detailed description of cooperative literature group members' assignments. The student assigned to be "literary luminary" identified three to five passages in that day's assignment for discussion or oral reading (Figure 8–6). The "vocabulary enricher" prepared a list of four to six unfamiliar words or word usages for discussion (Figure 8–7). The "discussion director" prepared five to eight questions about the assignment (Figure 8–8). The "checker" questioned each group member for completion of assignment, evaluated participation, and urged everyone to enter into the discussion (Figure 8–9). Discussions focused on daily independent reading assignments that were usually completed the day before at home.

In the beginning, Debbie carefully modeled each cooperative group assignment and helped students tie together trade and text learning through questions and discussions. Debbie devised these cooperative learning group roles because they contribute to students' learning in the manner she desires. It is important to note that you can devise your own cooperative learning group roles depending on what kinds of learning you want to take place within the groups.

Figure 8–6   Literary luminary for a cooperative learning assignment

Reading Assignment _____   Date _____   Name _____

LITERARY LUMINARY—guides oral reading for a purpose

Page	Reason (1–5)	Plan for Sharing Reading	Choices Could Include
			1. Good dialogue between characters
			2. Vivid description
			3. Setting a mood

			4. Examples of:
			    a. Simile/metaphor
			    b. Flashback or foreshadowing
			    c. Other literary device

			5. Other instance of the author's craft

Source: From Abraham, B., *Using Novels in the Classroom: A Management System.* Unpublished manuscript.

Such a system is admirably suited to teaching units, because a variety of trade books, each emphasizing a different aspect of the unit theme, will contribute much to the scope and depth of students' understanding. In Debbie's unit on Australia, one group of students reading *Devil's Hill* learned of the great distances between homesteads in central Australia and the effect this has on the people's lives. Another group looked at the multiethnic population of the country, including ethnic prejudices against the aborigines in *Fire in the Stone*. Another group of students read an interesting history of Australia in *The Valley Between*, while in *The Min Min*, students learned about the one-room schools, home correspondence courses, and boarding schools that are an important part of the country's school system.

Teaching With Trade and Text: A Symbiosis

Precisely how you develop plans for relating literature to themes and concepts in the text will depend on your individual style. Generally, you should be prepared to

Figure 8–7   Vocabulary enricher for a cooperative learning assignment

Reading Assignment _____   Date _____   Name _____

VOCABULARY ENRICHER—clarifies word meanings and pronunciations

Page	Word	Definition	Plan

Presentation Plan Possibilities
1. Have the group find the word and figure out the meaning from context clues.
2. Use the dictionary. Choose the correct definition.
3. Use a thesaurus. Find a synonym to substitute in the sentence.

Source: From Abraham, B., *Using Novels in the Classroom: A Management System.* Unpublished
manuscript.

use texts and trade books interchangeably throughout any teaching sequence. Toward that end, we recommend the following instructional combinations that are likely to deepen students' understanding of content material.

Use the Trade Book as a Schema and Interest Builder

Science.   A ninth-grade science teacher had her students read Jean George's (1959) *My Side of the Mountain* as a prelude to a unit on ecology. The story is about a boy who runs away from his crowded city life in New York to the Catskill Mountains, where he learns to live with nature. Young Sam Gribley's adventures and the lessons he learns set the stage for the theme of the ecology unit and class discussion by establishing an overall picture of how a human can live and thrive

Figure 8–8   Discussion director for a cooperative learning assignment

Reading Assignment _____   Date _____   Name _____

DISCUSSION DIRECTOR—asks questions to increase comprehension

Why do you think the author put _____ in this
   place in the story?

How is _____ like/different from _____?

If you had been _____ how would you have _____?

How did you feel about _____?

What happened after _____?

What do you think caused _____?

Compare _____.

If the author had left out _____
   how would the story have been changed?

Summarize _____.

Predict _____.

What happened that you think will be important later on?

Who? Where? When? _____

Source: From Abraham, B., *Using Novels in the Classroom: A Management System.* Unpublished
manuscript.

in harmony with nature. In addition, his story gave students a store of unusual, dramatic examples of the independence of species, food chains, and habitats, which they then read about in expository form in their science textbooks.

What a richly detailed schema these students developed for understanding and appreciating human dependence on nature for food. During the science unit, they often recalled Sam's adventures as they related to text content: his hard-won meals of dogtooth violet bulbs and dandelion greens and freshwater mussels dug from the bed of an icy stream; his reliance on Jesse C. James, the raccoon, which "could find mussels where three men could not" (p. 78); and Frightful, the falcon Sam trained to catch small game.

Biology.   Students in a tenth-grade biology class got to know O'Dell's (1960) stoic, insightful character Karana in *Island of the Blue Dolphins* before their ecology unit. The story of this Indian girl's 18-year struggle for survival alone on a small Pacific island provided an interest builder and a dramatic point of reference for the students who then read of habitats, food chains, and human impact on the environment. Karana makes an eloquent statement for respectful treatment of all living things.

Figure 8-9   Checker for a cooperative learning assignment

Reading Assignment _____   Day # _____   Name _____

CHECKER—checks for completion of assignments, evaluates participation, helps monitor discussion for equal participation

Names	Job	Done?	Participation or Cooperation	Read Assignment

Participation Key:
✓ for each answer
+ for other contributions and cooperative behaviors
– for interrupting, distracting, "goofing-off" incidents

Reading Key:
+ appears to have read
– little, if any, proof

Process Evaluation:
Our group _____
_____

Source: From Abraham, B., *Using Novels in the Classroom: A Management System.* Unpublished manuscript.

For a unit on the environmental degradation, a ninth-grade teacher prepared his students for their new learning with two trade books. He read aloud *The Voyage Begun* (Bond, 1981), a futuristic book about the potential dangers of environmental pollution on climate and how a young boy and girl learn to deal with and understand their new, altered world. He also shared with his class *A Walk in the Rainforest* (Pratt, 1992). Written and illustrated by a 15-year-old, this book contains colorful illustrations of tropical rainforest flora and fauna accompanied by an informative, ecology-minded text.

Physical Education.   Before starting the softball season, a physical education teacher read aloud to his students the interesting sports novel *The Curious Case of Sidd Finch* (Plimpton, 1988). He used this particular book because he wanted the "hot shots" in class to develop a little humility, and those students who lacked confidence to become aware of their own strengths in and outside of sports.

A group of senior high students who had volunteered to be counselors for summer camp were asked to read *Bless the Beasts and Children* (Sworthout, 1970) in their training class. The trainees had fun reading about the adventure and mischief the adolescent campers experienced in the rugged West. The book brought levity to the fact-filled 2-week class and served as a focal point for discussion about behavioral problems and health emergencies.

English.   In preparation for reading, studying, and doing dramatic interpretations of William Shakespeare's *Hamlet,* an English teacher had her 12th-grade students read Grant and Mandrake's (1990) picture book version of *Hamlet.* Lavishly illustrated, this work remains faithful to the story and retains much of the original dialogue and narration. Although the teacher knew there is no substitute for the actual Shakespeare, she nonetheless recognized the attraction of this illustrated book for introducing her students to the exciting world and remarkable ideas of *Hamlet.* In this way the book served as a bridge to the original, offering students a story with rich artwork and skillful expressions of Hamlet's anguish and torment.

Because you know which concepts and information will be met later in the textbook when choosing to read literature orally, you can easily highlight key, pertinent passages by reading them with particular emphasis or by reading them again after cuing the students. When trade books are read independently or in small groups, you can alert students to these passages before reading. You can also use discussion and demonstrate context strategies for learning terminology that appears in the trade book and later in the textbook.

One benefit of using good literature in content classes is that the interest factor is built in. Good narrative by its nature drives readers and listeners onward to discover what happens next. But you should not depend on reading alone to build schemata. Because students learn best through active participation, you should encourage discussion and written responses after daily reading sessions. Worthwhile topics could include favorite passages, alternate courses of action for characters, characters' personalities, and possible future developments in the story.

Use Trade Books to Extend Textbook Ideas

During reading, students can work in small groups to discuss particular issues focused on in the text and elaborated on in related trade books. Students can share what they have found to be particularly informative sections of the trade book or passages that support and extend the text. For instance, the teacher and class could read a section of text, then search trade books for additional and supporting information, as occurred in the following classroom examples.

Social Studies.   Eighth-grade students studying the Age of Exploration into the New World in their social studies texts also read in small groups Scott O'Dell's trilogy, *The Captive* (1979), *The Feathered Serpent* (1981), and *The Amethyst Ring* (1983), which chronicle the 16th-century world of the Maya, Aztec, and Inca empires. Students were asked to find passages in the trade books describing events from the indigenous people's point of view, a perspective often omitted in textbook treatments. Likewise, students found passages that helped to explain how and why a mere handful of Spaniards were able to overtake three enormous empires. As we have noted before, too often, the driving human forces behind important historical events are not made clear in textbook accounts. In O'Dell's trilogy, however, the reader is brought face-to-face with the greed and religious zeal that drove many explorers and their followers to fanatical behavior.

Music. A 12th-grade music teacher asked her orchestral class to read *Lohengrin* as they prepared for a performance of the overtures that accompany Wagner's enchanting opera. Much more than a libretto, *Lohengrin,* written by the composer, resembles a novella. Because of its length, the story of Lohengrin is well developed and character descriptions are rich. These features make the book ideally suited to instruction in musical interpretation. As the class read the book, they also worked on the operetta. Cooperative groups were formed on the bases of orchestral sections (strings, woodwinds, percussion, etc.). During each class session, groups were responsible for reflecting on the story, discussing plot and character, then, based on story interpretations, presenting possible musical interpretations. After whole-class discussions and teacher input, the student musicians attempted to operationalize their interpretations in rehearsals.

History. For the study of the American Revolution, a 10th-grade history teacher selected the following themes: Broaden the students' awareness of all the colonists attitudes toward the war, and sensitize students to the tragic consequences war brings its participants. She selected the trade book *My Brother Sam Is Dead* (Collier & Collier, 1974) to use in conjunction with text study. In this story, students learned about the hardships and realities of the war as told by Tim Meeker, a young boy who watches his loyalist father killed by bandits and his brother Sam unjustly accused of stealing by his comrade in the Colonial Army and hung.

As students read chapters in their textbook and trade book, they responded to study guides (discussed in Chapter 3) that were designed to help students see connections between material in both sources, apply their new learning beyond the parameters of the unit, and involve them in dynamic class discussions. In the first guide (Figure 8–10), students were asked to make inferences about the attitudes of story characters. In this way, students were helped to understand the variety of points of view on the war. With another study guide (Figure 8–11), students were asked to consider the human elements of war—so poignantly brought out in the trade book—by reminding them that the problems and conflicts the revolutionists faced are still very real today where other wars are being waged.

In a study of immigrants to the United States in the early 20th century, Tom read aloud to his juniors from the marvelous, award-winning book *Letters from Rifka* (Hesse, 1992). Rifka and her Jewish family flee Russia in 1919 to avoid Russian soldiers and a pogrom. Her dream to find a new, safe world is finally realized when the family arrives in America. Rifka records her journey in her treasured volume of Pushkin poetry, bringing the reader intimately close to her ordeal: humiliating examinations by doctors and soldiers; deadly typhus; separation from family, friends, and homeland; deadly ocean storms; detainment on Ellis Island; and the loss of her beautiful golden hair.

Figure 8–10   Study guide for *My Brother Sam Is Dead*

Directions: Listed across the page are 9 events or statements from *My Brother Sam Is Dead*. Listed down the left side are the names of characters involved in the story plot. In each box indicate whether that character would agree or disagree with the words stated above. Use the symbols in the key below. You must make some inferences to answer the questions. Be prepared to support your answers with examples from the book.

Key: **A** = Agree with **D** = Disagree **X** = Doesn't apply **?** = Not enough info	Children should respect and obey their parents.	Battle of Lexington and Concord.	Men should be free to govern themselves.	Render unto Caesar the things that are Caesar's.	I'm an Englishman but have more say in government as a colonist.	The end justifies the means.	I'm interested in making a living but not in fighting a war.	I'm just against wars.	Declaration of Independence.
Sam Meeker, rebel soldier									
Mr. Meeker, Sam's father									
Mrs. Meeker, Sam's mother									
Tim Meeker, Sam's brother									
Mr. Beacher, minister									
Betsy Read, Sam's girlfriend									
Col. Read, Betsy's father									
Mr. Heron, Meekers' neighbor									
General Putnam									
Captain Betts									

While studying the details and facts of immigration in their textbooks, students in Tom's class were discovering the human drama of immigration through the words in Rifka's diary. Tom had his students trace Rifka's journey on a map of Europe and the United States. Students compared immigration procedures on Ellis Island as discussed in the textbook with Rifka's experiences. He also had them adopt the persona of an immigrant and create a record of that person's experiences in the form of a diary or personal travelog modeled after Rifka's. Students were given regular opportunities to read entries from their diaries to the class.

Figure 8–11   Study guide for *My Brother Sam Is Dead*

"Principle, Sam? You may know principle, Sam, but I know war. Have you ever seen a dear friend lying in the grass with the top of his skull off and his brains sliding out like wet oats? Have you ever looked into the eyes of a man with his throat cut and the blood pouring out between his fingers, knowing that there was nothing you could do, in five minutes he would be dead, yet still trying to beg for grace and not being able because his windpipe was cut in two? Have you ever heard a man shriek when he felt a bayonet go through the middle of his back? I have, Sam, I have. I was at Louisbourg the year before you were born. Oh, it was a great victory. They celebrated it with bonfires all over the colonies. And I carried my best friend's body back to his mother—sewed up in a sack."

Both men had their own principles. Think about what your principles might be about war and the exercise of our freedoms. Immense human sacrifice was made by both sides during the American Revolution. Thomas Paine, a patriot, wrote, "The cause of America is in a great measure the cause of all mankind." What do you think he means by this? Was there another way besides war to achieve the same end? "Could the United States have made its way without all that agony and killing?" ask James and Christopher Collier.

Part I. Pretend you are a United States Senator. Indicate whether you would vote yes or no on the suggested imaginary bills on the floor of the Untied States Senate. Give your reason.

U.S. Senate Bill, proposed	*Reason*
_____ The U.S. Government should lift the arms embargo for Bosnian Muslims.	
_____ The U.S. Government should cut spending on nuclear arms.	
_____ The U.S. Government should create a fund to give aid to other countries' rebels or patriots.	

Write a bill of your own to be voted on.

Mathematics.   Lori had been struggling with her geometry students to help expand their perceptions of geometry and to look for real-life parallels to geometrical terms, postulates, and theorems. Her efforts did little to leaven low student interest, until she became bold and decided to have her class read and discuss novels. She began her search for appropriate literature with some incredulity, but with the help of a local reference librarian, soon discovered several books that appeared ideally suited to teaching geometry, including Abbot's *Flatland* (1927), Hinton's *An Episode of Flatland* (1907), and Dewdney's *The Planiverse* (1984). She finally chose *Flatland*, a 19th-century British novel of science fiction, as an important tool in trying to humanize students' understanding of geometry.

In *Flatland*, all of the characters are two-dimensional geometric figures that represent different social classes. The first part is essentially a social satire. In the second part, the main character travels to other dimensions to describe the relative merits of different points of view. *Flatland* can be read for its straight geometrical descriptions as well as for its social commentary and satire.

Lori found *Flatland* could be incorporated into her geometry course without ignoring any of the basic material. She tied the book to a unit in the textbook dealing with geometrical models of the universe. Class discussion centered on the basic plot, why it was written, its social context, details of Flatland, other lands and their inhabitants, and the symbolism. In small groups, students were asked to brainstorm solutions to problems in Flatland (not explained by the author) such as rain and snow patterns, locomotion, food, writing, and so on. Then the whole class compared their solutions. As a writing activity, students were asked to pick a known person and tell which Flatland class (geometrical figure) he or she would be in and why.

Lori's geometry unit was very well received. Many students asked that more novels be used in the class. Lori found her efforts to be worthwhile because she was able to get to know her students better, how they think and feel, as a result of the many opportunities to interact during the unit. She also accomplished her goal of humanizing the learning of geometry.

French.   Helping a group of freshmen develop an appreciation for the similarities and differences in French and American cultures, Faith had her students read *Mystery of the Metro* (Howard, 1987). In this story, a 16-year-old American girl finds herself alone in France and is forced to deal with all of the necessities of getting by in a foreign country. The story also has a tinge of mystery that makes it even more engaging. As students read the book, Faith had them compare the French styles of eating, transportation, and other customs with the American way of life. Students were also required to research a particular aspect of French culture that presented the main character in the book with problems and report back to the class.

Current Events.   Glen's senior class was focusing on the former system of apartheid in South Africa. Resources for the unit included government and United Nations reports, essays by Nelson Mandella, music lyrics by black South African folk song writers, and two masterful novels written by Norman Silver. *No Tigers in Africa* (Silver, 1990) tells the story of Selwyn Lewis and his white racist upbringing in Cape Town, South Africa. When his family moves to England, however, Selwyn's new experiences force him to confront his racism and look within himself to find moral solutions to prejudice. In *An Eye for Color* (Silver, 1991), Basil Kushenovitz narrates interconnecting stories about growing up white and Jewish in Cape Town. About his ambivalent position in a racist culture, Basil says that like a lizard, "My one eye sees one thing, and my other eye sees something quite different." Basil must try to reconcile his split vision—between his comforts and others' deprivation; between what is expected of a white man and what he himself is willing to become. Glen's goal in having his students read both of Silver's honestly painful novels was to rivet them to the compelling human stories of apartheid, making it possible for them to understand that racist systems leave victims on either side of the color/culture fence.

Science.   An eighth-grade teacher captured her students' attention and enthusiasm for learning by using the illustrated informational book, *Looking Inside Sports Aerodynamics* (Schultz, 1992). Filled with young teens' favorite sports figures, from Michael Jordan in basketball to Monica Seles in tennis, this colorful, fun book deals with unseen forces that affect objects in motion. By combining sports and science, the teacher found that students learn the facts of aerodynamics and understand it principles more thoroughly than when the textbook is the sole resource.

In another classroom, Gail taught a unit on the consequences of science and technology through the use of science fiction. Her goal was to promote problem-solving skills and help students clarify values regarding scientific technology. Knowing that science fiction can motivate students to take a greater interest in science (Kindler, 1982), Gail used *Star Trek: The Next Generation* (Bornholt, 1989) to instigate discussion on controversial issues associated with cloning. In the story, members of the Enterprise spaceship, while on a planet populated by original clone settlers, are asked to allow their own tissues to be used to spawn a new generation of clones to replace a line that is malfunctioning. The crew members refuse but find their tissues have been stolen while they were rendered unconscious. They return to the planet and destroy their clone look-alikes. The colony claimed that without the new clones they would die out in a few generations.

Given these story events, Gail poses the following question to her students and asks them to take a stand on a values continuum: Did the Enterprise crew members have the right to destroy the clones?

Pro-choice   **Right-to-life**
Do not provide tissue for cloning   Provide tissue for cloning

First, students were asked to write their positions on their own. Then they went to the board and plotted their positions on the values continuum by writing their names along it. This was followed by small group interaction to crystalize their positions and respond to position of others. The activity concluded with class discussion. Gail has found science fiction to be a rich resource for teaching science because it motivates students to become more active learners and thinkers.

Art.   Many students who are not blessed with artist's hands can learn something of how the artist sees the world through related trade books (Stover, 1988). Cal, a high school art teacher, began to recognize the connection between good books and art appreciation after reading sleuth books by Gash and Malcolm relating to crimes in the art world. This led him to investigate books for adolescents that would help students who struggle with drawing and painting assignments gain some insights into the way artists see the world and approach compositions. In his search he found several good books and began using them in his art classes. Among students' favorites are *Julie's Daughter* (Rodowsky, 1985); *In Summer Light* (Oneal, 1986), contemporary adolescents learn about art while grappling with typical adolescent concerns; *Linnea in Monet's Garden* (Bjork & Anderson,

1985), fictional characters visiting Paris to see the paintings of Monet; and *I, Juan de Pareja* (de Trevino, 1965), Juan is the slave and friend of the Spanish painter Velasquez who becomes a painter himself under the tutelage of his master. Cal has read these books aloud to his students, drawing their attention to the central theme of the artist's struggle to capture a vision on canvas. In addition, he has found that his students come to care deeply for the engaging characters who populate these books, thus, learning things from them about artistic expression that he himself cannot teach.

Use Follow-up Activities That Allow Students to Personalize New Trade/Text Knowledge

Because **follow-up activities** often help students to assimilate concepts and information and allow you to evaluate students' learning and to check for misconceptions, they are essential to a complete teaching and learning experience with trade books and textbooks.

With writing, drama, and art, all viable discourse forms, and with the array of electronic and graphic media available in today's schools, follow-up activities that help students synthesize textbook and trade book learning can be as diverse as the people who create them. The following strategies, which are drawn from the same classroom experiences referred to throughout this chapter, are representative of the unlimited possibilities for rewarding follow-up activities. Moreover, they facilitate deep and meaningful comprehension of the critical unit themes and concepts.

Writing. Writing activities can be as simple as on-the-scene descriptions of places or events mentioned briefly in the text and detailed in a trade book, or letters to historical figures from students who assume the persona of fictional characters. Both activities allow students to use factual knowledge in a personal way. A more involved writing activity is composing dialogue between historical figures and fictional characters. One teacher had students write dialogue between Piri, from *Upon the Head of the Goat* (Siegal, 1981) and Hitler, while the science teacher asked students to present conversation between the fictional Sam Gribley (George, 1959) and an industrial polluter. These composing activities elicited responses in which concepts, issues, and information were reviewed and reconsidered. As an overall review of the Australian unit, students wrote and illustrated an informational picture book containing facts from both sources. Fact sheets were written about the Aztec chieftain Montezuma as one culminating activity for students studying exploration of the New World. Students finishing their unit of the American Revolution assumed the persona of a character from *My Brother Sam is Dead* (Collier & Collier, 1974) and composed a short diary from April 1775 through April 1776. They also wrote personal letters from Tim Meeker to George Washington explaining his feelings about the war and its effects on the Meeker family.

Drama. Drama, unrehearsed and without an audience, serves students well in providing nonthreatening active contexts for trying out new roles and language forms and experiencing different perspectives. Students can extemporaneously reenact scenes or events mentioned in their reading or use text material and stories to provide models for original scenes pertaining to the same concepts. Informal, on-the-spot interviews of characters or figures met in texts or trade books allow students to play with newly acquired content-area ideas, concepts, and facts as they formulate questions and answers. Interviewers armed with facts as reported in their texts and the knowledge of the characters from trade book reading interviewed peers posing as Friedrich (Richter, 1970) and his German friend as they lived through different stages of the Nazification of Germany; Karana (O'Dell, 1960) in her island hut; Piri (Siegal, 1981) in the Jewish internment camp awaiting her passage to Auschwitz; Julian Escobar (the main character, a young seminarian, in *The Captive*, O'Dell, 1979) in the Mexican jungle; and the Redding townspeople gathered to watch the execution of Sam Meeker. For the World War II unit, some students interviewed local people who actually lived in Europe during the war as a means of personalizing and extending their knowledge of that era.

Radio plays are a natural adjunct to reading and writing. In this dramatic form, students select a scene or invent a probable scene from a historical event, write a script with dialogue and action, and tape-record it with sound effects for later "broadcast." Free of the demands of staging and acting, students can concentrate on accurate representation of facts, characters' motives, and appropriate language production. Imagine the language and composing skills, thinking, and relevant concepts and information called into play by students who reconstructed the scene surrounding Pissaro's decision to burn his ships off the Mexican coast to prevent his fearful, disgruntled soldiers from deserting. Drama—an enjoyable, valuable form of composition—is too seldom used in our secondary school classrooms.

We recommend activities that require students to plan, think, and in many cases, write and revise. Although these can be time-consuming processes, we believe much is gained from higher-order follow-up activities, including abundant oral and written language production; opportunities for independent thinking and decision making; and application of newly acquired concepts, ideas, and information. As you begin and continue to integrate trade books into your curriculum, we think you will agree that the benefits of such an integration more than justify the time it requires.

Promoting Lifelong Reading Habits

We now shift our attention away from specific instructional strategies that combine textbook and trade book learning to ways in which classroom teachers can help students develop the reading habit, encouraging them to read outside of school as well as inside the classroom for information, self-growth, and the sheer pleasure of reading.

In Chapter 1, we described the growing phenomenon of aliteracy—capable readers choosing not to read. We argued that the seeds of aliteracy are planted when reading lessons become drudgery; when the books students must read are uninspiring or have little connectedness to their real-world needs, concerns, and interests; and when reading is perceived as a separate subject instead of as a functional tool for intellectual and personal growth. Unfortunately, many young adults who enter junior and senior high school rarely read, not because they can't but because they won't. Some have given up reading altogether and will likely become nonreading adults (Reed, 1988).

Given that many adolescents are reluctant readers, all teachers have a responsibility for doing more than teaching the content in their subject areas. Teachers must try to reach students by developing curricula that encourage them to read interesting and personally meaningful books and that help them realize that reading for its own sake can be a pleasurable and rewarding experience.

What Classroom Teachers Can Do to Keep Students Reading

Classroom teachers who employ strategies similar to those described in this chapter will go a long way toward encouraging students already in the reading habit to read even more and toward rekindling a desire to read among students whose interest has faded. Along with these strategies, there are many additional ways to promote independent reading.

Discover and Use Students' Interests.   In Chapter 4 we offered some suggestions for assessing students' interests to introduce them to informative and exciting books that match their interests. We reiterate that it is important for you to discover the particular interests of the students in your classroom, not only to turn them on to your subject but to turn them on to reading.

A simple sentence-completion inventory, such as those suggested in Chapter 4 and the example that follows, can reveal a great deal about what students find pleasurable. Remember that students who may be nonreaders or reluctant readers will have little to say in response to questions or incomplete statements about reading. Therefore, interest inventories should reveal more than reading interests; they should uncover students' real-world interests, concerns, needs, dreams, hobbies, and so on.

Teachers who use journals often get to know their students in ways that would be impossible with simple inventories and questionnaires. In journals, students often disclose important aspects of their lives related to community, family, relationships, as well as what makes them laugh and cry. With this information a teacher is better able to respond with appropriate suggestions for reading material that speaks to their real-world concerns. For instance, a teacher who learned that one of her students was pregnant responded in the young woman's journal with suggested books about pregnancy, such as *Teen Pregnancy: The Challenges We Faced, The Choices We Made* (Ewy & Ewy, 1985), an honest guide through the practical, moral, and legal issues associated with childbirth and parenting.

Other teachers have used letters from reluctant readers to gain insights into their reading and outside-school interests (Isakson, 1991). Receiving letters from students and writing letters back to them makes it possible for the teacher to offer book suggestions in a nonthreatening and confidential way. One student confided in a letter to his teacher that he loved "stuff" about the Civil War but was having a very difficult time finding books on the topic that were easy for him to read. The teacher loaned him a copy of *Civil War: America Becomes One Nation* (Robertson, 1992), a photographic picture book written in a lively and accessible style—just right for the student. He eventually wrote back that it was one of the best books about the Civil War he had ever read and wondered if the teacher had more suggestions.

Demonstrate That Reading Is Valued.   Teachers who are bored with their own texts can hardly be expected to entice students into the "literacy club." Likewise, if students perceive that only the teacher and the text possess the important and correct ideas and information, they will likely remain uninvolved and disinterested readers.

Creating an atmosphere in the classroom in which you and your students are free to share enthusiasm for books is the best way we know to demonstrate that reading is valued. To do this, time must be allocated for building and browsing the classroom library and visiting the school library to self-select books, magazines, newspapers, for recreational reading, sharing books, and gathering students' responses and reactions to books.

Sanacore (1992) recommends cluttering up the classroom with as much print material as possible. In an environment where students are surrounded by reading material of all varieties, they are more likely to browse and read some of these materials. Instead of becoming anxious over what students choose to read, we should be reminded of Nell's (1988) discovery that as readers become more experienced in reading for pleasure, they tend to select appropriate materials. Making the environment conducive to reading by arranging a few comfortable reading spots with good seating and lighting and adding colorful posters, book jackets, and mobiles for decoration will make it clear to students that you value pleasurable, personal reading (Clary, 1991).

Within a print-rich classroom, there must also be time for pleasure reading. We strongly recommend a **sustained silent reading (SSR)** program as a useful strategy to encourage the leisure reading habit. SSR provides you and your students time to just read in an atmosphere free of assignments, grades, and reports. Students are allowed to read anything that interests them. For many, SSR may be the only free reading time all day. Ideally, the entire school should be involved in SSR, although you and your classroom can have a successful program even if the whole school is not involved. SSR programs have been shown to promote more positive attitudes toward reading (Levine, 1984; Sanacore, 1988). In the following sections are a few guidelines for your classroom SSR program.

Give Students Assistance in Finding Something to Read.   In time, most will come prepared for SSR with material selected in advance. Others, particularly reluctant readers, may need help in finding something to read. Talk with these students about their interests, and allow them to visit the classroom or school library to select a book, magazine, newspaper, or other reading material that matches their interest.

Accept Any Reading Material That Students Bring for Sustained Silent Reading. Avoid the tendency to push your tastes on students, even if they have selected material you consider to be of poor literary quality. The key is that you are providing a supportive environment for students to read material that is meaningful to them. One qualifier: Many teachers experienced with SSR programs find that they must eventually make it very clear that certain material is absolutely inadmissible, such as pornography. You may want to head off any problems before they occur by restricting certain materials that are clearly inappropriate for the SSR program.

Never Link Reports or Grading to Sustained Silent Reading. SSR is free reading. The best way to undermine this intent is by turning SSR into schoolwork. Occasionally, school-related activities will flow naturally from SSR reading. For instance, a student may use a book being read in SSR for a research project or story writing, but these activities should never become requirements. SSR should allow students in your classroom to explore the pleasures of reading. Your support of the program will clearly demonstrate that you value daily reading of personally meaningful and interesting materials.

Use as Much Time as You Can Allow for Sustained Silent Reading. Certainly, for adolescents, SSR periods of 15 minutes or more should be the goal. Keep in mind that those 15 minutes may be the only time all day that many students read self-selected materials simply for pleasure or personal use.

Read Aloud to Students. We mentioned earlier in this chapter that reading aloud is one way to integrate trade books into secondary content classrooms. Reading aloud to students on a regular basis is also an excellent way to motivate them to read and is a highly pleasurable experience for listeners of any age (Daisey, 1993). Jim Trelease, the noted storyteller, says teachers should read aloud "to reassure, to entertain, to inform or explain, to arouse curiosity, and to inspire—and to do it all personally" (1989, p. 2). We recommend that you try to re-create the same intimate atmosphere of a parent reading a favorite story to a child (Mathews, 1987). In a warm, trusting context, you and your students can "get lost" in books. Read-aloud resources can range from short, appealing magazine articles to full novels. Sharing with students a variety of materials helps them expand their tastes and explore a wide diversity of material.

Make Reading Fun. Many teachers and parents are quick to point out that reading cannot possibly compete with television viewing as a leisure time activity. It is well documented that most adolescents spend from a few to several hours per day watching TV (Neuman, 1986). It is also apparent that reading performance is negatively correlated to TV viewing, especially for those who watch 4 or more hours daily (Neuman, 1988). A surprising finding by Neuman, however, is that students choose to watch TV during their leisure time because it is more interesting than other activities, such as reading. In other words, take TV out of the life of students who are disinterested in reading, and those students will fill the TV void with other nonreading activities. Get those students more excited about books, however, and they will consciously make time for reading, even if it means eliminating some TV viewing hours. One way to help students actively choose reading as a leisure-time activity is to make it fun.

We must remember that junior and senior high school students enjoy playing with language and should be encouraged to read books that are fun. Reed (1988) recommends that teachers, as well as parents, should suggest humorous young adult books such as joke books and, yes, even comic books, especially for reluctant readers, to keep them active members of the literacy club. These books can act as a bridge to more sophisticated reading materials.

A seventh-grade teacher we know demonstrates how fun reading can be through read-alouds. Using regionalized versions of well-known fables and fairy tales from such books as Chase's *Grandfather Tales* (1948), *Jack Tales* (1943), and Jacobs's *Cajun Night Before Christmas* (1973), she involves students in role plays to her compelling narration. The texts and her interpretations often leave the class full of laughter. She has noted the influence of the read-alouds on her students' own enthusiasm for reading these and other humorous books.

Make Reading a Real-Life Experience.   As we have emphasized throughout this chapter, your goal as a teacher is more than inculcating the "stuff" of your subject area. You must also be involved in reaching students through reading to help them take responsibility for their own literacy development beyond the schoolroom. This can be accomplished by taking every opportunity to bring real-world reading materials into the classroom, so that, through interesting and meaningful classroom activities, adolescents come to understand how reading needs to be a part of their adult lives. Newspapers, magazines, and various other print sources found in the adult world should be used in daily classroom instruction and made available in the classroom library or reading corner.

A prime example of integrating everyday reading materials into classroom instruction comes from a literature teacher who was helping his students understand *metaphor*. He knew that metaphors are often found in newspapers. And because they are inexpensive, easy to obtain, and contain articles that are generally short and concise, newspapers are a very good source for figurative language instruction.

The teacher began by distributing to small groups of students headlines that used metaphorical language, such as "Still Limping, Oil Patch Exits Intensive Care," and "Experts Zero In on Magic Bullet to Kill Cancer Cells." Using a reciprocal teaching strategy (explained in Chapters 2 and 3), the teacher modeled a question-asking and -answering process out loud to demonstrate for students how he interpreted the metaphors in the headlines. For instance, with the first headline, he began by asking "What is an oil patch?" Then he dug into the article until he found information that helped him answer the question. The oil patch is a group of four states whose net worth and economic stability depend heavily on the production and sale of oil— namely, Louisiana, Oklahoma, Colorado, and Texas.

The next question he asked was, "In what way could four oil-producing states exit intensive care?" He pointed out how the statement clearly made no sense if interpreted literally, which, by default, made it a metaphor. This question led immediately to his next question, "Who would normally exit, 'limping,' from the intensive care ward?" Students were quick to respond by saying a sick or injured person who is getting better but is basically still ill or injured. In this way students began to see the similarities between the "oil patch" and a patient just released from intensive care.

At this point, the teacher asked students working in their groups to come up with an explanation of the metaphor. Most were able to explain that the oil-producing states were in trouble but were in far better financial shape than they were a few years ago, just as the hospitalized person who limps out of intensive care is still in trouble but in better physical condition than not long before.

The teacher went on to engage students in discussion concerning why the author chose to use a metaphorical headline in the first place. To make the article more attractive and "catchy," was one explanation. Another was that the author was "teasing" readers to entice them to read the article. The teacher pointed out that by linking the troubled economies of distant states with something familiar—hospitals, illness—the author was trying to make his subject accessible to more readers.

There are many more examples of teachers who routinely integrate real-life reading materials into their content instruction to help students see connections between literacy development inside and outside the classroom boundaries.

- A health teacher has students bring in menus from restaurants and cookbooks from home when working on food preparation and nutrition.

- A business education teacher for his unit on career explorations brings in several examples of actual employment applications. He also urges students who may be applying for part-time jobs to bring in their applications.

- A chemistry teacher asks students to bring into class labels from household cleaning products and foods that indicate that certain chemicals are being used.

- A government teacher uses popular news magazines to relate text topics to current events.

- An accounting teacher asks students to bring in actual bills and account statements to teach accounting terms and budgeting.

- A math teacher asks students to write/create math problems using tables, maps, and graphs from the local newspaper.

The list could go on and on, because the possibilities for integrating everyday reading materials into the content classroom are virtually limitless.

According to LaBlanc (1984), adolescents today live in a "right-now" world of instant food, appliances, entertainment, and information. Unfortunately, the technology that makes life easier for young adults is also decreasing their motivation to develop literacy skills beyond the classroom. To help students see the importance and utility of real-world literacy, we recommend that teachers bring into the classroom familiar, everyday texts that students encounter outside school. These strategies, along with strategies that emphasize the personal growth benefits and pleasure of leisure reading, are the best ways we know to encourage young adults to make reading an integral part of their lives.

Case Study Revisited

Remember, Linda, the history teacher? She was preparing a unit on "Immigration to the United States," and we asked you to think of trade book strategies that might be helpful to her as she developed activities for her students. Write your suggestions now.

Linda taught the unit using a variety of sources, including their history textbook, Mitsumasa Anno's *Anno's U.S.A.* (1983), Riki Levinson's *Watch the Stars Come Out* (1985), Paula Fox's *The Slave Dancer* (1973), and a special issue of *Time* (Grunwald, 1985) from July 8, 1985, devoted to immigration past and present.

The class began the study of immigration by reading, analyzing, and discussing *Anno's U.S.A.* in small groups and then as a class. Each student was asked to look for historical and literary events, figures, and ideas found within the book. This wordless picture book was a favorite among many of Linda's students. Some of the students borrowed the book over and over again, impressed that the Japanese author knew so much about the United States but they knew so little about the country and history of Japan. *Anno's U.S.A.* provided Linda's American history classes with an excellent introduction to the topic of immigration through detailed and accurate illustrations.

Linda then introduced *The Slave Dancer* and *Watch the Stars Come Out* to her classes to help them center their attention on black and Jewish immigration. She divided each class into small groups and asked them to read *Watch the Stars Come Out*. As she circulated among the groups, they talked about what they read and what they saw in the illustrations. As each group finished, she asked them to write down their reactions to what they read: what they liked and did not like, what the illustrations brought to the text, what the illustrations told them that the text did not, and their overall impressions. At the same time, during their regular American history curriculum, students were discussing Adolph Hitler's rise to power in Germany, and her students were becoming more and more interested in Jews in both Europe and the United States. They discussed pogroms, anti-Semitism, and Hitler's plans to create a master race. Linda's students thoroughly enjoyed reading *Watch the Stars Come Out* and participating in lively discussions on trans-Atlantic travel by young children without parental supervision and guidance, procedures on Ellis Island, and life on Hester Street in New York City at the turn of the century. This engaging picture book provided a refreshing contrast to their regular pre-World War II textbook reading and class discussion.

During this time, Linda also read *The Slave Dancer* to both classes, so that her students would have a clearer understanding of black immigration. Through it, students learn about Jesse, a New Orleans boy who is kidnapped and taken aboard a slave ship where he's forced to play his fife so the slaves will dance and not lose their physical condition. Students also learned a wealth of information about how slaves were obtained in Africa and the routes taken to bring them to the United States. Her students enjoyed the novel immensely. In discussion groups, they explained the role of African tribal chiefs who sold blacks to white captains like Cawthorne (the captain of the ship in the story); they described the living conditions aboard the slave ship; and they debated the reasons for slavery in America.

The next activity also involved small-group and then class discussion as she asked students to brainstorm possible ways for them to share the material they found in *Anno's U.S.A., Watch the Stars Come Out,* and *The Slave Dancer.* After they compiled a list of activities and projects, she asked each student to pick an activity or project to do individually and share it with the class. (Figure 8–12 shows the list of activities the students brainstormed.) As a class, they focused their attention on the specific contributions of Jews and African-Americans to the United States. Students were asked to center their individual research on one positive contribution made by an African-American or an American Jew, or one positive contribution that American blacks or Jews as a group have made to our culture.

After students had completed the trade books and Linda had completed reading *The Slave Dancer* to the classes, they turned their attention to the issue of cultural diversity, its advantages and disadvantages, and the specific contributions and problems that have resulted from America's brand of cultural diversity. Using the special immigration issue of *Time* magazine, both classes focused on African-Americans and Jews. These ideas were handled in a number of living discussions. Topics included anti-Semitism and racism in the last decade, the recent arrests of white supremacy group members, U.S. Supreme Court decisions, the Ku Klux Klan and the American Nazi Party, superiority, inferiority, economic disparity, and even the firing and censorship of baseball officials after their racist remarks about black athletes.

The classes charted the problems that both groups of immigrants have faced in American society and the ways in which society has sought to address and solve those problems. Linda's students did not affix blame to any one racial or ethnic group; rather, they recognized that we are all responsible for the problems and for finding the solutions.

Figure 8–12   **Project choices for immigration unit**

Anno's U.S.A.

1. Draw a map of the United States to show Anno's route.
2. Draw time line to accompany the pages of the book.
3. Write a text for several pages of the book. Choose an age group and audience to write it for.
4. Analyze a page with historical and literary explanations.
5. Write a list of questions to ask the author and then draft them into a letter.
6. Choose some activity or paper to explain an incident or character found on a page of the book.
7. Add a double-page spread to update the book to 1987.
8. Add a double-page spread to include the history of Pearl City.
9. Construct a model of a page or part of a page.
10. Share the book with a younger student and provide the student with explanations.
11. Design a cover or a book jacket for *Anno's U.S.A.*

Watch the Stars Come Out

1. Write a list of questions and possible answers for the narrator.
2. Dramatize the above interview and tape record it.
3. Contact a recent immigrant, develop a list of questions, interview the immigrant, and then write a report of the interview.
4. Write a description/explanation/list of the narrator's first week in the United States.
5. Write a diary as the narrator of life aboard ship.
6. Read and then discuss the book with younger students.
7. Research some aspect of immigration (transportation, routes, conditions aboard ship, Ellis Island, etc.) and prepare a written report.
8. Design a cover or a book jacket for *Watch the Stars Come Out.*
9. Research and write a short paper on why Jews immigrated to the United States.
10. Research conditions in one European country that led to the immigration of some of its Jewish citizens to the United States.
11. Research the contributions made by a Jewish immigrant after he or she came to the United States.

The Slave Dancer

1. Design a cover or a book jacket.
2. Design a picture book based on one aspect of the book.
3. Write a letter to the main character expressing your thoughts and opinions about slave trading.
4. Write a book review.

Summary

This chapter has been devoted to two themes: (a) strategies for combining trade book and textbook instruction in the content classroom and (b) strategies for helping students develop lifelong reading habits.

First, we presented a theoretical rationale, specific recommendations, and practical considerations for integrating young adult books and textbooks in the classroom. We have shown that the practical use of trade books in content classrooms can be supported by theories of learning. Trade books can help students build on past literacy successes, engender interest and motivation, and develop schemata.

In this chapter we provided an in-depth explanation of how trade books and textbooks can be used together. Specific instructional recommendations are made for (a) developing a unit overview and identifying key themes and concepts within the unit topic, (b) choosing trade books to help teach concepts, (c) teaching with textbooks and trade books, and (d) following up a unit of study with exciting learning activities.

The union of textbook and trade book is feasible and has produced elaborate processing of textual information, greater enthusiasm for learning, and long-term recall in field tests that we have conducted in the junior and senior high school (Brozo & Tomlinson, 1987). Probability of success with this approach is enhanced when teachers responsible for content-area subjects look for opportunities to integrate trade books with their texts and when the literacy support staff work with classroom teachers to help bring about such an integration. Moreover, using trade books in content classrooms should not be perceived as a device or gimmick to bring about interest in a topic on Monday only to be forgotten by Friday. To use the trade books and textbook effectively, you need to make long-range plans, carefully considering how each unit's themes and salient concepts will be developed, and how trade books and text will interplay from the introduction to the conclusion of the unit.

Good literature, once discovered, sells itself. Students return again and again to favorite books, and teachers who know good young adult literature find ways to use it in their classes. The key is knowing the literature. Unfortunately, many teacher training and certification programs still offer literature courses as electives only. We endorse the trend toward making these courses mandatory and further suggest that all content-area methods courses include a literature component to increase the likelihood that students will graduate with skills and knowledge related to using trade books across the curriculum. Most importantly, we recommend that you establish and maintain an independent reading program of literature geared to the students and subject you teach.

The content areas deal with interesting, vital information; but if you rely on textbooks as your sole teaching resource, you may render this information dry and lifeless. Use trade books in conjunction with texts to help ensure that students are more actively involved in learning and that the vitality and spirit inherent in the content-area material are kept alive. In later chapters, you will discover once again how young adult literature can play an integral role in content-area learning.

Finally, this chapter discussed ways in which the classroom teacher can demonstrate the importance and pleasure of developing independent reading habits. Students who are led to see the connection between their real-world needs, concerns, and interests and books, newspapers, magazines, and the myriad print sources in the adult world will likely remain active, lifelong members of the literacy club.

References

Atwell, N. (1987). *In the middle.* Portsmouth, NH: Heinemann.

Brandsford, J., & Vye, N. (1989). A perspective on cognitive research and its implications for instruction. In L. Resnick & L. Klopfer (Eds.), *Toward the thinking curriculum: Current cognitive research.* Alexandria, VA: Association of Supervision and Curriculum Development.

Brown, J., Collins, A., & Duguid, P. (1989). Situated cognition and the culture of learning. *Educational Researcher, 18,* 32–42.

Brozo, W. G., & Tomlinson, C. (1986). Literature: The key to lively content courses. *The Reading Teacher, 40,* 288–293.

Brozo, W. G., & Tomlinson, C. (1987). A trade book/textbook approach versus a textbook-only approach on student learning and attitudes during a social studies/history unit. Paper presented to the College Reading Association, Baltimore, Maryland.

Carlsen, G., & Sherrill, A. (1988). *Voices of readers: How we come to love books.* Urbana, IL: National Council of Teachers of English.

Clary, L. (1991). Getting adolescents to read. *Journal of Reading, 34,* 340–345.

Daisey, P. (1993). Three ways to promote the values and uses of literacy at any age. *Journal of Reading, 36,* 436–440.

Dillon, D. (1989). Showing them that I want them to learn and that I care about who they are: A microethnography of the social organization of a secondary low track English Reading classroom. *American Educational Research Journal, 26,* 227–259.

Eccles, J., & Wigfield, A. (1985). Teacher expectations and student motivation. In J. B. Dusek (Ed.), *Teacher expectancies.* Hillsdale, NJ: Erlbaum.

Ellis, W. G. (1987). To tell the truth or at least a little non-fiction. *ALAN Review, 14,* 39–41.

Frager, A. (1993). Affective dimensions of content area reading. *Journal of Reading, 36,* 616–622.

Frew, A. (1990). Four steps toward literature-based reading. *Journal of Reading, 34,* 98–102.

Fuhler, C. (1991). Add spark and sizzle to middle school social studies: Use trade books to enhance instruction. *The Social Studies, 82,* 234–237.

Graff, H. F. (1980). *The free and the brave.* Chicago: RandMcNally.

Grunwald, H. (Ed.). (1985, July 8). Special immigration issue: The changing face of America. *Time, 126*(1).

Guzzetti, B., Kowalinski, B., & McGowan, T. (1992). Using a literature-based approach to teaching social studies. *Journal of Reading, 36,* 114–122.

Huck, C. S. (1982). "I give you the end of a golden string." *Theory into Practice, 21,* 315–321.

Huck, C. S. (1986). To know a place for the first time. *Theory Into Practice, 25,* 12–15.

Huck, C., Hepler, S., & Hickman, J. (1987). *Children's literature in the elementary school,* (4th ed.). New York: Holt, Rinehart & Winston.

Isakson, M. (1991). Learning about reluctant readers through their letters. *Journal of Reading, 34,* 632–637.

Kindler, L. (1982). The relative effectiveness of narrative and expository forms of written presentation in developing selected cognitive abilities in science students. *Dissertation Abstracts International, 33,* 5577–A.

LaBlanc, E. P. (1984). *Everyday reading: Motivating activities for improving reading, vocabulary, and study skills, grades 7–12.* Glenview, IL: Scott, Foresman.

Levine, S. G. (1984). USSR-A necessary component in teaching reading. *Journal of Reading, 27,* 394–400.

Levstik, L. (1990). Research directions: Mediating content through literary texts. *Language Arts, 67,* 848–853.

Maria, K. (1990). *Reading comprehension instruction: Issues and strategies.* Parkton, MD: York Press.

Mathews, C. (1987). Lap reading for teenagers. *Journal of Reading, 30,* 410–413.

Mathewson, G. C. (1985). Toward a comprehensive model of affect in the reading process. In H. Singer & R. Rudell (Eds.), *Theoretical models and processes of reading,* 3rd. Ed. Newark, DE: International Reading Association.

McGowan, T., & Guzzetti, B. (1991). Promoting social studies understanding through literature-based instruction. *The Social Studies, 81,* 16–22.

McNeil, J. D. (1987). *Reading comprehension: New directions for classroom practice,* 2nd ed. Glenview, IL: Scott, Foresman.

Nell, V. (1988). *Lost in a book: The psychology of reading for pleasure.* New Haven, CT: Yale University Press.

Neuman, S. B. (1986). Television, reading and the home environment. *Reading Research and Instruction, 25,* 173–183.

Neuman, S. B. (1988). The displacement effect: Assessing the relation between television viewing and reading performance. *Reading Research Quarterly, 23,* 414–440.

Peterson, R., & Eeds, M. (1990). *Grand conversations.* Richmond Hill, Ontario: Scholastic-TAB.

Reed, A. J. S. (1985). *Reaching adolescents: The young adult book and the school.* New York: Holt, Rinehart and Winston.

Reed, A. J. S. (1988). *Comics to classics: A parent's guide to books for teens and preteens.* Newark, NJ: International Reading Association.

Renner, S., & Carter, J. (1991). Comprehending text: Appreciating diversity through folklore. *Journal of Reading, 38,* 602–604.

Sanacore, J. (1988). Schoolwide independent reading: The principal can help. *Journal of Reading, 31,* 346–353.

Sanacore, J. (1990). Creating the lifetime reading habit in social studies. *Journal of Reading, 33,* 414–418.

Sanacore, J. (1992). Encouraging the lifetime reading habit. *Journal of Reading, 35,* 474–477.

Smith, J. (1993). Content learning: A third reason for using literature in teaching reading. *Reading Research and Instruction, 32,* 64–71.

Smith, V., Scott, J., & Coskrey, W. (1990). *Teaching the science in science fiction.* Paper presented at the meeting of the American Association for the Advancement of Science, New Orleans, LA.

Stover, L. (September, 1988). What do you mean, we have to read a book for art class? *Art Education,* 8–13.

Swiebold, G. (1984). Textbooks do need trade books: One librarian's case study. *Top of the News, 41,* 93–98.

Trelease, J. (1989). *The new read-aloud handbook.* New York: Penguin.

Vye, N., Rowe, D., Kinzer, C., & Risko, V. (1990). *The effects of anchored instruction for teaching social studies: Enhancing comprehension of setting information.* Paper presented at the meeting of the American Educational Research Association, Boston, MA.

Young Adult Books

Abbot, E. (1927). *Flatland.* Boston: Little, Brown.

Anno, M. (1983). *Anno's USA.* New York: Philomel.

Asimov, I. (1966). *Fantastic voyage.* Boston: Houghton Mifflin.

Beattie, O., & Geiger, J. (1992). *Buried in ice: The mystery of the lost arctic expedition.* Toronto: Madison Press Books.

Bjork, C., & Anderson, L. (1985). *Linnea in Monet's garden.* New York: Farrar, Straus & Giroux.

Bond, N. (1981). *The voyage begun.* New York: Atheneum.

Bor, J. (1963). *The Terezin requiem.* New York: Alfred A. Knopf.

Bornholt, J. (1989). *Star trek, the next generation.* New York: Dell.

Burgess, A. (1962). *The wanting seed.* New York: W. W. Norton.

Caudill, R. (1988). *Tree of freedom.* New York: Puffin Books.

Chaneles, S. (1974). *Three children of the Holocaust.* New York: Avon.

Chase, R. (1943). *Jack tales.* Boston: Houghton Mifflin.

Chase, R. (1948). *Grandfather tales.* Boston: Houghton Mifflin.

Chauncey, N. (1960). *Devil's hill.* New York: Franklin Watts.

Clark, M. T. (1969). *The min min.* New York: Collier.

Collier, J. L., & Collier, C. (1974). *My brother Sam is dead.* New York: Scholastic.

de Trevino, E. (1965). *I, Juan de Pareja.* New York: Farrar, Straus & Giroux.

Dewdney, A. K. (1984). *The planiverse.* New York: Poseidon Press.

Edmonds, W. (1991). *The matchlock gun.* New York: Troll.

Ewy, D., & Ewy, R. (1985). *Teen pregnancy: The challenges we faced, the choices we made.* New York: New American Library.

Forbes, E. (1945). *Johnny Tremain.* Boston: Houghton Mifflin.

Fox, P. (1973). *The slave dancer* (E. Keith, Illus.). New York: Bradbury.

George, J. C. (1959). *My side of the mountain.* New York: E. P. Dutton.

Grant, S., & Mandrake, T. (1990). *William Shakespeare's Hamlet.* New York: Berkley.

Hesse, K. (1992). *Letters from Rifka.* New York: Henry Holt.

Hinton, C. H. (1907). *An episode in flatland.* London: Swan Sonnenschein.

Howard, E. (1987). *Mystery of the metro.* New York: Random House.

Hunt, I. (1965). *Across five Aprils.* New York: Grosset & Dunlap.

Jacobs, H. (1973). *Cajun night before Christmas.* New York: Pelican.

Kantor, A. (1971). *The book of Alfred Kantor.* New York: McGraw-Hill.

Lagerlof, S. (1912). *The wonderful adventures of Nils* (V. S. Howard, Trans.). New York: Doubleday, Page.

Levin, I. (1977). *The boys from Brazil.* New York: Dell.

Levinson, R. (1985). *Watch the stars come out* (D. Goode, Illus.). New York: E. P. Dutton.

Lowry, L. (1989). *Number the stars.* Boston: Houghton Mifflin.

Meltzer, M. (1976). *Never to forget: The Jews of the Holocaust.* New York: HarperCollins.

Mowat, F. (1979). *Never cry wolf.* New York: Bantam.

O'Dell, S. (1960). *Island of the blue dolphins.* Boston: Houghton Mifflin.

O'Dell, S. (1979). *The captive.* Boston: Houghton Mifflin.

O'Dell, S. (1981). *The feathered serpent.* Boston: Houghton Mifflin.

O'Dell, S. (1983). *The amethyst ring.* Boston: Houghton Mifflin.

Oneal, Z. (1986). *In summer light.* New York: Bantam.

Pelgrom, E. (1980). *The winter when time was frozen* (M. Rudnik & R. Rudnik, Trans.) New York: William Morrow.

Plimpton, G. (1988). *The curious case of Sidd Finch.* New York: Ballantine.

Pratt, K. (1992). *A walk in the rainforest.* Nevada City, CA: DAWN Publications.

Richter, H. P. (1970). *Friedrich* (E. Kroll, Trans.). New York: Holt, Rinehart & Winston.

Robertson, J. (1992). *Civil War!: America becomes one nation.* New York: Alfred A. Knopf.

Rodowsky, C. (1985). *Julie's daughter.* New York: Farrar, Straus & Giroux.

Rose, A. (1977). *Refugee.* New York: Vail-Ballou Press.

Schultz, R. (1992a). *Looking inside sports aerodynamics.* Santa Fe, NM: John Muir Publications.

Schultz, R. (1992b). *Looking inside the brain.* Santa Fe, NM: John Muir Publications.

Seltzer, D. (1979). *Prophecy.* New York: Ballantine.

Sender-Minsky, R. (1986). *The cage.* New York: Bantam.

Siegal, A. (1981). *Upon the head of the goat.* New York: Farrar, Straus & Giroux.

Silver, N. (1990). *No tigers in Africa.* New York: E. P. Dutton.

Silver, N. (1991). *An eye for color.* New York: E. P. Dutton.

Sworthout, G. (1970). *Bless the beasts and children.* New York: Pocket Books.

Thiele, C. (1974). *Fire in the stone.* New York: Harper & Row.

Thiele, C. (1982). *The valley between.* Adelaide: Rigby.

Wells, H. G. (1966). *The island of Dr. Moreau.* New York: Airmont.

9

Strategic Learning Across the Content Areas

Shifting the responsibility for learning from the teacher to the student and improving the capabilities of students for engaging in self-directed learning might be expected to have benefits for both students and teachers. First, with respect to teachers and schools, these changes might provide an economical way to increase total learning without the need to allocate additional teaching or instructional time. . . . Giving students more responsibility for their learning might also be expected to reduce somewhat the burden that teachers bear for effecting student achievement. Having students share in this responsibility might be expected to reduce teachers' anxiety that they alone are the cause of students' successes and failures.

—Thomas, Strage, and Curley (1988)

As the preceding quotation suggests, students who are strategic in their learning will profit, as will their teachers. Students will profit because the use of study strategies is highly correlated to their academic achievement (Zimmerman & Pons, 1988). The same strong correlations between achievement and strategy use have also been found in college settings (e.g., Nist, Simpson, Olejnik, & Mealey, 1991).

As defined in Chapter 2, study strategies are deliberate, planned, and conscious activities that students select to achieve a particular goal. As such, strategies can be "examined, reported, and modified" (Garner, 1988, p. 64). Students typically employ study strategies when they need to retain material for the purpose of taking a test, writing a paper, participating in class discussion, or any other demonstration of their learning. When does the need for strategy training begin? As soon as students are required to retain material for a later purpose, typically, when they encounter their first expository textbook—around fourth grade.

Given the restraints of time, the strategies we teach students should incorporate the processes that characterize strategic learning. Researchers (e.g., Thomas, Rohwer, & Wilson, 1989) have suggested that these cognitive and metacognitive processes include the following:

1. Select important ideas and transforming them into your own words.
2. Reorganize and elaborate on these ideas.
3. Ask questions concerning the significance of targeted information and ideas.
4. Monitor when you know and when you do not understand.
5. Establish goals and define your tasks.
6. Evaluate plans and the usefulness of the strategies you selected.

Because of the importance of these cognitive and metacognitive processes, the strategies we share in this chapter will reflect these underlying processes.

We should also note that this chapter is an extension of Chapter 3 because both describe and discuss how to build active learners. Whereas Chapter 3 emphasizes teacher-generated strategies that encourage elaborative processing of text and reflection (e.g., anticipation guides, interlocking guides, and study guides), this chapter emphasizes student-initiated strategies that promote strategic reading and independent learning. In particular, this chapter is devoted to ways of incorporating strategy training into your classroom instruction.

Case Study

Khaled is a ninth-grade English teacher who has been required by his department chairperson and the district-level Language Arts Coordinator to teach "study strategies" to his students. They have provided him a workbook that contains the SQ3R method and other techniques for improving vocabulary, time management, and reading rate. Khaled has organized his curricula so that Mondays are reserved for study skill instruction. During class, students complete the workbook pages by reading the brief passages and answering questions. As the students work, he walks around the room to answer questions and help students. Unfortunately, his students have complained bitterly about these activities on Monday. Even more disheartening is the fact that Khaled's students have not seen the connection between the workbook activities and their other courses. Students seem to be reading, listening, and studying in the same way in his English class, and other teachers report the same. That is, students still seem to be passive memorizers and learners. Khaled believes study skills are important for his students, but he is growing increasingly frustrated.

To the Reader: As you read and work through this chapter on study strategies, decide what Khaled might do to improve his approach. Consider the strategies we examine and the conditions necessary for students to become strategic learners.

Guidelines for Teaching Study Strategies

Determine the Demands of the Criterion Task

Imagine that you are training to run a machine in a factory, and you prepare for your job by reading a manual about how to operate the machine. You read the manual a couple of times, skimming over it before you begin working. Then, you are put on the machine and told to get started. Every few minutes you need to consult the manual; eventually, the machine breaks down, and your boss is at your throat. The reason for your failure? A clear mismatch between how you trained and the task's demands.

Now imagine that in preparing for a test about a chapter in her psychology textbook, an 11th grader reads her book, puts key terms related to Sheldon's body types on flashcards, and rehearses the definitions and characteristics of endomorphs, mesomorphs, and ectomorphs. The test question asks, "Critique Sheldon's theory of personality type and human morphology by pointing out strengths and limitations of the theory." The student pleads with her teacher after receiving a failing grade, "But this wasn't in the book." The reason for the student's failure? A clear mismatch between how she trained and the task's demands.

When we were high school teachers, time and again students came to us with complaints similar to this psychology student's. "I failed my history test," a student said once. "I even studied for 3 days! The teacher tricked us—she asked questions that weren't in the book."

"Okay, but how did you study?"

Well, I read the chapter two times and tried to remember everything I could about World War I."

After looking over the student's exam, it was plain to see that he had studied and remembered facts, but the exam questions, in the form of short essays, asked him to draw conclusions and critically evaluate. On further investigation, it was discovered that the history teacher had announced in advance the kind of test and types of question the students would have. The primary reason this student failed was not because of a "trick" test, but because of a mismatch between how he had processed the material he was studying and the processing demands required by the history exam.

This incident and the examples preceding it point out the importance of the principle of **transfer appropriateness**. This principle states that the higher or more appropriate the match between a study process and a task, the more easily information can be transferred to long-term memory. A few years ago, J. R. King, Biggs, and Lipsky (1984) and, more recently, Simpson, Stahl, and Hayes (1989) verified through separate research studies that perhaps the best way to prepare for an essay-type examination, for instance, is by creating written summaries of the important material in the text. Because summary writing and essay exam writing both require a similar type of product (writing) and a similar level of processing (synthesizing), there is a high match between the study process and the exam, which leads to positive testing outcomes.

Imagine that a student is studying for a biology test by using flashcards with the names of bones on one side and their locations on the other. The test asks students to match bones with their locations. In this case, we would expect a positive outcome. There is a clear match between the level and type of processing of the study strategy and the exam. Even though the level of processing of the materials is a literal, factual level, the exam questions are at the same level. In short, the strategy matches the task.

We do not need research to tell us that some study processes or training methods are more appropriate for certain tasks than others. It is often a matter of common sense. Yet, we all have observed teachers who feel so strongly about one study method or system that they will force it on students as the panacea for all learning. The key to an effective study strategy is how well matched it is with the **criterion task** (i.e., the test, paper, discussion, demonstration). The more closely matched these two, the greater likelihood of positive results on the criterion task.

All teachers should provide clear and explicit information about what students are expected to learn as a result of their study and how that learning is to be demonstrated, and they should assist students in study processes that help them meet these expectations. More importantly, students need to be shown that it is acceptable for them to seek information about the nature of their tasks and other ways they will be held accountable for their learning. With that information, they then can make informed decisions as to which study strategy they should employ.

Develop Flexible Strategies and Knowledge of When and Why to Use Them

In Chapters 2 and 3, we described active learners as those who have knowledge (i.e., declarative, procedural, and conditional) and control of strategies. Here, we reiterate that active learners need to develop a repertoire of adaptive, flexible strategies and an ability to engage the most appropriate ones to match the processing demands and content areas they are reading and studying. To do this, we need to teach students the *when*, or best specific applications of the strategy; the *whys*, or advantages; the limitations; and the *hows*, or steps of the strategy. No single study strategy or method is effective in all circumstances.

Create Situations So Students Can Transfer Strategies to Realistic Content-Area Tasks

Students need real, meaningful purposes for reading and studying. To teach them how to take notes in a particular way that has little to do with how they are actually supposed to organize and process the material in your class and other classes may mean that they will know how to take notes your way, but they will find no reason to do so. What good is it that students can list the steps of a strategy or complete a workbook activity using the strategy? As we have said many times, strategies should never be taught in isolation from authentic reading and study tasks.

One way to increase the likelihood that students will actually use the strategies they are taught is by linking strategy training to learning across the content areas. A nearby high school provides us an example of the approach. The high school requires all incoming freshmen to take a reading and study skills course during their first quarter. The course is designed to teach the new ninth graders how to read and study their textbooks, manage their time, and prepare for and take tests. They are taught to take notes from the text and lectures in a specific form, called the Cornell or split-page method (Pauk, 1985). Split-page notes are taken on note paper that is divided into two columns; the left side for key idea statements or questions, and the right side for the details of the lecture (this method is explained in greater detail later in this chapter). Here is what is so special about the way students in this high school learn this strategy: Although they are taught and practice the strategy in reading class, they are given the opportunity to apply it in their biology class. Biology teachers reinforce this method of note taking by talking to their students about how split-page notes can be taken for text content and for their lectures. To facilitate this process, they show students examples of their lecture material organized in the split-page format, and they constantly remind and encourage students to use the method.

Bob, the teacher in this reading course, is a former graduate student of ours. We asked him to conduct some informal research to determine if the freshmen, who had completed his reading course their first quarter, were continuing to take split-page notes in the last quarter of school. Near the end of the year, he met with each of his former students and, without advance warning, asked them to open their notebooks so he could spot any evidence that the method was being used. To his delight, and ours, many students were still taking split-page notes for their biology lectures. In contrast, however, only a few students were using the strategy in their other courses. It seemed clear to us that students were taking split-page notes in biology a full three quarters after they had been taught the strategy because Bob and the biology teachers were actively encouraging students to do so. Perhaps the split-page notes strategy was appropriate for the freshmen's other courses, but they were not spontaneously transferring the strategy. What we learn from this example is that one of the best ways to make study strategies a functional part of school learning is to get all teachers involved in reinforcing the strategies in their content areas. As you plan ahead to teach a particular strategy, meet with other teachers to explain your intentions and garner their support. In short, all teachers must carefully orchestrate strategy transfer.

Take the Time to Develop Students' Strategic Expertise

Stahl (1983), in his comprehensive analysis of over 100 textbook systems, discovered that one of the principal factors of success with a given system is providing students enough time to master the strategy. Most study strategies involve complex processes that cannot be mastered in short training sessions or artificial exercises packaged in workbooks. Admittedly, students may learn the steps of a strategy from such instructional approaches, but they will not gain the conditional and procedural knowledge necessary for them to transfer the strategy to their own tasks.

We believe it is critical that any teacher interested in training students to use study strategies accept this principle; otherwise, the teacher and the class may give up on a strategy, in spite of its potential, too early, before students have had a chance to develop control and expertise.

Validated training approaches and models (e.g., Garner, 1988; Stahl, King, & Henk, 1991) are numerous, but they do agree that instruction should be direct, informed, and explanatory. In other words, students can be trained to employ a strategy if they receive intensive instruction over a reasonable period of time that is characterized by (a) strategy explanations and rationales (i.e., steps, tactics, advantages); (b) strategy modeling and talk-throughs by the instructors; (c) examples from real texts and tasks that students will encounter; (d) guided practice with real texts, followed by specific, qualitative feedback; (e) debriefing sessions that deal with questions, student doubts, and fix-up strategies; (f) frequent independent practice opportunities across appropriate texts; and (g) guidelines on how to evaluate a strategy's success or failure.

We have found that it takes at least a few weeks before students begin to feel comfortable with a particular strategy. One way we have found to facilitate this process is by allowing students to practice the strategy with material that is easy to understand. In this way, students avoid overcrowding the cognitive workbench and can focus most of their attention on learning the strategy. Gradually, we increase the difficulty of the material, until students can demonstrate that they can apply the strategy to their own textbooks. This may take several weeks, but the time is well spent because our primary goals of study strategy training are to develop students' strategic expertise and ultimate independence in learning.

Encourage Students to Modify Strategies to Meet Personal Needs and Styles

It never fails. After a semester of teaching study strategies, say a lecture note-taking system, none of the students' notes look exactly like ours or like anyone else's in the class. But this should be expected, because there are no prototypes, no answer keys. We all make choices and decisions based on what we think is the most important information to include in our notes, and we modify the format to fit those perceptions. Students need to be able to make these choices and changes. After all, each of our study needs is personal, and what better time to learn how to make personal adaptations than when students are being trained to use study strategies. Help students develop ownership of the strategies by allowing them to be their own best informants about how study strategies should be modified to meet their needs.

The fundamental point is this: Do not be too prescriptive, mechanical, or formulaic when teaching students study strategies. Otherwise, you shift emphasis away from your intention of having students modify study processes to making judgments about products.

Know the Study Strategies You Teach

We could restate the principle "know the study strategies you teach" by saying, "practice what you preach." In our experience, students respond most favorably to strategy instruction when the teacher is credible and enthusiastic. This means that you must be very familiar with the strategies you offer students. If you plan to teach your students a text-study system, for instance, you need to know the system inside and out, know its strengths, limitations, and applications. One way to gain this knowledge is to learn and practice the system with your school reading. If you are taking university course work, use the strategy you are teaching your students in your own studying. Then, when students have questions about the strategy, you will be able to answer them from firsthand experience. Examples of your own strategies can also be very illuminating for students, because students often hold the misconception that "sophisticated readers" can read and remember everything on the first try. One of our graduate students shared with her students the chart she had created to learn the different theories of reading as one way of explaining the strategy of comparison and contrast charts. Students are sensitive to your attitudes about what you teach; if you can demonstrate your belief in the value and utility of study strategies, they will respond to your enthusiasm.

Use Homework to Reinforce Study Strategies

The topic of homework is often overlooked in secondary reading-methods textbooks. Yet, anyone who is or has been a high school teacher knows that students who study, study at home. In fact, high school students equate studying with time outside the classroom spent poring over books and notes in preparation for tests.

Interesting correlational data have been accumulated by the National Assessment of Educational Progress (NAEP) that relate homework with reading achievement. According to two major NAEP reports (*The Reading Report Card,* 1985; *Learning to be Literate in America,* 1987), the amount of homework students do seems to be related to their reading and writing proficiency. With regard to high school populations, increasing time spent on homework is systematically related to academic achievement (Keith, Reimers, Fehrmann, Pottebau, & Aubey, 1986). The authors of these reports conclude that students who study harder are likely to increase their levels of literacy over those who do not. They recommend that teachers take a more serious attitude toward homework for all groups of students.

While these correlational data seem to point in the direction that more homework is better, we contend that homework, in and of itself, does not necessarily promote and extend classroom learning, in spite of the chidings from national educational figures and major national reports. We briefly take up this topic here because we believe that homework, when appropriately assigned, can play an important role in reinforcing students' developing study strategies. Our data for this discussion do not come from empirical research but, rather, from anecdotal evidence, actual interviews with high school classroom teachers, as well as from our teaching experience.

Classroom teachers interested in helping students see the connection between how they read and study their textbooks, and the course expectations and requirements should assign homework that asks students to integrate particular strategies with the learning of the course content. For example, a biology teacher who wants her students to learn the different glands and hormones in the endocrine system could assign homework requiring them to create a map to summarize those concepts. In class, the students could brainstorm what information might be contained in the maps (e.g., locations, functions) and examine possible formats. The following day students could meet in groups to compare and discuss their maps and identify any ambiguous information. She could also give the students a pop quiz about the endocrine system, allowing them to use their newly created maps. In this way, the teacher receives feedback on how students are progressing in their mastery of the study strategy simultaneously with how well they are learning the course content.

In addition to these ideas for using homework as a vehicle for applying newly learned study strategies, we offer the following guidelines for assigning strategy homework:

- Study strategy homework assignments should be made as a result of careful initial planning of a unit's themes and concepts.
- Homework should be related to the amount of instruction given and time spent teaching a study strategy.
- If study strategy homework is given, it should be to all students, and adjustments should be made for various ability levels.

- Homework should be used as feedback on students' progress toward strategy expertise.
- Study strategy homework should be meaningful and functional.
- Specific feedback should be provided on students' homework assignments in a timely fashion.

Students frequently perceive homework as an infringement on their time for extracurricular activities, part-time jobs, or recreation. When homework is given judiciously and when it is meaningfully related to the course expectations, there is a greater chance that it will be completed. In turn, students who practice applying strategies to their course content will become competent readers and successful independent learners.

Based on these guidelines of effective study strategy instruction and the processes characterizing strategic learners, we next share some of the strategies that content-area teachers can incorporate into their classroom routine.

Basic Processes and Strategies

One basic strategy that students often overlook is the effective use of the textbook. We have known college students who have carried their psychology textbook around for 6 weeks, not knowing that there was a glossary in the back or that a list of key terms was included at the end of each chapter. If students can learn how their textbook is organized and capitalize on those features as they read and study, they can increase their concentration, understanding, and remembering.

Knowing the Format and Organization of a Textbook

Carolina, a history teacher, had attended a district workshop where the speaker stressed the importance of introducing the format and organization of textbooks to students. Before the workshop, she had assumed, as had many other teachers, that most students take the time to explore their textbooks once they receive them. Like most, she had merely handed out her textbook and assigned the first chapter of reading. Taking part of a class period to explain the "obvious characteristics" of a textbook seemed a bit unnecessary, but she decided to give it a try. She began her discussion by explaining that textbooks contain only the theories, perspectives, and conclusions of certain scholars under contract from a publisher. She then asked the students to read the title page and preface of their textbook to determine information about their authors. The students discovered that three individuals had written their text. After a discussion of the three, Carolina then stressed that the content of all their readings would be filtered through the biases and personal opinions of the authors.

After that brief philosophical orientation, which many students found intriguing, Carolina then distributed a textbook introduction activity designed to further orient her students to their textbook (Figure 9–1). She had learned in the workshop that many students neither know where important textbook parts are located nor how they function. She therefore paired her students and gave them 15 minutes to familiarize themselves with the parts of the textbook through the questions on the activity sheet. Each history chapter, as the students soon discovered, had a general introduction; a summary that listed key ideas; and boldfaced headings, subheadings, and italicized words. Carolina closed the period with a discussion of how these aids could help them as they read and studied their first assignment.

Carolina received positive feedback from her students on this lesson and decided to incorporate it into her "beginning of the year" routine. We know some school districts that insist that all teachers take the time during the first week of school to introduce their textbook with some activity like the one in Figure 9–1. The form can obviously be modified to fit any content-area textbook. What Carolina and many other teachers hope is that students will become critical and savvy consumers of text who will conduct their own "get-acquainted" activities before they begin reading.

Figure 9–1   Getting acquainted with your textbook

Title of textbook _____
Author(s) _____
Copyright date _____ Has the book been revised? _____

1. Read carefully and completely the **preface.** Summarize briefly what it says.
2. Find the **table of contents.** Answer these questions after studying the table of contents:
    a. Are the chapters broken down into many or few subheadings?
    b. List five or six major topics included in the table of contents.
3. Find the **index.** On what page does it begin? Name two or three types of information you find there.
4. Find the **glossary.** How can the glossary help you?
5. Find the **appendix.** What type of information can you find in it?
6. Find one **bibliography** in your text. List two authors or titles that interest you.
7. Examine Chapter 1. Check the organizational features available with this textbook:
    a. Introduction _____
    b. Marginal notes _____
    c. Italicized or underlined words _____
    d. Boldface headings _____
    e. Pictures _____ Graphs _____ Maps _____ Charts _____
    f. Internal summaries _____ Summary _____
    g. Questions at the end _____

Previewing

> Dominique and Turkessa were preparing to go to a performance of the local symphony. As they were dressing, Turkessa suggested they read about the composer, Bach, to learn about his life and musical philosophy. Dominique rummaged through their stacks of books in the basement and eventually found the trusty music appreciation text he had used years ago in undergraduate school. He read aloud about Bach as they finished dressing and continued reading to Turkessa as she drove downtown. They arrived at Symphony Hall early and read further from the program about the compositions to be performed that evening. By the time the first note sounded, they had established a context for the music that greatly aided their interpretation and appreciation of what they heard.

It is this kind of context setting that is at the heart of the **previewing strategy**. Students often seem to begin a reading assignment much like those people who entered Symphony Hall and scurried to find their seats just before the conductor's entrance on the stage. The music rushed over them, but because they did not plan for listening, they may not know what the composer intended to communicate with his music. Likewise, when students are expected to gain a complete understanding of their text but approach their reading by opening their books to the beginning of the reading assignment and simply plow forward, they fail to prepare for the flood of words they encounter and may find themselves in the middle of the chapter, unsure about what the author is trying to convey.

To prepare for the reading assignments, students should be taught how to preview. The previewing strategy is a logical follow-up to learning the format and organization of a textbook because it requires students to know and use those features. As indicated in Figure 9–2, as students preview they note the introductory paragraphs, summaries, topic markers or boldface headings, visual aids, summaries, and questions or problems provided by the author. Once students have previewed these text aspects, they then need to take a moment to reflect on the information they have just obtained, allowing the ideas to sink in. They might ask themselves such questions as these: What is the chapter about? What are some key vocabulary words I will learn? How should I read this chapter and divide up this task? With a mental framework of the key ideas and information in the text, students can employ appropriate strategies, and their reading can proceed more purposefully and appropriately.

So why should students preview? Because students may initially resist such a strategy, it is important to discuss the advantages of previewing with them. In these discussions stress the fact that previewing provides a meaningful organization of the material to be learned. As students read introductory paragraphs and look over headings and subheadings, a mental outline will be formed of the major topics and subtopics. This information will provide students with the data they need to make judgments about their readiness to learn the material, the difficulty of the material, and the actions they may need to take to learn the material. In addition, when students take the time to preview their textbooks before they read,

Figure 9–2 Important textbook features to be previewed

- *Table of contents.* A look through the table of contents for a chapter provides students with a broad level of organization.
- *Topic markers within the chapter.* These markers provide the reader with a more specific view of the organization of the chapter. Students should look over titles, headings, and subheadings and concurrently ask themselves these questions: How much do I already know about this topic? What does the author expect me to learn from this chapter? How are the topic markers related? The following topic markers, from a chapter in a history textbook over the Civil War, are listed in the order in which they appeared in the text to demonstrate how much students can learn about the material from merely surveying these markers.

  1. Bloodshed
       Fort Sumter Leads to War
          Other Southern States Secede
          The Border States
       The North Against the South
          The Northern Position
          The Southern Position
       Surprise at Bull Run

  2. The Real War Begins
       Machinery of Modern War
          New Guns
          Better Warships
       Early Battles
          The Battle of Shiloh
          A Naval Blockade
          The Peninsula Campaign
          Antietam

  3. The Goals of War Change
       England Remains Neutral
       Slavery Becomes the Main Issue
       The Emancipation Proclamation
       Drafting Begins

- *Introductory paragraphs and summaries.* Students can gain a great deal of information about the purpose of the chapter, the author's goals, and the major concepts by reading these sections of text. With this information in mind, students can focus their attention while reading about these important ideas.
- *Graphs, diagrams, and pictures.* Students should be shown that authors include visuals to highlight important information and ideas.
- *Questions or problems.* Textbook authors often include questions for consideration at the beginning of a chapter and/or questions at the end of a chapter that help students reflect on what they have read. Keeping these questions in mind will help students focus their reading on important information.

they should observe an improvement in their reading fluency, concentration, and comprehension (Neuman, 1988).

As a strategy, previewing is neither relevant nor appropriate for all texts and tasks. Some texts are not considerately organized, and many literature anthologies do not contain textbook markers or summaries. Hence, students will need to modify the preview strategy (i.e., read the first sentence of each paragraph when there are no textbook markers) or select a more appropriate strategy. Occasionally, some teachers may not want their students to read and study an entire chapter but instead may assign students to memorize some specific processes, steps, or formulas. For example, if a chemistry teacher told her class that all they would be required to know from Chapter 3 in their textbook was the symbols and atomic weights for five specific elements, extensive previewing would not be appropriate. This example points again to the importance of students' knowing what they will accountable for as a result of reading and studying so that they can employ the most relevant study strategy.

Previewing, although not a panacea, certainly will engage students in more active reading and learning. Moreover, previewing is one of those strategies that can be initially introduced by teachers, modeled and reinforced, and then gradually shifted to the students for their own responsibility and control.

Once students have previewed their text and started their reading, they must be able to identify and transform key ideas using their own words. In the next section, we deal with that essential process and strategy.

Summarizing

When you ask your colleague in the hall, "How are you?" and she says, "Fine," she is summarizing—categorizing her collective experiences and feelings and labeling them with a single word. When you ask a fellow student about the weather and he says, "Gloomy," this also is a summary, the selection of a single word that embraces a variety of weather characteristics.

All of us summarize many times during the course of a day. **Summarizing** is condensing information and ideas; it is getting to the heart of a matter, and without it, communication might be tediously protracted. Imagine those two simple questions being answered by a litany of feelings, emotions, and experiences, and by a detailed description of every weather feature. Despite our experience with summarizing, many students find it difficult to summarize what someone else has written (Brown & Day, 1983).

The ability to summarize text is perhaps one of the most essential and sophisticated reading skills (Wittrock, 1990; Wong, Wong, & Perry, 1986). In fact, if you were to return to Chapter 2 and review the five theoretical principles that characterize active learners, you would note that summary generation involves students in all these principles of active learning. Because summarization involves students in so many cognitive and metacognitive processes, a great deal of time can be required to develop expertise in summarizing. If, however, students can learn how to construct a summary using their own words, their understanding and metacognition will be enhanced (Wittrock, 1990). In addition, students can use their self-generated summaries to study and prepare for examinations. For example, Simpson and Nist (1990) found in their research that students who had been trained to summarize and annotate key ideas performed significantly better on three different content-area exams than a similar group of subjects who used traditional study methods (e.g., rereading, outlining). Even more interesting was the finding that the students who had summarized and annotated spent one-half as much time studying as did their counterparts.

The process of constructing summaries has been found to be rule governed (Brown & Day, 1983); that is, the mental steps involved seem to be the same from person to person. These rules have been turned into steps and have been used effectively to train students in summary writing:

1. Delete unimportant and redundant information.
2. Categorize information.
3. Select or create key idea statements.
4. Synthesize ideas across paragraphs.

These steps are a logical place to begin teaching students how to summarize. Loris, a ninth-grade English teacher, uses these steps and extensive modeling to teach summarization to her students. Mindful of process writing, Loris begins summary-writing instruction by emphasizing the process of constructing written summaries, thereby releasing students from the burden of worrying about correct structure and perfect grammar, and allowing them to focus on learning the process.

After the class discusses what a summary is and looks over examples, Loris passes out a short article and, without having previously rehearsed it, begins reading and thinking aloud as she works through the summary-writing process. She believes that to demonstrate the summarizing process with brand-new text is to give students a glimpse of how she struggles to make meaning and to reveal the genesis of her summary thinking. Loris has discovered that by giving only polished summaries, she misses the opportunity to teach them the strategies she used to construct them, the process of working from confusion to understanding (Pradl, 1987).

A ninth grader in the class offered Loris his history textbook and asked her if she would make a summary for a subsection from his reading assignment for the upcoming week. Selecting a short section entitled "The Yellow Press," Loris made copies and distributed them the next day. Without rehearsing, she then modeled the entire summary-writing process, talking out loud about how she made sense of the text and the decisions behind what to include in her summary. Compare the textbook segment with Loris's think-aloud while modeling the summarizing process.

The Yellow Press

While supporters of the rebel cause were active in the United States, newspaper tycoons William Randolph Hearst and Joseph Pulitzer were carrying on a circulation war. Each was determined that his paper would outsell the other. So both began to play up Spanish "atrocities." Legitimate accounts of suffering in the concentration camps were mixed with fake stories of wells being poisoned and little children being thrown to the sharks. American correspondents, who were not allowed to enter areas where fighting was going on, would sit around the bars of Havana and make up reports about battles that never took place. One, artist Frederic Remington, who had been illustrating reporters' dispatches, cabled Hearst saying that war between the United States and Spain seemed very unlikely. Back came Hearst's reply, "You furnish the pictures and I'll furnish the war."[*]

Loris's Think-Aloud

Loris: Remember that I'm looking at this section without having read what comes before, so I'm reading it in isolation. . . . You would have read the entire chapter. But I can clearly see by looking at the other sub-headings on these couple of pages that the topic is about Cuba and its struggle for independence from Spain around the turn of the century.

Okay, right from the start, the term "yellow press" means something like bad journalism or false reporting. This is something I just already know, so I'm thinking that the section will describe false reports about the Cuban–Spanish war. I don't remember much about that time in history except for Teddy Roosevelt and his Rough Riders, so I'll have to read on to find out which side the press is writing bad news about. (*Loris reads the first three lines aloud.*)

I know of Hearst and Pulitzer and the fact that they made their fortunes in the newspaper business. Remember Patti Hearst? She's part of that family . . . and you've heard of the Pulitzer Prize for journalism and fiction writing, haven't you?

I've learned here that they were reporting falsely about the Spanish to make them look bad and capitalize on all the Cuban supporters in the United States who might buy their papers. I figured this out because it said they wanted "to outsell the other" so they played up Spanish "atrocities." Atrocities are terrible acts of inhumanity, like the Nazis' concentration camps . . . and the word is in quotes, which

[*]Source: Adapted from Jordan, W. D., Greenblat, M., & Bowes, J. S. (1985), *The Americans, the History of a People and a Nation*, Evanston, IL: McDougal, Littell. Copyright 1985. Adapted by permission of the publisher.

tells me that it's being used in a sarcastic or exaggerated way. (*Loris reads the next sentence.*)

These are examples of the exaggerated stories about how the Spaniards were supposedly torturing helpless Cubans . . . throwing babies to sharks . . . and poisoning water. Because these are specific examples, I probably won't include them in my summary. (*Loris reads the last three sentences.*)

Okay, so the reporters made up the false stories . . . and the last example points up how far Hearst was willing to go. He would actually lie about a war between the U.S. and Spain just to sell more papers.

I noticed Remington was an illustrator. . . . He's famous for his paintings of Western scenes, cowboys and Indians. . . .

Now I'm going back to write a summary for this. First, I'm thinking about what the overall point is . . . something like how newspapers reported lies during the Cuban war of independence just to sell more papers. With this idea in mind, I'm going to *delete* some specific details here, like the fake stories of atrocities and the fact that the reporters sat in bars and thought up their stories . . . and even the last example about Hearst and a make-believe war. (*As she reported aloud on her thinking, she went to the board and crossed out the lines she wished to delete.*) Instead I want to group or *categorize* these things with an expression like, well I could use this one: "The press printed false stories about Spanish atrocities."

So I might say in my summary (*Loris writes using a grease pencil and overhead transparency, while saying the words aloud*): "During the Cuban war of independence, major U.S. newspapers were competing with one another to sell the most papers. To do this, some papers printed false stories about Spanish atrocities."

Now, if it's important to remember that Hearst's and Pulitzer's papers were the primary ones engaged in false reporting, then I suppose they should be mentioned in the summary.

Student: You said that when we summarize we should also look for topic sentences if the author gives them to us, so couldn't you just take the first three lines of that section, since they say just about what you've said?

Loris: They do sound similar, don't they? If those three sentences said it all for you, then I guess there would be no reason why you couldn't use them. But one thing I'm trying to encourage you all to do is to put the information into your own words as much as possible . . . because by paraphrasing you can usually save on words and condense even more. I suppose if I were summarizing this entire chapter, then mention of the Cuban war of independence in my first sentence would not be necessary either, and I could cut it out.

As this session demonstrates, allowing students to eavesdrop on her thinking and decision making provided students a model for interacting with Loris in the construction of summaries for other pieces of text. Working together, struggling together, they marked up and deleted information, created topic sentences, and tied together remaining ideas into condensed paragraphs.

As we mentioned earlier, it is important to begin strategy training with text that is relatively easy for students to understand so that they can concentrate on learning the strategy instead of being bogged down by simply trying to understand what they are reading. Loris likes to begin training by providing students with articles from popular magazines that are interesting and well organized. Eventually, students bring in their own articles to summarize, and gradually their practice includes passages and chapters from their school textbooks.

Like other teachers who have taught students how to summarize, Loris uses a variety of activities to teach and reinforce the steps of summarization. Once students feel somewhat comfortable summarizing, Loris asks them to share their own summaries with their classmates to help each other. In Figure 9–3 is a record of Cheng, Juan, and Andrea, members of Loris's class, discussing Juan's summary of an article about a radical high school principal from New Hampshire.

Loris has also given students models of summaries to evaluate. We have used this activity and have found it productive to provide students two or three versions of a summary and ask them to rank them from best to worst and to provide a rationale for their decisions. This activity can be done in pairs or in small groups.

Studying From Summaries

Hidi and Anderson (1986) have identified two types of summaries—reader based and writer based. **Reader-based summaries** are produced for someone else, probably a teacher. In contrast, **writer-based summaries** are produced by students for themselves, presumably for their study and reflection. Hare (1992) points out that writer-based summaries are different in that they are not bound by convention and form, probably include personal elaborations and comments, and use abbreviations or phrases rather than complete sentences. Students should probably learn how to construct both types of summaries. More importantly, students should be taught how to use their summarizations as a means of studying and learning content-area concepts.

Index Cards.   One obvious way of using summarization for studying is to have students read and test themselves on their summaries. To facilitate even more active learning, we have found it useful to have students place their summaries on **index cards** so they can test themselves. The index card in Figure 9–4 illustrates how one student in a driver's education course organized his summaries for study. Note that he put the key term on the front of the card with the main heading or superordinate idea that the term represented. On the back of the card he placed his summary, making sure he used his own words.

Figure 9–3 Cooperative group interaction during summary writing

Juan's Summary

Dennis Little took over as principal of Thorne High School six years ago. Before he came and got involved the dropout rate was high, reading and math scores were below average. Now that everything is up, the townspeople and the school board are trying to get rid of him because he is very intimate with students.

Cheng asked why the townspeople would want to get rid of Little when their students were doing better.

Juan: He's too close with the students.

Cheng: But it says here that he knows all the students and helps them out . . . like the girl who got pregnant when she was a junior and he helped her graduate and now she's in college.

Andrea: Sounds like a great principal to me. Ours just tells us to go to class, and stuff like that.

Cheng: That's what I mean . . . if he's doing such a great job why do they want to get rid of him?

Juan: I think this town is weird . . . they don't know how good Little is.

Andrea: I think what Cheng is asking is, is it only because Little's close to the students that they want him out, or is there something else?

Juan looked back over the article, studying certain sections intently.

Juan: It's a small town, they're set in their ways . . .

Cheng: Yeah, that's what I think. So how can you say that in your summary?

Juan: Something like, because he's so different and the town is so . . .

Andrea: Conservative.

Juan: Yeah, conservative, they want him out even though students like him, and more are going to college.

Cheng: And fewer drop out, and they have higher reading and math scores like you said already.

Juan: Okay, anything else you think I should change?

Andrea: I think you should say how Little made the change, you know, like where it says he raised discipline and academic standards.

Cheng: And he puts students first.

After assisting Juan with other minor concerns, his partners helped him rewrite his summary to read:

Dennis Little took over as principal of Thorne High School six years ago. Before he came, the dropout rate was high, and reading and math scores were below average. By requiring high academic standards and discipline, and getting involved in students' lives, Little's students have made big improvements. Even though they have improved, the conservative townspeople and school board think Little doesn't set a good example and they are trying to get rid of him.

There are several advantages to having students use index cards for their summaries. Most importantly, index cards are formatted so that students can test themselves or have another individual test them. Index cards also discourage students from becoming wordy and copying verbatim from the text because they are limited in size. Finally, students can group index cards in categories, thus further enhancing their understanding of how ideas relate to each other.

Figure 9–4   Using index cards for summaries

HYDROPLANING

In heavy rain or slush, the wheels of the car leave the road and climb up on the tough film of water. You can determine if this will happen by examining the surface. If you see a clear reflection on the pavement and patches of standing water or rain dimples, then you are in trouble. When this occurs, you have no traction, which is necessary for safe steering and braking. To avoid hydroplaning, you should slow down when it is raining, be alert, and keep good tread on your tires and plenty of air in your tires.

Textbook Annotations.   If students are permitted to write in their textbooks, another format they can use is **textbook annotations**—summarizing in the margins of their chapters. The college freshmen in the Simpson and Nist (1990) study wrote summaries in the margins of their history, sociology, and psychology textbooks. Simpson and Nist used the checklist in Figure 9–5 to provide the students qualitative feedback about their annotations. Checklists can also help students objectively evaluate their own work and strategies.

Split-Page Format.   Another format for recording and organizing students' summaries of textbook content is the **split-page format**. With this format, students record their abbreviated summaries on the right-hand side of a piece of paper and place on the left-hand side the term or concept represented by their notes. The notes in Figure 9–6 illustrate how the strategy can be applied to biology.

Figure 9–5 Annotation evaluation checklist

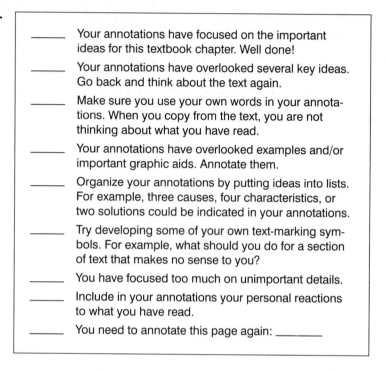

_____ Your annotations have focused on the important ideas for this textbook chapter. Well done!

_____ Your annotations have overlooked several key ideas. Go back and think about the text again.

_____ Make sure you use your own words in your annotations. When you copy from the text, you are not thinking about what you have read.

_____ Your annotations have overlooked examples and/or important graphic aids. Annotate them.

_____ Organize your annotations by putting ideas into lists. For example, three causes, four characteristics, or two solutions could be indicated in your annotations.

_____ Try developing some of your own text-marking symbols. For example, what should you do for a section of text that makes no sense to you?

_____ You have focused too much on unimportant details.

_____ Include in your annotations your personal reactions to what you have read.

_____ You need to annotate this page again: _____

Bob, a 10th-grade biology teacher, teaches his students the split-page format. He begins his instruction by asking the sophomores to read a chapter from their biology textbook and take notes on it in their usual fashion. This assignment provides him and his students some self-assessment data. Samples of actual notes produced by students are put on the overhead and analyzed. Bob asks students to consider the note samples relative to the goals of studying, which stimulates discussion of the relevance and transfer appropriateness of note-taking strategies. When he introduces split-page notes, he first describes the format; then, unrehearsed, he creates a set of notes. In this way, students get an inside view of Bob's own thoughts and decisions during the note-taking process, similar to Loris's way of introducing her students to the summary-writing process. In so doing, he models appropriate learner actions in creating and studying split-page notes.

1. He considers his purpose for reading, what he is expected to understand as a result of studying the content.

2. He previews the text, paying special attention to sections that may provide information relevant to his purpose.

3. He reads first, then decides what are the important concepts and supporting information.

4. He "boils down" the information by putting it into his own words, and he abbreviates whenever possible.

Chapter 7: Reproduction : Heredity

7.5 Terminology

Alleles (uh LEE uhlz)	— forms genes take — dominant or recessive — transmit hereditary traits
genotype (JEE nuh type)	— genetic formula — includes both alleles — example: R n
phenotype (FEE nuh type)	— trait determined by genotype — visible trait or physical characteristic — example: blue eyes
homozygous (hoh moh ZY guhs)	— two alleles — both the same — example: R R

Figure 9–6   Sample of split-page notes

5. He uses the split-page format to record the important concepts or terms in the left column and supporting information (e.g., examples, characteristics, definitions) in the right column.

6. He leaves extra space in the right-hand column before he makes each new entry in the left column for additional information picked up later in his reading or in class.

7. He demonstrates how he would study the notes by covering the right column and using the left-column entries as recall prompts, and vice versa.

Bob continues to model and encourage, working first with simple passages, and then gradually, as their expertise grows, assigning students to take notes from more difficult and lengthy sections of their biology textbooks. To reinforce the usefulness of taking notes from their textbook, Bob occasionally permits students to use their notes during quizzes, though he never informs them of this in advance. When students see that their effort in stating ideas in their own words has helped them in doing well on quizzes, they then become "believers."

Summarizing and taking notes from expository text, regardless of the format, involve students in several elaborative reading and thinking processes. Hence, they cannot be mastered in a week or two. We emphasize the point that if you believe a study strategy is worth teaching, students should be given the opportunity to learn it well. More importantly, students need to develop facility with the strategy so that they can personalize it to the task and course in a controlled and comfortable manner.

Mapping

Carol, a learning disability resource-room teacher, was working recently with her students on study strategies. Instead of talking to them about strategies, she spent the day meeting with students individually to discover what their study needs were and how they were presently trying to meet those needs. While sitting with Mark, a congenial, conscientious 12th grader, she listened as he tried to explain the characteristics and relationships among the three major aspects of Freud's theory of personality. He was studying for a test in his psychology course. As Mark moved back and forth from *id* to *ego* to *superego*, Carol soon became lost and said, "I need to see what you're talking about, can you draw me a picture?" As Mark drew and Carol questioned, they created a diagram to represent Freud's theory (Figure 9–7). When finished, they both looked at the diagram they had created and realized they had taken their understanding of the material to a new level. The diagram was an attempt to infer and make clear the organization and relationships in the content. Mark and Carol then talked about how students can create diagrams of complex material to use as study aids. Mark agreed that drawing out how ideas are related forces students to get their thoughts together.

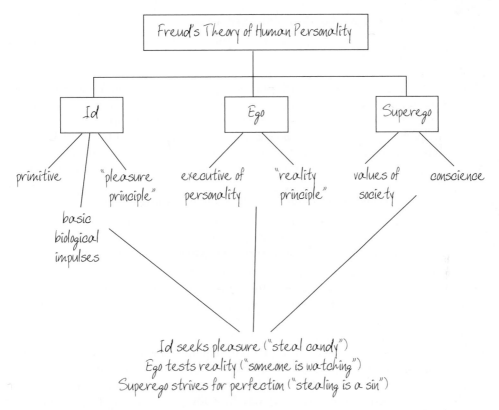

Figure 9–7   **Map for Freud's theory of human personality**

Mark's discovery that creating a diagram of the material helped organize his thinking and provided him a useful study aid is perhaps the best way to learn the value of the **mapping strategy**. Moreover, research has clearly demonstrated that it is a valuable strategy (Berkowitz, 1986). Like other elaborative study processes, however, mapping should not be taught as a series of steps that when followed will automatically lead to greater comprehension and retention. Instead, students should discover through experimentation an approach to mapping that is personally meaningful and appropriate to the study task. The reason for this is that there is actually no set way to map content—the material itself, the individual style and preference of the reader, and the study demands will all influence any map design. Notice how the specific designs of the examples of maps in Figure 9–8 to 9–10 differ yet retain these common features:

- The major theme, topic, or concept is emphasized.
- Other important ideas, concepts, and terms are boxed, circled, or otherwise set off in some way.

- Lines are used to connect related ideas.
- Information becomes more specific as map lines radiate from the major theme or topic.

We encourage students who prefer to create maps and other diagrammatical representations of text to develop a sensitivity to the clues the author provides to the organization of the content so that they can create the most accurate and useful map. For example, some content may best be represented by a cycle or flow chart, whereas other content may be best summarized in a tree diagram. The following suggestions have also helped students as they map sections from their textbooks:

1. Read and think about the text before beginning to map.
2. Make sure you do not crowd the information in your map because you want a memorable and precise image to study from. Consider the use of legal-size paper or computer paper because they are larger.
3. The act of constructing a map is a way of studying, but you will learn even more if you review your map by talking through the ideas. Better yet, see if you can construct another map from memory as a way of testing yourself.

Our experiences with teaching the mapping strategy have led us to believe that students either initially love the strategy or find it confusing and cumbersome. Hence, we have found it useful to encourage students to "try out" the strategy before rejecting it as a possible way to study. The best way to encourage students in trying out any strategy is to begin with some very structured practice on easy, high-interest material. With the mapping strategy, you can provide initial structure by asking students to complete a skeletal or unfinished map in small groups or pairs. Students can then discuss the experience and brainstorm ways to study from their finished product.

You may remember that a graphic organizer, useful as both a readiness strategy (see Chapter 5) and a vocabulary strategy (see Chapter 6), is a visual representation of the key vocabulary and concepts in a text that the teacher creates and provides to students. Although maps often strongly resemble graphic organizers, the major difference between the two is that maps are student generated. This is a critical difference. Providing students with organizational aids will promote learning; however, teaching students how to generate their own strategies will ensure that they become successful independent learners. As teachers, we need to determine how to walk that fine line between providing and promoting content-area learning.

Other Organizational Study Strategies

In Chapter 3, "Comprehension Strategies," we discussed charting as one strategy for helping students determine the relationships between ideas and organize their important likenesses and differences. Charting can also be a student-initiated

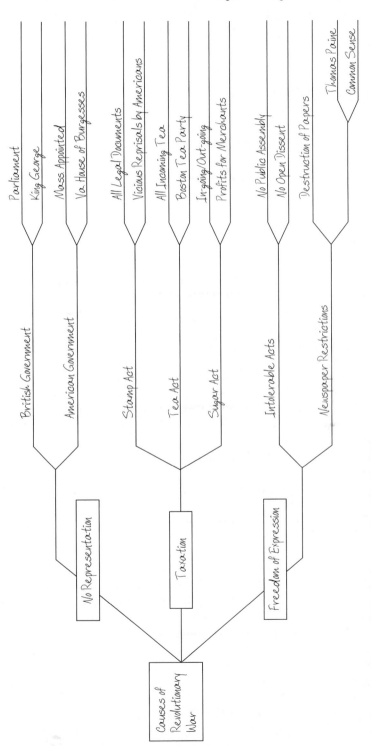

Figure 9–8   Map for the causes of the Revolutionary War

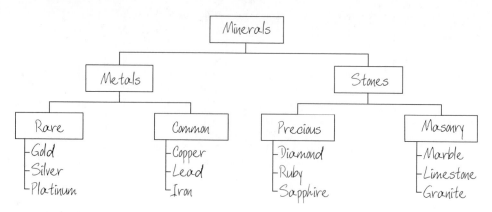

Figure 9–9   Map for minerals

strategy for studying and preparing for tests. The example in Chapter 3 of the various hormones secreted by the pituitary gland was created by the teacher and given to the students partially completed; however, students could have created that chart for their personal study. Of course, as with any study strategy, students must be taught the steps in making a chart as well as the advantage of charting. The chart in Figure 9–11 was created by one student to compare and contrast the presidencies of John Kennedy and Lyndon Johnson. Of course, the most difficult step of constructing a chart is the generation of the ideas for the vertical axis, which will serve to compare and contrast theories or people. To facilitate this step for students, it sometimes helps to brainstorm a list of generic ideas or terms that can be used. For example, these generic terms work particularly well in compare/contrast charts: (a) influences, (b) backgrounds, (c) contributions, (d) criticisms, (e) major beliefs, (f) stages, (g) examples, and (h) characteristics. Note that some of these generic terms could also be used in creating a map for a concept.

Time Lines

Time lines can be used in any course where it is important for students to understand a sequence or chronology of events. As with charting, the act of constructing a time line helps students organize and synthesize ideas, especially if they come from multiple sources such as textbook, lecture, and newspaper article. In Kent's 11th-grade English class, he teaches a unit on the struggle for civil and economic rights in the United States by a variety of minorities. In this way he can ask his students to read a variety of essays, short stories, poems, and novels that illustrate differing perspectives and ideas. One of the unit activities that students can select is the time line. Charisse and Erik, two of Kent's students, created the time line in Figure 9–12 after viewing a television documentary and reading the book *The Autobiography of Malcolm X* (Haley, 1964). Their time line arranged

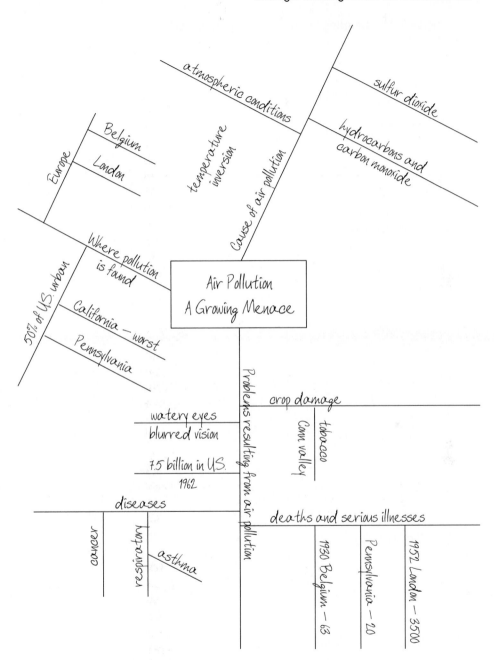

Figure 9–10   Map of a chapter on air pollution

Figure 9–11   **Charting to study and prepare for tests**

	JFK	LBJ
Background		
Political beliefs		
Civil rights		
Domestic policies		
Foreign policy		
Achievements, failures		

important events during the 1950s and 1960s in a vertical fashion, but time lines can also be visually arranged in a horizontal fashion. As with the chart or any other organizational strategy, Charisse and Erik learned a considerable amount of information merely from the decisions they had to make in formatting, identifying, and arranging the events.

Figure 9–12   Civil rights time line during the 1960s and early 1970s

1960	Sit-in at a lunch counter, Greensboro, NC.
1962	Meredith tries to enter U. of MS; Kennedy sends forces and two die, many are injured in disagreement.
1963	MLK campaigns against discrimination in Birmingham, AL; violence against peaceful demonstrators. Governor Wallace of AL tries to stop blacks from entering the U. of AL. Kennedy on television pleads for civil rights legislation. MLK leads (August) 200,000 peaceful demonstrators on the "March on Washington." Medgar Evans, a civil rights worker, is shot in MS. Explosion in a Baptist Church kills four black girls in Birmingham. Malcolm X becomes national spokesperson for black Muslims.
1964	Civil Rights Act of 1964. 24th Amendment. MLK wins Nobel Peace Prize. Voter registration effort begins in Mississippi; blacks and Northern whites work together; three are killed. Mississippi Freedom Democratic Party sends delegation to national Democratic Convention; refused seating. Malcolm X goes to England.
1965	Student Non-Violent Coordinating Committee (SNCC) launches new tactic, voter registration drives in AL; Black Panther Party is started. Violence in Selma, AL, as MLK, Malcolm X, and S. Carmichael register voters. Johnson sends through Congress Voting Rights Act of 1965. Riots in Watts, Los Angeles. Malcolm X is shot.
1966	Voter registration in Lowndes County, MS. SNCC and S. Carmichael criticize MLK's methods. Meredith begins march from Memphis to Jackson, MS (March Against Fear) and is shot. MLK and Carmichael continue march for him, and 4,000 blacks are registered to vote. This is the last great march in the South. The movement now moves North.
1967	Riots in Newark, NJ, and Detroit; 43 people die.
1968	MLK is killed.

In this section, we have shared a variety of study strategies that students can use to help them in selecting, transforming, and reorganizing key ideas. Many of these study strategies will also improve students' metacognitive awareness of what they know and what they do not know or understand. Because metacognitive awareness is an essential characteristic of active learners, in the next section, we discuss some additional study strategies that can be used to enhance secondary students' metacognition.

Strategies for Creating Metacognitive Awareness

Self-Questioning Strategies for Expository Text

Tom Newkirk says that our reading programs develop "polite readers" who are "deferentially literate. . . . Like good guests, they do not ask impertinent questions" (1982, p. 455). Many reading programs offer few opportunities for students to ask questions of the text, themselves, or the teacher. Instead, either the teacher asks the questions or the text provides questions after reading. These questioning practices convey a number of messages to students: (a) what appears in print is unassailable, (b) the teacher's and the text's questions are the important ones, (c) comprehension cannot be self-regulated. Yet the ability to ask and answer appropriate questions is crucial to becoming independent, self-monitoring readers and learners who can make sure that their purposes for reading are being met (Garner, 1988).

One strategy for increasing students' active processing of text is to teach them how to pose and then answer task-relevant questions about what they study. Because nearly every form of testing comprises questions, asking and answering questions while studying makes good sense. The key, of course, is knowing the kinds of questions to ask.

Students can learn how to ask thought-provoking questions by using high-utility stems as question starters (A. King, 1992). The following question stems are useful in most content areas:

1. In my own words . . . what does this term mean?
2. What are the author's key ideas?
3. What is an example of . . . ?
4. How would you use . . . to . . . ?
5. What is a new or different example of . . . ?
6. In my own words, explain why. . . .
7. How does . . . affect . . . ?
8. What are the results or consequences of . . . ?
9. What are the likenesses between . . . and . . . ?
10. How is . . . different from . . . ?

11. What are the advantages of . . . ?

12. What are the disadvantages/limitations of . . . ?

13. What are the functions of . . . ?

14. What are the characteristics of . . . ?

15. Do I agree or disagree with this statement: . . . ?

16. What were the contributions/influences of . . . ?

17. How would you evaluate . . . ?

King found that students working in pairs who generated elaborative answers to question stems like those in the preceding list perform better on a content-area objective test than their counterparts.

Students have options in how they organize and answer their questions about expository text. They could, as did the subjects in King's studies, meet in pairs and quiz each other. Students could also write their questions and answers in a format that encourages self-testing. One such format is the questions–answers strategy.

Questions–Answers Strategy.   The example in Figure 9–13 illustrates how one student used the **questions–answers strategy** to prepare for a test about water pollution in his ecology class. Notice that many of the questions use the generic stems. When the questions and answers are written and organized in this way, students

Figure 9–13   Question–answer strategy to prepare for a test

Questions	Answers
1. What is the major source of solid waste?	Agriculture
2. What is the effect of silting on our environment?	Silting reduces O_2 production and food supply for fish; also fouls spawning beds of fish.
3. What causes acid mine drainage?	
4. What is the danger of acid mine waste?	
5. Why was DDT banned?	
6. What chemical compound affects the central nervous system of humans and animals?	
7. What is the specific problem associated with thermal pollution?	
8. Give an example of a material that is NOT biodegradable.	

can test themselves by folding the paper in half and reading the questions aloud. They can also test each other because a permanent written artifact is available for them to share. Because the questions–answers strategy is written, it also can be handed in to teachers for their feedback. For example, by looking at the students' self-generated questions, teachers can determine what misconceptions for difficulties students are encountering with a particular concept.

Questions like the ones in Figure 9–13 do not spout from students' mouths at the first try. In fact, we have found that modeling, coaching, and specific feedback on the students' attempts are all necessary for students to learn how to ask and answer meaningful questions. One geography teacher we know distributes index cards to his students and requires them to write a question each day throughout the year. He collects the cards and then shares with the class some of the more probing and thought-provoking questions, using them as a stimulus for discussion. Although it may take time to teach this strategy, the results are worth the effort in that students learn how to control and monitor their own learning. In the next section, we discuss how this strategy can be modified to narrative text.

Narrative Text and Self-Generated Questions

In Chapters 2 and 3, we presented the idea that texts have predictable structures and that we can teach students to take advantage of inherent properties of text to improve their reading and studying. One way to capitalize on the predictable rhetorical structure of narratives is to ask and answer questions related to story elements. The following questions typify the kind of generic questions that could be asked:

1. Who is the main character?
2. What did you learn about the main character from his actions? From what he said? From what others said about him?
3. How is the setting important to this story? Could this story have taken place somewhere else?
4. What are the goals of the main character? supporting characters?
5. How does the main character attempt to accomplish these goals?
6. Is the main character successful in reaching his goals?
7. What is the author saying about human nature?

Singer and Donlan (1982) devised such a set of story-structure questions and taught them to 11th-grade students. They found that, when compared with a group of students who simply read and reread, the students who asked questions of the story elements have a more complete understanding of the stories.

A senior high literature teacher taught his students to use the story-structure questions as a basis for creating their own specific questions. The teacher made it clear that this questioning process could be useful for understanding the stories they would read in their literature text, which in turn would aid them in class discussion and on examinations. To reinforce the relevance of this study strategy, the connection between these criterion tasks and studying stories through questioning was made explicit by presenting students with typical discussion and exam questions and relating them to specific questions based on the story-structure questions. Modeling the process of question construction, the teacher talked through how he created specific questions to prompt his understanding of essential story elements for simple, familiar stories. He then asked students to work in small groups to generate questions for other simple, familiar stories. Gradually, students began working with the stories from their literature anthology. Figure 9–14 illustrates one group's set of questions developed specifically for Hemingway's "The Short Happy Life of Francis Macomber," a short story in their literature anthology.

What is most impressive about story-structure questions is that they reflect the student's attempt to personalize and control the questioning process. Students learned that questioning can be modified to match the structure of a story and to focus their attention on its most important aspects.

Figure 9–14   Story-specific questions based on story-structure questions for Hemingway's "The Short Happy Life of Francis Macomber"

The Leading Character

Who is Francis Macomber?
What do we learn about him from what Wilson and Margot say about and to him?
   What the author says about him?

The Goal

Why does Macomber want to kill the lion?
What does this reveal about Macomber's personality?

The Obstacles

What prevents Macomber from killing the lion?
Why does Macomber go after the buffalo with such a vengeance?

The Outcome

Why did Macomber run from the grass when the lion charged?
What does this reveal about his character?
Was Margot trying to shoot Macomber or the buffalo?

The Theme

Macomber's struggle is with himself and his own self-confidence. He also struggles with the forces of nature in the lion and buffalo. And he struggles with his wife because of what she thinks about him.

The Talk-Through

If you have ever verbally rehearsed what you wanted to tell the life insurance agent who kept pestering you with phone calls, you have conducted a talk-through. A **talk-through** is a study strategy that involves students in verbally rehearsing content-area concepts (Simpson, 1993). The study strategies previously discussed (e.g., summarizing, mapping) have relied on written artifacts, whereas the talk-through involves students in expressing and explaining themselves orally. In fact, the talk-through is very much like teaching, except the audience is imaginary. We tell students that when they conduct their talk-throughs they should imagine themselves giving a lecture on a topic to a very uninformed audience.

Given the fact that most of us have informally conducted talk-throughs to practice important information, it is not surprising to learn that talk-throughs, as a study strategy, can improve understanding and remembering of content-area concepts. Simpson's (1993) research demonstrated that students who had been trained to generate talk-throughs performed significantly better on an objective (i.e., multiple-choice and true–false) and essay exam than their counterparts. Even more interesting was the finding that these students predicted more accurately their overall performance on the test and on each individual item. In other words, the subjects who did talk-throughs were more metacognitively aware of their performance on the exam than their counterparts.

Talk-throughs can be used in any content area, but they must be tailored to the demands of the course. Depending on the course, a talk-through could contain any of the following information:

1. Key ideas, using the student's own words
2. Examples, characteristics, processes, steps, causes, effects
3. Personal or creative reactions
4. Summary statement or generalizations
5. Personal applications or examples

Consequently, what constitutes an effective talk-through in an American history class would probably differ from an effective talk-through in a geometry course or physical education course. For example, in history, students would want to include key terms like the Progressives, muckrakers, initiative, referendum, and recall, making sure that they also analyze the causes and effects of each.

Carolina, the history teacher whom we mentioned earlier in this chapter, has found that students profit from using the talk-through strategy in her course, especially if they learn it early in the year. She begins her lesson by demonstrating a talk-through. After her demonstration, Carolina talks her students through the steps in preparing and delivering a talk-through. The steps she teaches her students include the following:

1. Think about the key ideas and trends of the assigned material. Make sure you are using your own words.

2. Organize the key ideas in some way. This can be on an index card, but be brief because these notes are meant only to prompt your memory.

3. Find a quiet place, close your textbook or class notes, and use your card to deliver out loud your talk-through.

4. After practicing your first talk-through, check your card to make sure you were precise and complete. Ask yourself if you made sense.

5. Practice the talk-through several times until you can do it without looking at the card. Sometimes it helps to stand up, looking into a mirror as you speak. Some individuals prefer delivering their talk-through into a tape recorder so they can listen to it later. Others prefer to deliver their talk-throughs to friends or relatives.

Carolina usually follows up her demonstration and explanations with a very structured assignment that asks students to prepare a talk-through on one section of a textbook chapter. For example, the assignment in Figure 9–15 illustrates how she guides students through the section on Kennedy's confrontations with Cuba. The next day students meet in pairs to give their talk-throughs as she walks about the room to eavesdrop on the pairs. After students have practiced their talk-throughs, Carolina encourages students to discuss the experience as well as the content they studied.

Carolina knows that students must internalize the advantages of a targeted strategy if they are to transfer it to their own tasks voluntarily. Consequently, after having the students try out the talk-through strategy, she asks them to brainstorm the possible advantages. Her students usually generate a list of advantages that included the following: (a) Talk-throughs help me determine what information I know and what information is still unclear. (b) Talk-throughs improve my understanding of key terms because I am using my own words. (c)

Figure 9–15 Sample talk-through card

Use the outline below to guide you in the development of a talk-through card for Kennedy's Cuba Confrontations on pages 284–285.

1. The Alliance for Progress
   Goals?
   Success?
2. Bay of Pigs Plan From Eisenhower?
   Goals?
   Success?
   Results?
3. Kennedy's Reaction to Khrushchev's Placement of Missiles in Cuba
4. Khrushchev's Response to Kennedy
5. Results of the Cuban Missile Crisis (5–6 results)

Talk-throughs help store information in my long-term memory. (d) Talk-throughs make me more actively involved in my learning.

Depending on her students' abilities to summarize and synthesize, Carolina may repeat the structured lesson several times before asking them to independently practice the talk-through strategy. Once a comfort level with the talk-through is established, she designates 1 day a week for talk-through sessions, usually at the beginning of the hour while she is taking attendance and distributing papers. In this way, she learns a lot about her students. That is, she quickly learns which students are doing their reading and which students are having difficulty understanding concepts. She has also found the talk-through strategy to be an excellent warm-up activity for any writing she assigns in her history class.

Journals as a Way to Build Metacognitive Awareness

In Chapter 7 we discuss the role of journals in encouraging students to become more active learners. Another journal format can help students monitor their thoughts and processes as they read and study—the double-entry format (Calkins, 1986; Nist & Simpson, 1987). With this format, students use the left-hand column of an evenly divided note page to copy directly from the text quotations, statements, theories, definitions, and other things that are difficult to understand, interesting, of key importance, or require clarification. On the right-hand side, students record whatever thoughts, questions, or comments that come to mind as they attempt to make sense of what was copied. Figure 9–16 is an example of a double-entry format that one ninth-grade student, Chris, created for his reading and study skills course. The text he copied on the left side of the paper came from one of his government chapters because he was having difficulty in the course. Notice Chris's comments on the right side. By examining this journal entry, his reading teacher was able to determine the productive strategies he was using, as well as the specific difficulties he was having. More importantly, Chris also gained that information about himself through his writing. The last comment made by Chris was a very honest and perceptive observation about textbooks that typifies the feelings of some students who are very metacognitively aware. Those comments, however, do not occur as a result of one journal entry. As with all study strategies, students need time, guidance, and specific feedback with their double-entry journals if they are to learn anything from the experience.

Defining Tasks and Establishing Goals

With the study strategies discussed previously, we have focused on ways to increase students' monitoring of what they read. Another critical aspect of metacognition involves students in planning their own learning by defining the tasks they are expected to accomplish. Tasks have two features—a product and a process. The product of a task is what students must do to demonstrate their

Figure 9–16   Entry in a study-skills journal

Text	Responses to Text and Strategy Concerns
Political attitudes may exist merely as potential. They may not have crystal-lized. But they still can be very impor-tant, for they can be evoked by lead-ers and converted into action. Latent opinions set rough boundaries for leaders. . . . *Source:* J. Burns, J. Peltason, & T. Cronin (1984). *Government by the People* (p. 175), Englewood Cliffs, NJ: Prentice Hall.	I know that this section is supposed to define the key word *latent* because the boldface heading tells me this. How-ever, I am having problems finding a definition. Help! *Okay*—I think the second sentence helps me, but I will need to look up the word *crystallized*. I think, right now, that latent opinions are opinions not formed, but existing as potential for leaders and other people who wish to influence us. *Whew*! I will read on since our teacher has told us that authors often take several pages to define a word. This is hard work and I think the text-book authors made it even harder for us.

understanding. In a typical content-area class, that product might be an essay exam or a written report. What students must do to complete the report are the processes. For example, to complete a report in a biology class, students would have to be able to identify and locate sources in a library, summarize that infor-mation, and then synthesize the ideas into a written paper.

As you would expect, task definition is especially important if students are to appropriately choose and implement a strategy (Alexander & Judy, 1988). In high school many secondary teachers typically define tasks in a rather explicit fashion. For example, a sophomore English teacher we observed provided her students this task information:

> On Friday you will have an essay exam over the five short stories we have studied thus far. The essay questions will ask you to analyze how the themes of these short stories are alike and different. Your essays will be evaluated on how well you answer the ques-tion and provide specific examples of your points. I will not be grading on spelling and mechanics, but I do expect organization.

Some secondary teachers or college professors, however, are not so explicit. As a result, students become confused about what they should do to read and study and often give up or become extremely frustrated (Simpson & Nist, 1992). One strategy that helps students define tasks and set goals is the PLAE strategy (Simpson & Nist, 1984). **PLAE** is an acronym that stands for *preplan, list, activate,* and *evaluate.* With PLAE, students define the task and establish their goals, select the most appropriate strategies for the task, make a plan of study, put their plan into operation, and then evaluate the effectiveness of their plan once they have completed the task. We focus on the first step of PLAE, preplan. In Figure 9–17 you will find the questions that students should pose and then answer during their preplanning step of PLAE. If students do not know the answers to any of the questions, they should be encouraged to ask their teacher. Thus, with that information, they can determine which strategies are most appropriate and how long they must study. If, for example, students determine that the test is multiple choice (the product) and requires them to learn a lot of factual material (the process), they then know to select a study strategy that will allow them to focus on memory-level thinking. They also can set more realistic goals and estimations of how long they must spend reviewing and studying.

Though the preplanning step is meant for students, content-area teachers may wish to use these questions as guidelines in their own assignment making. One teacher we know starts the year using these questions to help her elaborate on the task. In fact, she even hands out the preplanning questions to the students to answer as she speaks. By the end of the first quarter, however, she has transferred the responsibility to the students. On a day she deems appropriate, she announces a test and says, "Any questions?" Though it took time to cultivate, students eventually realized that they were responsible for gathering the data that would guide their reading and studying.

Figure 9–17   Preplanning during PLAE (preplan, list, activate, and evaluate)

PREPLANNING STAGE: Step 1 (Gathering information about the test and setting my goals.)

1. When is the test? (date, day, time)
2. Specifically, what are my other obligations that week?
3. What does the test cover?
4. How many items or questions will there be on the test?
5. What kind of test will it be?
6. What type of questions will be asked? Factual or memory questions? Inferential? Applied?
7. How much does the test count in the total evaluation process?
8. What is my goal for a grade on this test?
9. How much time do I need to spend studying, reciting, and reviewing?
10. How will this study change my regular schedule? Explain how I will find extra time.

Case Study Revisited

Return to the beginning of the chapter where we described Khaled, the English teacher assigned to teach study strategies. After having read this chapter, you probably have some ideas about how he could be more creative and effective in his teaching. Take time now to write your suggestions.

Khaled decided that his present approach of using a workbook to teach study strategies needed modification. His most important realization was that he had no idea what strategies his ninth graders needed to know to be successful learners in their other courses. Khaled therefore decided to talk with his colleagues and visit some of the classes during his planning period to determine the tasks or academic demands they required of their students. He also borrowed textbooks from each of the teachers and read a chapter in each. By doing this, he determined what the students were asked to read.

Armed with this information and comments from the students, he decided to downplay the importance of the workbook. As he explained to his department chairperson, "The students do not like the workbook, and neither do I. Commercial materials are not relevant to what students are being asked to do in their other courses. They do not typically read short passages and answer questions about the main idea and tone. If I am to teach students how to study, then I should teach them using the materials they are expected to master."

During the school year, Khaled also read a few articles about the teaching of study strategies in professional publications such as the *Journal of Reading*. From his reading, he realized that he needed to teach strategies more directly rather than merely assigning students to complete activities. One teaching technique he found particularly intriguing was modeling, or the think-aloud. After looking through the units he used to teach, he decided that he would probably have to teach less material but in more depth if he wanted his students to modify and transfer the strategies to their own courses.

During the summer, Khaled planned his curriculum, making sure he would emphasize some generic strategies such as knowing the parts of a textbook that students could use in all classes. He also included some content-specific strategies such as how to read and solve a word problem in mathematics. Overall, he knew his goal was to show his students how to become more active learners rather than passive memorizers.

We caught up with Khaled at the end of the first quarter, and he filled us in on what he perceived, thus far, to be the successful units as well as the failures. On the positive side, Khaled thought his unit on teaching his students how to use their textbook and how to preview was well received by the students and other ninth-grade teachers. In fact, the civics teacher was so thrilled that her students this year knew how to use the index, appendix, and glossary for her textbook that she agreed to reinforce the preview strategy in her class.

Khaled and his students also thought the unit on solving mathematical problems was successful. By thinking through the processes he had used to solve problems, Khaled devised these seven steps, which he taught to all his students:

1. Read the problem carefully, underlining key words or phrases.
2. Reword the problem with the necessary facts.
3. Ask yourself, What do I have to solve? What is unknown?
4. Translate the reworded problem to an equation.
5. Solve the equation.
6. Check the answer by substituting the answer in the equation. Ask yourself, Does this answer make sense?
7. State the answer to the problem clearly.

Khaled kept these seven steps on his bulletin board and distributed them to every student on a bookmark. Throughout the first 9 weeks, he provided think-alouds and demonstrations. The following example is typical of his verbal reporting during problem solving:

This is the problem. Watch the overhead as I read it aloud. "As a chef's assistant in a fancy restaurant, Kendra earns in 1 year a salary of $19,000. This is two fifths of the head chef's salary. What is the head chef's salary?"

First, I will reword the problem. Two fifths of the head chef's salary is Kendra's salary. I was able to reword the problem because I knew that the word *this* in the second sentence referred to Kendra's salary (he points to the word and the referent). Look for words like *this*. Please notice how I took out the extra words and reduced the problem to just the necessary facts and words.

Second, I will translate these 10 words into symbols and numbers to create an equation. My goal for this problem is to find the chef's salary, which I do not know. Thus, I will represent this *unknown* with an X. I do know Kendra's salary: It is $19,000. I also know that two fifths of the chef's salary, or 2/5 of X or 2/5 *times* X is $19,000. Or stated in another way, 2/5 times X = $19,000 or 2/5(X) = $19,000

I used the parentheses to stand for "multiplied by." Now we are ready to solve the problem.

Now, you may have already figured out the chef's salary without the first step of rewording and the second step of translating. Problems can be answered without these two critical steps. However, the type of problems you will be solving in Mr. Maxwell's algebra class demand that you learn how to reword and translate before you try to solve. So, please indulge yourself and me by doing these two steps on the next three story problems that appear on the overhead. I will give you 6 minutes to reword and set up equations. I do not care if you solve them at this time. The answer is not important. The process or steps are.

Khaled also spent considerable time teaching his students to summarize sections in their textbooks. He learned, however, not to have students practice a difficult and new process with material they find demanding. The first time he taught summarization, he had assigned the students to summarize a section from their biology textbook. The lesson was a complete disaster. Some students did not do it, and others became frustrated and resorted to almost verbatim copying from their textbook rather than paraphrasing. After analyzing the problem, Khaled realized that his students were struggling with the processes of summarization and certainly did not need the added factor of a difficult text to confound the situation. He replaced the assignment with a high-interest and well-organized article about gene splicing from the newspaper. The easier and more considerate material made all the difference in the assignment.

As Khaled looks to the next quarter, he is excited. His students participate more in class and do not complain as much about their assignments, even though they are probably doing more than what they did when they completed workbook pages. Many of his students are reading and listening more actively, but some are not. With those students he hopes to discover how they read and think about text through the use of the double-entry journal. He also plans to introduce the strategy of mapping to the students who have resisted the idea of summarizing. The first quarter has taught Khaled many things, but most importantly, he has realized that students will not be able to transfer study strategies to their own tasks if they only complete workbook activities.

Summary

Study strategies should be taught as processes instead of as a series of steps that when followed will automatically produce greater learning and retention. We have emphasized the learner as an important part of strategy instruction. Without opportunities for learners to help shape the particular study strategies they are being taught, we run the risk of offering students a series of meaningless formulas that have little relevance to students' genuine study needs. This has important implications for the teacher who wishes to foster successful independent learners. Your role should be to inform students of each study process and its best possible applications and then to guide them in developing personally meaningful adaptations that transfer to actual study tasks.

We purposely limited our presentation to a few effective study-reading processes because we wish to reinforce the idea that it takes a great deal of time to develop expertise in them. We also made it clear that no single text-study strategy will be appropriate for every study need. Consequently, students should be encouraged to learn a core of flexible, meaningful study processes so they can select the most appropriate one to fit their purposes and tasks. Finally, we have tried to stress that the development of strategic and active learning should be the goal of every high school curriculum.

References

Alexander, P. A., & Judy, J. E. (1988). The interaction of domain-specific and strategic knowledge in academic performance. *Review of Educational Research, 58,* 375–404.

Berkowitz, S. (1986). Effects of instruction in text organization on sixth-grade students' memory for expository reading. *Reading Research Quarterly, 21,* 161–178.

Brown, A. L., & Day, J. (1983). Macrorules for summarizing texts: The development of expertise. *Journal of Verbal Learning and Verbal Behavior, 22,* 1–14.

Burns, J., Peltason, J., & Cronin, T. (1984). *Government by the people.* Englewood Cliffs, NJ: Prentice-Hall.

Calkins, L. M. (1986). *The art of teaching writing.* Portsmouth, NH: Heinemann.

Garner, R. (1988). *Metacognition and reading.* Norwood, NJ: Ablex.

Hare, V. C. (1992). Summarizing text. In J. Irwin & M. Doyle (Eds.), *Reading/writing connections: Learning from research* (pp. 96–118). Newark, DE: International Reading Association.

Hidi, S., & Anderson, V. (1986). Producing written summaries: Task demands, cognitive operations, and implications for instruction. *Review of Educational Research, 56,* 473–493.

Jordan, W. D., Greenblat, M., & Bowes, J. S. (1985). *The Americans, the history of a people and a nation.* Evanston, IL: McDougal, Littell. Copyright 1985. Used by permission of the publisher.

Keith, T. Z., Reimers, T. M., Fehrmann, P. G., Pottebau, S. M., & Aubey, L. W. (1986). Parental involvement, homework, and TV time: Direct and indirect effects on high school achievement. *Journal of Educational Psychology, 78,* 373–380.

King, A. (1992). Enhancing peer interaction and learning in the classroom through reciprocal questioning. *American Educational Research Journal, 27,* 664–687.

King, J. R., Biggs, S., & Lipsky, S. (1984). Students' self-questioning and summarizing as reading study strategies. *Journal of Reading Behavior, 16,* 205–218.

National Assessment of Educational Progress. (1985). *The reading report card.* Princeton, NJ: Author.

National Assessment of Educational Progress. (1987). *Learning to be literate in America.* Princeton, NJ: Author.

Neuman, S. B. (1988). Enhancing children's comprehension through previewing. In J. E. Readence & R. S. Baldwin (Eds.), *Dialogues in literacy research. Thirty-seventh yearbook of the National Reading Conference* (pp. 219–224). Chicago: National Reading Conference.

Newkirk, T. (1982). Young writers as critical readers. *Language Arts, 59,* 451–457.

Nist, S. L., & Simpson, M. L. (1987). Facilitating transfer in college reading programs. *Journal of Reading, 30,* 62–625.

Nist, S. L., Simpson, M. L., Olejnik, S., & Mealey, D. L. (1991). The relation between self-selected study processes and test performance. *American Educational Research Journal, 28,* 849–874.

Pauk, W. (1985). *How to study in college* (3rd ed.). Boston: Houghton Mifflin.

Pradl, G. (1987). Close encounters of the first kind: Teaching the poem at the point of utterance. *English Journal, 76,* 66–69.

Simpson, M. L. (1993, December). *An examination of elaborative verbal rehearsals and their impact on college freshmen's cognitive and metacognitive performance.* Paper presented at the National Reading Conference, Charleston, SC.

Simpson, M. L., & Nist, S. L. (1984). PLAE: A model for planning successful independent learning. *Journal of Reading, 28,* 218–223.

Simpson, M. L., & Nist, S. L. (1990). Textbook annotation: An effective and efficient study strategy for college students. *Journal of Reading, 34,* 122–131.

Simpson, M. L., & Nist, S. L. (1992). A case study of academic literacy tasks and their negotiation in a university history course. In C. Kinzer & D. Leu (Eds.), *Literacy research, theory, and practice: Views from many perspectives. Forty-first Yearbook of the National Reading Conference* (pp. 253–260). Chicago: National Reading Conference.

Simpson, M. L., Stahl, N. A., & Hayes, C. G. (1989). PORPE: A research validation. *Journal of Reading, 33,* 22–28.

Singer, H., & Donlan, D. (1982). Active comprehension: Problem-solving schema with question generation for comprehension of complex short stories. *Reading Research Quarterly, 17,* 166–186.

Stahl, N. A. (1983). A historical analysis of textbook-study systems (Doctoral dissertation, University of Pittsburgh). *Dissertation Abstracts International, 45,* 480A. (University Microfilms No. 84–11, 839)

Stahl, N. A., King, J. R., & Henk, W. A. (1991). Enhancing students' notetaking through systematic, self-directed training and evaluation procedures. *Journal of Reading, 34,* 614–623.

Thomas, J. W., & Rohwer, W. D., & Wilson, M. (1989, March). *Hierarchical models of studying.* Paper presented at the meeting of the American Educational Research Association, San Francisco.

Thomas, J. W., Strage, A., & Curley, R. (1988). Improving students' self-directed learning: Issues and guidelines. *Elementary School Journal, 88,* 313–326.

Wittrock, M. C. (1990). Generative processes of comprehension. *Educational Psychologist, 24,* 345–376.

Wong, B. Y., Wong, R., & Perry, N. (1986). The efficacy of a self-questioning summarization strategy for use by underachievers and learning-disabled adolescents in social studies. *Learning Disabilities Focus, 2,* 20–35.

Zimmerman, B. J., & Pons, M. M. (1988). Construct validation of a strategy model of student self-regulated learning. *Journal of Educational Psychology, 80,* 284–290.

10

Expanding Literacy for Students With Special Needs

Only as we meet our students, observe them intelligently, and use them as informants are we able to draw from the potential curriculum appropriate and suitable objectives, assignments and strategies. Teachers with their students create, change, and are in charge of curriculum.

All the fuss about knowing students, both in general and specifically, comes from the belief that learning occurs when it is personalized and positive, and when it focuses on the strengths and unique abilities of individuals.

—Dorothy Watson (1988)

In previous chapters of this book, we have laid down the foundations for effective reading instruction and literacy development for secondary students. In many ways, these instructional foundations find their most powerful expression in applications for students with special needs. These students should receive our best strategies and not simply more structure, more routines, more basic remedial lessons. Special needs students, such as those who are culturally different, those who speak another language or a dialect, those who are poor readers, or those with specific learning disabilities, make up a varied and diverse group. Consequently, blanket generalizations about these students are inappropriate (Poplin,

1984). Yet, these students can be taught to become better readers, thinkers, and language users if we apply our knowledge of literacy and language development to them as we do to other so-called "normal" or "regular" students (Brodinsky & Keogh, 1989; Morgan & Hosay, 1991; Squires & Inlander, 1990). For students with special needs, as for all students, literacy development should be seen as a process of meaning making, in which reading and writing are vehicles for helping students make sense of their world, and the classroom is the supportive environment where growth in literacy occurs (Miller, 1993). Throughout this chapter, therefore, we will be emphasizing approaches that capitalize on what special needs students bring to the classroom, in terms of their needs, prior knowledge, experiences, beliefs, and culture.

Case Study

Rene is a biracial young woman of an Asian mother and a Hispanic father. She is in the 11th grade and attends a high school in a major urban center in the Midwest in a community of ethnic and socioeconomic diversity. The school is a large, decaying fortress-looking building with no windows. Its grounds are littered and unattended. Rene has been in special education classes since the third grade. She recalls with bitterness the experience that led her to initiation into special classes:

> It was the first or second day of school. My mom was real sick, she was having a miscarriage I think. I was really afraid. I thought she was going to die. Anyway, the teacher would write a word on the board, erase it, then go around the room and call on someone to say the word and spell it. Well, she finally called on me, but I wasn't paying attention because I was so upset about my mom. I had to stand up . . . I just couldn't remember the word. The class started laughing, and the teacher told me to sit down and for not paying attention I would have to write the word 50 times. It seems like from that time on I started having a lot of trouble reading, and they put me in special ed.

As an 11th grader, Rene was still in a special reading class. The class comprised 23 students—all but two were ethnic minorities. The classroom was small, cramped, and cluttered. During the winter, the radiators generated stifling heat and clanged uncontrollably. According to the teacher of this special reading class—a former shop teacher with 4 graduate hours of reading from a nearby university—students were supposed to be working on their own in self-paced workbooks and programmed materials. Reading kits with 25-year-old copyright dates and some programmed spelling and phonic books were stacked irregularly on the one small bookcase next to the teacher's desk. Very few of these materials were being used, however. Most of the students were either sleeping, listening to music on headphones, or talking quietly. On one of our visits, the teacher spent the period balancing his checkbook.

Rene used the time to visit with the only other female in the class. She commented on her experiences in remedial reading:

> It's a joke. I'm wasting my time in there. Nobody works, we just catch up on what's going on, you know, who's pregnant, who's going with who and stuff. Mr. Willis hates it too, so he just says "Don't bother me and I won't bother you." That's cool, but my reading is still bad and I have to take general courses because they're the only ones I can pass.

Rene commented on how she gets by in her other classes, such as history, science, and math, where reading assignments are required for successful class performance.

> Math's no problem for me. I've always been good in math. History is harder. I sit next to my girlfriend, Stella. She's real smart, she tells me what to do. I don't like that teacher . . . I never look at him and he never calls on me.

To the Reader: When reflecting on this challenging scene of dysfunctional teaching and learning in a disadvantaged, urban setting, consider ways Mr. Willis's class could become a place for meaningful literacy opportunities. How could Rene be "reached"? How could her reading class be restructured so that it is no longer a "waste of time" for students like Rene? Be prepared to write down your ideas and recommendations after reading this chapter.

How Does It Feel to Be a Reader With Special Needs?

To fully empathize with special needs students, we would have to be able to trade places with them, "crawl into their skin," see the world from their eyes. Anyone who has journeyed to another country and has experienced trying to communicate and get by in a brand-new culture where English is not spoken can begin to appreciate the frustrations some special needs students experience as they grapple to understand new, complex language forms in secondary school classrooms and textbooks. For obvious reasons, we cannot entirely come to know the feelings and experiences these students have when trying to learn, although we can help you come closer to understanding these students through a simulation. Read the following passage; then write in your own words what you believe is the correct interpretation of the section.

The Correct Interpretation of the Thirty-Fourth Section

The thirty-fourth section refers to the construction thereof adopted by the local tribunals, and to rights of things having a permanent locality, and other matters immovable and intraterritorial in their nature and character. It never has been supposed that the section did apply, or was intended to apply to questions of a more general nature, not at all dependent upon a fixed and permanent operation, as, for example, to the construction of written instruments, where the state tribunals are called upon to perform, that is, to ascertain upon general reasoning and legal analogies what is the true exposition of the instrument.

Based upon this interpretation, it seems to us that it would be at least as reasonable to assume an intent that the power should be imperative as to property known to be productive but which later becomes unproductive. We think under the facts of this case the existence of an intent that the power of sale was to become imperative upon failure of productivity with likelihood of continuance of that status, is the correct interpretation of the thirty-fourth section.

Now that you have read the passage and written your own interpretation of the "thirty-fourth section," how does it feel to be a remedial reader? We are only half serious when we ask this question, because we know you are not a remedial reader—most of the time. Occasionally, however, we all encounter texts that leave us totally bewildered, confused, and frustrated. This is how many special needs students must feel when they try to read textbooks filled with abstract concepts, unfamiliar vocabulary, and for which they have little interest or prior knowledge. As you work through the remainder of this chapter, keep in mind your experiences with "the thirty-fourth section," remember what it felt like to have little or no meaning to grab onto in the passage, and then, perhaps, you will see more clearly the relevance and importance of the ideas and strategies we recommend for helping special needs students expand their literacy.

Instructional Guidelines for Teaching Special Needs Students

In this chapter, we define students with special needs as those who require extra teacher attention to become competent language users and to excel as active, independent learners. Although we will not discuss every category of special need, we hope you will gain a sense of how the guidelines and methods of effective reading and writing instruction set forth in previous chapters and in this chapter may be applied to meet the literacy needs of these special students.

Special Needs Students Need More Than Pull-Out Time in a Resource Room

In her learning disabilities resource room, Carol provides sound reading and study skills assistance, but she cannot take care of all the literacy needs of her students. Much of her time outside of class, therefore, is spent in consultation with subject area teachers to discover ways to work cooperatively. She often finds this aspect of her work the most challenging because many teachers feel that the 45 minutes these students spend in resource daily is all the time they need. The result of this attitude is that classroom teachers give up responsibility for assisting the language and literacy development of their special needs students. Resource should play a supplementary and support role and not replace the work of the classroom teacher, who should be highly involved. The key concern here is that without coordination between the reading and writing instruction in resource and the kind that occurs in other classrooms, special needs students will likely continue to experience difficulty learning content-area subject matter and adequate reading strategies.

Lack of coordination can lead to another problem—the failure to adequately demonstrate how special needs students can transfer their reading and writing skills learned in resource to reading tasks in other classrooms and outside of school. Classroom teachers can facilitate transfer by helping students apply text study processes to their own textbooks reading and other assignments. Working with the resource teacher, the classroom teacher can discover the particular needs of each special student and plan for valuable reading and writing opportunities for these students. By taking time to integrate reading and study skills instruction into their content lessons, teachers will assist special needs students without singling them out or making them feel inferior.

Instruction Should Emphasize Meaningful Reading and Writing Experiences Over Skill Mastery

Poor readers are often penalized. They are usually recycled through a regimen of basic skills instruction that failed to produce reading competency in the first place (Herber & Nelson-Herber, 1987). Basic skills instruction that focuses on spelling accuracy and word attack and requires memorizing rules and performing mechanical behaviors fails to capitalize on how language is learned best (Brozo & Brozo, in press; Goodman, 1986). As for minority students, Reyhner and Garcia (1989) point out that many teachers falsely assume these students can be successfully diagnosed with standardized reading tests and then treated prescriptively through "basic" skills instruction. This approach "focuses a teacher's efforts on testing and remediation rather than on finding meaningful reading materials and culturally appropriate ways to teach and motivate students" (Reyhner & Garcia, 1989, p. 86). Poor readers and students from divergent cultures can expand their literacy skills when they are given opportunities to explore their own interests through meaningful reading and writing experiences (Field & Aebersold, 1990).

You probably recall the story we told earlier in this book about the young man who was diagnosed as learning disabled in the second grade because of his inability to read. To refresh your memory, just when special education and reading teachers were ready to give up on him, his seventh-grade math teacher discovered that the young man had a great interest in magic. The teacher gave him books on magic, which he struggled through initially but eventually began reading with growing confidence. Soon he was able to apply his increasing reading skills to his school textbooks. The young man went on to graduate from high school and, finally, from the University of Illinois. We remind you of this story to demonstrate the power of meaningful learning.

It should not be assumed that students with special needs require inordinate structure and routines to expand their language and literacy skills. Using reading and writing as vehicles for helping them explore personal interests and satisfy cultural needs can increase their language competencies and motivate them to become better language learners.

Each Student's Unique Contribution Should Be Valued

In *Seeking Diversity*, Linda Rief (1992) says about her junior high students, "I don't believe any one system of learning works for every child. Everyone learns differently. As a teacher I believe my job is to find out what works best for each child" (p. 3). In valuing student diversity, we discover ways to reach and teach young adults that are personally meaningful and culturally responsive. Banks puts it this way:

> When teachers have gained knowledge about cultural and ethnic diversity, looked at that knowledge from different ethnic and cultural perspectives, and taken action to make their own lives and communities more culturally sensitive and diverse, they will have the knowledge and skills needed to help transform the curricular canon as well as the hearts and minds of their students. (1991, p. 140)

In contrast to this open, diversity-seeking stance is the very definite message that is communicated to students, especially those with special needs, when the teacher and the text completely dominate and control instruction. The message is that only the teacher and text can ask the questions, only their questions are worth asking, students cannot learn from one another, and the students' job is to answer questions correctly. A vice grip on the curricular controls denies the important individual contributions each student can make to the development of literacy in the classroom. More significantly, it reinforces feelings of inferiority because students learn that their ideas, attitudes, and experiences have little value.

As stated many times before in this book, the process of meaning making, whether in reading or writing, depends on an individual's perceptions and is enhanced through students' interaction and cooperation within the social context of the classroom. Literacy theory refers to classrooms as **interpretive communities** (Harste, 1986; Fish, 1980) made up of individuals who share many approaches to life and models of reality but who also hold separate and unique models of reality based on interactions in other interpretive communities outside the classroom (home, community, church, social groups, etc.). Through cooperative grouping and other forms of student interaction where they can share thoughts, feelings, and experiences, students question and expand their own models of reality and learn to value each other's cultures, perceptions, and input. This student-centered approach to language learning assigns a great deal of value to the social interactions within the classroom. When special needs students see that their input is valued because it has helped reshape someone else's perceptions about a text, this gives them the chance to be recognized as successful thinkers and learners.

All Dialects of a Language Should Be Valued

What do you call a person who knows two languages?
Bilingual.
What do you call a person who knows one language?
An American.

We found this graffiti on a university corridor, and it occurred to us that ethnocentricity rooted in monolingualism is so prevalent in our society that it cannot help but creep into our schools and classrooms. It also occurred to us that it is not necessarily bilingualism that marks a speaker as being less of an American but which ethnic group is speaking. For instance, why do the speech patterns of many African-Americans, rural Southerners, Eastern European immigrants, or Hispanic immigrants receive a negative response, whereas descendants from Western Europe find that their speech patterns are quite acceptable, for example, those with French, Swedish, or German accents? Pietras claims that understanding and accepting language variation is "more a matter of which racial, ethnic, or social group is doing the speaking than it is of language variation per se" (1984, p. 240). The serious danger to an illogical response to language variation is that some teachers may judge students negatively just by the sound of their speech. In fact, research in teacher expectancy suggests that low expectations about a student's ability to learn are unconsciously formed based on dialects and use of language (Au et al., 1984).

According to linguists (Barnitz, 1980; Labov, 1982), all of us who speak English use a dialect or version of the English language. Teachers who understand this, who are knowledgeable about language, fail to be swayed by dialects; instead, they incorporate this information into their curriculum to help students understand the functions of language and literacy in all aspects of everyday communication and social interaction.

To be sure, issues of dialect are often highly charged and controversial and rarely clear-cut. Lisa Delpit (1988), an African-American educator, suggests that schools fail students of color when schools ignore the importance of the ability to use "standard" forms of English. She asserts that standard English, the form of English used by the dominant culture, becomes a power lever for students of color and nonstandard dialect users as they attempt to advance economically and politically. Without this ability to shift their speaking and writing into the dialect of the dominant culture, students will find few avenues of advancement. Delpit quotes an angry African-American mother, who discovered that the school her son was attending placed little or no emphasis on teaching students standard forms of English, as saying "My son already knows how to be Black!" (1988, p. 285).

From another perspective, those of us who are privileged, who may be white, and are members of the dominant culture are asked to change our perceptions of what constitutes appropriate language use (Arnold & Swadener, 1993). Swadener (1990) poses these stirring questions:

- "What if teachers and teacher educators were required to show evidence of bi- or multi-cultural competence, rather than merely mastery of dominant culture approaches to pedagogy and mastery of "general knowledge," drawing entirely from Eurocentric traditions?" (p. 34)
- "What if those of us who are monolingual were considered at risk?" (p. 35)

Although all dialects of a language should be valued, situation and purpose may require a certain form of the language. Perhaps the responsible position is to respect variant forms of language, while helping students use the dialect expected of them when they participate in the institutional life of our society, especially as it applies to writing standard English.

Engage Students in Literacy Experiences That Reverse Cycles of Passive Failure and Learned Helplessness

The constructs of *passive failure* and *learned helplessness* come from a line of psychological inquiry known as **attribution theory** (e.g., Covington & Omelich, 1979; Weiner, 1979). This theory posits that students' performance on a task is influenced by their perceptions of the causes of past behavior. Researchers (Butkowsky & Willow, 1980; Diener & Dweck, 1978) have found that students who attribute their performance to stable, controllable factors, such as "effort," maintain their effort in the face of failure. Students who attribute performance to uncontrollable factors, such as "luck," the "task," the "teacher," and "ability," are likely to give up in the face of failure.

Whether they are aware of it or not, teachers generally treat less successful students differently than their more successful peers (Robinson & Good, 1987), which makes it easier for less successful students to attribute their failure to low ability. Johnston and Winograd (1985) have described teacher behaviors that apparently contribute to students' feelings of helplessness and passivity. The list of teacher behaviors, derived from classroom observation research by Good and Brophy (1984), suggests that teachers reinforce passive failure when they

1. Give less successful students the answers or shift to another student instead of refocusing or readjusting the question.
2. Reward inappropriate behavior or answers.

3. Criticize less successful students more often for failure.

4. Praise less successful students less frequently for success.

5. Pay less attention to and interact less with less successful students.

6. Wait less time for less successful students to answer questions.

7. Demand less from less successful students.

8. Come to the aid of less successful students more quickly.

9. Give terminal feedback more often.

10. Interrupt more often before the end of a sentence during oral reading.*

The teacher–student interactions in this list communicate to students that they cannot exert control over their own learning, reinforcing feelings of incompetence. We are not sure that any of us can totally eliminate differential behaviors from our interactions with students. Nonetheless, it is important to become more sensitive to these behaviors so that we can try to modify them. Indeed, it has been shown that when teachers are made aware of behaviors and attitudes that potentially may have negative effects on students, they can change (Brophy & Good, 1985).

Students' feelings of incompetence often have their roots in reading experiences in very early grades and become so entrenched that they persist right into adulthood. In a study of a population of college upper-classmen who had been diagnosed as learning disabled as early as grammar school, Brozo and Curtis (1987) found that these students continued to view themselves as failures. This was evidenced by statements they made about themselves:

I see it as stuff I wasn't born with.
I'm not smart.
There's not a lot I can do to change myself.

The key to helping students break the cycle of passive failure in reading is to force their attention to the connection between effort and outcomes. Less successful learners who have become helpless or passive need to accept more responsibility for their failure and success. Metacognitive strategies, such as those discussed in Chapters 3 and 9, that make students aware of what they are doing during learning will help them know when effort pays and when it does not. Getting students actively involved in the learning and teaching process through cooperative learning, for instance, is essential for developing independence and a sense of control over their literacy (Rhodes & Dudley-Marling, 1988). When placed in the role of teacher, students see that they are valued and respected for their strengths, rather than ignored or hounded because of their disabilities and disruptions (Watson, 1988). We should also provide these students with engaging texts and opportunities to explore personal connections and real-world applications through the use of all the communications systems: reading, writing, speaking, and listening.

---

*Adapted from Johnston & Winograd, 1985, p. 285.

E. Garcia (1990) promotes the following list of curriculum principles for moving linguistically and culturally "diverse" secondary students beyond passivity and engaging them in meaningful learning:

- The more diverse the students we teach, the more content must be related to the student's own environment and experience.

- The more diverse the students, the more the curriculum should involve students in active rather than passive learning experiences.

- The more diverse the students, the more the curriculum should offer opportunities for students to apply new learning in meaningful contexts.

- The more diverse the students, the more the curriculum should deemphasize excessive practice and drill while providing for a greater proportion of time for informal activities such as group work on projects.

- The more diverse the students, the more the curriculum should be integrated to provide students opportunities for in-depth study of topics and for skill application.

Promote New, Positive Ways of Communicating About Special Needs Students

Our professional education discourse is replete with labels. Unfortunately, although labels are used by professionals to better understand and communicate about behavioral, psychological, and sociological phenomena, they can also stigmatize and engender self-fulfilling prophecies of student failure. The field of reading has been especially responsible for promoting a lexicon of pejorative labels. Consider the terms used over the past century about students who demonstrate reading difficulty such as "congenital word blindness," "reading retarded," and "disabled reader." Is it possible that the very words and terms we use to describe students influence our expectations about them and, in turn, influence the brand and type of instruction they receive? In attempting to answer this question, let's consider the growing use of the term *at risk*.

The pervasiveness of the term *at risk* hardly needs an introduction. The language of "risk" has gained such currency in educational circles these days that it can be found as the focus of special journal issues, conferences, and national centers for research. In a recent ERIC search, Swadener (1990) reported uncovering as many as 1,047 citations using the "at risk" descriptor! What does it mean to be at risk? Does it signal a useful way of identifying students for assistance who would otherwise fail, or is it just another labeling device that perpetuates a deficit view of literacy education?

Ironically, one of the first applications of the at-risk label was to African-Americans at a time when they were not legally educated. African-American children were referred to as children "at risk" of literacy (Swadener, 1990). Over the last century, educators and public officials have most often framed the problem of poor school achievement by at-risk students in the following ways (Cuban, 1989):

- Students who perform poorly in school are responsible for their performance. They lack ability, character, and motivation.

- Families from certain cultural backgrounds fail to prepare their children for school and provide little support for them in school. They are poor, lack education, and do not teach their children what is proper and improper in the dominant culture.

Notice how these first two explanations locate problems of being at risk in the students and families themselves. From this deficit perspective, students are presumed to have an affliction or disease that must be treated. Using the medical metaphor, students at risk need "immunization" and treatment in the form of special classes and tracks or compensatory pull-out programs.

But what if we reframed the issue of *at risk* whereby schools and political institutions acknowledged their responsibility in helping to create living and learning conditions that bring about failure for certain students and their families? Remember Rene, the student we focused on in this chapter's case study? We believe the very learning conditions she was subject to in her special reading class were contributing to, not alleviating, her "risk" status. McDermott and Gospodinoff contend:

> Without learning how to read, there are few other paths for upward mobility for minority children in modern nations. . . . If we wanted a mechanism for sorting each new generation of citizens into the advantaged and the disadvantaged, into the achieving and underachieving, we could have done not better than to have invented the school system we have. (1979, p. 192)

Pellicano says that the at-risk label "reflects the dysfunctions of both the larger society and the school" (1987, p. 49). From this perspective, schools that are inflexible to the linguistic and cultural needs of their students may be creating conditions that breed academic failure and unsatisfactory student performance. Elkind's (1983) notion of the "curriculum-disabled child" is useful for conceptualizing how teaching practices and curricula can actually increase the likelihood of students' reading and learning failure in school (Polakow & Brozo, 1993).

So we see that labels themselves can be deceiving. Some labels, such as "at risk," may do little more than blame the victims and perpetuate conditions of failure both at home and in school. In recognition of this problem, all of us can make efforts to reverse the detrimental effects of labeling and deficit-driven instruction. We can begin this reversal process by changing the educational vernacular used to describe students with special needs. For instance, it has been demonstrated that by transposing our deficit-laden language to a language of hope for and expectation of success teachers can make profound differences in the ways students perceive, use, and grow into literacy (Brozo, 1991). Terms such as "disabled reader" or "learning disabled" can be replaced by language that refers to ways literacy progress can be improved for students or, better yet, completely turned around to become "at promise" of literacy growth (Lee & Neal, 1992–1993). We believe that an at-promise view of special needs students will lead to more interesting and meaningful teaching and learning.

Reading and Writing Strategies for Special Needs Students

As we stated earlier, the strategies advocated in this chapter for expanding literacy levels of readers with special needs follow naturally from those described and demonstrated in previous chapters. For all readers, be sure to include the readiness activities of Chapter 5, the vocabulary strategies of Chapter 6, and the comprehension activities from Chapter 3. Writing experiences (Chapter 7), opportunities to read, listen and respond to young adult trade books (Chapter 8), and study skills training (Chapter 9) are essential for helping special needs students become enthusiastic and independent readers and writers. In addition to activities in the preceding chapters, the strategies that follow are particularly useful for meeting the literacy needs of special students.

Sustained Silent Reading and Writing

In Chapter 8 we introduced the **sustained silent reading (SSR)** strategy for promoting the reading habit. We once again extol its virtues by demonstrating how SSR, as well as **sustained silent writing**, can be particularly helpful for special needs students.

We agree with Frank Smith (1985), who says that students improve their reading and writing by reading and writing. Sustained silent reading and writing provide daily uninterrupted silent time for personal and pleasure reading and writing. This time not only helps poorer readers improve but promotes positive attitudes toward reading and themselves as literate young adults.

A local high school has an exemplary SSR program that has had a very positive influence on special needs readers. Immediately after lunch, every day, all other activities cease, and everyone reads for 20 minutes, including teachers, the principal, secretaries, the custodial and food service staff, and any visitors to the school. Even a work crew that was doing repairs to the roof of the school during a 2-week period got into the act, taking out their books, newspapers, and magazines to read with the rest of the school.

Judith teaches 10th-grade journalism. She finds the most challenging aspect of the SSR program is helping reluctant readers, who claim they do not like reading, choose just the right book. She knows that the right book can often get a student hooked on reading. She recalls how one of her former "poor" readers literally discovered his "calling" after reading a book on paleontology. He went on to major in anthropology in college and is currently studying artifacts of cave-dwelling Native

Americans in Colorado. Judith attributes this student's self-discovery to the fact that he was able to find the book in her well-stocked classroom library, which contains paperbacks from a variety of genres that appeal to students of varying abilities and interests and, most importantly, provides opportunities for personal choice. She has acquired books and magazines in a number of ways, including garage sales, library benefit book sales, thrift shops, student donations, and money from bake sales, which she has used to take advantage of several paperback suppliers' good discounts. She regularly gives personal introductions to new books with book talks, suggests three or four books that might appeal to particular students, and lets students know what she is reading for enjoyment by sharing her current book and why she likes it. After the SSR period, she allows students to talk about their books if they wish. Students are also allowed to talk to their friends about their interests and to recommend titles. Time is also provided for browsing through books that were discussed or introduced. The key, says, Judith, is that book sharing and recommendations are pressure free; students therefore realize that they can make free choices about the books they would like to read instead of being told what to read and that reading can be personally enjoyable instead of punitive.

A nearby suburban junior high school has a sustained silent writing program that operates much like the SSR program we just described. Everyone in school writes for 15 minutes during a set time, in this case, after lunch. The program has been most successful in stimulating reluctant writers to write. By engaging in personally meaningful writing experiences, students establish the habit of writing, which improves their writing skills and helps them develop healthy attitudes about writing. Many students keep journals or make diary entries during this time. Some write letters or "to do" lists. No one, however, does homework or work-related writing because the intent of the program is to help students see the pleasurable and personally meaningful side of writing.

In her eighth-grade language arts classroom, Madelyn, like the other teachers in the building, does not restrict what her students write during sustained silent writing. However, she helps reluctant writers find personally meaningful reasons for writing by suggesting and demonstrating a variety of purposeful written exchanges. Two of her writing strategies we find particularly stimulating for special needs readers and writers include **message board** and **dialogue journals**.

Message Board: Encouraging Purposeful Writing

Kurt,

Yesterday I was talking with Sean and he told me that extinct animals have been found frozen in ice. I don't believe him, do you?

Neal

Neal,

It's true. I saw a show about it. They found one of them long haired elephants. There's a book in the resource center that has pictures of them. Want to see?

Kurt

Kurt,
Okay. What are you doing 6th period? I got study hall, but Mr. Williams will let me go to
the library.

Neal

And so go the typical kinds of exchanges students pin to the message board.
Madelyn explains that many of her poor writers have never enjoyed writing so
much since she introduced the message board and allowed them to write notes
(which are forbidden in most classrooms) to one another and to her.

As we demonstrated in Chapter 7, reading and writing, indeed, all of the language systems, complement and support each other. When Madelyn's students
write, they read what they are writing: They read to regain their train of thought
or their momentum, to check the "sound" of their text, to check for errors, or for
any of a variety of reasons. When given real-world reasons to communicate, students will take the time to edit and revise and clean up spelling and punctuation
errors (Rhodes & Dudley-Marling, 1988).

Dialogue Journals

In addition to face-to-face conferencing with her poor writers, Madelyn corre-
sponds with them about their writing, reading, and personal concerns in **dialogue
journals** (Wells, 1992–1993). Using an approach developed by Nancie Atwell
(1984, 1987), she gives reluctant writers a folder with the following letter inside:

> This folder is a place for you and me to talk about books, reading, authors, writing, and
> us. You write letters to me, and I'll write letters back to you. In your letters, talk with me
> about what you've read. Tell me what you thought and felt and why. Tell me what you
> liked and didn't like and why. Tell me what these books meant to you and said to you.
> Tell me about your interests and dreams, what you do when you're outside of school.
> Ask me questions or for help. And write back to me about my ideas, feelings, and
> questions.

The writing folder provides Madelyn a forum for getting to know her special
needs students as readers and writers and as people with real-life concerns, interests, experiences, strengths, weaknesses, self-concepts, hang-ups, and gripes. She
can exploit what she learns about these students by introducing them to books
and engaging them in writing experiences that match their interests and experiences. Through the dialogue journal, she can offer specific advice and suggestions,
as well as carry on a dialogue from one interested reader/writer/person to another.
The journals are ungraded and free of red pen marks and circles highlighting
spelling, syntax, and punctuation errors. Instead, Madelyn subtly influences student writing and attention to these errors by using their misspelled words in her
own responses, spelling them correctly.

As her class grew increasingly excited about an upcoming field trip to a
museum downtown, Madelyn read and responded to lots of journal entries about

the trip. In one of the journals, a very shy young lady talked about how depressed she was because she wouldn't be able to go on the trip because her mother didn't have the money. Madelyn was so moved by the student's concern that she wrote back: "Ask your mother if she'll allow you to go if I pay your way." A broad smile on the girl's face the next day gave away the answer. Without the opportunity to communicate through the journal, it's likely that Madelyn would never have learned of her student's problem. The dialogue journal makes it easier for special needs students to follow through on their natural impulses to use language to communicate genuine feelings, ideas, needs, desires, and interests.

Exploring Personal Connections to Text

Several summers ago, Carol, the special education teacher, was teaching special needs students in a small junior high in rural Illinois. Just a few days into the teaching term, she became frustrated with their antipathy toward reading and their inability to generate more than a few lines when given writing assignments. We talked about ways she could find out who her students were outside of school—their experiences and interests, their concerns and attitudes. With this knowledge, she could begin to identify texts that would help them make links between their personal lives and why they read.

She began by revealing herself to the group through the "My Bag" strategy (discussed in Chapter 5). To refresh your memory, the strategy involves filling a bag with personal items and symbols that represent aspects of your personality, interests, experiences, and beliefs. Students empty the bag, then make guesses and ask questions as they pass around the items. This strategy has often been used as a catalyst for writing based on questions and interests others have about a particular aspect of one's personality or experiences.

Carol first emptied her bag, which contained a picture of a female runner, a copy of an Agatha Christie mystery, a photograph of her husband, some sheet music, and an old brooch. After talking about the items and answering questions, the students wanted to know more about the brooch. The next day, Carol read aloud a theme that described how the brooch came from her grandmother and brought back many wonderful memories of summer visits to her grandparents house on the Missouri river. Students then revealed themselves with their bags. They had great fun with this strategy, and Carol discovered some very useful information about each student.

Another strategy she used to help students get closer to text, to transact with text, and to find personal connections with text was a **reader-response heuristic**. This strategy, which was discussed in detail in Chapter 7, involves creating an essay based on three questions about text:

1. What aspect of what you read excited or interested you the most?
2. What are your feelings and attitudes about this aspect of the text?
3. What experiences have you had that help others understand why you feel the way you do?

This response heuristic gives readers an opportunity to present their own personal visions of literacy by writing expressive and explanatory prose in response to what they read. When the heuristic is used as a catalyst for writing, it can, with revisionary assistance from other writers and the teacher, yield a sophisticated essay (Brozo, 1988). The response heuristic should guide the writer in the development of an essay with specific personal support for feelings and assertions. Examples and illustrations should come from the reader's experiences, beliefs, knowledge, and perceptions of the text. In contrast, traditional, formal essays require writers to support stances and claims with information accessible to all writers, with little concern for personal validation. Yet, it is through a personal connection that a text is made meaningful and memorable.

Carol modeled the essay-writing process by sharing her own essay, which was a response to an article about sons and daughters dealing with their aging, infirm parents, and by sharing the decisions that went into creating the essay. She explained her attitude that children should accept responsibility for their parents when they grow old and helpless, and she related this attitude to an anecdote that captured the special relationship she has with her mother. She shared the article with the class, read her personal response, and talked through her reasoning processes in reading, writing, and revising. She also answered students' questions about her response.

Colt, a hulking, slow-moving 14-year-old could barely finish two sentences in a 45-minute period. When Carol discovered from the "My Bag" strategy that he had a motorcycle, she found a human interest article in the paper related to bikes and invited him to read it and respond to it, if he liked, in a manner similar to how she responded to her article. The newspaper clipping was about motorcycle gang members who were out for a Sunday ride when they came upon the scene of an accident. A car had veered off the road and plunged into a small lake. A dozen or so people were standing on shore watching as the car's hood dipped below the surface. One of the bikers dashed off his bike and ran down to the scene. Quickly surmising the problem, he screamed at the crowd in bewilderment: Why hadn't anyone tried to save the people in the car? The crowd had been unable to act. He kicked off his boots and dove in the water. Before long, he bobbed up with two children in his arms, and then a woman came to the surface. Only when they were near shore did some of the people help them out of the lake. The biker gathered his boots, had a few parting criticisms for the crowd, got on his bike, and left.

Carol could not help noticing at the end of the period that Colt was still working. He had written two full pages! He said he wanted to take it home and finish it. The next day Colt raised his hand when Carol invited members of the class to share what they had written. Slowly and methodically, he described the contents of the article, then he moved into his personal response. "Bikers get a raw deal . . . " it began. Colt went on to read his moving essay about how important it is to be brave, like the biker in the article. He related an experience of finding someone, on one of his rides, who had flipped a dirt bike and broken his arm. His essay went on to describe how he positioned the boy on his own bike seat, sat behind him so he could reach around holding the handle bars and keep the boy from falling and rode to the emergency room. Colt concluded his essay by saying "Bikers should be treated with respect because you never know when you might need a brave one to come along."

We have known for some time that individual perceptions (Anderson, 1984) and cultural schemata (Pritchard, 1990) shape one's comprehension. Providing special needs students with vehicles for responding to the texts they read that begin with references to the text and then move into personal narratives helps these readers explore the roots of their perceptions. In supportive classrooms, teachers can exploit the reader-response heuristic as a catalyst for reading and writing.

By the end of the summer, Colt and the other students had written several essays that tied their experiences to an aspect of the texts they read. Their written products grew longer and more sophisticated as a result. More importantly, these students began to view themselves differently as readers. Colt's comments on one of the last days of school are revealing:

> I've changed the way I feel about reading things. . . . I never cared about reading before . . . now I look for something that interests me . . . something I can connect to.

Trade Books

We emphasized in Chapter 8 that abundant reading of quality young adult literature provides a powerful means of helping students acquire information, gain insights into themselves and others, and enrich their leisure hours. It is also clear that bringing young adults into contact with trade books is a very effective means of helping them learn language, extend vocabulary, and come to grips with new and complex syntax. From improving young women's self-concept (Miller, 1993) to giving teen mothers a second chance at literacy (Doneson, 1991), providing regular opportunities to hear, read, and respond to quality young adult trade books can make it possible for all special needs students to become better language learners and users.

Picture Books and Wordless Books.   We often associate picture books and wordless books with very young readers. Yet, these books can be used profitably with poor readers and culturally different readers at the secondary level to help them develop a sense of story, make predictions, produce language, generate their own texts, and build schemata. Picture books can also be used to sensitize all students to issues of diversity. Furthermore, Bishop and Hickman point out that "Picture books are a source of personal pleasure and aesthetic satisfaction for all ages" (1992, p. 4). "We also value picture books, fiction and nonfiction alike, for what they can teach us through their content" (p. 5).

The list in Figure 10–1, compiled by Carol Gilles and colleagues (1988), represents an excellent assortment of picture books and wordless books especially created for secondary students.

Figure 10-1   Wordless books and picture books for young adults

Laurie Anderson *The Package*	John S. Goodall *An Edwardian Christmas* *An Edwardian Holiday* *An Edwardian Summer* *Shrewbettina's Birthday* *Story of an English Village* *The Ballooning Adventure of* *Paddy Park*	Uri Shulevitz *Dawn* *Treasure*
Mitsumasa Anno *Anno's Animals* *Anno's U.S.A.* *Anno's Britain* *Anno's Italy* *Anno's Journey* *Dr. Anno's Magical Midnight* *Circus*		Peter Spier *Noah's Ark* Brinton Turkle *Deep in the Forest* Mircea Vasiliu *What's Happening*

Frank Asch
Topsy Turvies: Pictures to
   Stretch the Imagination
George's Store
	John Hamburger
	The Lazy Dog
	
	Fernando Krahn
	The Flying Saucer Full of
	   Spaghetti
	The Great Ape
		Lynd Ward
		The Biggest Bear
		The Silver Pony
		The Wild Pilgrimage

Linda *The Blue Balloon*		Holden Wetherbee *The Wonder Ring: A Fantasy* *in Silhouette*
Julie Brinckloe *The Spider Web*	Mercer Mayer *Frog Goes to Dinner* *Oops* *Two Moral Tales*	
Eric Carle *The Very Long Train*		Peter Wetzel *The Good Bird*
Ruth Carroll *The Dolphin and the Mermaid*	Guilermo Mordillo *The Damp and Daffy Doings* *of a Daring Pirate Ship*	Brian Wildsmith *Brian Wildsmith's Circus*
Giovannetti *Max*	Kjell Ringi *The Winner*	

Source: From C. Gilles, M. Bixby, P. Crowley, S. Crenshaw, M. Henrich, R. Reynolds, & D. Pyle, *Whole Language Strategies for Secondary Students* (pp. 145–146), New York: Richard C. Owen, 1988. Used by permission.

Chris uses picture books with high school English as a Second Language (ESL) students as a catalyst for oral language production and writing. He first gives personal introductions to several books by sharing the pictures and eliciting responses and predictions about the stories and characters. Then, small groups of two or three students select a picture book for which to write a story, script, or text to be shared with the class. Some students sit in an "author's chair" with class members gathered around and read their texts while holding up the pictures for all to see. Others give dramatic interpretations of the pictured events and characters in the books using their scripts as guides. Chris eventually types what the students have written and places them with the picture books in the class library.

Elley (1981) has demonstrated that we can speed up the learning of English in bilingual contexts if we exploit the use of good stories. He recommends building up a stock of materials geared to the students' natural curiosity, their love of narrative, of excitement, of humor, and the easy identification with characters like themselves. Picture books allow students to interpret the events of stories and the personalities and motives of characters from their own cultural perspectives and experiences, while experimenting with the English language.

According to Stotsky, "Teachers are responsible, in a highly multireligious and multiethnic society, for creating and cultivating common ground through the literature they teach in all its many forms" (1992, p. 56). As we stated in Chapter 8, many important stories of cultural victimization and ethnic prejudice often go unmentioned or are only hinted at in content-area textbooks. Trade books may be the only sources that examine these issues closely and in personal terms. For example, in the picture book *Encounter* (Yolen, 1992), the author describes how the Taino Indian culture and civilization were all but lost after Columbus landed on their beaches.

The number of multicultural trade books written by ethnically diverse authors is on the rise (Farris, 1993), so that it's possible for most junior and senior high teachers to find quality picture books covering a range of important topics. Picture books are an excellent way to introduce cultures to students. For example, Amelda had her eighth graders read two recent picture books, *The Fortune-Tellers* (Alexander, 1992) and *Red Thread* (Young, 1993), so they could compare Camaroon and Chinese cultures regarding young men, their need to understand what the future holds for them, and marriage. Her students also explored their own beliefs about the future and marriage.

Dean's freshmen explore trickster tales from a variety of Native American cultures as a way of demonstrating what is considered antisocial behavior in these particular cultures. In their exploration, they have read about tricksters called "Raven" by Native American tribes of the Pacific Northwest and "Coyote" by tribes in the Southwest in *Song for the Ancient Forest* (Luenn, 1993) and called "Iktomi" by Plains Indians, as illustrated in *Iktomi and the Boulder: A Plains Indian Story* (Goble, 1988).

Numerous books have African-American characters and themes, which is due largely to the growing pool of talented African-American authors and illustrators. During African-American history month, Sylvia worked with two excellent picture books. In *Follow the Drinking Gourd* (Winter, 1989), students learned about slavery and how slaves escaped from their masters. In Hopkinson's (1993) *Sweet Clara and the Freedom Quilt,* Sylvia's students discovered how slaves hand sewed quilts in designs that served as a map of the Underground Railroad.

Picture books have been used to present the wonderful diversity among cultures both within and outside our borders. Secondary school teachers who involve their students in reading, writing, discussing, and listening to these books have found that all students develop greater empathy and understanding of other cultures. This is critical in light of our criticisms of many typical textbooks that fail to adequately deal with issues of diversity and multiculturalism.

Nonfiction Trade Books Promoting Cultural Pluralism

> A people's dream died at Wounded Knee
> The nation's hoop is broken and scattered.
> There is no center any longer, and the
> sacred tree is dead.

These words—spoken by Black Elk, an Oglala medicine man—open the first chapter of *A Boy Becomes a Man at Wounded Knee* (Wood & Afraid of Hawk, 1992). In this haunting and exciting photographic picture book, we follow the story of Wanbli Numpa Afraid of Hawk, an 8-year-old Sioux, as he journeys with his Lakota tribe 150 miles from his reservation to Wounded Knee Creek. The trip is the fifth and final one taken on the anniversary of the Wounded Knee massacre foretold by a medicine man as the only way to mend the "sacred hoop" and restore the dreams and hopes of the Lakota (Sioux) nation. Wanbli Nampa tells of braving 50-degree below zero temperatures and treacherous mountainous terrain along the way as a ritual of sharing the suffering borne by his ancestors.

Nonfiction trade books such as *A Boy Becomes a Man at Wounded Knee* are ideally suited to the cultural and personal interests of certain special needs students. The goal is to find just the right book to "reach" them in ways the textbook and packaged curriculum never could (J. Garcia, Hadaway, & Beal, 1988).

An interesting and easy-to-read biography of Colin Powell, *Colin Powell: A Man of War and Peace* (Senna, 1992) could bring joy and inspiration to many special needs young adults. Two recent books that deal with the horror and reality of drug addiction (*The House That Crack Built*, Taylor, 1992) and homelessness (*No Place to Be: Voices of Homeless Children*, Berck, 1992) would be excellent sources for helping special needs students better understand these growing social problems and help them explore ways of improving their own lives and the lives of others.

Reading Aloud.   Special needs students, particularly bilingual students, need to become familiar with written English, which differs, of course, from spoken English. Poor readers need to know that reading is more than drill sheets and workbooks. Therefore, daily experiences with listening and responding to literature is extremely important for these students for developing knowledge about and interest in language. Jim Trelease, in talking about the importance of reading aloud to students, says that

> Reading aloud . . . stimulates their interest, their emotional development, and their imagination. There is also a fourth area which is stimulated by reading aloud and it is a particularly vital area in today's world . . . language. They will speak the language primarily as they have heard it spoken. (1985, p. 11)

Students who are exposed to excellent works of young adult literature through regular read-alouds will also develop reading and writing schemata. These schemata will help them understand more complex language structures in their reading and will help them create richer written discourse.

Our concerns about language development of special needs students are rooted in the fact that many of them, especially poor readers, have role models who do not stimulate language growth or come from homes where language experiences are not encouraged. In such cases, your classroom may be one of the few environments these students have for language development opportunities. We urge you to take advantage of this opportunity by exposing students to quality literature.

We have found the list of books in Figure 10–2 to be excellent read-alouds for young adult readers with special needs. These read-aloud books should be used to stimulate discussion, writing, and further reading. The ideas and suggestions in Chapter 8 will provide you with options for helping special needs students respond to and extend their experiences with literature.

Figure 10–2 Read-aloud books for young adults

Eth Clifford
The Rocking Chair Rebellion

Walder Dean Myers
Won't Know Till I Get There

Lois Lowry
A Summer to Die

Madeleine L'Engle
A Ring of Endless Light

Alice Childress
A Hero Ain't Nothin' but a Sandwich

Virginia Hamilton
M. C. Higgins, the Great

Sibley Lampman
The Potlach Family

Lawrence Yep
Child of the Owl

Ivan Southall
Josh

R. R. Knudson
Zanbanger
Zanboomer

Mel Cebulash
Ruth Marini, Dodger Ace
Ruth Marini of the Dodgers

Thomas Dygard
Rebound Caper
Winning Kicker

Rosemary Wells
When No One Was Looking

Barbara Cohen
Thank You, Jackie Robinson

Otto Salassi
And Nobody Knew They Were There

Jack London
The Call of the Wild

Robert Newman
The Case of the Baker Street Irregular

Robert Newton Peck
The Day No Pigs Would Die

T. Ernesto Bethancourt
The Dog Days of Arthur Cane

Willie Morris
Good Old Boy

Allan W. Eckert
Incident at Hawk's Hill

James L. Collier & Christopher Collier
Jump Ship to Freedom
My Brother Sam Is Dead

Lois Duncan
Killing Mr. Griffin

Patricia Beatty
Lupita Manana

Jean George
My Side of the Mountain

Anne Holm
North to Freedom

Paul Fleischman
Path of the Pale Horse

Robert Murphy
The Pond

Scott O'Dell
Sarah Bishop
Sing Down the Moon

Felicia Holman
Slake's Limbo

Harry Mazer
Snow-Bound

Elizabeth George Speare
The Witch of Blackbird Pond

Bob Greene
American Beat

Judith Gorog
A Taste for Quiet and Other Disquieting Tales

The most commonly asked question we receive from teachers who work with special needs students is, How can my ESL and remedial students who are reading well below grade level understand these stories? Daniel Fader (Fader, Duggins, Finn, & McNeil, 1976) supplies the most convincing answer to this question. Based on his work with delinquent boys at the W. J. Maxey Boy's Training School in Michigan, where he helped transform them from disinterested, nonreaders into willing and excited readers, he says:

> Semi-literate readers do not need semi-literate books. The simplistic language of the life-leached literature inflicted upon the average schoolchild is not justifiable from any standpoint. Bright, average, dull—however one classified the child—he is immeasurably better off with books that are too difficult for him than books that are too simple. . . . Reading is a peculiarly personal interaction between a reader and a book . . . but *in no case* does this interaction demand an understanding of every word by the reader. The threshold . . . even in many complex books, can be pleasurably crossed by many simple readers. (Fader et al., 1976, p. 106; emphasis in original)

Young Adult Books With Characters Who Have Special Needs.   Students with special needs are like us all. They have complex personalities and are as talented in many areas and as untalented in just as many areas as any other people. They exhibit all of the emotions and in the same proportions as other people, and, therefore, literature should portray them realistically. Characters with disabilities, for instance, should be respected and not pitied. "They should be shown coping with their disability," says Marsha Rudman (1984), "rather than being rewarded with a miraculous cure because of their positive thoughts and/or good behavior."

An excellent way to draw special needs students into the literacy club is by finding young adult books that interest them, that deal with themes relevant to their personal situations. Again, these books can be used most profitably when tied to the kinds of learning experiences suggested in Chapter 8. Students should receive personal introductions to books, the books should be used as catalysts for small-group and whole-class interactions and discussions, and students should be provided plenty of opportunities for extending their understanding through personal research, writing, and additional reading.

Figure 10–3 is a list of books that we and other teachers have found to be of great interest to adolescents with special needs. These fiction and nonfiction books deal with typical problems special needs students must face.

Charles, a physical education teacher, has his students who are preparing to work in summer camps and recreation programs read *The Acorn People* (Jones, 1976). This true story about a group of handicapped children at summer camp explores how counselors first react to them. Slowly, the counselors realize how human the new campers are and how much they share. He has found the book serves a useful purpose in sensitizing his students to the emotional and physical sides of working with special needs kids with mobility impairments. Dean's senior sociology students read Miklowitz's (1987) *Secrets Not Meant to Be Kept*, a trade book that creatively deals with the very sensitive but current social problem of child sexual abuse. Dean contends that this personalized view of child abuse

Figure 10–3   Young adult books with special needs topics

Geoffrey Austrian
The Truth About Drugs

Avi
Sometimes I Think I Hear My Name

Janet Bode
Rape: Preventing It; Coping with the Legal, Medical, and Emotional Aftermath

Betsy Byars
The Summer of the Swans

Vera and Bill Cleaver
Me Too

Robert Cormier
I Am the Cheese

N. B. Dorman
Laughter in the Background

Linna Due
High and Outside

Lois Duncan
A Gift of Magic

Mel Glenn
Class Dismissed: High School Poems

Virginia Hamilton
The Planet of Junior Brown
Sweep Whispers, Brother Rush

Deborah Hautzig
Second Star to the Right

Florence Parry Heide
Growing Anyway Up

Irene Hunt
The Lottery Rose

Margaret Hyde
Cry Softly! The Story of Child Abuse
Knowing About Alcohol
Mind Drugs

Ann Irwin
One Bit at a Time

Norma Johnston
Of Time and Seasons

M. E. Kerr
Dinky Hocker Shoots Smack

Ursula K. LeGuin
Very Far Away From Anywhere Else

Jane Claypool Miner
Why Did You Leave Me?

Joyce Slayton Mitchell
See Me More Clearly: Career and Life Planning for Teens With Physical Disabilities

Jocelyn Riley
Only My Mouth Is Smiling

Harriet Savitz
Run, Don't Walk

Marlene Shyer
Welcome Home, Jellybean

Colby Rodowsky
What About Me?

Ivan Southall
Let the Balloon Go

helps make real the facts and statistics reported in the textbook and brings his students to a new level of awareness of and empathy for victims of abuse.

"Other Englishes"

Literature for ethnic and racial minority students should represent the emotional and intellectual reality of a world that is important to them (Pugh, 1989). Reyhner and Garcia (1989) argue that these students can benefit from reading materials that are linguistically and culturally related to their backgrounds. McKay (1982) asserts that literature that is both thematically relevant and linguistically accessible to ethnic and racial minorities can motivate them to read and provide "an ideal vehicle for illustrating language use and introducing cultural assumptions."

A rich source of literature for helping ethnic and racial minorities learn more about themselves, expand their knowledge of English, and extend reading for its own sake is the material written in "**other Englishes**"—literature written in English by non-native English speakers. The result is an English shaped by native styles, tempos, and themes, yet still quality English (Pugh, 1989). Much of this

Figure 10–4   Examples of literature written in and for students who speak "other Englishes"

Ashabranner, B. (1986). *Children of the Maya: A Guatemalan Indian odyssey*. New York: Dodd, Mead.

Desai, A. (1982). *Games at twilight and other stories*. New York: Penguin.

Fernando, L. (1968). *Twenty Malaysian stories*. Singapore: Heinemann Educational Books.

Haverstock, N. (1987). *Nicaragua in pictures* (Visual Geography Series). Minneapolis, MN: Lerner Publications.

Ludwig, E. (1971). *The Chicanos: Mexican American voices*. Baltimore: Penguin.

Narayan, R. K. (1985). *Under the banyan tree and other stories*. New York: Viking Penguin.

Nuccio, R. (1986). *What's wrong, who's right in Central America? A citizen's guide*. New York: Facts on File Publications.

Perera, V. (1986). *Rites: A Guatemalan boyhood*. San Diego, CA: Harcourt Brace Jovanovich.

Qoyawayma, P. (1964). *No turning back: A Hopi Indian woman's struggle to live in two worlds*, as told to V. F. Carlson. Albuquerque, NM: University of New Mexico Press.

Ridenour, R. (1986). *Yankee Sandinistas: Interview with North Americans living and working in the new Nicaragua*. Willimantic, CT: Curbstone Press.

Santos, B. (1979). *Scent of apples*. Seattle, WA: University of Washington Press.

---

literature deals with a dilemma that ethnic and racial minorities face daily—the tension in non-Western immigrant families in which the parents' past is in one culture and the children's future is in another. Figure 10–4 contains a partial list of a growing body of literature by authors of other Englishes, as well as books appropriate for students who speak other Englishes. (The Appendix is an extensive list of works in English by non-native speakers.)

Once beginning the search, the responsive teacher will soon tap into a rich vein of trade literature that can help special needs students learn more about themselves and their disabilities, link them with their immediate culture, dissipate the effects of cultural discontinuity, spark interest in further reading, and demonstrate the power and promise of literacy.

Verbal Reports

In Chapters 3 and 9, we demonstrated the value of modeling for and eliciting from students **verbal reports** of thought processes while they occur during reading and writing. The goal of this strategy is to make readers more aware of how they make sense of what they read. According to our best knowledge about poor readers, from research and teacher observations, they lack knowledge about themselves as learners and lack metacognitive awareness of their reading strategies

(Wong, 1988). Helping these students verbalize thoughts while reading can lead to a level of self-awareness necessary for recognizing the demands of the reading task—to engage the most appropriate strategies—and for recognizing when comprehension is breaking down—to engage fix-up strategies (Dana, 1989; Gentile & McMillan, 1992; Reyes & Molner, 1991; Young & Bastianelli, 1990).

To effectively demonstrate comprehension processes for special needs students, you need to become aware of your own cognitive activity during reading. To describe your mental activity in terms your students will understand and eventually be able to model, you need to learn the **language of process.** To illustrate what we mean, Figure 10–5 contains examples of *content statements,* essentially,

Figure 10–5 The language of process

- **Making and Checking Predictions**
  Content Statement: Okay, based on the title and this first subheading, I think the author is going to explain why the number of nurses is declining.
  Metacomment: What I'm doing now is *predicting* what the text is going to be about, and as I read further I can check to see if my predictions need to be changed.

- **Using Contextual Strategies for Word Learning**
  Content Statement: It says here that the Romans had *agrarian* laws giving all citizens equal shares of land . . . so agrarian probably refers to land or agriculture.
  Metacomment: See how I'm using *context clues* right within this sentence to figure out what the word *agrarian* means.

- **Imaging**
  Content Statements: I can picture this guy, Ian, trapped in a mine shaft, with no light, and not knowing which way to turn.
  Metacomment: By *creating an image* in my mind of the events of the story, I can almost see them happening, and they become more understandable.

- **Linking Prior Knowledge to Text**
  Content Statement: The truck broke down on their way to California. That reminds me of the time I was driving to Boston and . . .
  Metacomment: I'm thinking about something in my *prior knowledge and experience* that I can relate to what I'm reading so I can better understand it.

- **Verbalizing Points of Confusion**
  Content Statement: The text says that the sun is actually slightly closer to the earth during the winter than it is during the summer.
  Metacomment: This is very *confusing* to me. It makes more sense to me to think about it in just the opposite way.

- **Demonstrating Fix-Up Strategies**
  Content Statement: (Same as previous content statement)
  Metacomment: Maybe I wasn't paying close enough attention to the explanation on this page. . . . I'm going to *reread* this section about the earth's orbit around the sun and its relationship to the seasons.

paraphrases of the text, and *metacomments,* statements that describe how the reader thinks about and makes meaning of the text. Notice how the metacomments describe as accurately as possible the type of processing the reader is engaged in, so that students can clearly see the relationship between these processes and the comprehension strategies they are being taught to use.

As we indicated in Chapters 2 and 3, you will undoubtedly discover that attempting to talk about how you make sense of a text is not very easy at first. Sophisticated readers, such as you and I, process text so automatically that we are hardly aware of our own mental operations during comprehension. Helping poor readers develop conscious control of their text-processing strategies will require that they "see" what goes into effective comprehension. Verbal reporting can help them see how a sophisticated reader negotiates a text and derives meaning.

In the next section, "Case Study Revisited," we reconsider the problems of dysfunctional teaching in Rene's remedial reading class. You will also read about a teacher who employs a number of the strategies discussed in this chapter to expand the literacy levels of her remedial readers.

Case Study Revisited

We hope by now you have had a chance to give some thought to Rene's situation. We're sure it became obvious as you read this chapter that a variety of potentially very effective literacy strategies can be used with special needs students. The fact that Mr. Willis is providing very little in the way of meaningful literacy experiences for Rene and the class is, we believe, largely inexcusable. Here is your chance to suggest ways of transforming Rene's special reading class to make it a more culturally and intellectually responsive environment for language learners. Take a moment to write your suggestions now.

We next offer our suggestions for making over Mr. Willis's classroom. To do so, we describe the outstanding work of a remedial reading teacher who we believe embodies what it means to teach meaningful literacy to special students.

Carolyn teaches remedial reading in a suburban high school. Many of her students are non-native English speakers, and all of her students have histories of poor academic achievement. In her classroom, she has created a literacy environment that supports authentic uses of print. She also regularly demonstrates for students her own comprehension processes, thereby allowing them to observe effective reading and writing strategies. Carolyn believes that development in reading and writing can take place only in environments where students regularly engage in reading and writing, and where there are frequent opportunities for students to read and write whole, meaningful texts.

Students who enter her classroom are immersed in a language-rich environment characterized by the following:

- A reading center: a comfortable corner of the classroom, crammed with fiction and nonfiction books, magazines, newspapers, pamphlets, taped stories, high interest/easy reading books, and other sources of printed material
- Displays of students' work: including stories, themes, essays, and artwork
- Functional reading opportunities: including a message board for exchanging notes and information among students and between Carolyn and her students, lunch menus, part-time job notices, classified ads, and more

Carolyn demonstrates how reading and writing can be functional and enjoyable. Fifteen minutes of every class are devoted to reading aloud from young adult books. Students have enjoyed the experiences of hearing and discussing books such as *A Hero Ain't Nothin' but a Sandwich* (Childress, 1973), *Just Like Martin* (Davis, 1992), and *The Chocolate War* (Cormier, 1974). Another 15 minutes of each class period are set aside for SSR, time for Carolyn and her students to read anything they like.

Carolyn not only writes to her students on the message board and through response journals, but she also writes with them by collaborating on such projects as letter and report writing, a class diary, and language experience stories.

Carolyn helps her students see themselves as growing and maturing into literacy by providing frequent opportunities to read and write what they choose, which helps consolidate their less than sophisticated strategies. In this way, they can more readily self-correct and teach themselves.

Carolyn exploits students' own concerns, interest, and individual needs to know more about certain topics through reading and writing. Students are asked to respond to books being read in class by finding links between the text and their own personal experiences. For instance, two of her students, Raymond and Renque, teamed up to write a compelling piece about their experiences as "graffiti artists" in response to an editorial Carolyn read to the class about the influence of the media on public opinion. Raymond and Renque argued that newspapers gave graffiti artists a bad reputation by erroneously linking their activity to gangs.

Modeling and demonstrating the editing process begins early in the year in Carolyn's classroom. Daily, she makes overheads of her own and students' writing, and for 10 minutes or so, she edits them for the whole class to see, commenting aloud as she works through a piece. Students are encouraged to take notes on what they observe and keep them in a special section of their notebooks labeled "Editor's File," which will also contain procedures and editor's marks. Gradually, as students develop a feel for the editing process, she receives more and more comments about the writing displayed on the overhead. As students' writing is displayed and edited by the class, they become sensitized to their own strengths and weaknesses with conventions and focus attention on weak areas during the writing process.

As students develop skill in the editing process, Carolyn establishes an **editor's table** (Burke, 1985), where students rotate the responsibility for editing their own and other's writing before it is prepared for publication. Carolyn reports that as students take turns at the editors table she begins to see substantial growth in their own work. We strongly endorse this process of helping special needs students learn by assuming the role of teacher.

To establish a close relationship between the regular and remedial programs, Carolyn meets frequently with her students' subject-area teachers. From them, she discovers as much as possible about her students' strengths and weaknesses in each subject area and learns about the content and type of instruction they receive. Her efforts have led to collaboration with teachers on various units of study. For example, she worked with a history teacher during his unit on the Reconstruction because several of her students were in the history class. She gathered the history teacher's notes and other materials on the topic. In her classroom, she introduced the students to Armstrong's book *Sounder* (1972) and Smothers' book *Down in the Piney Woods* (1992), which were used as vehicles for helping students connect with and assimilate many of the concepts and details related to race relations during that period in American history.

Carolyn says her classroom is a place where students can take risks and learn to take advantage of the power and joy of literacy. All of her students come to her with histories of negative and maladaptive attributions for their failure as readers and learners. In her class, however, they are given abundant opportunities to view themselves as successful and competent communicators. This feeling of competence has a way of leavening their global self-concepts and generalizing across school subjects.

Summary

We have stressed that special needs students should receive our best strategies if we are to help them become effective language users. We asserted that reversing the "deficit-driven" language and perceptions of special needs students could help change the face of literacy instruction these students are offered. We agree with Allington, Boxer, and Broikou (1987), who recommend that instruction in remedial and special language programs move away from workbooks and skills exercise that fractionalize literacy learning and leave few or no opportunities for teacher–student interaction. Instead, we have described methods that emphasize meaningful, whole, and enjoyable reading and writing experiences. Meaningful literacy experiences should include those that are personally and culturally relevant to the students as well as those that assist students in applying effective reading and writing strategies to subject-area learning. Special needs students and those who teach them should be involved in demonstrations of and interactions throughout the process of comprehending and constructing whole texts. Finally, special needs students should be led to discover the enjoyment and power of mastering language forms.

References

Allington, R. L., Boxer, N. J., & Broikou, K. A. (1987). Jeremy, remedial reading and subject area classes. *Journal of Reading, 30,* 643–645.

Anderson, R. C. (1984). Role of reader's schema in comprehension, learning, and memory. In R. C. Anderson, J. Osborn, & R. Tierney (Eds.), *Learning to read in American schools: Basal readers and content texts.* Hillsdale, NJ: Lawrence Erlbaum.

Arnold, M., & Swadener, E. B. (1993). *Savage inequalities* and the discourse of risk: What of the white children who have so much green grass? *The Review of Education, 15,* 261–272.

Atwell, N. (1984). Writing and reading literature from the inside out. *Language Arts, 61,* 240–252.

Atwell, N. (1987). *In the middle.* Portsmouth, NH: Heinemann.

Au, K., Tharp, R., Crowell, D., Jordan, C., Speidel, G., & Calkins, R. (1984). KEEP: The role of research in the development of a successful reading program. In J. Osborn, P. Willson, & R. C. Anderson (Eds.), *Reading education: Foundations for a literate America.* Boston: D. C. Heath.

Banks, J. (1991). Multicultural literacy and curriculum reform. *Educational Horizons,* Spring.

Barnitz, J. G. (1980). Black English and other dialects: Socio-linguistic implications for reading instruction. *The Reading Teacher, 33,* 779–786.

Bishop, R. S., & Hickman, J. (1992). Four or fourteen or forty: Picture books for everyone. In S. Benedict & L. Carlisle (Eds.), *Beyond words: Picture books for older readers and writers.* Portsmouth, NH: Heinemann.

Brodinsky, B., & Keogh, K. (1989). *Students at risk: Problems and solutions.* (ERIC Document Reproduction Service No. ED 306 642)

Brophy, J., & Good, T. (1985). Teacher behavior and student achievement. In M. Wittrock (Ed.), *Third handbooks of research on teaching.* New York: Macmillan.

Brozo, W. G. (1988). Applying a reader-response heuristic to expository text. *Journal of Reading, 32,* 140–145.

Brozo, W. G. (1991, October). *Who is at risk?: A critical literacy perspective.* Paper presented at the annual meeting of the College Reading Association, Washington, DC.

Brozo, W. G., & Brozo, C. L. (in press). Literacy assessment in standardized and zero-failure contexts. *Reading and Writing Quarterly.*

Brozo, W. G., & Curtis, C. L. (1987). Coping strategies of four successful learning disabled college students: A case study approach. In J. Readence & R. S. Baldwin (Eds.), *Research in literacy: Merging perspectives, Thirty-sixth Yearbook of the National Reading Conference.* Rochester, NY: National Reading Conference.

Burke, C. L. (1985). Editor's table. In J. Harste, K. M. Pierce, & T. Cairney (Eds.), *The authoring cycle: A viewing guide.* Portsmouth, NH: Heinemann.

Butkowsky, I., & Willow, D. (1980). Cognitive-motivational characteristics of children varying in reading ability: Evidence for learned helplessness in poor readers. *Journal of Educational Psychology, 72,* 408–422.

Covington, M., & Omelich, C. (1979). Effort: The double-edged sword in school achievement. *Journal of Educational Psychology, 71,* 169–182.

Cuban, L. (1989). The "at-risk" label and the problem of urban school reform. *Phi Delta Kappan, 70,* 780–801.

Dana, C. (1989). Strategy families for disabled readers. *Journal of Reading, 33,* 30–35.

Delpit, L. (1988). The silenced dialogue: Power and pedagogy in educating other people's children. *Harvard Educational Review, 58,* 280–298.

Diener, C., & Dweck, C. (1978). An analysis of learned helplessness: Continuous changes in performance, strategy, and achievement cognitions following failure. *Journal of Personality and Social Psychology, 34,* 451–462.

Doneson, S. (1991). Reading as a second chance: Teen mothers and children's books. *Journal of Reading, 35,* 220–223.

Elkind, D. (1983). The curriculum-disabled child. *Topics in Learning and Learning Disabilities, 18,* 71–78.

Elley, W. (1981). The role of reading in bilingual contexts. In J. Guthrie (Ed.), *Comprehension and teaching: Research reviews.* Newark, DE: International Reading Association.

Fader, D., Duggins, J., Finn, T., & McNeil, E. (1976). *The new hooked on books.* New York: Berkley.

Farris, P. (1993). *Language arts: A process approach.* Dubuque, IA: Brown & Benchmark.

Field, M. L, & Aebersold, J. A. (1990). Cultural attitudes toward reading: Implications for teachers of ESL/bilingual readers. *Journal of Reading, 33,* 406–410.

Fish, S. (1980). *Is there a text in this class? The authority of interpretive communities.* Cambridge, MA: Harvard University Press.

Garcia, E. (1990, November–December). *An analysis of literacy enhancement for middle school Hispanic students through curriculum integration.* Paper presented at the annual meeting of the National Reading Conference, Miami.

Garcia, J., Hadaway, N., & Beal, G. (1988). Cultural pluralism in recent nonfiction tradebooks for children. *The Social Studies,* November/December, 252–255.

Gentile, L., & McMillan, M. (1992). Literacy for students at risk: Developing critical dialogues. *Journal of Reading, 35,* 636–641.

Gilles, C., Bixby, M., Crowley, P., Crenshaw, S., Henrich, M., Reynolds, R., & Pyle, D. (1988). *Whole language strategies for secondary students.* New York: Richard C. Owen.

Good, T., & Brophy, J. (1984). *Looking into classrooms* (3rd ed.). New York: Harper & Row.

Goodman, K. (1986). *What's whole in whole language?* Portsmouth, NH: Heinemann.

Harste, J. C. (1986). Good readers as informants: What it means to be strategic. Paper presented at the annual meeting of the National Reading Conference, San Antonio, TX.

Herber, H. L., & Nelson-Herber, J. (1987). Developing independent learners. *Journal of Reading, 30,* 584–588.

Johnston, P., & Winograd, P. (1985). Passive failure in reading. *Journal of Reading Behavior, 17,* 279–301.

Labov, W. (1982). Objectivity and commitment in linguistic science: The case of the black English trial in Ann Arbor. *Language and Society, 11,* 165–202.

Lee, N., & Neal, J. (1992–1993). Reading rescue: Intervention for a student "at promise." *Journal of Reading, 36,* 276–283.

McDermott, R., & Gospodinoff, K. (1979). Social contexts for ethnic borders and school failure. In A. Wolfgang (Ed.), *Nonverbal behavior.* New York: Academic Press.

McKay, S. (1982). Literature in the second language classroom. *TESOL Quarterly, 16,* 529–536.

Miller, D. (1993). The literature project: Using literature to improve the self-concept of at-risk adolescent females. *Journal of Reading, 36,* 442–448.

Morgan, R., & Hosay, J. (1991). Making students better readers. *Vocational Education Journal,* March, 32–33.

Pellicano, R. (1987). At risk: a view of "social advantage." *Educational Leadership, 44,* 47–49.

Pietras, T. (1984). Cultural variation and textbook publication vis-à-vis jelly beans and designer genes. In R. C. Anderson, J. Osborn, & R. Tierney (Eds.), *Learning to read in American schools: Basal readers and content texts.* Hillsdale, NJ: Lawrence Erlbaum.

Polakow, V., & Brozo, W. G. (1993). Special section editors' introduction. *The Review of Education, 15,* 217–221.

Poplin, M. (1984). Summary rationalizations, apologies and farewell: What we don't know about the learning disabled. *Learning Disabilities Quarterly, 7,* 130–134.

Pritchard, R. (1990). The effects of cultural schemata on reading processing strategies. *Reading Research Quarterly, 25,* 273–295.

Pugh, S. (1989). Literature, culture, and ESL: A natural convergence. *Journal of Reading, 32,* 320–329.

Reyes, M., & Molner, L. (1991). Instructional strategies for second-language learners in the content areas. *Journal of Reading, 35*, 96–103.

Reyhner, J., & Garcia, R. (1989). Helping minorities read better: Problems and promises. *Reading Research and Instruction, 28*, 84–91.

Rhodes, L., & Dudley-Marling, C. (1988). *Readers and writers with a difference: A holistic approach to teaching learning disabled and remedial students.* Portsmouth, NH: Heinemann.

Rief, L. (1992). *Seeking diversity.* Portsmouth, NH: Heinemann.

Robinson, R., & Good, T. (1987). *Becoming an effective reading teacher.* New York: Harper & Row.

Rudman, M. (1984). *Children's literature: An issues approach.* New York: Longman.

Smith, F. (1985). *Reading without nonsense.* New York: Teachers College Press.

Squires, N., & Inlander, R. (1990). A Freirian-inspired video curriculum for at-risk high-school students. *English Journal*, February, 49–56.

Stotsky, S. (1992). Whose literature? America's! *Educational Leadership, 49*, 53–56.

Swadener, E. B. (1990). Children and families "at risk": Etiology, critique, and alternative paradigms. *Educational Foundations*, Fall, 17–40.

Trelease, J. (1985). *The read aloud handbook.* New York: Penguin.

Watson, D. (1988). Knowing where we're coming from: The theoretical bases. In C. Gilles, M. Bixby, P. Crowley, S. Crenshaw, M. Henrich, R. Reynolds, & D. Pyle (Eds.), *Whole language strategies for secondary students.* New York: Richard C. Owen.

Weiner, B. (1979). A theory of motivation for some classroom experiences. *Journal of Educational Psychology, 71*, 3–25.

Wells, M. C. (1992–1993). At the junction of reading and writing: How dialogue journals contribute to students' reading development. *Journal of Reading, 36*, 294–303.

Wong, B. (1988). Metacognition and learning disabilities. In T. Waller, D. Forest, & E. MacKinnon (Eds.), *Metacognition, cognition, and human performance.* New York: Academic Press.

Young, P., & Bastianelli, C. (1990). Retelling comes to Chiloquin high. *Journal of Reading, 34*, 194–196.

Young Adult Books

Alexander, L. (1992). *The fortune-tellers.* New York: E. P. Dutton.

Armstrong, W. (1972). *Sounder.* New York: Harper & Row.

Berck, J. (1992). *No place to be: Voices of homeless children.* Boston: Houghton Mifflin

Childress, A. (1973). *A hero ain't nothin' but a sandwich.* New York: Avon.

Cormier, R. (1975). *The chocolate war.* New York: Dell.

Davis, O. (1992). *Just like Martin.* New York: Simon & Schuster.

Goble, P. (1988). *Iktomi and the boulder: A Plains Indian story.* New York: Orchard.

Hopkinson, D. (1993). *Sweet Clara and the freedom quilt.* New York: Alfred A. Knopf.

Jones, R. (1976). *The acorn people.* New York: Bantam.

Luenn, N. (1993) *Song for the ancient forest.* New York: Atheneum.

Miklowitz, G. (1987). *Secrets not meant to be kept.* New York: Dell.

Senna, C. (1992). *Colin Powell: A man of war and peace.* New York: Walker.

Smothers, E. F. (1992). *Down in the piney woods.* New York: Alfred A. Knopf.

Taylor, C. (1992). *The house that crack built.* San Francisco: Chronicle Books.

Winter, J. (1989). *Follow the drinking gourd.* New York: Alfred A. Knopf.

Wood, T., & Afraid of Hawk, W. N. (1992). *A boy becomes a man at Wounded Knee.* New York: Walker.

Yolen, J. (1992). *Encounter.* San Diego: Harcourt Brace Jovanovich.

Young, E. (1993). *Red thread.* New York: Philomel.

11

Becoming an Effective Literacy Professional

I have to learn beyond my classroom. I have to put myself in situations that challenge my thinking, my comfort. I take courses that push my knowledge. I find myself hiding behind other students, hoping the professor won't call on me because I'm having trouble understanding the vocabulary and the concepts. But I push myself to figure it out. I listen hard. I reread. I rewrite what I think. And I try to relate it all to my experiences. I have to be a learner in and out of my classroom so I won't lose sight of what it's like for my students—so I will continue to hear their voices.

—Linda Rief (1992)

Just as effective reading does not result from prescriptive teaching, effective teaching cannot be achieved by following a set of prescriptions. What makes literacy professionals effective is often what makes them unique. They create classroom learning environments and engage students in experiences that break from tradition, that make learning exciting and memorable. The strategies in this book, then, should be viewed as examples of possibilities that when modified to fit your needs, your students' needs, and the context will lead to greater learning and enthusiasm for learning.

This chapter deals with several important issues related to literacy professionalism as it concerns secondary classroom teachers and student literacy. First, we explore personal, contextual, and political factors that influence teachers' use of innovative reading and learning strategies. Within this discussion, we propose a model of teacher change. We then discuss how teacher reflections and classroom action research can provide teachers insights into themselves, their evolving philosophies of teaching, and their students. We also present collaborative strategies for solidifying support between teachers and students, parents, other teachers, and administrators. We argue that through these collaborative relationships, teachers become more effective at gaining students' enthusiasm for learning, increasing content-area learning, and expanding literacy. As part of this discussion, we present what we believe to be the most effective role a literacy professional can play in an overall secondary school reading and writing program. Finally, we share ideas about how literacy professionals can become more knowledgeable and critical consumers of computer technology.

Literacy Innovations in the Content Classroom: Challenges to Change

Those of us who teach content-area reading courses for undergraduate and graduate preservice and in-service teachers from a variety of subject-area disciplines are engaged in a constant struggle of convincing our students that the methods we advocate have validity. A ubiquitous concern is that we are being hypocritical as teachers of teachers if we tell our students to teach content in a way that makes it personally meaningful and functional to their students, while we discuss and demonstrate strategies that are not functional or personally meaningful to our own students (Short & Burke, 1989).

Several researchers (O'Brien, 1988; Ratekin, Simpson, Alvermann, & Dishner, 1985; Ruddell & Sperling, 1988; Smith & Feathers, 1983; Stewart & O'Brien, 1989) have offered explanations for why classroom teachers do not practice the strategies learned in content reading courses. Collectively, these reasons include the following:

- Teachers construct simplified approaches to content instruction based on the perceived constraints of their particular school setting.
- Teachers view content reading and writing strategies as instructionally worthless because they were learned from lecture and textbooks, essentially in isolation from real classroom settings with groups of students. They have not been able to try out the strategies, observe them in practice, or make judgments and decisions about them.
- The organization and power structure of schools inhibit teachers' attempts to try new ideas such as content reading and writing strate-

gies. Preservice teachers are also acutely sensitive to the potential ramifications of nonconformity and innovation.

- Teachers perceive that content reading and writing strategies encroach on valuable time spent covering content.

- Teachers perceive that content reading and writing instruction does not produce measurable gains on standardized tests, where such tests are seen as the most important gauge of successful teaching.

To determine your own attitudes and beliefs about teaching reading and writing strategies in your classroom, follow the directions in Figure 11–1 to complete the inventory of attitudes and beliefs about implementing reading and writing strategies in your content classroom.

Figure 11–1   Inventory of attitudes and beliefs about implementing reading and writing strategies in your content classroom

Directions: Read the following statements and decide whether you strongly agree (SA), agree (A), are undecided (U), disagree (D), or strongly disagree (SD) with each statement. Use the abbreviations and write your response in the space to the left of the statement.

_____ 1. The principal and other teachers will disapprove if I employ many reading and writing strategies in my classroom.

_____ 2. I will not have time to implement reading and writing strategies in my classroom, because I must spend most of the class time teaching the content.

_____ 3. In the secondary school, the teaching of reading should be the responsibility of the reading teacher and the teaching of writing should be the responsibility of the English teacher.

_____ 4. Students should already know how to read my textbook when they enter my class.

_____ 5. If I give reading assignments, I should not have to help my students read and learn from the material I assign.

_____ 6. Writing can be used in my classroom to improve learning.

_____ 7. I am very aware of the reading and writing needs of my students and am in the best position to teach to those needs relative to the course content.

_____ 8. If students in my class cannot read my textbook, it is not my responsibility to show them how.

_____ 9. It is just as important for my students to learn how to learn as it is for them to learn content information.

_____10. I believe the language systems (reading, writing, speaking, listening) can be used as vehicles for learning the subject matter.

Strategy, Teacher, and Organizational Characteristics Influencing the Knowledge and Use of Reading and Writing Strategies

Ruddell and Sperling (1988) have identified teacher, strategy, and structural characteristics that influence the extent to which reading and writing strategies are implemented in the classroom. These are discussed in the following paragraphs.

Strategy

For any new strategy to be effectively incorporated into practice, teachers must perceive it in one or more of the following ways:

1. The new strategy must have an advantage over alternatives. We believe it has been made abundantly clear in this book that when strategies for reading, writing, and literacy development are integrated within the content classroom, a number of advantages over traditional instructional delivery systems can be realized. Students can improve content acquisition by improving the process of acquiring the content. They can become more motivated to learn, remember, and apply the content when innovative language-learning strategies are used as vehicles for expanding knowledge. The teacher can become more enthusiastic and involved in the teaching/learning process when there are abundant opportunities for demonstrations, multidirectional interactions, reflections, and personal and group explorations.

2. The new strategy must be compatible with what the teacher already knows or believes. What do you know and believe about teaching reading in the secondary school? In this book we have attempted to expand your understanding of the reading process as well as knowledge about how best to teach reading and writing within the secondary school classroom. Figure 11–2 is a table adapted from Ruddell and Sperling (1988) that summarizes what we know about skilled readers and writers and implications for teaching based on this knowledge. We believe their summary may also serve as a summary for the reading and writing processes and strategies discussed in this book.

3. The new strategy must not be too complex to be acted on. Although it is true that the reading process comprises many complex interactions, we have tried to point out that it is also true that teachers can be effective if they recognize self-evident truths about learning. For instance, it does not take volumes of research to tell us that students will be more motivated to read and learn if we give them something interesting to read. By the same token, students will become better language users if we give them plenty of opportunities to use language in meaningful and functional ways. We have purposely tried to eliminate unnecessary complexity from our discussions and not laden our explanations of reading and writing processes and strategies with dense, abstract theoretical terminology, because we believe that theory and practice are transactional (Lee & Patterson, 1987; Stansell & Patterson, 1987). In other words, reading theory ought to be grounded in experi-

Figure 11–2   Skilled readers and writers and instructional implications

Reading	Writing	Implications for Practice
We learn to comprehend written text using prior knowledge—life experience as well as academic.	We construct written text using prior knowledge and experience.	*Reading.* Connecting students' prior knowledge and experience to reading content. *Writing.* Using students' own life and school experiences as topics for writing or the basis for developing content for more general topics.
We develop basic perceptual and decoding processing to a level of automaticity, freeing attention for text analysis and construction of meaning.	We master convention of style and mechanics to a level of automaticity, freeing attention for construction of meaningful content.	*Reading.* Attending to meaning of text, allowing decoding skills to develop in the service of meaning. *Writing.* Attending to development of ideas in writing, allowing skills in style and mechanics to develop in the service of communicating ideas.
Our reading purpose and the nature of the text material influence our self-monitoring and comprehension of text.	We learn to write guided by our own writing purposes, the nature of our material, and awareness of audience.	*Reading.* Introducing students to notions of genre and reading for different purposes based on reading genre. *Writing.* Having students write in different genres to achieve a variety of real-world communicative purposes, addressing real readers other than the teacher.
Our attitudes and interests focus and sustain attention, leading to improved understanding and lifelong development of values.	Our attitudes toward writing as a valuable communicative process serve to focus and sustain attention while composing and lead to lifelong writing development.	*Reading.* Giving students books and articles to read that address their individual interests and curiosities. *Writing.* Valuing students' own ideas, including their own experience and knowledge, to be communicated through their writing.
We modify our knowledge in assimilating and comprehending new text-based information and related aesthetic experiences.	We modify our knowledge in the process of writing it down.	*Reading.* Encouraging student predictions about story outcomes and using these predictions to emphasize reading as a discovery process. *Writing.* Having students write for the sole purpose of discovering their ideas and working out solutions to problems.

Adapted from R. B. Ruddell & M. Sperling (1988), "Factors Influencing the Use of Literacy Research by the Classroom Teacher: Research Review and New Directions," in J. Readence & R. S. Baldwin (Eds.), *Dialogues in Literacy Research* (pp. 322–323), Chicago: National Reading Conference. Used by permission of the author.

ence (Harste, 1988). In this connection, we have tried to demonstrate what competent language teachers and users do to facilitate text comprehension.

4.   The new strategy must be tried out and/or observed in practice. For some of you who have yet to enter a classroom, nearly every teaching strategy discussed by a professor or presented in a textbook must seem a bit hollow and leave you a bit incredulous. We are especially sensitive to these reactions among students. Although the laws of physics prevent us from projecting you into an actual classroom/instructional setting, we have tried our best to offer realistic applications for the strategies discussed. The constant references to actual classroom practices and anecdotal evidence for the successful implementation of strategies are intended to help you see how the strategies worked in one setting and reflect on the possibilities for you and your classroom.

Teacher

Ruddell and Sperling claim that teachers are highly likely to accept and put into practice innovative literacy strategies if they (a) view themselves as supportive and productive; (b) have open lines of communication in the classroom and with colleagues and others in the profession; (c) are self-initiating, cooperative, and highly motivated; and (d) are intellectually curious. Giroux and McLaren (1986) recommend that teachers explore the ramifications of the cultural/political role of schooling—how schools define teachers' roles as technicians and students' roles as passive receptors of information. Through this exploration, Giroux and McLaren claim, teachers can actively transform their perceptions of themselves and of students.

Organization

Several factors related to the organizational system of the school, including communication networks through which teachers obtain new information about reading and writing, can strongly influence how much a teacher knows about innovative reading and writing strategies and whether knowledge is translated into practice.

The Ease or Difficulty of Access to Professional Development Opportunities.   The ease or difficulty of access to professional development opportunities is directly related to how much support is provided a teacher for professional development as reflected by a school's formal policies that structure a teacher's time and activities. For instance, ease of access to professional workshops and conferences and access to professional journals can dramatically influence a teacher's knowledge and use of reading and writing strategies. Some systems have formal policies in place that provide for many opportunities for professional development, whereas others are less formalized and less abundant (Sperling, 1982).

The Extent to Which Change Agencies Are Highly Formalized. In the complex organizational system of many schools, responsibility for change is often centralized and highly formalized. In some school systems, boards, superintendents, and principals are the exclusive change agencies responsible for implementing formal policies related to such issues as standardized testing and textbook adoptions, which in turn influence curriculum choices and changes. It has been found that in organizations where the change agencies are not so formalized, innovative teaching strategies are more easily and quickly implemented in classrooms.

According to Cuban (1982) and O'Brien (1988), before teachers will take full advantage of content literacy strategies, they should be informed of the realities of school organizations in which they must function on a day-to-day basis. They should be given the opportunity to explore reasons behind an organization's resistance to change and the social and political constraints that define school policy and acceptable and unacceptable teaching practices.

Supporting Meaningful Change in Teacher Practice

As you might infer, promoting change in the ways secondary school teachers integrate and apply content-area literacy strategies is not always a simple or clear-cut process. Educational innovations do not happen in schools merely because teacher educators or school administrators say they should. The expanding literature on teacher change suggests that ignoring teachers' beliefs (Richardson, Anders, Tidwell, & Lloyd, 1991), the structure and organization of schools (Hargreaves, 1984; Little, 1987), teachers' personal attributes (Smylie, 1988), and teachers' knowledge of the realities of their own teaching situations—referred to as practical knowledge (Liston & Zeichner, 1991)—in the change process could lead to disappointing results.

Researchers involved in exploration of how educational innovations are adopted and used by teachers have begun to paint a more detailed picture of the variables involved in the change process. For instance, teachers are no longer viewed as intractable, unknowledgeable, and blindly resistant to innovation. Instead, teacher change involves a complex blend of variables from personal attributes of teachers to the structure of the organizations within which they work. To more fully understand the interrelationships among these variables, Richardson (1990) proposes that the following questions should be explored:

- Who is in control of change?

    Teachers should feel a genuine sense of investment in the change process.

    Teachers should see a relationship between their efforts and change outcomes.

Teachers should be provided opportunities to reflect on their practical knowledge, theoretical frameworks, and activities associated with the educational innovation.

- What is significant and worthwhile practice?

  Teachers must be actively involved in making judgments about which changes are worthwhile and significant.

- What is the context of change?

  Individual teacher change should be viewed within the culture and norms of teachers, administrators, other school personnel, and students in a particular school.

Given these questions, we present a model for promoting meaningful change in teacher practice in Figure 11–3.

The model suggests that changes in teaching practices are most likely to come about when teachers' own beliefs, attitudes, theories about learning and teaching, and their everyday knowledge about the realities of teaching are taken into account when an educational innovation is introduced to them. Structural support refers to all of the ways school administrators and staff can support each other in the change process, including providing necessary and desired resources and providing time to collectively problem solve and commiserate. A critical component of this model is the need for teachers to reflect on the change process to regularly assess the efficacy of the educational innovation and the ways in which it is being implemented.

Figure 11–3 A model for promoting meaningful change in teaching practice

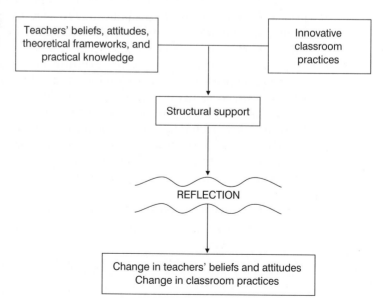

Characteristics of Effective Teachers

Although we know that effective teaching cannot be distilled, bottled, and taken as an elixir, we do know that effective secondary classroom teachers exhibit certain general characteristics that can serve as guidelines for helping you become a better teacher.

Effective Teachers Are Reflective Teachers

Reflective teaching is a powerful way to consider your teaching carefully and to become a more thoughtful and alert student of teaching (Cruickshank, 1987). Valverde provides a very useful operational definition of *reflection:*

> The teacher must examine his/her situation, behavior, practices, effectiveness, and accomplishments. Reflection means asking basic questions of oneself. The basic and comprehensive question during reflection is, What am I doing and why? . . . Reflection then, is an individual's needs assessment and continued self-monitoring or satisfaction with effectiveness. As with any type of evaluation, reflection should be formative, that is, periodic, constructive and deliberate. (1982, p. 86)

Reflective teachers do not rely on routine, tradition, and authority to simplify their professional lives, nor do they uncritically accept the everyday reality of schools. Instead, they constantly and carefully reconsider beliefs and practices (Grant & Zeichner, 1984).

Reflection allows the teacher to examine critically the assumptions that schools make about what are and are not acceptable goals and practices. According to Posner (1985), although teachers must work within some constraints, they often accept as predetermined by authority or tradition far more than is necessary. Although we have seen that school structures do place constraints on teachers' policy and decision making, a fair degree of latitude exists, nonetheless. For instance, teachers within the same school will vary widely on such matters as evaluation and classroom management practices, goals, political beliefs, treatment of special needs students, and adherence to textbooks. We believe there is ample room for teachers to exercise their professional prerogative and individuality in teaching.

Urging you to be a reflective teacher, then, is urging you to depend on yourself as a decision maker and to trust your judgments of what you know and believe.

Reflection and Developing a Personal Philosophy of Teaching.   Reflective thinking can be a tool for helping you develop and refine your personal philosophy of teaching, your professional identity. Reflection forces you to engage in inquiry about teaching that ultimately requires self-analysis and appraisal. If you reflect on your professional experience throughout your career, your personal philosophy of teaching will evolve over the years. This evolution is a sign of professional growth.

One way to become a reflective teacher, to determine where you stand and what you believe relative to your specific secondary school environment is by recording events and your analysis of them in a **Reflective Thinking Journal (RTJ)**. Keeping a daily or weekly journal allows you to keep track of events and privately reflect on what they mean to you and what they mean within a broader context. What happened? Why did it happen? What was my role? What beliefs did my actions reflect? Did my actions reflect beliefs and assumptions about which I was not aware? Did the consequences of my actions raise doubts or reinforce beliefs? How should I want to act in the future based on what happened (Posner, 1985)?

An RTJ not only can lead you to discoveries about how you teach; it can help you teach. It can offer you a way to think strategies through, to plan their implementation, to question the social and dynamic conditions that will influence the success of the strategy, to appraise its effectiveness, and to reconsider and modify strategies (Janesick, 1983).

We suggest the format depicted in the sample RTJ in Figure 11–4. Any format is adequate, however, if it helps you focus on particularly significant events and facilitates recording necessary information about events and analysis of events. A discussion of the components of the RTJ follows.

Figure 11–4   A Reflective Thinking Journal: Sample format and entry for an 11th-grade earth science classroom

Event	Analysis Reflections
I began chapter 7 a little differently today. Instead of jumping into the text like I normally do, I asked the class to write before they read the chapter. The chapter was concerned with important environmental issues related to nuclear power, and I asked students to get together in small groups and talk about possible solutions to the nuclear energy problems and then write a short paper discussing their solutions. Collective groans went up when I explained the assignment. It took a few students several minutes to find a group. As I moved around the room, I discovered that many students were not participating in the group discussions; some were staring out the window or had their heads on the desk; some were talking about anything but the topic. I asked them to hand in their papers at the end of the period—I got 7 out of 27 back!	I'm not sure what happened, but this strategy of writing before reading sure fell on its face. I felt embarrassed and confused. I wanted to demand that students get involved and take advantage of this "fun," different approach to the chapter, but it didn't make any sense to try that. They seemed just as confused and unenthusiastic as I must have appeared. As I think some more on it, I'm beginning to realize that I came out of nowhere with this exercise. The class has done very little group work and not much writing other than term papers and reports. Maybe if we try this again—but move into it more gradually and I prepare the class for writing—I might get a better response. I think I also have to get clearer in my head why I'm asking students to do this in the first place. I read that it was a good idea; perhaps I need more information.

Events.   Select one or two events that you felt were significant. It may be significant because what you tried to teach or what you observed bothered you (as in the case with the earth science teacher's concern about trying a prereading writing assignment); excited you; caused you to rethink your initial ideas, plans, or goals; or convinced you that your initial ideas were valid. Whether your events reflect successful or unsuccessful experiences, or something in between, they are significant if they provide fodder for reflection and learning.

Describe the significant event(s) in detail. Think about what you felt during the event, your perceptions of your students responses to your actions and words, and who or what significantly influenced and shaped the outcome of the event(s). Rich description here will provide you the material you need for further analysis and reflection in the other section of the journal.

Analysis/Reflection.   In this section of the journal, you should include discussion of *why* the event was significant to you and how you interpret it. Posner points out the critical importance of this section:

> Try to figure out what you accomplished, identify problems that emerged and how you plan to follow up, and distill from the episodes what you learned. This last point is the most important. You may have learned what works in this situation and what does not. If so, describe what you conclude. But you may also have learned something about your philosophy of teaching (your perspective). Does the episode confirm your ideas or force you to reconsider them? Maybe initial ideas you held rather dogmatically depend, to a large extent, on the situation that affected the applicability of the ideas? (1985, p. 25)

After analysis and reflection, you may be left with more questions than answers. We view questions as an essential part of the inquiry process of reflective thinking. The RTJ can be used to search for answers to your questions, explore your evolving feelings and philosophy about teaching, and help you modify approaches over time.

To help you "experience" reflective thinking, please take a moment for a reflective thinking exercise. Set up a piece of notebook paper in the format shown in Figure 11–4, using the headings "Event" and "Analysis/Reflection." Fill in this "page" of an RTJ based on one of the following: (a) a strategy you implemented in your classroom, (b) a strategy you observed a teacher implement, or (c) a recent classroom experience in which you were a student. Try to provide a full description of the event and a complete analysis of and reflection on the event.

In summary, reflective teaching is a process that causes teachers to think deeply about their experiences and calls on them to self-assess and produce insights and new perspectives that will guide their practice.

Effective Teachers Use the Research Process as a Learning Process

Effective teachers expand their knowledge about their practice and themselves in many ways. They learn by reading the professional literature, by observing students in their own classrooms, by observing teachers and students in other class-rooms, by reflecting on their observations alone and with others, and by sharing their knowledge and experience. They also learn through systematic investiga-tions of their teaching effectiveness (Strickland, 1988). According to Harste (1988), "As a learning process, nothing beats research."

Teacher researchers, interested in improving practices within their own set-tings, undertake research to better understand their students, themselves, and their particular educational environment. In simple terms, teacher researchers use research to do a better job of teaching (Applebee, 1987).

Classroom action research is research undertaken by teachers to improve practice. It can also be used to provide verification and produce evidence that cer-tain strategies are making a difference (Duckworth, 1986). You and most teachers work hard and are constantly searching for new methods and strategies to improve instruction, but rarely do you gather the kind of proof about the effec-tiveness of your strategies that makes superintendents, principals, and other teachers take notice. As a result of action research, your teaching practices improve, and support for your efforts increases. This type of research also encour-ages ownership of strategies as well as improvement in student achievement. Effective teachers view teaching as research.

Judith Green (1987) suggests a seven-phase plan for helping teachers conduct research in their classrooms: (a) Identify an issue, interest, or concern; (b) seek knowledge; (c) plan an action; (d) implement an action; (e) observe the action; (f) reflect on the observations; and (g) revise the plan. For you to better understand classroom action research and how it works, we discuss the seven phases in some detail.

Phase I: Identify an Issue, Interest, or Concern.   Strickland and Cullinan (1986) have discovered several reasons why teachers conduct classroom research: (a) They want to learn more about an aspect of their students' reading and writing develop-ment. (b) They want to observe the reading and writing development of certain students (e.g., special needs students). (c) They want to observe over time stu-dents' responses to and development of particular strategies. (d) They want to observe the effect of the learning environment on student development. (e) They want to determine differences in students' responses to and development of vari-ous strategies.

For example, Michael, an 11th-grade history teacher, was dissatisfied with the departmental unit tests that had been developed before he joined the faculty. He felt they placed too much emphasis on memory of detailed information and not enough emphasis on understanding concepts. After presenting his concerns to the history faculty and gaining their general support, he decided to test some alternative teach-ing strategies to determine how well students learned important history concepts.

Phase II: Seek Knowledge.   A variety of sources are available for acquiring informa-tion about teaching strategies, including (a) college undergraduate and graduate courses and notes; (b) professional books, journals and magazines; (c) university faculty; (d) district curriculum specialists; (e) professional conferences, workshops, and in-service training; and (f) colleagues.

For example, Michael began to seek information related to teaching concepts in history. He got the idea for teaching history using a thematic unit approach centering around critical concepts from an undergraduate history methods class. He found reinforcement for the idea from presentations at a state social studies conference and from a class project in a graduate content-area reading class. Returning to the handouts and texts from the presentations and courses, he began putting together a unit plan on the Civil War. In addition, he consulted with his former university professors and the district curriculum specialist, and he brainstormed with a colleague in the history department to round out the particulars of the unit and ways in which students' knowledge of concepts could be assessed. Michael decided to focus his instruction on helping students apply their understanding of the concept of civil war to examples of civil strife that have occurred before and since and are occurring today around the globe (i.e., in the former Soviet Union and Yugoslavia).

Phase III: Plan an Action.   In this phase the teacher researcher should refine research goals. One way to do this is to pose questions that the classroom research might help answer. Brainstorm as many questions as possible related to the issue, interest or concern of the research. During this phase, plan how the action will be observed or assessed.

For example, Michael formulated three main questions:

1. Will students acquire the basic factual information of the Civil War (e.g., battles, generals, dates, places)?
2. Will students demonstrate an understanding of the concept, *civil war*?
3. Will students exhibit greater enthusiasm for this unit over previous ones?

To answer the first question, the existing questions on the departmental unit test would be used. In this way, his students' performance could be directly compared with the performance of students in other classes.

To answer the second question, Michael wrote some additional questions for the unit test that required knowledge and application of the critical concept. In addition, he designed an assessment that required students to generate a personal essay that would provide insights into their ability to apply their knowledge of the concept.

To answer the third question, Michael designed an attitude and interest inventory that would be given students at the conclusion of the unit. The inventory asked students to reflect on their learning experiences during the unit and decide how they felt about them and how they compared with other learning experiences in other history units.

Phase IV: Implement the Action.   The plan that has been devised to investigate an issue, interest, or concern should be put into action. A plan of action in classroom action research generally involves a teacher trying out a strategy or series of strategies related to the five reasons for classroom research outlined in Phase I. The strategies may be new, or they may be existing. In both cases the teacher desires information about students' responses to the strategies and their effectiveness.

For example, during the unit, Michael engaged his class in a variety of learning experiences intended to help students explore the concept of *civil war*. As students read and learned about our Civil War, they also learned about civil strife in other countries and at other times in history using fiction and nonfiction trade books, current events magazines, films and videos, discussions and debates, and many other strategies.

Phase V: Observe the Action.   Teacher researchers employ a variety of data-gathering methods as part of their investigations. The most common methods include observations, field notes, teacher and student journals and learning logs, interviews, and questionnaires. Normally, teachers gather feedback and interpret student responses throughout an investigation period as a part of everyday classroom assessment.

For example, Michael kept a daily log of classroom events in which he recorded observations, perceptions, and reflections. The log provided him a means of formative evaluation concerning how well he was teaching the critical concept and the extent to which students were learning it. The log was also used to monitor students' enthusiasm and interest in the unit. With this information, he was able to make ongoing adjustments to the unit plan.

Phase VI: Reflect on Observation.   In this phase, data collected through various methods to provide information for the teacher researcher concerning the issue, interest, or concern should be collated. Teacher researchers typically analyze data informally; however, formal analyses are made in more tightly structured investigations.

For example, Michael analyzed data from four primary sources: (a) his daily log, (b) the end of unit department test, (c) his end of unit essay test, and (d) the attitude inventory. At the conclusion of the unit, all students from all the history classes took the departmental test, the essay test, and the attitude inventory. Results clearly demonstrated that Michael's students came away from the Civil War unit with not only a collection of newly learned details but also the ability to recognize other examples of civil strife and explain their significance. Students in the other history classes seemed only to be able to demonstrate memory of detailed information.

Phase VII: Revise the Plan.   A scrutiny of the results of the investigation should lead to some important decision making. The teacher researcher should ask, Were the investigation's questions answered? Is more information needed? Was useful unanticipated information obtained? Answers to these questions will help the teacher determine whether or not students benefited, further investigations should be planned, new strategies should be implemented, or changes in the way data are collected and analyzed should be made.

For example, Michael's demonstration of the effectiveness of a concept approach to teaching history content led to several important changes. It helped solidify the history faculty's resolve to place a more balanced emphasis on critical concepts and important details; departmental goals were revised; cooperation increased among the history faculty; and changes were made to the unit tests. In addition, the principal made more money available to the history department for trade books and other alternative resources.

Why do we encourage classroom action research? To reiterate, we believe there are many benefits to individual teachers and teacher teams conducting classroom-specific research, including the following:

- Provide verification that instructional practices work.
- Promote more open-mindedness among the faculty and the administration to try "new ideas."
- Expand instructional possibilities and enhance a teacher's own teaching.
- Develop ownership of specific strategies based on theory and research.
- Help teachers learn more about themselves and their students.
- Build a teachers' self-confidence and feelings of empowerment.

In short, we concur with the words of Dorothy Strickland (1988):

> In an age when our nation is calling for excellence in teaching, there is no more promising trend than the teacher-as-researcher movement. The demystifying of research, professionalization of teaching, and empowering of teachers are part of the plan. (p. 763)

Effective Teachers Employ Innovative Strategies That Link Content and Literacy Learning

All of the ideas in this book for expanding reading, writing, and other language processes are suggestions, ways of demonstrating possibilities. These suggestions come from our own work, research, and most prominently from the exceptional teachers who have developed them and used them successfully. They are to be considered guidelines, because, obviously, not all will work in your particular setting, and not all of the suggested strategies will work in precisely the ways we describe. Effective teachers are constantly on the lookout for new ideas, suggestions, and strategies that they can modify and adapt to their particular needs. This process of modification and adaptation is innovation. In fact, we expect that the strategies we suggest will take on new shapes and forms in the hands of generative teachers.

For example, a 10th-grade music teacher who wished to incorporate trade books into her music classes was having difficulty finding appropriate young adult fiction books that dealt with music themes. She solved this problem by locating and bringing in the original stories for the suites her students were performing.

Together, they read the stories, analyzed them, and based much of their musical interpretation on what they learned about the characters and the action. In another example, a ninth-grade science teacher created a language-rich environment in his classroom by establishing a class library, including a variety of science textbooks and information books dealing with many different topics, science magazines, young adult fiction books with science themes, picture books, biographies of scientists, and other young adult books unrelated to science but available to students who simply wished to read. Next to the shelved books was an old, overstuffed couch, a couple of beanbag chairs, and a table with chairs for relaxation reading and personal research. Students were given opportunities during nearly every class period to use the class library to work on personal and class projects and to simply read as their interests dictated.

To restate our key point, you do not become an effective teacher by simply following the suggestions of others. Teaching effectiveness will result if you create new strategies, based on reframing and expanding on existing strategies that are more ideally suited to the needs and interests of you and your students.

Effective Teachers Understand Literacy Processes

A common concern among the teachers we meet is expressed in this question, "How can I stay abreast of all the new trends and developments in the fields of reading and writing?" In response, we strongly advocate that teachers take graduate courses in reading or as part of a graduate or certification program and attend workshops and conferences on reading and writing. Another inevitable answer we must give to this question is that to become aware of current teaching developments in reading and writing, you must read the professional literature. We admit, however, that trying to decide what professional literature to read can be a daunting task. Some guidelines follow.

Become a member of the International Reading Association (IRA) and the National Council of Teachers of English (NCTE). As a member of either of these organizations, you can receive a journal that deals with reading and writing issues, concerns, and practical teaching suggestions for secondary students. Secondary-level IRA members find the *Journal of Reading* most helpful for presenting many fresh ideas each month on such topics as teaching vocabulary, writing in the content areas, and using young adult literature. NCTE's *English Journal* is most appropriate for secondary teachers looking for ideas and strategies to facilitate students' written expression. Select two or three articles from these journals every month, and read them closely. Integrate the ideas and suggestions into your instructional plans, and modify them to meet your particular needs. In this way, you will gain regular exposure to the current perspectives on reading/writing processes and developing skill at translating ideas and other's suggestions into your own personally meaningful and useful strategies.

Another benefit of membership in IRA and NCTE is the availability of discounted books on a wide range of reading/writing topics, most of which can be purchased only through these professional organizations, and new books are added annually. As you peruse the IRA or NCTE catalog, you will undoubtedly find three or four publications on topics of interest. Regularly reading these publications will help to expand your knowledge about reading and writing processes and provide you with many more strategies for developing these language processes and helping students use them as vehicles for learning your classroom content.

International Reading Association
   800 Barksdale Road
   P.O. Box 8139
   Newark, DE 19714-8139

National Council of Teachers of English
   1111 Kenyon Road
   Urbana, IL 61801

Given the staggering numbers of journals that publish reading and writing articles, and the professional texts that appear annually, we suggest that you ease into the current literature in a modest way. Set aside a couple of hours per week to devote to reading journals and books. After reading a journal article or book, jot down notes about the topics on an index card, and file it so you can consult it when you need some ideas for teaching course content using reading and writing strategies. Your file categories might include "Developing Prior Knowledge," "Developing Vocabulary," "Teaching Text Study Strategies," or "Writing in the Content Areas."

A second common concern, related to the one just discussed, is expressed in the question, "How do I determine whether reading strategies are appropriate for my students and based on sound theory and research?" This concern, dealing with how to choose appropriate, sound, and research-based strategies for teaching reading and writing, is not easily answered. Perhaps the biggest challenge for the concerned professional is to determine the most important criteria related to a research study or methods paper: Is the research based on actual practice in actual school settings with students like mine, or is it based on populations of students and conducted in contexts dissimilar to my own?

It is safe to say that because of the mind-boggling numbers of research studies and reports that continually appear in the professional literature, many literacy professionals, including those in higher education, do not always know what is "research based." To confound matters, articles appearing in the same journal often contain conflicting findings. So it is not surprising to find many concerned teachers confused about how best to teach reading and writing.

One way of breaking through the confusing maze of reading research is to follow our advice in previous sections of this chapter in our discussion of reflective teaching and classroom research. Begin defining your personal philosophy about teaching language processes. Your philosophy will be influenced by what you have learned and are learning about reading and writing from course work, journals, textbooks, other teachers, your students, and most importantly, your own class-room research experiences and reflections. Then, look for and generate strategies that are consistent with your evolving knowledge about yourself and your students and the best conditions for teaching and learning.

We certainly hope that your developing philosophy encompasses beliefs similar to our own:

1. Students grow in language when it is whole, meaningful and functional.
2. All classrooms should immerse students in a language-rich environment.
3. The learning environment should be arranged in such a way as to promote and encourage regular and frequent student–student interactions.
4. Teachers should demonstrate the reading, writing, and learning processes they expect their students to acquire.

These beliefs have guided the selection of strategies for this book. If your beliefs about language development are similar, then it should be easy for you to modify and adapt many of the strategies contained in this book to help improve your ability to develop your students' content knowledge and literacy. Also, as you read about other strategies that may derive from a different philosophical base, you will be better able to decide what, if any, aspects of the strategies can be adapted for your use and what can be left out of your instructional practices.

Effective Teachers Establish Personal Reading Programs

Secondary teachers often protest when we suggest that they should read several young adult books every year so that they can use good books to enlist their students in the "literacy club," as Frank Smith (1985) terms it. "We haven't the time," they respond. "We're too busy with our required work to read all those books."

We are not naive; we understand the time constraints placed on secondary school teachers. Teaching often entwines itself around teachers' entire lives so that outside the classroom they are thinking about their students, their existing methods of instruction, new ways to improve their instruction, as well as grading papers and preparing lessons. Yet many teachers also have a family, children, house chores, cooking, and may even be taking additional university courses. Teachers lead incredibly busy lives! However, reading young adult books may be as integral to your role as a teacher as any other teaching-related activity.

We can reach adolescents in many ways. Experienced and insightful teachers often discover how to capitalize on subtle teaching moments that are not a part of a preconceived lesson or curriculum. We know, for instance, that young adults can be dramatically influenced by teachers who simply show genuine concern for them as individuals with real-world needs and problems. Often, a book recommended to a teenager by a concerned teacher can make a significant difference in the young adult's life, their way of viewing a problem or relationship, their strategies for coping with a personal difficulty, or their interest in knowing more about a topic. It is not uncommon for us to learn from our undergraduate and secondary reading students that certain books that really moved them as teenagers were recommended by teachers. One student recalled how in 10th grade he was talking with his history teacher, whom he regarded as a friend, about the difficulty he was having in geometry. The teacher suggested that he read the book *The Planiverse* (Dewdney, 1984), which describes life in a two-dimensional world. The student became very excited about the ideas in the book and began approaching his geometry lesson with renewed enthusiasm, which helped him pass the course. Another student recounted how her music teacher, who knew her mother had recently died, passed her the book *When the Phone Rang* (Mazer, 1985), which tells the story of three teenagers who have to deal with the tragic death of their parents. It wasn't the book itself that really made a difference in her ability to cope, she said, but that her teacher cared enough for her that she suggested the book.

Young adult books can obviously play a more direct role in lesson planning and content-area instruction, as demonstrated in Chapters 8 and 10. Because of the tremendous influence these books can have on students' lives, we recommend that all teachers become knowledgeable about how to use adolescent literature to grab students' interests in the topic of study, to help them learn the content information in a more palatable way, and to reach them by introducing them to books that relate to their needs outside of the classroom. To get started on a personal reading program, we suggest that you take as little as 15 minutes a day to read a young adult book. Try reading the book before bed. We think you will discover that this kind of teaching preparation is much easier and exciting than traditional school-preparation tasks. You will have the pleasure of enjoying quality literature while you learn about the power of books for reaching the students in your classroom.

The following is a list of where you can find young adult books for your own reading and for stocking your classroom library:

- Locally owned bookstores and bookstore chains
- Supermarkets, drugstores, and discount department stores
- Used bookstores
- Libraries (will often sell duplicate or unused books at a fraction of the original cost)
- Book fairs
- Book clubs (paper and illustrations are often inferior, but the prices are low)
- Garage sales

Effective Teachers Collaborate With Students, Teachers, Parents, and Administrators

Many people share an interest in your students' reading, writing, and learning development, including the students themselves, other teachers, parents, and school administrators. The prospects of students becoming active learners and developing life-long reading habits greatly increase when all concerned work collaboratively to help students use literacy for information and pleasure. And with these collaborative efforts, your teaching effectiveness increases as well.

Following are suggestions for developing collaborative relationships with teachers, parents, administrators, and students.

Let All Interested Groups Know Your Expectations for Reading, Writing, and Learning.   To work collaboratively, it isn't necessary to convert others to your approach to teaching, but it is important that they are made aware of the nature of your curriculum and the rationale behind it. Otherwise, suspicion, distrust, and confusion may develop. Before others make judgments about you based on piecemeal or incorrect information, share with them as honestly and as accurately as possible your teaching philosophy and classroom strategies.

Make Sure Students Understand Your Expectations for Them as Readers, Writers, and Learners.   Students must "revalue" reading and writing as meaningful, functional processes that can be used as vehicles for learning and expanding on subject matter. All the strategies discussed in this book have been intended to help you incorporate into your content curriculum learning experiences that demonstrate this revaluing of literacy.

Develop Collaborative Relationships With Students.   Rhodes and Dudley-Marling put it well when they said, "We can teach but we can't force learning; learning is a student's prerogative" (1988, p. 273). Secondary students should be used as curricular informants and should be allowed a hand in determining course topics, materials, learning experiences, projects, and evaluation. Involving students in course decisions will encourage cooperation and commitment; they will be vested in the learning process. Without students' active involvement, the chances of expanding their content knowledge as well as their literacy skills are greatly diminished.

Develop Collaborative Relationships With Parents.   Parents play a vital role in the literacy development and motivation of students (Bates & Navin, 1986; Schuck, Ulsh, & Platt, 1983). Teachers and parents can work together to facilitate students' literacy at home. Most of the suggestions that teachers make to parents should be reminders of how parents have been supporting literacy at home for generations. When support for literacy at school is provided at home, students receive a vital message regarding the importance of reading and writing (Shuttleworth, 1986). Parents in turn can be useful informants about their students' attitudes, interests, hobbies, and other behavioral and personality insights that the teacher can use when selecting trade books and planning research projects.

One of the best ways parents can be involved in their adolescent son's or daughter's literacy development is by encouraging and modeling personally meaningful reading. Adolescents who daily "catch their parents in the act" of reading—whether its an executive in Los Angeles with the *Wall Street Journal,* a hog farmer in Illinois with the farm report, or a teacher in Florida curled up on the couch with a mystery novel—are likely to develop positive attitudes about reading (O'Rourke, 1979). Encourage parents to make sure they let their adolescents observe them reading. Instead of ordering and demanding them to read, parents should set an example for their adolescents of the importance and joy of literacy.

Another way to involve parents in the literacy development of their sons or daughters is to encourage them to make a variety of reading materials available in the home. A student in one of my graduate reading courses told me recently how she had been struggling to get her 12-year-old son to read. She had subscriptions to youth and teen magazines, but he wouldn't read them. She handed him one book after another only to have each rejected. One day she left Wilson Rawls's (1961) *Where the Red Fern Grows* on his bedstand. Later that night she noticed light spilling out from under the door. To her delight, she found her son engrossed in the book. She almost had to wrestle it from him to get him to go to sleep. The next day a blizzard kept students at home, and he picked up the book on waking and stayed in bed until he was finished. "Man, that was a great book," he said, "Are there any more like that?"

Indeed, there are many more outstanding young adult books that can make the difference in the lives of adolescents as to whether or not they become lifelong readers. In Figure 11–5 are guidelines adapted from Reed (1988) for helping parents select books for adolescents.

The best way to assist adolescents in developing the reading habit is to be a model. As adolescents observe influential adults reading functional and meaningful materials and observe adults' selection processes, they are likely to imitate this behavior. Teachers and parents can work together to discover what adolescents will enjoy reading and use thoughtful and sensitive guidance to help them become mature readers.

Develop Collaborative Relationships With Other Teachers.   In Chapter 9 we described how Bob, a reading and study skills teacher, teamed up with a biology teacher to help reinforce instruction in the split-page method of note taking. The beneficiaries of their collaboration were brand-new freshmen grappling with the demands of high school textbook reading. This example of cooperative planning between teachers demonstrates the power of collaboration as an effective way to influence teachers' beliefs about reading, writing, and learning.

A great deal of demands are placed on classroom teachers, and more seem to mount yearly. Although most teachers are interested in incorporating effective reading, writing, and learning strategies into their plans, real or perceived constraints limit how much they can do in this area. One way teachers can support each other is by collaborating on thematic units. For example, an eighth-grade history teacher teamed up with the language arts teacher on a World War I unit.

Figure 11–5 A parents' guide to selecting books for adolescents

1. Use the book lists in Chapters 8 and 10 as guides.
2. Check local bookstores, and public and university libraries for the best source of books.
3. Consult librarians, bookstore clerks, university faculty, and teachers who are knowledgeable about young adult books.
4. Become a keen observer of your adolescent's interests, including favorite television shows, hobbies, leisure-time activities, and the kinds of books he or she had read and enjoyed in the past.
5. Consider how well your daughter or son reads when deciding the appropriateness of young adult books.
6. Take a close look at the books to determine whether they match your adolescent's interests.
7. Enroll your son or daughter in a young adult book club.
8. Be sure the main character in the book approximates the age of your adolescent. Characters who are too young are likely to be poorly received; characters who are a bit older are often preferred.
9. Try to make a variety of books available to your adolescent, then allow her or him to select a favorite one.
10. Don't impose your tastes on your adolescent; use your child's selection to guide you in selecting or purchasing future books.
11. Don't jam the books down your adolescent's throat or lay on a thick, hard sales pitch.
12. Try to increase gradually the literary quality of books.
13. Avoid the tendency to make reading a requirement at home; be patient.
14. Try to gradually induce your adolescent to select young adult books. Help by (a) encouraging regular visits to the public library and bookstore, (b) introducing librarians and clerks who are knowledgeable about young adult books and sensitive to the needs of adolescents, (c) purchasing and sharing annotated bibliographies of young adult books (see the reference guides in Chapter 8), (d) discussing the book your young adult is reading, and (e) suggesting books your young adult might enjoy.

Adapted from A. J. S. Reed (1988), *Comics to Classics: A Parent's Guide to Books for Teens and Pre-teens*, Newark, DE: International Reading Association.

In the language arts classroom, students read *No Hero for the Kaiser* (Frank, 1986), wrote responses and themes related to the book and what they were learning in the history class, researched their own family histories to determine who fought in the war, built charts relating battles described in their history books to the effects of the battles on the characters in the trade book, and engaged in many other literacy experiences designed to integrate trade and text reading. This support of the history teacher's unit led to greater student learning of details and concepts related to World War I, as well as increased enthusiasm for the unit on the part of the students and the teachers alike. In this way, the history teacher had time to cover the content he felt was important, while the language arts teacher engaged students in functional and meaningful literacy experiences. And in the process, everyone benefited.

A few secondary schools have a reading specialist to serve students and teachers. If your school has such an individual, introduce yourself immediately to discover what specific services the specialist can offer you to help your students. The reading specialist can take referrals of students from your class who are having difficulty learning your content-area concepts. The specialists will often team teach with you to develop effective study strategies for learning material from course texts and class notes. The specialist might conduct demonstration lessons for your students on certain strategies, such as mapping or the survey procedure using your content materials. The reading specialist can also provide you with teaching ideas for students who have been mainstreamed into your classroom.

Finally, you should develop an effective relationship with your school librarian. Librarians can be invaluable friends and colleagues when you plan units and projects with your students. Librarians are excited about identifying relevant resources for your upcoming topics. They can provide your class helpful presentations and demonstrations in using reference material, accessing computer data bases, and conducting research. Finally, as mentioned in Chapter 8, librarians are your best link to quality young adult books.

Develop Collaborative Relationships With Administrators. In most buildings, school administrators (principals, supervisors, etc.) possess a great deal of decision-making power. Therefore, they can be important allies. The extent to which they share their power may depend on how actively you cultivate cooperative relationships with them.

We recommended earlier that to begin you should make clear your expectations for the learning environment in your classroom. Most administrators are happy to hear of your innovative efforts and are more likely to provide support if they are kept abreast of the reading, writing, and learning strategies you are attempting to incorporate into your classroom. Principals can play an instrumental role in developing and implementing a sustained silent reading or writing program. They can find revenues for alternative resources, such as trade books, and can provide the necessary support for book drives, sales, and other plans you devise for finding books and raising money for books. Administrators can help create a supportive environment for teacher collaboration and classroom research. With your cooperation, they can help arrange important and enlightening in-service training, and facilitate parent–teacher programs. They can also make critical links to community resources for donations of reading, writing, and other curricular materials.

The more you communicate with administrators about your students' growth, the greater the chance they will appreciate your efforts, understand your needs, and support your curricular changes.

One last word about collaboration. We do not want to give the impression that students, parents, teachers, and administrators are the only individuals who can contribute to the overall learning and literacy development of your students. We recommend that you also develop links with other members of the community who can assist you, including local poets, writers, musicians, senior citizens, retired teachers, university student volunteers, and others. Sometimes persistent inquiry can lead to the discovery of some wonderful local resources. Recently, for example, one of our students, an English teacher, while preparing a unit on the Arthurian Legend, found out about a local group of actors known as the "Guild of Creative Anachronisms." Several members came into his classroom dressed in Arthurian garb and gave an exciting and informative demonstration on life, culture, and music during that period and place in history. This strategy enlivened the unit and provided his students a truly unforgettable experience.

Effective Teachers Are Knowledgeable of the Uses and Limitations of Computer Technology

In Chapter 7, we described how microcomputers equipped with word processors can facilitate the writing process for students. Word processing is only one use of the ever-expanding applications of computers for classroom use. We believe that computer technology will likely play a much more prominent role in the classroom of the future. Therefore, it is imperative that secondary school teachers learn more about this technology and remain open to potential instructional applications of computers in their classrooms.

Although computer use is becoming more widespread in our nation's secondary schools (Beynon & Mackay, 1993), a 1988 Office of Technology Assessment study found that today's classrooms are far less computerized than factories and offices (Rogers & Sandza, 1988). According to Weinstein and Roschwalb (1990), in schools today, the computer is becoming almost as common as the blackboard. Yet, these researchers argue, certain computer technologies, such as telecommunications, continue to go largely underused in schools. This situation is attributable in large part to limited funding and reluctant teachers who perceive computer technology as inconvenient and are skeptical of its effectiveness. Because many of the newer computer technologies have only recently been introduced into schools, and because the research base, although growing, is limited, the verdict is still out on the long-range implications of computer-related instruction. Reinking argues, however, that resistance to computer technology is not unlike resistance to any new idea, "Pondering the relationship of computers to language processes may be hampered by our familiarity with conventionally printed text" (1987, p. 3).

Computer Technology Today and in the Future

Developments in computer hardware and software increase at such dizzying rates that the present and future seem to be one and the same. In the first edition of this book, we predicted that trends in schools' use of computer technology most likely to expand in the future would include (a) data bases, (b) telecommunications, and (c) multimedia. More than 4 years later, it is safe to say that these same educational applications of computer technology will become increasingly sophisticated, user-friendly, and commonplace in American secondary schools.

Data Bases

Data bases are extremely versatile computer programs that allow students to collect, organize, and retrieve information. Similar to phone books, recipe files, and catalogs, data bases enable students to classify and sort data and search for specific topics and information quickly and easily. Currently, many libraries store reference materials including encyclopedias in data bases. One of the more interesting developments in data base technology is the compact laser disk, similar to audio CDs, with storage capacities of hundreds of millions of bits of information. Called CD-ROM, one small diskette can hold up to 250,000 pages of information. Some school libraries have entire encyclopedias stored on a single compact disk along with an extensive index that allows searchers to access the information within seconds.

Following are brief descriptions of how data bases have already been used by secondary school teachers to improve motivation and learning in the content classroom.

An eighth-grade social studies teacher had her class compile a data base on current events using information from local newspapers about happenings in countries around the world. Each student was assigned 10 newspaper articles per quarter, which were summarized in a data base field that included country, subject, date, title, publication, and student's name. At the conclusion of the year, the class organized their articles into their own encyclopedia containing more than 2,000 newspaper articles.

In another classroom, 10th graders engaged in a letter-writing campaign to political prisoners, which grew out of a unit on Amnesty International, and built data bases to keep track of their prisoners. They entered such information as the reason for the arrest, the length of the prison term, the current length of imprisonment, the reason for incarceration, health status, and addresses of persons or groups to contact. With the data base, they could monitor changes with their political prisoner, update information on any prisoner as information became available, and analyze the information for patterns such as similarities among charges brought against the prisoners.

With the development of software such as Apple's Hypercard and erasable optical disks, it will be possible to create and use data bases containing an immense amount of information. For instance, software technology has now made it possible to store as much as the equivalent of 400 books on a single plastic cartridge no larger than a paperback book. Although it may be a few years before this technology is in more general use in our schools, we can safely speculate on exciting classroom applications. Imagine a biology student working at a computer terminal or work station on a research paper about ecosystems. In the middle of the paper, the student needs more information about the related concept of ecological succession. On the same terminal using Hypercard or some variation, the student accesses "ecosystems" in an encyclopedic data base, and narrows the topic using subtopic descriptors to locate specific information about "succession." Notes are taken on the topic, or the desired information is printed, then the student returns to the research paper to incorporate the newly retrieved information.

A list of companies with quality instructional data base software follows:

Active Learning Systems
P.O. Box 1984
Midland, MI 48640

Apple Computer, Inc.
20515 Mariani Avenue
Cupertino, CA 95014

Broderbund
17 Paul Drive
San Rafael, CA 94903

CBS Software
One Fawcett Place
Greenwich, CT 06836

Claris Corporation
440 Clyde Ave.
Mountain View, CA 94043

Cue Softwap, Inc.
P.O. Box 2087
Menlo Park, CA 94026

Conduit
The University of Iowa
Oakdale Campus
Iowa City, IA 52242

Educational Testing Service
Rosedale Rd.
Princeton, NJ 08451

ESSi
P.O. Box 8543
Wichita, KS 67208

Glorier Electronic Publishing
Sherman Turnpike
Danbury, CT 06816

Lotus Development Corporation
55 Cambridge Parkway
Cambridge, MA 02142

McGraw-Hill
School Division
1221 Avenue of the Americas
New York, NY 10020

MECC
3490 Lexington Ave.
St. Paul, MN 55126

Microsoft
10700 Northrup Way
Bellevue, WA 98009

Mindscape, Inc.
Educational Division
3444 Dundee Road
Northbrook, IL 60062

Oryx Press
2214 North Central
Phoenix, AZ 85004

Scholastic, Inc.
730 Broadway
New York, NY 10003

Sensible Software, Inc.
335 E. Big Beaver Rd.
Troy, MI 48084

Sunburst
39 Washington Ave.
Pleasantville, NY 10570

Toucan Software
338 Commerce Dr.
Fairfield, CT 06430

Telecommunications

Another current trend that is expected to grow in the future is telecommunications. The **telecommunications** technology involves electronic communication of information using computers. Although telecommunications have been in use for some time in business and industry, a growing number of telecommunications applications are being explored in schools. Massive webs of phone lines, bulletin board systems, and international networks are now available to bring a world of people and information within reach for teachers and students (Watson, 1990). Electronic bulletin boards are being used to receive messages; exchange lesson plans, tests, and entire teaching units; and order materials for classes.

Students who were foreign exchange students have returned to the United States and continued their learning through electronic sharing with the students they visited.

Using an international network called FREDMail, junior high students in West Virginia established computer pen pals in Moscow.

In another case, students kept track of a U.S. Coast Guard "tall ship" during a training journey. Students gathered updates on its movements and activities through the SAILING forum, which can be accessed through a telecommunications network. The topic was of great interest to the students and included a variety of related learning experiences. Students researched more about the ship. They adopted a sailor or cadet aboard ship and exchanged letters and pictures. They read books such as *Mutiny on the Bounty* because the Coast Guard ship was following a route similar to Captain Bligh's. Log sheets were kept, while weekly updates via computer and mail were received. Students learned about time zones and the international date line, and they developed map skills. Telecommunications technology stimulated and supported the students' exploration of a 20th-century sailing voyage.

A group of 10th-grade biology students in Massachusetts used the National Geographic Society's Kids' Net to tap into a national science project. Kids' Net was designed for science classrooms around the country to share in-class science experiments. The students tried various experiments with seeds that had been sent into space aboard the space shuttle to see how space travel had affected them. After collecting data on their experiments, the students sent their results across the country through Kids' Net telecommunications.

Multimedia

The use of multimedia technology in the classroom is in its infancy but likely will be used more widely in the near future. **Multimedia** technology involves blending video, graphics, sound, and computers along with other technologies to enhance the presentation of information and ideas. Interactive video disk technology allows teachers and students to control video information through the computer. Any particular segment of the disk can be accessed quickly and easily without having to scan the entire disk. In a physics class, for instance, while reading, writing, or answering questions about subatomic particles from a computer screen, students can call up moving video images that further demonstrate and explain how these particles are detected by cyclotrons. Teachers are beginning to discover the potential of this teaching tool. Software is currently available that allows teachers to create their own interactive programs using this technology.

Accessing Information About Computer Technology

Because of the rapid developments in computer technology, keeping up with innovations in hardware, software, and related technologies is a daunting task, especially for busy teachers. Perhaps the most challenging task for the classroom teacher is the selection of appropriate software. While microcomputers have the potential for improving teacher effectiveness, this can only occur when quality computer programs are put in the hands of quality teachers. Concern about quality software is especially critical for those of us promoting the integration of literacy processes into secondary content classrooms.

It is generally accepted that most software can, at best, cover only a small portion of the curriculum (Rude, 1986). The vast majority of currently available computer programs are not actually designed to instruct students but, rather, to drill them on material presented previously. More significantly, few programs are available that provide instruction based on an interactive model of the reading and writing process (Dobrin, 1990; Michigan Reading Association, 1989). Given these limitations, we recommend that software be selected on the basis of the extent to which it contains meaningful content and can be used for purposeful learning. In addition, software programs should require active participation by the learner and emphasize elaborative thinking instead of repetitive drill.

One fairly easy way to find appropriate software is by reading reviews of software in educational computing and general microcomputer magazines as well as in professional journals. A list of some of the more popular and relevant publications follows:

Adult Literacy and Technology
    Adult Literacy and Technology Project
    Penn State University
    248 Calder Way, Suite 307
    University Park, PA 16801

Byte
    70 Main Street
    Petersborough, NH 03458

Classroom Computer Learning
    19 Davis Drive
    Belmont, CA 94002

Classroom Computer News
   Box 266
   Cambridge, MA 02138

Computers in the Schools
   The Haworth Press
   75 Griswald Street
   Binghamton, NY 13904

Computers, Reading and Language Arts
   Modern Language Publishers, Inc.
   1308 E. 38th Street
   Oakland, CA 94602

The Computing Teacher
   Department of Computer and Information Science
   University of Oregon
   Eugene, OR 97403

Creative Computing
   Box 789-M
   Morristown, NJ 07690

Educational Computer
   Box 535
   Cupertino, CA 95015

Educational Technology
   720 Palisade Avenue
   Englewood Cliffs, NJ 07632

Electronic Education
   Suite 220
   1311 Executive Center Drive
   Tallahasee, FL 32301

Electronic Learning
   902 Sylvan Ave
   Englewood Cliffs, NJ 07632

Journal of Reading
   International Reading Association
   800 Barksdale Rd
   P.O. Box 8139
   Newark, DE 19714-8139

PC
   Ziff-Davis Publishing Co.
   One Park Ave
   New York, NY 10016

T.H.E. Journal—Technological Horizons in Education
  Information Synergy, Inc.
  2922 South Daimler Street
  Santa Ana, CA 92705

Teaching and Computers
  Scholastic, Inc.
  902 Sylvan Avenue
  Englewood Cliffs, NJ 07632

Tech Trends
  Association for Educational Communications and Technology
  1126 Sixteenth Street NW
  Washington, DC 20036

We believe that in the years ahead, effective teachers will be recognized by their knowledge of and expertise in educational applications of computer technology. We advocate that secondary school teachers in training and in the field today strive to increase their understanding of and facility with this new technology so as to ensure that computers are used to increase meaningful learning in the content areas.

Summary

This chapter was devoted to issues related to teacher professionalism. We organized the chapter around factors that influence the degree of literacy instruction that classroom teachers provide and around characteristics of effective teachers.

We know that secondary teachers must deal with real and perceived constraints on what they can do in the classroom. We suggested that innovative literacy strategies are likely to find their way into the classrooms of teachers who (a) are able to explore their own beliefs, theories, and practical knowledge when preparing to implement an innovative literacy practice; (b) are provided the necessary support from administrators and staff to follow through with implementation; and (c) are given plenty of opportunities to reflect on the change process.

We describe characteristics of effective teachers that contribute significantly to students' achievement and attitudes. In particular, we have much to learn about teaching effectiveness from teachers who are reflective; who test their strategies in classroom action research; who understand the importance of providing literacy instruction within the content classroom; who develop collaborative relationships with students, parents, teachers, and administrators; and who strive to increase their knowledge about classroom applications of computer technology.

References

Applebee, A. (1987). Musings . . . teachers and the process of research. *Research in the Teaching of English, 21,* 5–7.

Bates, G., & Navin, S. (1986). Effects of parental counseling on remedial readers' attitudes and achievements. *Journal of Reading, 30,* 254–257.

Beynon, J., & Mackay, H. (1993). *Computers into classrooms: More questions than answers.* London: Falmer Press.

Cruickshank, D. R. (1987). *Reflective teaching: The preparation of students of teaching.* Reston, VA: Association of Teacher Educators.

Cuban, L. (1982). Persistent instruction: The high school classroom, 1900–1980. *Phi Delta Kappan, 64,* 113–118.

Dobrin, D. (1990). A limitation on the use of computers in composition. In D. Holdstein & C. Selfe (Eds.), *Computers and writing: Theory, research, practice.* New York: The Modern Language Association.

Duckworth, E. (1986). Teaching as research. *Harvard Educational Review, 56,* 481–495.

Grant, C., & Zeichner, K. (1984). On becoming a reflective teacher. In C. Grant (Ed.), *Preparing for reflective teaching.* Needham, MA: Alyn & Bacon.

Giroux, H. A., & McLaren, P. (1986). Teacher education and the politics of engagement: The case for democratic schooling. *Harvard Educational Review, 56,* 213–238.

Green, J. L. (1987). *Colloquial materials.* Unpublished manuscript. Columbus: The Ohio State University.

Hargreaves, A. (1984). Experience counts, theory doesn't: How teachers talk about their work. *Sociology of Education, 57,* 244–254.

Harste, J. C. (1988). Tomorrow's readers today: Becoming a profession of collaborative learners. In J. Readence & R. S. Baldwin (Eds.), *Dialogues in literacy research. Thirty-seventh Yearbook of the National Reading Conference.* Chicago: National Reading Conference.

Janesick, V. (1983). *Using a journal to develop reflection and evaluation options in the classroom.* Paper presented at the annual meeting of the American Educational Research Association, Montreal.

Lee, S., & Patterson, L. A. (1987). *The nature of transactional theory: Not static, but dynamic.* Paper presented at the annual meeting of the National Reading Conference, St. Petersburg, FL.

Little, J. (1987). Teachers as colleagues. In V. Richardson-Koehler (Ed.), *Educators' handbook: A research perspective.* New York: Longman.

Liston, D., & Zeichner, K. (1991). *Teacher education and the social conditions of schooling.* New York: Routledge.

Michigan Reading Association. (1989). Using computers in reading instruction. *Michigan Reading Journal, 22,* 48–50.

O'Brien, D. G. (1988). Secondary preservice teachers' resistance to content reading instruction: A proposal for a broader rationale. In J. Readence & R. S. Baldwin (Eds.), *Dialogues in literacy research. Thirty-seventh Yearbook of the National Reading Conference.* Chicago: National Reading Conference.

O'Rourke, W. J. (1979). Are parents an influence on adolescent reading habits? *Journal of Reading, 22,* 240–243.

Posner, G. J. (1985). *Field experience: A guide to reflective teaching.* New York: Longman.

Ratekin, N., Simpson, M., Alvermann, D., & Dishner, E. (1985). Why teachers resist content reading instruction. *Journal of Reading, 28,* 432–437.

Reed, A. J. S. (1988). *Comics to classics: A parent's guide to books for teens and preteens.* Newark, DE: International Reading Association.

Reinking, D. (1987). *Reading and computers: Issues for theory and practice.* New York: Teachers College Press.

Rhodes, L., & Dudley-Marling, C. (1988). *Readers and writers with a difference: A holistic approach to teaching learning disabled and remedial students.* Portsmouth, NH: Heinemann.

Richardson, V. (1990). Significant and worthwhile change in teaching practice. *Educational Researcher, 19,* 10–18.

Richardson, V., Anders, P., Tidwell, D., & Lloyd, C. (1991). The relationship between teachers' beliefs and practices in reading comprehension instruction. *American Educational Research Journal, 28,* 559–586.

Rief, L. (1992). *Seeking diversity: Language arts with adolescents.* Portsmouth, NH: Heinemann.

Rogers, M., & Sandza, R. (1988, October 24). Computers of the '90's: A brave new world. *Newsweek,* pp. 52–57.

Ruddell, R. B., & Sperling, M. (1988). Factors influencing the use of literacy research by the classroom teacher: Research review and new directions. In J. Readence & R. S. Baldwin (Eds.), *Dialogues in literacy research. Thirty-seventh Yearbook of the National Reading Conference.* Chicago: National Reading Conference.

Rude, R. (1986). *Teaching reading using microcomputers.* Englewood Cliffs, NJ: Prentice-Hall.

Schuck, A., Ulsh, F., & Platt, J. (1983). Parents encourage pupils (PEP): An innercity parent involvement reading program. *The Reading Teacher, 36,* 524–527.

Short, K., & Burke, C. (1989). New potentials for teacher education: Teaching and learning as inquiry. *The Elementary School Journal, 90,* 193–206.

Shuttleworth, D. (1986). Parents-as-partners. *Education Canada, 26,* 41–43.

Smith, F. (1985). *Reading without nonsense.* New York: Holt, Rinehart & Winston.

Smith, F. R., & Feathers, K. M. (1983). Teacher and student perceptions of content area reading. *Journal of Reading, 26,* 348–354.

Smylie, M. A. (1988). The enhancement function of staff development: Organizational and psychological antecedents to individual teacher change. *American Educational Research Journal, 25,* 1–30.

Sperling, M. (1982). Policies influencing writing episodes. *Working papers for the NIE study of the Teaching of Writing in Secondary Schools.* Berkeley, CA: Bay Area Writing Project, University of California at Berkeley.

Stansell, J. C., & Patterson, L. A. (1987). Teachers are researchers: A new mutualism. *Language Arts, 64,* 717–721.

Stewart, R. A., & O'Brien, D. G. (1989). Resistance to content area reading: A focus on preservice teachers. *Journal of Reading, 32,* 396–401.

Strickland, D. S. (1988). The teacher as researcher: Toward the extended professional. *Language Arts, 65,* 754–764.

Strickland, D. S., & Cullinan, B. (1986). Literature and language. *Language Arts, 63,* 221–225.

Valverde, L. (1982). The self-evolving supervisor. In T. Sergiovanni (Ed.), *Supervision of teaching.* Alexandria, VA: Association for Supervision and Curriculum Development.

Watson, B. (1990). The wired classroom: American education goes on-line. *Phi Delta Kappan, 72,* 109–112.

Weinstein, S., & Roschwalb, S. (1990). Is there a role for educators in telecommunications policy? *Phi Delta Kappan, 72,* 115–117.

Young Adult Books

Dewdney, A. K. (1984). *The planiverse.* New York: Poseidon Press.

Frank, R. (1986). *No hero for the Kaiser.* New York: Lothrop, Lee & Shepard.

Mazer, H. (1985). *When the phone rang.* New York: Scholastic.

Rawls, W. (1961). *Where the red fern grows.* New York: Doubleday.

Appendix

Literature in and for Students Who Speak "Other Englishes"

	Type	Region
Abiakam, J. (n.d.). *The game of love: A classical drama from West Africa.* Onitsha, Nigeria: J. C. Brothers Bookshop.	Play	Nigeria
Achebe, C. (1959). *Things fall apart.* New York, Astor-Honor.	Novel	Nigeria
Achebe, C. (1969). *No longer at ease.* Greenwich, CT: Fawcett.	Novel	Nigeria
Achebe, C. (1985). *African short stories.* Portsmouth, NH: Heinemann.	Stories	Nigeria
Achebe, C. (1988). *Anthills of the Savannah.* New York: Anchor Press.	Novel	Nigeria
Achebe, C. (1989). *Arrow of God.* New York: Anchor Books. (Original work published 1974)	Novel	Nigeria
Achebe, C. (1989). *A man of the people.* New York: Anchor Press. (Original work published 1966)	Novel	Nigeria
Allen, P. G. (1983). *The woman who owned the shadows.* Boston: Beacon Press.	Novel	Native American (Laguna-Sioux)
Allen, P. G. (1986). *Recovering the feminine in American Indian traditions.* Boston: Beacon Press.	Nonfiction	Native American (Laguna-Sioux)
Allen, P. G. (1989). *Spider woman's granddaughters.* Boston: Beacon Press.	Stories	Native American (Laguna-Sioux)
Amadi, E. (1971). *The great ponds.* London: Heinemann.	Novel	Africa
Amadi, E. (1972). *The concubine.* London: Heinemann. (Original work published 1965)	Novel	Africa
Amand, M. R. (1970). *Untouchable.* Delhi: Orient. (Original work published 1935)	Novel	India
Anorue, J. C. (n.d.). *The complete story and trial of Adolph Hitler.* Onitsha, Nigeria: J. C. Brothers Workshop.	Play	Nigeria
Chan, A. B. (Ed.). (1983). *Gold mountain: The Chinese in the new world.* Vancouver: New Star Books.	Poetry	China
Coffer, J. O. (1989). *The line of the sun.* New York: Harper & Row.	Autobiography	Puerto Rico
Colon, J. (1961). *A Puerto Rican in New York and other sketches.* New York: Mainstream.	Stories	Puerto Rico
Day, L. B. (1874). *Govinda samanta or history of a bengal raivat* (2 Vols.). London: Macmillan. (Reprinted 1878 under the title *Bengal peasant life*)	Novel	India
Desai, A. (1980). *Clear light of day.* New York: Harper & Row.	Novel	India

	Type	**Region**
Desai, A. (1982). *Games at twilight and other stories.* New York: Harper & Row.	Stories	India
Dinh, T. V. (1983). *Blue dragon, white tiger: A Tet story.* New York: TriAm Press.	Nonfiction	Vietnam
Erdrich, L. (1984). *Jacklight.* New York: Holt, Rinehart & Winston.	Poetry	Native American (Chippewa)
Erdrich, L. (1984). *Love medicine.* New York: Holt, Rinehart & Winston.	Novel	Native American (Chippewa)
Erdrich, L. (1986). *The beet queen.* New York: Holt, Rinehart & Winston.	Novel	Native American (Chippewa)
Erdrich, L. (1988). *Tracks.* New York: Holt, Rinehart & Winston.	Novel	Native American (Chippewa)
Ekwensi, C. (1961). *Jagua Nana.* Greenwich, CT: Fawcett.	Novel	Nigeria
Ekwensi, C. (1962). *Burning grass.* London: Heinemann.	Novel	Nigeria
Ekwensi, C. (1966). *The drummer boy.* Cambridge, England: Cambridge University Press.	Novel	Nigeria
Ekwensi, C. (1966). *Lokotown and other stories.* London: Heinemann.	Stories	Nigeria
Ekwensi, C. (1969). *The people of the city.* Greenwich, CT: Fawcett. (Original work published 1963)	Novel	Nigeria
Ekwensi, C. (1971). *The passport of Mallam Ilia.* Cambridge, England: Cambridge University Press. (Original work published 1960)	Novel	Nigeria
Ekwensi, C. (1975). *Restless city and Christmas gold: With other stories.* London: Heinemann.	Stories	Nigeria
Ekwensi, C. (1986). *Jagua Nana's daughter.* Nigeria: Spectrum.	Novel	Nigeria
Fernando, L. (1968). *Twenty-two Malaysian stories.* Kuala Lumpur: Heinemann.	Stories	Malaysia
Gonzalez, N. V. M. (1961). *The bamboo dancers.* Denver: A. Swallow.	Novel	Philippines
Gonzalez, N. V. M. (1964). *Selected stories.* Denver: A. Swallow.	Stories	Philippines
Gonzalez, N. V. M. (1977). *Children of the ash-covered loam and other stories.* Manila: Bookmark.	Stories	Philippines
Hagedorn, J. (1990). *Dogeaters.* New York: Pantheon.	Novel	Philippines
Harth, D., & Baldwin, L.(Eds.). (1974). *Voices of Aztlan: Chicano literature of today.* New York: New American Library.	Poetry, stories	Mexico/US
Javellana, S. (1976). *Without seeing the dawn.* Quezon City, Philippines: Alemar-Phoenix.	Novel	Philippines
Latin American Literature Review Press (Ed.). (1991). *Scents of wood and silence.* Pittsburgh, PA: Latin American Literature Review Press.	Stories	Latin America
Lim, C. (1978). *Little ironies: Stories of Singapore.* Singapore: Heinemann.	Stories	Singapore
Lim, C. (1980). *Or else the lightning god and other stories.* Singapore: Heinemann.	Stories	Singapore

	Type	Region
Ludwig, E. (Ed.). (1972). *The Chicanos: Mexican-American voices.* Baltimore, MD: Penguin Books. (Original work published 1971)	Poetry, stories	Mexico/US
Momaday, N. S. (1968). *Journey of Tai-Me.* New York: Harper & Row.	Novel	Native American (Kiowa and Cherokee)
Momaday, N. S. (1969). *The house made of dawn.* New York: Harper & Row.	Novel	Native American (Kiowa and Cherokee)
Momaday, N. S. (1969). *The way to rainy mountain.* New York: Ballantine.	Novel	Native American (Kiowa and Cherokee)
Momaday, N. S. (1974). *Angle of geese and other poems.* Boston: D. R. Godine.	Poetry	Native American (Kiowa and Cherokee)
Momaday, N. S. (1987). *The names: A memoir.* Tucson: University of Arizona Press. (Original work published 1976)	Autobiography	Native American (Kiowa and Cherokee)
Momaday, N. S. (1989). *The ancient child: A novel.* New York: Doubleday.	Novel	Native American (Kiowa and Cherokee)
Naipaul, V. S. (1964). *The mystic masseur.* New York: Penguin. (Original work published 1957)	Novel	Trinidad
Naipaul, V. S. (1967). *A flag on the island.* New York: Macmillan.	Stories	Trinidad
Naipaul, V. S. (1969). *A house for Mr. Biswas.* New York: Penguin. (Original work published 1961)	Novel	Trinidad
Naipaul, V. S. (1972). *The overcrowded barracoon.* London: Andre Deutsch.	Stories	Trinidad
Naipaul, V. S. (1975). *Guerrillas.* London: Andre Deutsch.	Novel	Trinidad
Naipaul, V. S. (1979). *A bend in the river.* New York: Alfred A. Knopf.	Stories	Trinidad
Naipaul, V. S. (1984). *Finding the center: Two narratives.* New York: Alfred A. Knopf.	Novel	Trinidad
Narayan, R. K. (1966). *The guide.* New York: New American Library.	Novel	India
Narayan, R. K. (1967). *The vendor of sweets.* New York: Viking.	Novel	India
Narayan, R. K. (1970). *A horse and two goats.* New York: Viking.	Stories	India
Narayan, R. K. (1972). *The dark room.* Delhi: Hind Pocket Books.	Novel	India
Narayan, R. K. (1972). *Lawley Road and other stories.* Delhi: Hind Pocket Books.	Stories	India
Narayan, R. K. (1972). *Next Sunday.* Delhi: Hind Pocket Books.	Novel	India
Narayan, R. K. (1974). *My days.* New York: Viking.	Novel	India
Narayan, R. K. (1974). *The reluctant guru.* Delhi: Hind Pocket Books.	Novel	India
Narayan, R. K. (1976). *The painter of signs.* New York: Viking.	Novel	India
Narayan, R. K. (1985). *Under the banyan tree and other stories.* New York: Viking.	Stories	India

	Type	Region
Nau, C. (Ed.). (1977). *Singapore writing.* Singapore: Woodrose Publications.	Poetry, stories	Singapore
Neihardt, J. G. (1961). *Black Elk speaks.* Lincoln: University of Nebraska Press.	Novel	Native American (Oglala-Sioux)
Okara, G. (1970). *The voice.* London: Heinemann.	Novel	Nigeria
Ong, J. (1975). *Run tiger run.* Kuala Lumpur: Eastern Universities Press.	Novel	Malaysia
Orfalea, G. (1988). *Before the flames: A quest for the history of Arab Americans.* Austin, TX: University of Texas Press.	Nonfiction	Syria
Panunzio, C. (1921). *The soul of an immigrant.* New York: Macmillan.	Novel	Italy
Qoyawayma, P. (E. White). (1964). *No turning back: A Hopi Indian woman's struggle to live in two worlds,* as told to V. F. Carlson. Albuquerque, NM: University of New Mexico Press.	Novel	Native American (Hopi)
Rao, R. (1963). *Kanthapura.* London: Oxford University Press. (Original work published 1943)	Novel	India
Rao, R. (1965). *The cat and Shakespeare: A tale of India.* New York: Macmillan.	Novel	India
Rao, R. (1968). *The serpent and the rope.* Delhi: Hind Pocket Books.	Novel	India
Riis, J. (1909). *The old town.* New York: Macmillan.	Novel	Denmark
Riis, J. (1957). *How the other half lives.* New York: Hill & Wang.	Nonfiction	Denmark
Rolvaag, O. E. (1929). *Giants in the earth: A saga of the prairie.* New York: Harper.	Novel	Norway
Rolvaag, O. E. (1929). *Peder victorious.* New York: Harper & Brothers.	Novel	Norway
Rivera, E. (1983). *Family installments.* New York: Macmillan.	Novel	Puerto Rico
Santos, B. (1979). *Scent of apples.* Seattle, WA: University of Washington Press.	Novel	Philippines
Seng, G. P. (1972). *If we dream too long.* Singapore: Island Press.	Novel	Singapore
Singh, K. (1983). *The interview and other stories.* Singapore: Chopmen Publishers.	Stories	Singapore
Tan, K. S. (1972). *Son of Singapore.* London: Heinemann.	Novel	Singapore
Thumboo, E. (Ed.). (1970). *The flowering tree: Selected writings from Singapore/Malaysia.* Singapore: Educational Publications Bureau.	Poetry, stories	Malaysia, Singapore
Thumboo, E. (Ed.). (1976). *The second tongue. An anthology of poetry from Malaysia and Singapore.* Singapore: Heinemann.	Poetry	Malaysia, Singapore
Tutuola, A. (1953). *The palm-wine drinkard.* London: Greenwood Press. (Original work published 1952)	Novel	Nigeria
Tutuola, A. (1954). *My life in the bush of ghosts.* New York: Grove Press.	Novel	Nigeria
Tutuola, A. (1987). *Pauper, brawler, and slanderer.* London: Faber and Faber.	Novel	Nigeria
Ulasi, A. L. (1973). *Many things you no understand.* London: Collins (Fontana).	Novel	Nigeria

	Type	Region
Yeap, J. K. (1975). *The patriarch.* Singapore: Times Printers.	Novel	Malaysia
Yeo, R. (Ed.). (1978). *Singapore short stories.* Singapore: Heinemann.	Stories	Singapore
Yezierska, A. (1920). *Hungry hearts.* New York: Grosset & Dunlap.	Stories	Poland
Yezierska, A. (1923). *Children of loneliness.* New York: Grosset & Dunlap.	Novel	Poland
Yezierska, A. (1925). *The bread givers.* Garden City, NY: Doubleday, Page.	Novel	Poland
Yezierska, A. (1927). *The arrogant beggar.* Garden City, NY: Doubleday, Page.	Novel	Poland
Yezierska, A. (1932). *All I could never be.* New York: Harper.	Novel	Poland
Yezierska, A. (1950). *The red ribbon on a white horse.* New York: Harper.	Novel	Poland

Name Index

Abbot, E., 261
Abersold, J., 327
Abraham, B., 254, 255, 256, 257
Abrahamson, R., 46
Afflerbach, P., 53, 106, 108
Afraid of Hawk, W.N., 342
Alexander, L., 341
Alexander, P., 22, 27, 29, 72, 87, 315
Allington, R., 350
Altwerger, B., 12
Alvermann, D., 21, 22, 28, 37, 129, 131, 204, 356
Anders, P., 174, 361
Anderson, L., 263
Anderson, R., 20, 128–129, 132, 158, 339
Anderson, T., 22, 23, 25
Anderson, V., 295
Anno, M., 271
Applebee, A., 201, 205, 206, 216, 221, 366
Armbruster, B., 22, 23, 25, 29
Armstrong, W., 350
Arnold, M., 330
Arnothy, C., 130
Aronson, E., 92
Arter, J., 95
Asimov, I., 252
Atwell, N., 41, 240, 336
Au, K., 329
Aubey, L. W., 286
Auten, A., 159

Baird, W., 87, 125
Baker, I., 27, 30, 137
Baker, L., 29
Baldwin, R. S., 37, 163, 174
Banks, J., 328
Barnitz, J., 329
Bartlett, B., 23
Bastianelli, C., 347
Bates, G., 374
Baum, D., 137
Bauman, J., 53
Beal, G., 342
Bean, J., 214
Bean, T., 37, 115, 209, 214
Beattie, O., 252
Beck, I., 20, 127, 153, 155, 156, 157, 158, 162, 192
Becker, E., 11
Belanoff, P., 96
Berck, J., 342
Berkowitz, S., 301
Beynon, J., 378
Biggs, S., 282
Bishop, R., 339
Bissex, G., 81
Bixby, M., 340
Bjork, C., 263
Blumer, H., 9
Bond, N., 257
Bor, J., 247, 249
Bornholt, J., 262
Bos, C., 174
Bowen, B., 232
Bowes, J., 293

Bowles, B., 163
Boxer, N., 350
Brandsford, J., 20, 21, 243, 250
Brannon, L., 1
Bridgeman, B., 229
Brodinsky, B., 323
Broiku, K., 350
Brophy, J., 330, 331
Brostoff, A., 221
Brown, A., 29, 53, 54, 72, 73, 291, 292
Brown, J., 250
Brown, P., 157, 188
Brown, R., 27, 87, 94, 103
Brozo, C., 94, 327
Brozo, W., 2, 7, 14, 24, 56, 94, 95, 108, 158, 213, 214, 243, 274, 327, 331, 333, 338
Burgess, A., 252
Burke, C., 350, 356
Burns, J., 315
Butkowsky, I., 330
Buxton, W., 125
Byers, B., 221

Calfee, R., 81
Calkins, L., 4, 41
Calkins, R., 314
Camp, R., 95
Campbell, J., 7
Camperell, K. B., 24, 118
Carey, R., 85
Carlsen, G., 241
Carlson, S., 229

Subject Index

About the Authors

William G. Brozo earned his bachelor's degree from the University of North Carolina and his master's and doctorate from the University of South Carolina. He has taught reading and language arts in junior and senior high school in the Carolinas. Before joining the faculty of the College of Education at Texas A&M University—Corpus Christi, he was a member of the reading faculties at Eastern Michigan University, Georgia State University, Northern Illinois University, and Northeastern Illinois University. Dr. Brozo has authored numerous articles that have appeared in reading and related journals. He also regularly speaks at professional meetings around the country and meets frequently with teachers and administrators to discuss ways of infusing classrooms with exciting literacy strategies. Dr. Brozo has recently served on the editorial boards of the *Journal of Reading, Reading Research and Instruction,* and the *Kentucky Reading Journal.* He believes that the biggest challenge for classroom teachers is not only to develop skillful readers, writers, and thinkers, but also the desire among students to use literacy for personal and academic growth by making it an integral part of their lives.

Michele L. Simpson received her bachelor's and master's degrees from the University of Northern Iowa and her doctorate from Arizona State University. She taught English and speech in junior and senior high schools in Iowa, Illinois, and Michigan before beginning one of the first high school developmental reading programs in Iowa. She was recognized as the Iowa Reading Teacher of the Year, the first secondary teacher to win such an award, and also served as a Reading and Language Arts Consultant for an Area Education Agency in Iowa. She has taught reading methods at the universities of Northern Iowa and Georgia. Dr. Simpson has co-authored two textbooks for college reading and study strategy programs and has contributed several chapters for edited textbooks. She regularly makes presentations at conferences across the United States and publishes in reading journals. She has been a regular editorial board member for *Reading Research and Instruction,* the *Journal of Reading Behavior,* and the *Journal of Reading.* Dr. Simpson's current research is focused on the conditions that foster students' transfer of strategies to their own learning tasks. As a 1994 recipient of the Elva Knight Research Award from the International Reading Association, she hopes to examine strategic transfer in history courses. To keep in tune with the public schools, she collaborates with her husband, Tom, a middle school reading teacher.